Captive Hearts

Shojo Beat

Story & Art by
Matsuri Hino

Vol. 5

Captive Hearts
Vol. 5

CONTENTS

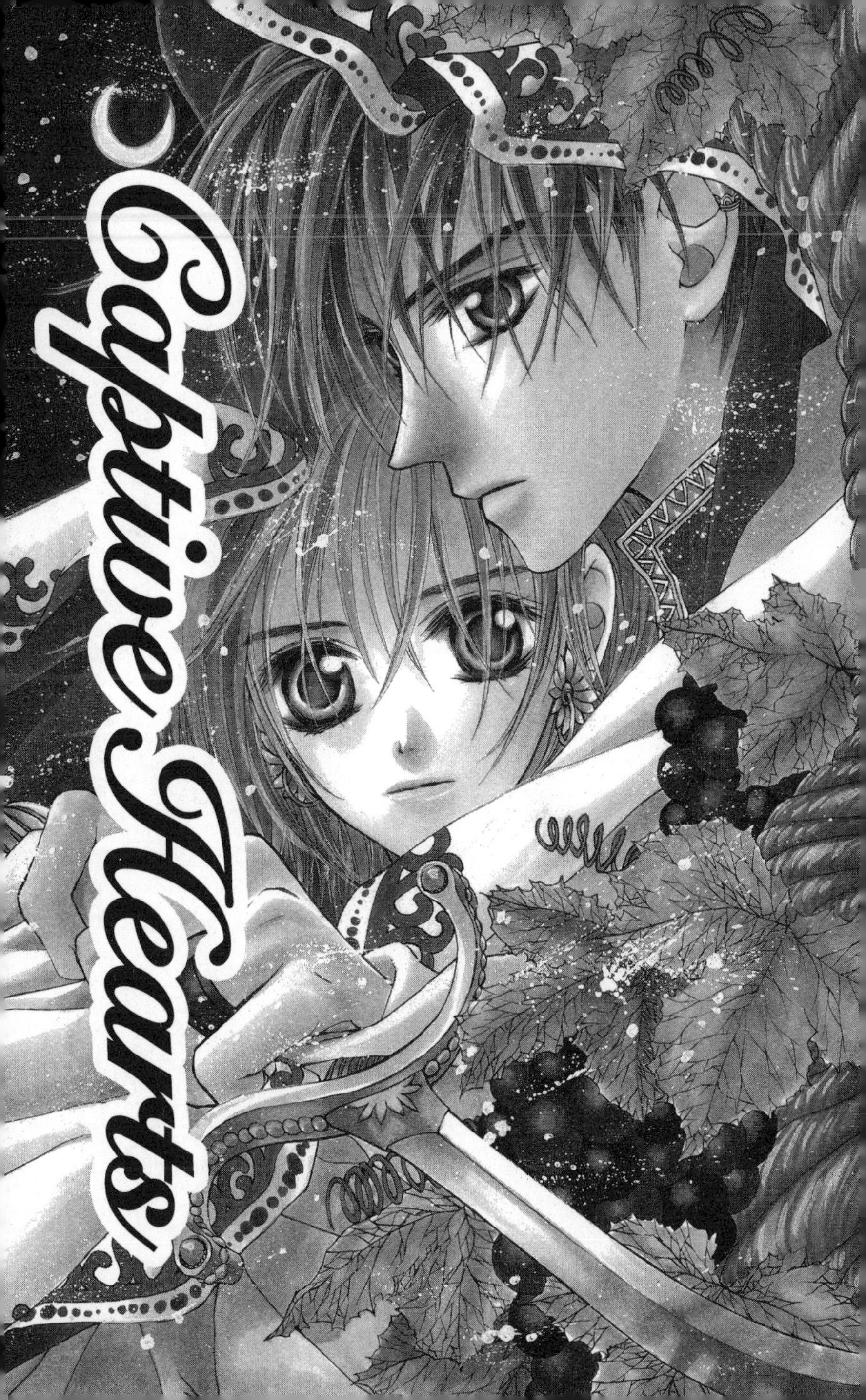
Captive Hearts

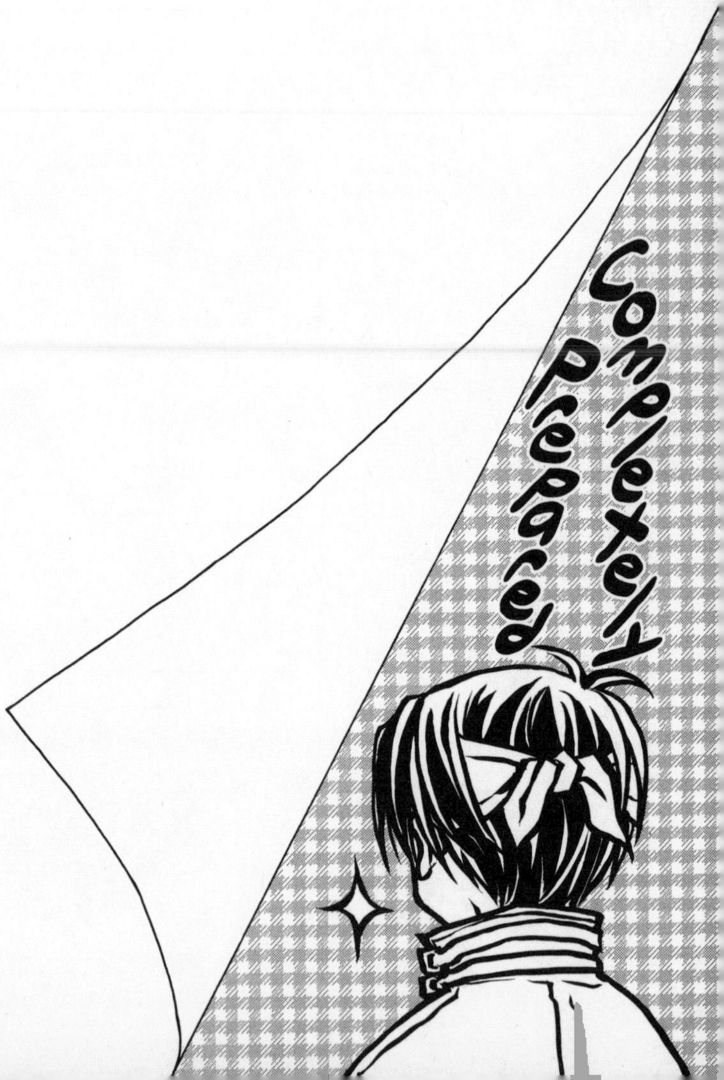
Completely Prepared

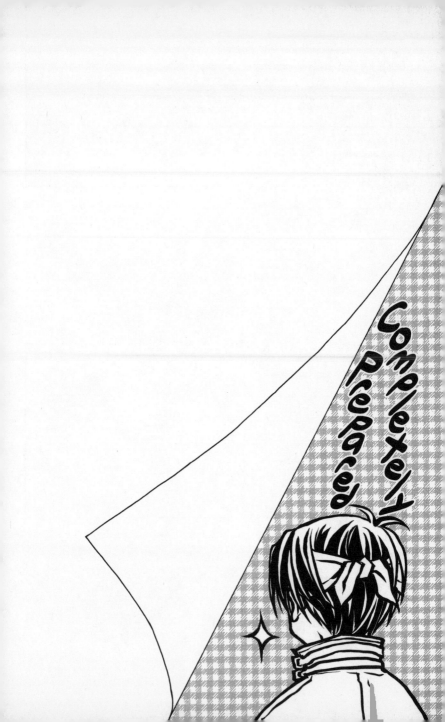

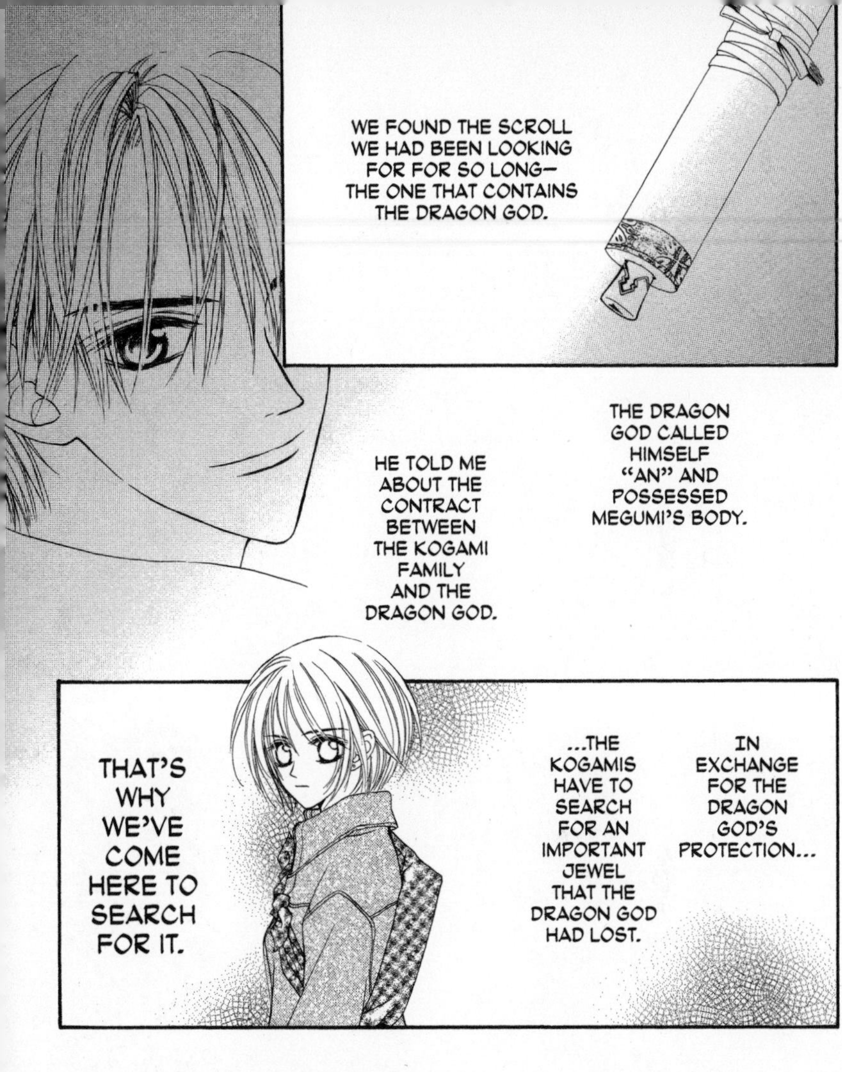
WE FOUND THE SCROLL WE HAD BEEN LOOKING FOR FOR SO LONG—THE ONE THAT CONTAINS THE DRAGON GOD.
THE DRAGON GOD CALLED HIMSELF "AN" AND POSSESSED MEGUMI'S BODY.
HE TOLD ME ABOUT THE CONTRACT BETWEEN THE KOGAMI FAMILY AND THE DRAGON GOD.
IN EXCHANGE FOR THE DRAGON GOD'S PROTECTION...
...THE KOGAMIS HAVE TO SEARCH FOR AN IMPORTANT JEWEL THAT THE DRAGON GOD HAD LOST.
THAT'S WHY WE'VE COME HERE TO SEARCH FOR IT.

Backstory ① I thought about this part of the story taking place in China since the beginning. It's like the "happily ever after" in a fairy tale. After I wrote the first part of *Captive Hearts* and was given the chance to do a series, I suggested that the characters go to China, break the curse and live happily ever after. But at the time, I wasn't given enough pages, so now I'm happy I have the opportunity to see it through! I feel like I just had a huge weight lifted off my shoulders! (Laughs) By the way, I originally wanted Hiryu-kun (who debuted in volume 2) to be in the China story.

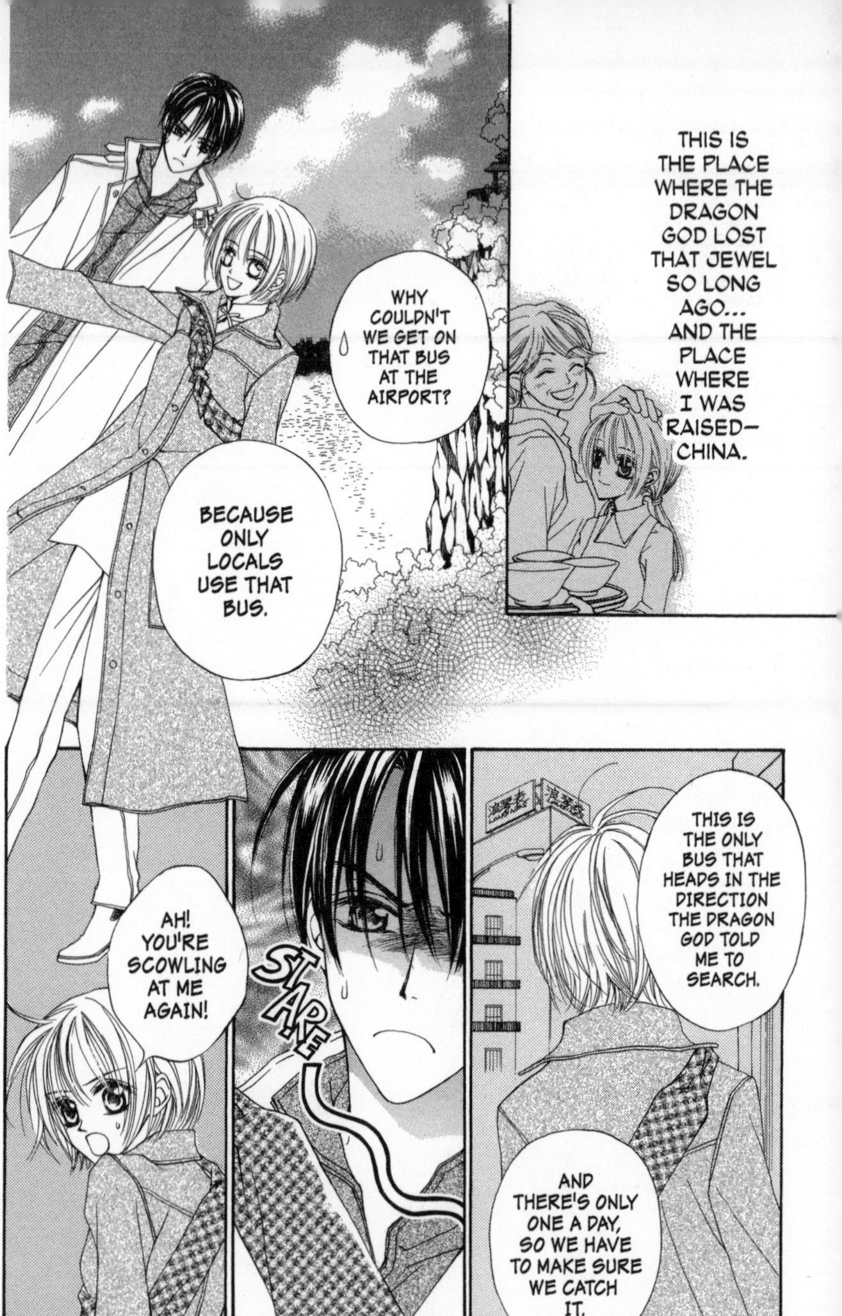
THIS IS THE PLACE WHERE THE DRAGON GOD LOST THAT JEWEL SO LONG AGO... AND THE PLACE WHERE I WAS RAISED—CHINA.
WHY COULDN'T WE GET ON THAT BUS AT THE AIRPORT?
BECAUSE ONLY LOCALS USE THAT BUS.
THIS IS THE ONLY BUS THAT HEADS IN THE DIRECTION THE DRAGON GOD TOLD ME TO SEARCH.
AND THERE'S ONLY ONE A DAY, SO WE HAVE TO MAKE SURE WE CATCH IT.
STARE
AH! YOU'RE SCOWLING AT ME AGAIN!

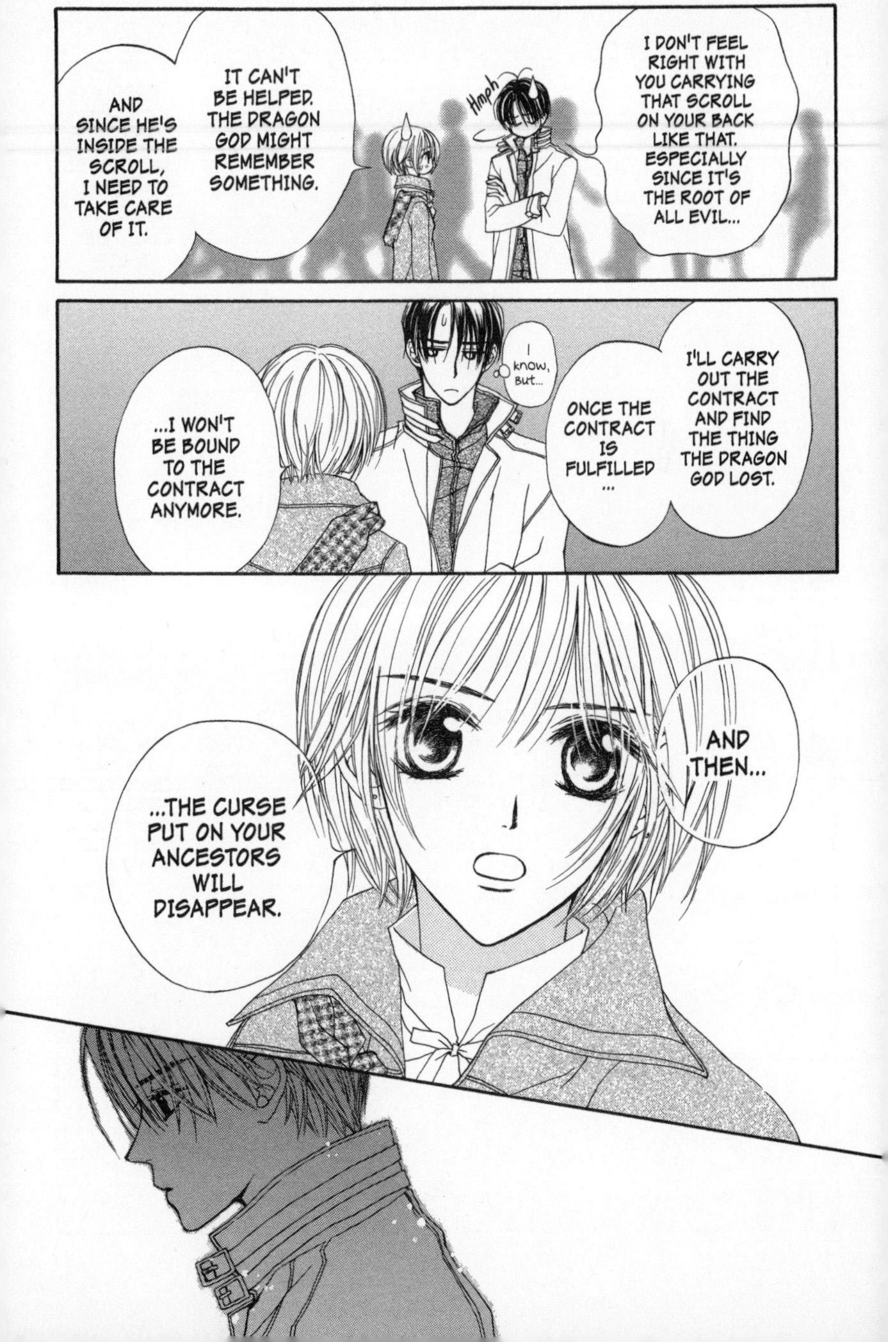
I DON'T FEEL RIGHT WITH YOU CARRYING THAT SCROLL ON YOUR BACK LIKE THAT. ESPECIALLY SINCE IT'S THE ROOT OF ALL EVIL...
Hmph
IT CAN'T BE HELPED. THE DRAGON GOD MIGHT REMEMBER SOMETHING.
AND SINCE HE'S INSIDE THE SCROLL, I NEED TO TAKE CARE OF IT.
I'LL CARRY OUT THE CONTRACT AND FIND THE THING THE DRAGON GOD LOST.
I know, but...
ONCE THE CONTRACT IS FULFILLED...
...I WON'T BE BOUND TO THE CONTRACT ANYMORE.
AND THEN...
...THE CURSE PUT ON YOUR ANCESTORS WILL DISAPPEAR.

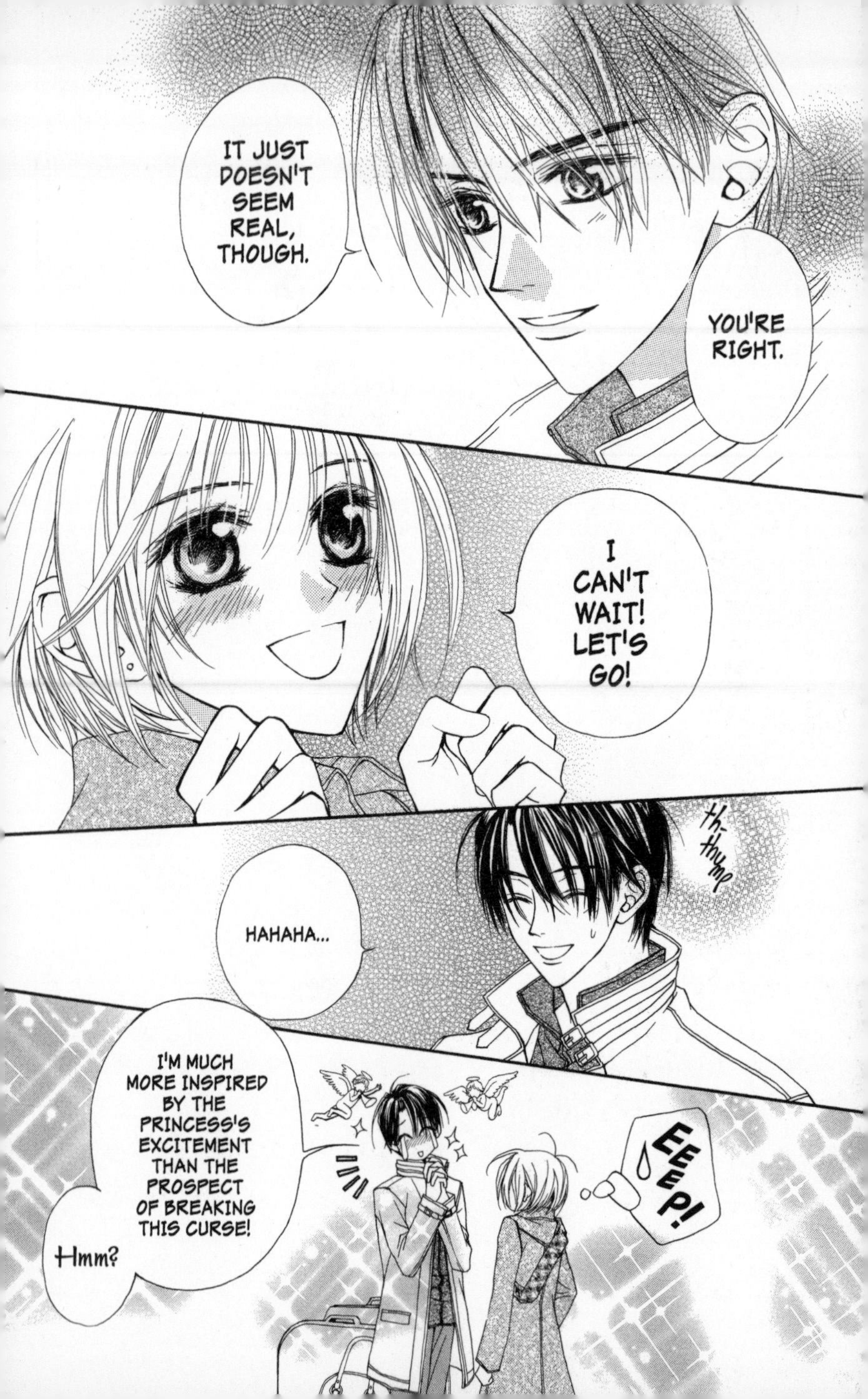

YOU'RE RIGHT.
IT JUST DOESN'T SEEM REAL, THOUGH.
I CAN'T WAIT! LET'S GO!
th-thump
HAHAHA...
I'M MUCH MORE INSPIRED BY THE PRINCESS'S EXCITEMENT THAN THE PROSPECT OF BREAKING THIS CURSE!
Hmm?
EEEP!

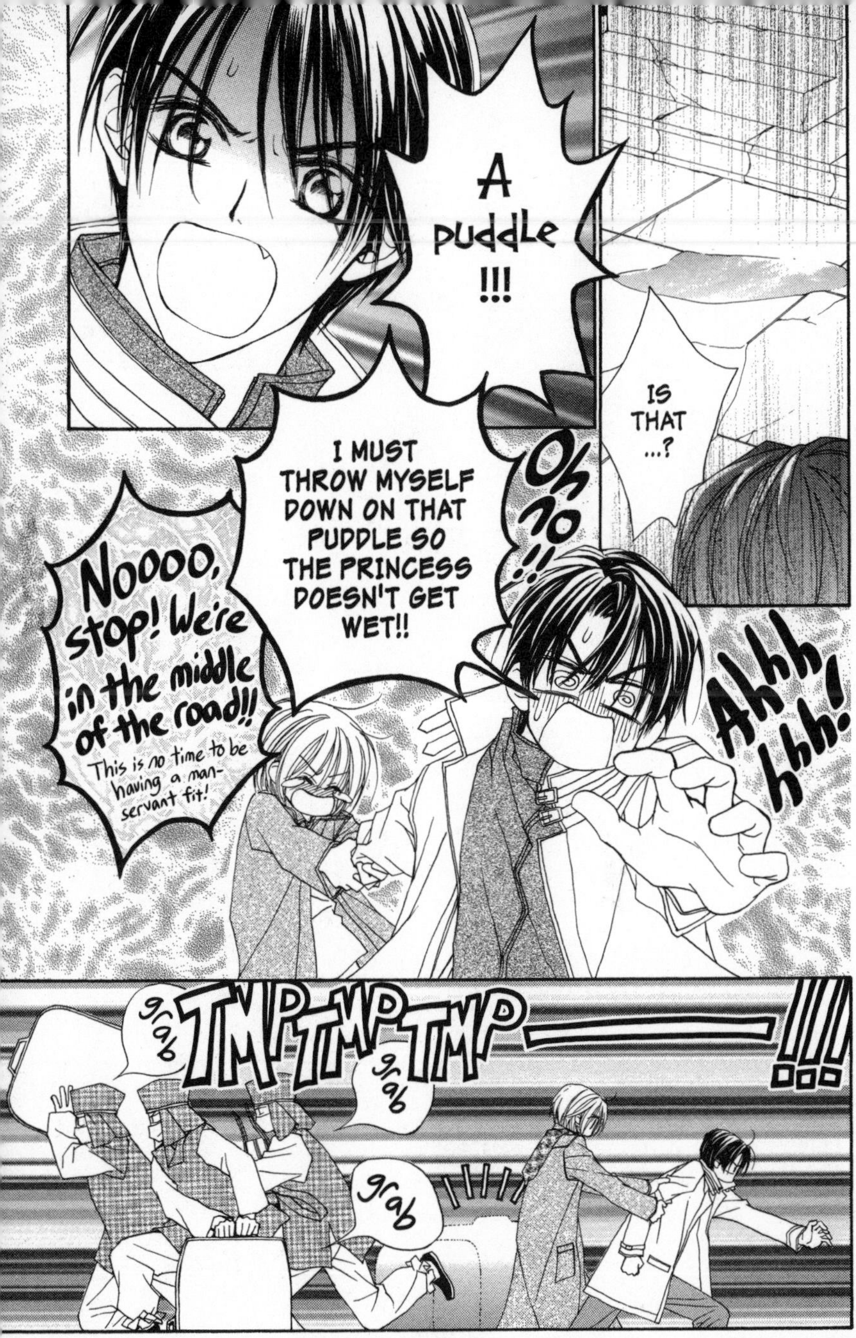
IS THAT ...?
A puddle !!!
I MUST THROW MYSELF DOWN ON THAT PUDDLE SO THE PRINCESS DOESN'T GET WET!!
Oh no!!
Ahhh hhh!
Noooo, stop! We're in the middle of the road!!
This is no time to be having a man-servant fit!
TMP TMP TMP———!!!
grab
grab
grab

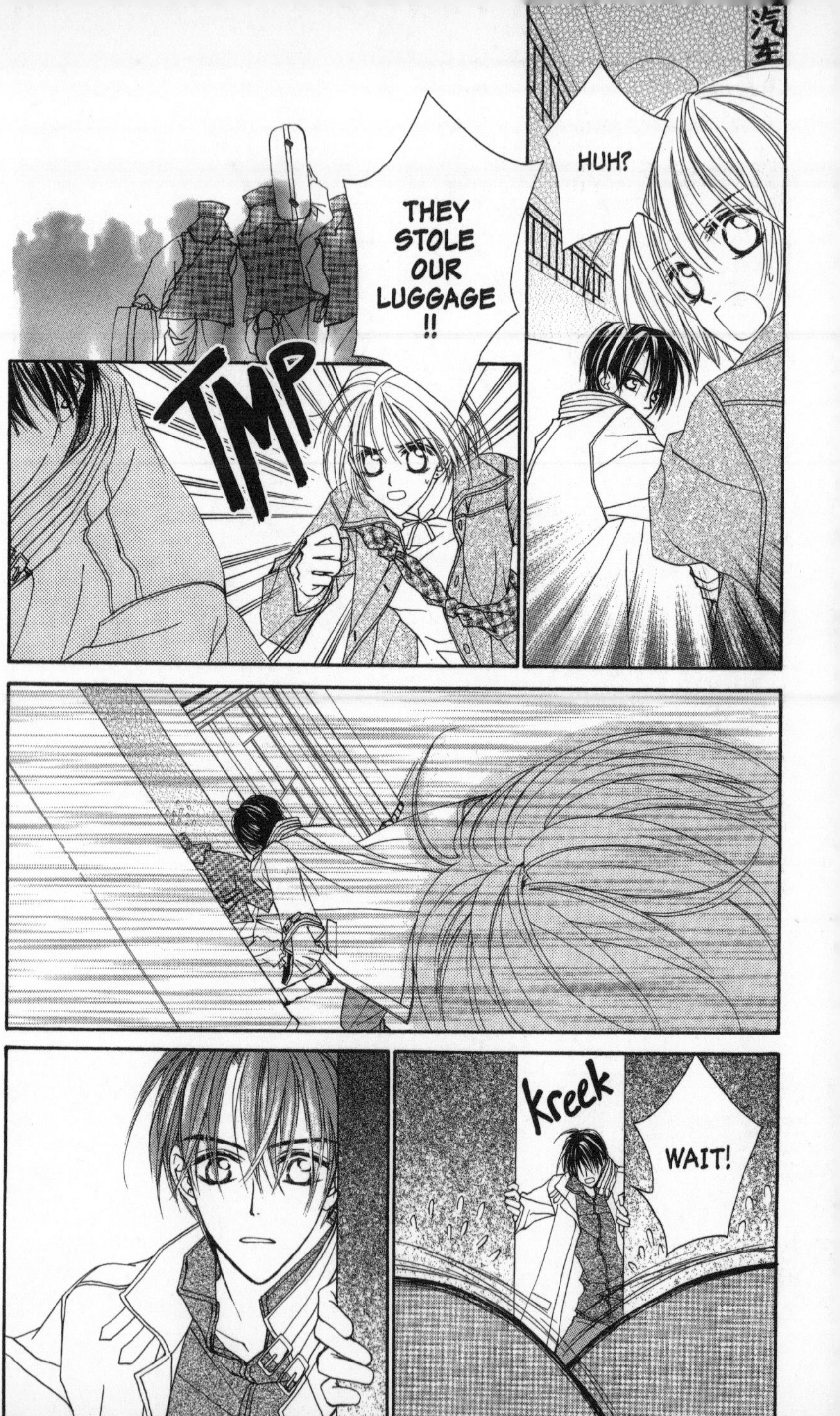
HUH?
THEY STOLE OUR LUGGAGE !!
TMP
kreek
WAIT!

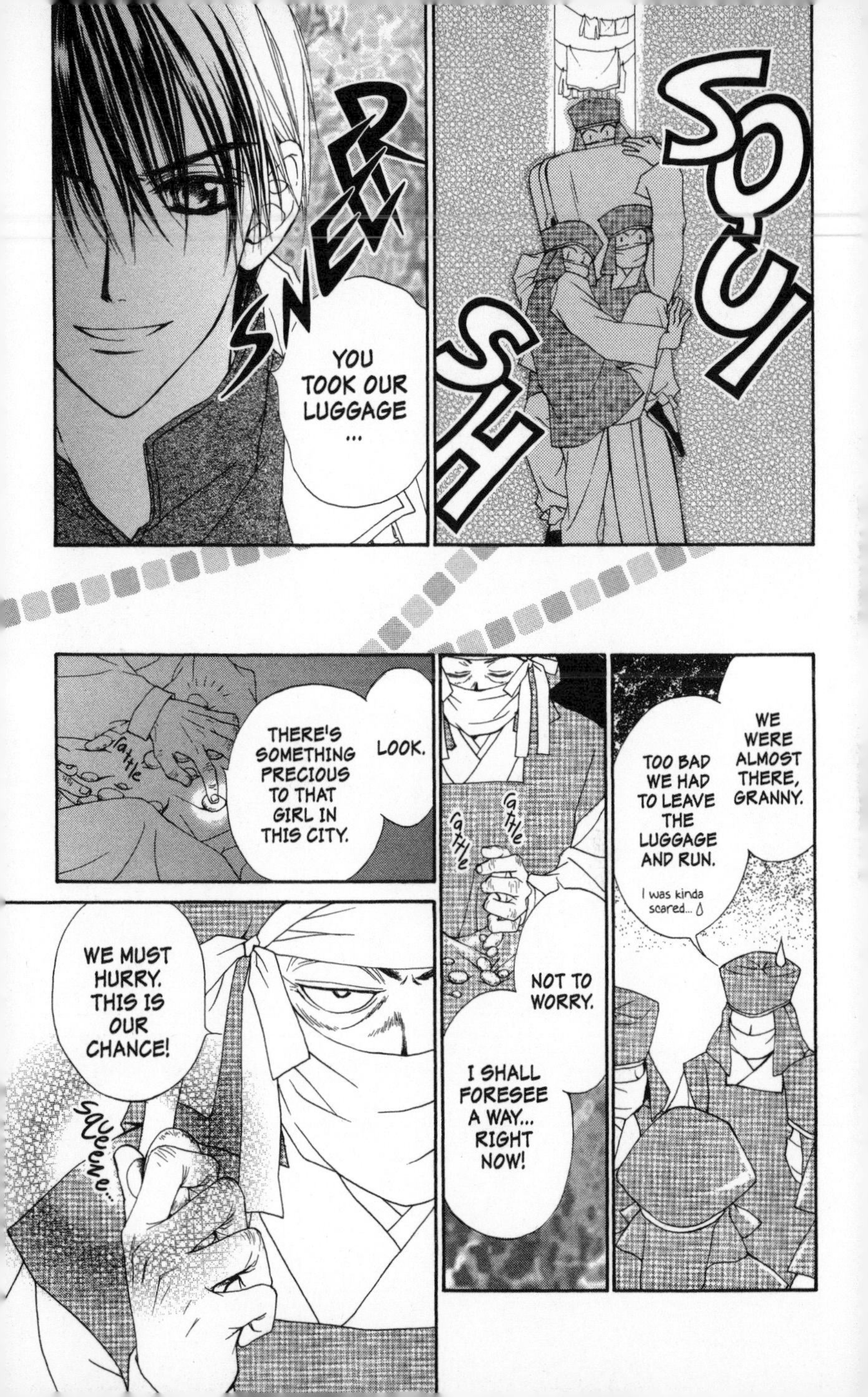
SQUISH
SNEER
YOU TOOK OUR LUGGAGE ...
WE WERE ALMOST THERE, GRANNY.
TOO BAD WE HAD TO LEAVE THE LUGGAGE AND RUN.
I was kinda scared...
rattle
rattle
NOT TO WORRY.
I SHALL FORESEE A WAY... RIGHT NOW!
LOOK.
THERE'S SOMETHING PRECIOUS TO THAT GIRL IN THIS CITY.
rattle
WE MUST HURRY. THIS IS OUR CHANCE!
squeeze...

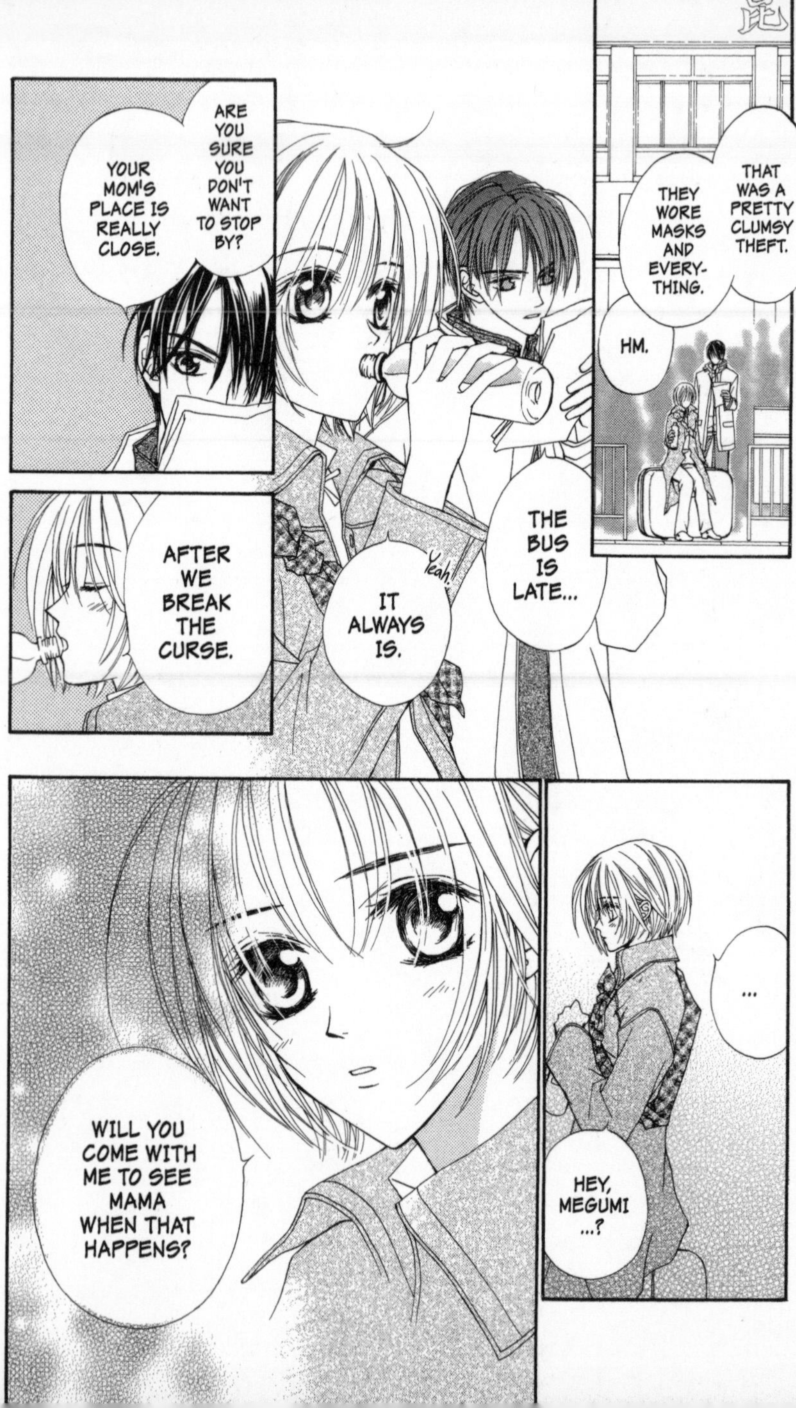

THAT WAS A PRETTY CLUMSY THEFT.
THEY WORE MASKS AND EVERYTHING.
HM.
THE BUS IS LATE...
Yeah.
IT ALWAYS IS.
ARE YOU SURE YOU DON'T WANT TO STOP BY?
YOUR MOM'S PLACE IS REALLY CLOSE.
AFTER WE BREAK THE CURSE.
...
HEY, MEGUMI ...?
WILL YOU COME WITH ME TO SEE MAMA WHEN THAT HAPPENS?

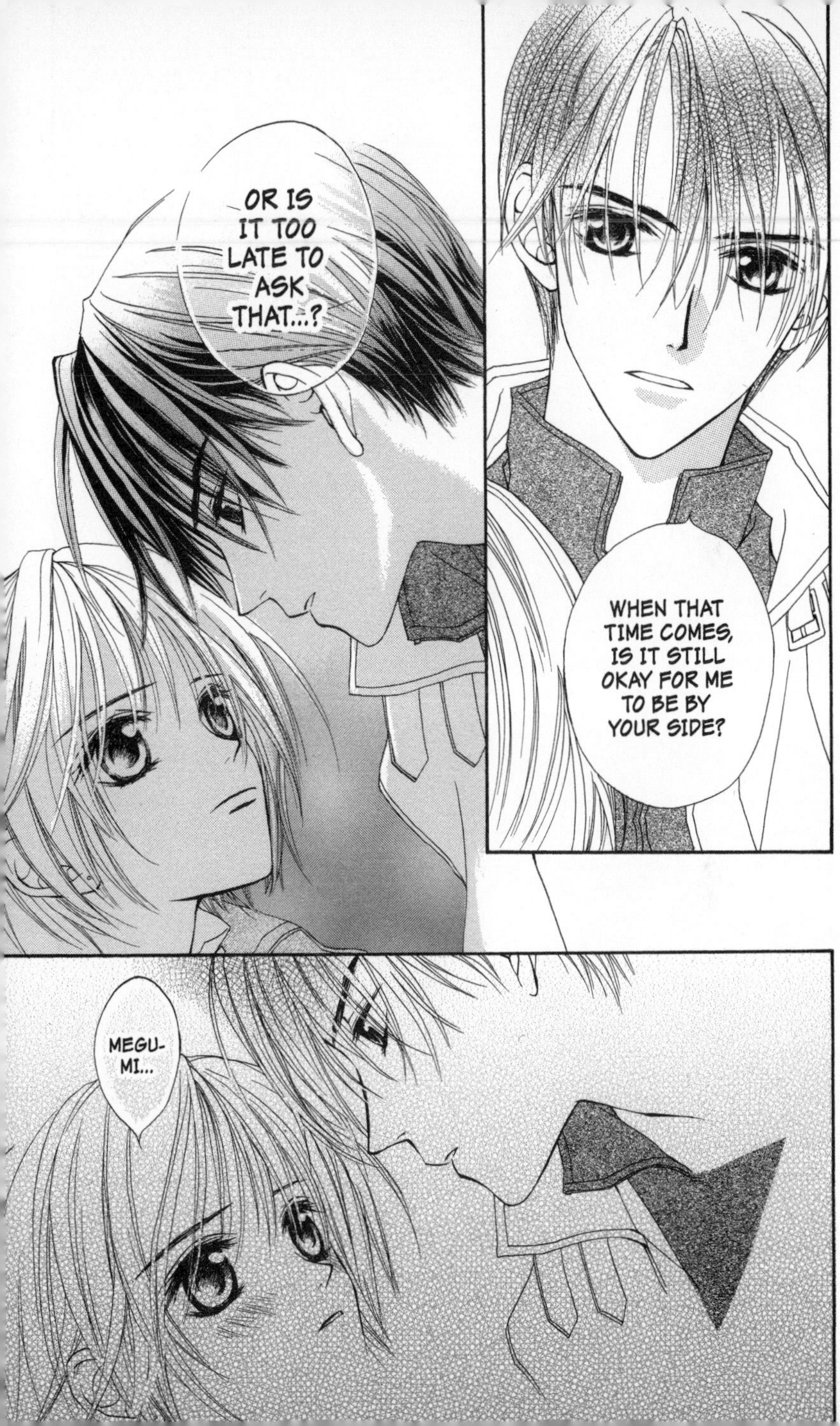
WHEN THAT TIME COMES, IS IT STILL OKAY FOR ME TO BE BY YOUR SIDE?
OR IS IT TOO LATE TO ASK THAT...?
MEGU-MI...

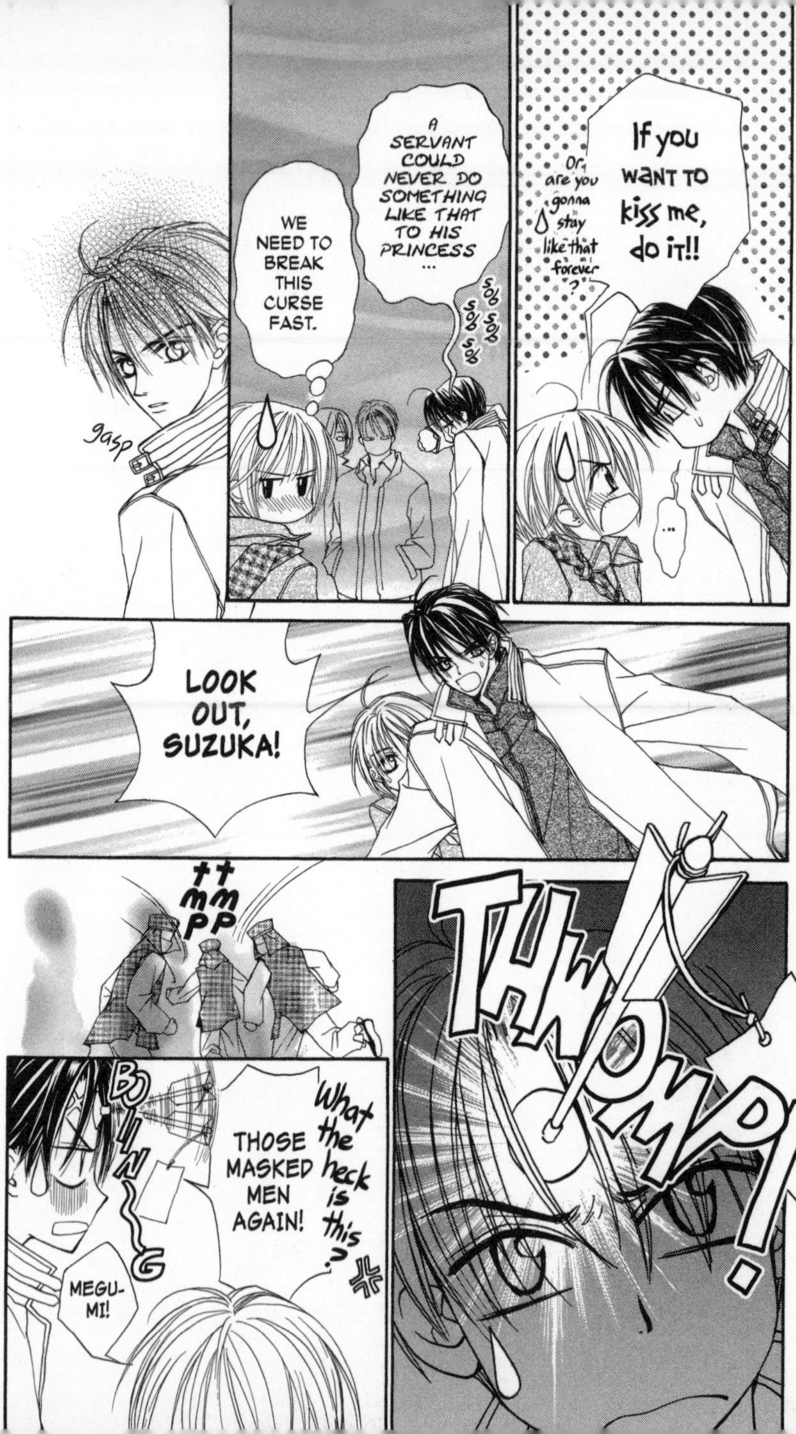

If you want to kiss me, do it!!
Or are you gonna stay like that forever?
...
A SERVANT COULD NEVER DO SOMETHING LIKE THAT TO HIS PRINCESS...
sob sob sob sob
WE NEED TO BREAK THIS CURSE FAST.
gasp
LOOK OUT, SUZUKA!
THWOMP!
tmp tmp
What the heck is this?
THOSE MASKED MEN AGAIN!
BOING
MEGUMI!

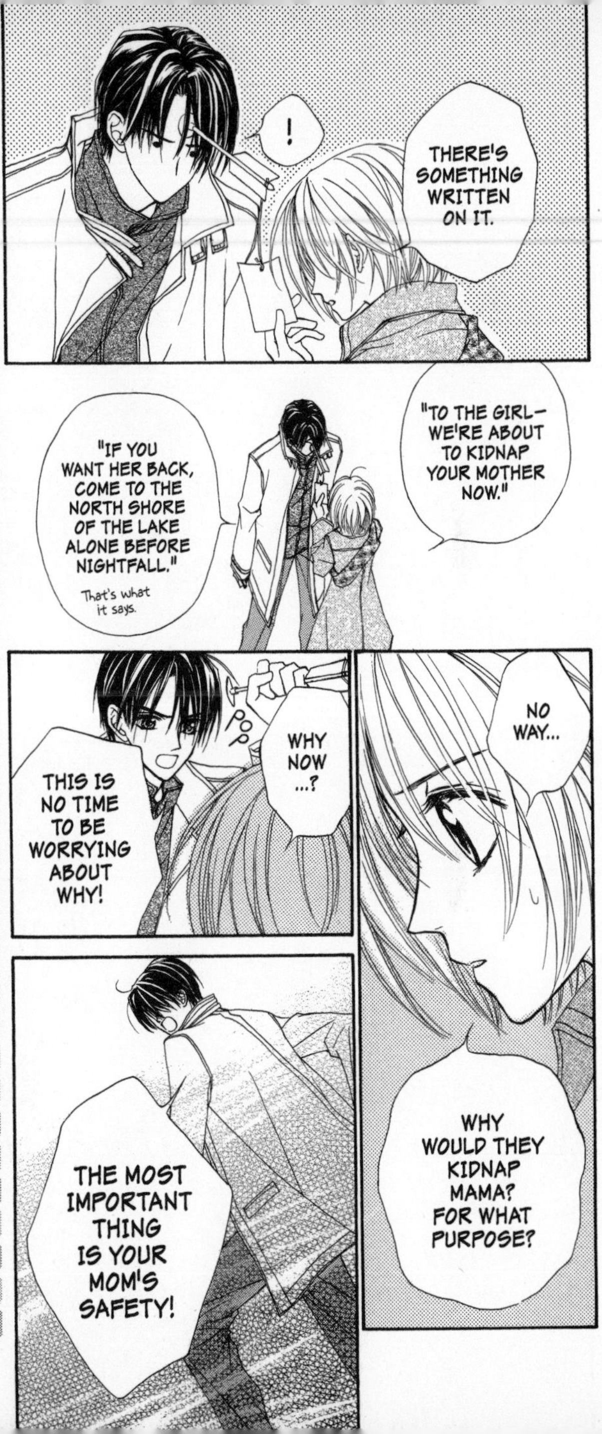
THERE'S SOMETHING WRITTEN ON IT.
!
"TO THE GIRL— WE'RE ABOUT TO KIDNAP YOUR MOTHER NOW."
"IF YOU WANT HER BACK, COME TO THE NORTH SHORE OF THE LAKE ALONE BEFORE NIGHTFALL."
That's what it says.
NO WAY...
WHY WOULD THEY KIDNAP MAMA? FOR WHAT PURPOSE?
WHY NOW ...?
POP
THIS IS NO TIME TO BE WORRYING ABOUT WHY!
THE MOST IMPORTANT THING IS YOUR MOM'S SAFETY!

Greetings

Thanks for picking up this book.

After three years, this is the final volume of *Captive Hearts*. I went as fast as I could! ♪

Looking back, I realize that these past three years have really been packed with no room to spare, full of happy times and sad times...

Whenever I look at the stack of letters I received from everyone, I get so touched. So many people read the story from the very beginning or started in the middle! Of course it doesn't matter how many people there are, but it does make me genuinely happy. Knowing that so many people are reading my work makes me feel so glad I became a professional manga artist.

I'm unbelievably behind on answering letters, plus I have to get the book organized... ;;

I'll just take things one at a time.

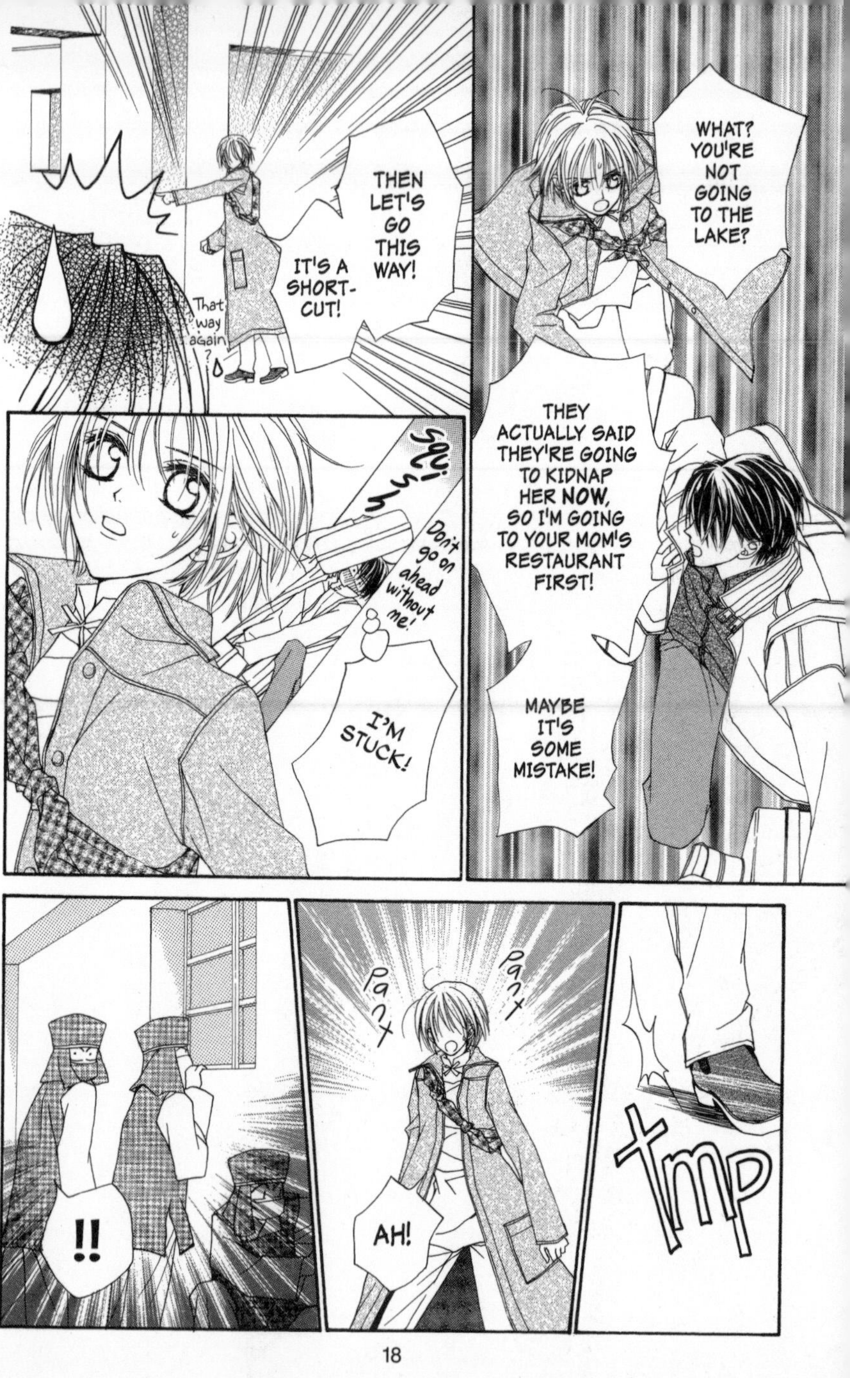

WHAT? YOU'RE NOT GOING TO THE LAKE?
THEY ACTUALLY SAID THEY'RE GOING TO KIDNAP HER NOW, SO I'M GOING TO YOUR MOM'S RESTAURANT FIRST!
MAYBE IT'S SOME MISTAKE!
THEN LET'S GO THIS WAY!
IT'S A SHORT-CUT!
That way again?
squish
Don't go on ahead without me!
I'M STUCK!
tmp
Pant
Pant
AH!
!!

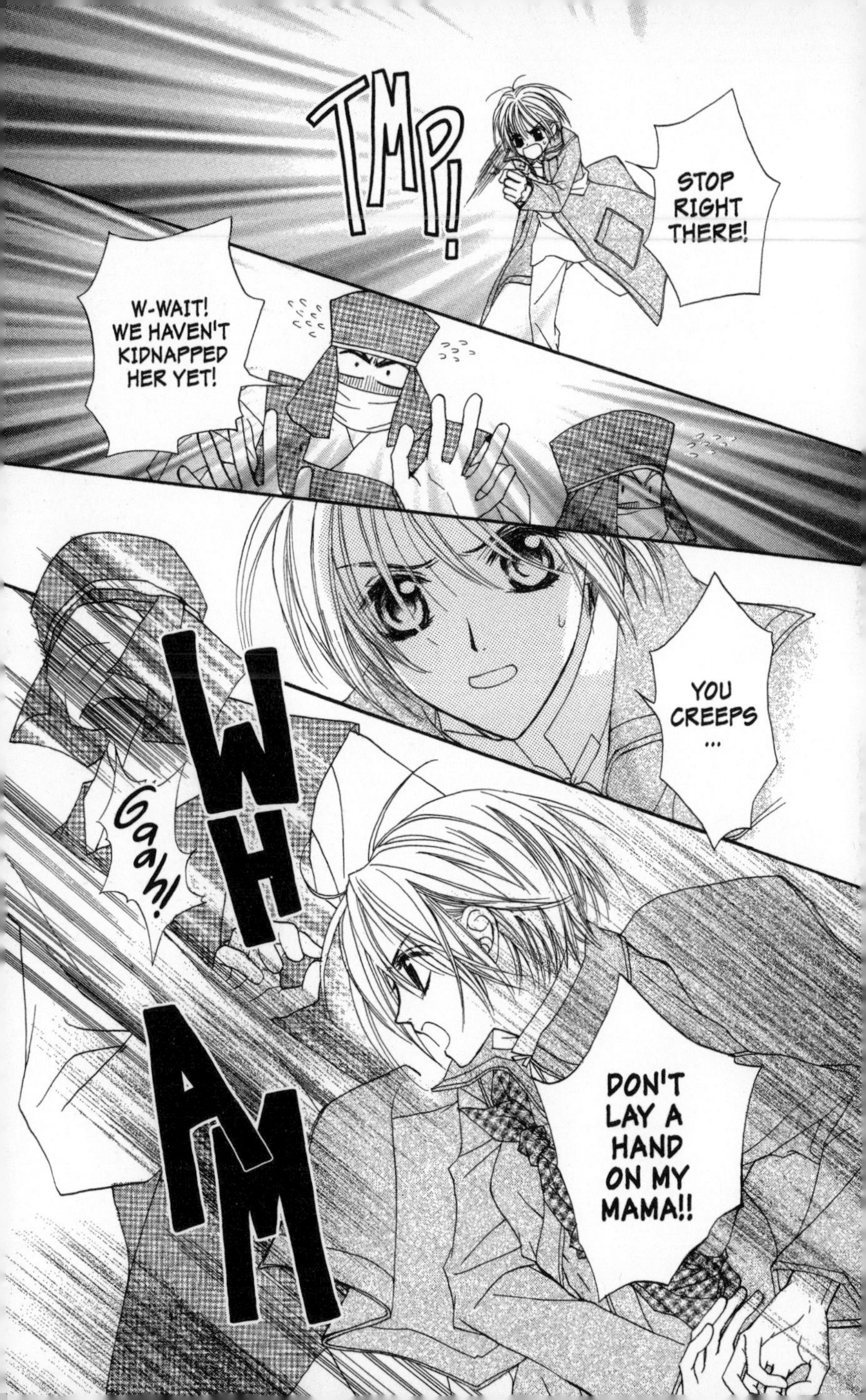
TMP!!
STOP RIGHT THERE!
W-WAIT! WE HAVEN'T KIDNAPPED HER YET!
YOU CREEPS ...
WHAM
Gaah!
DON'T LAY A HAND ON MY MAMA!!

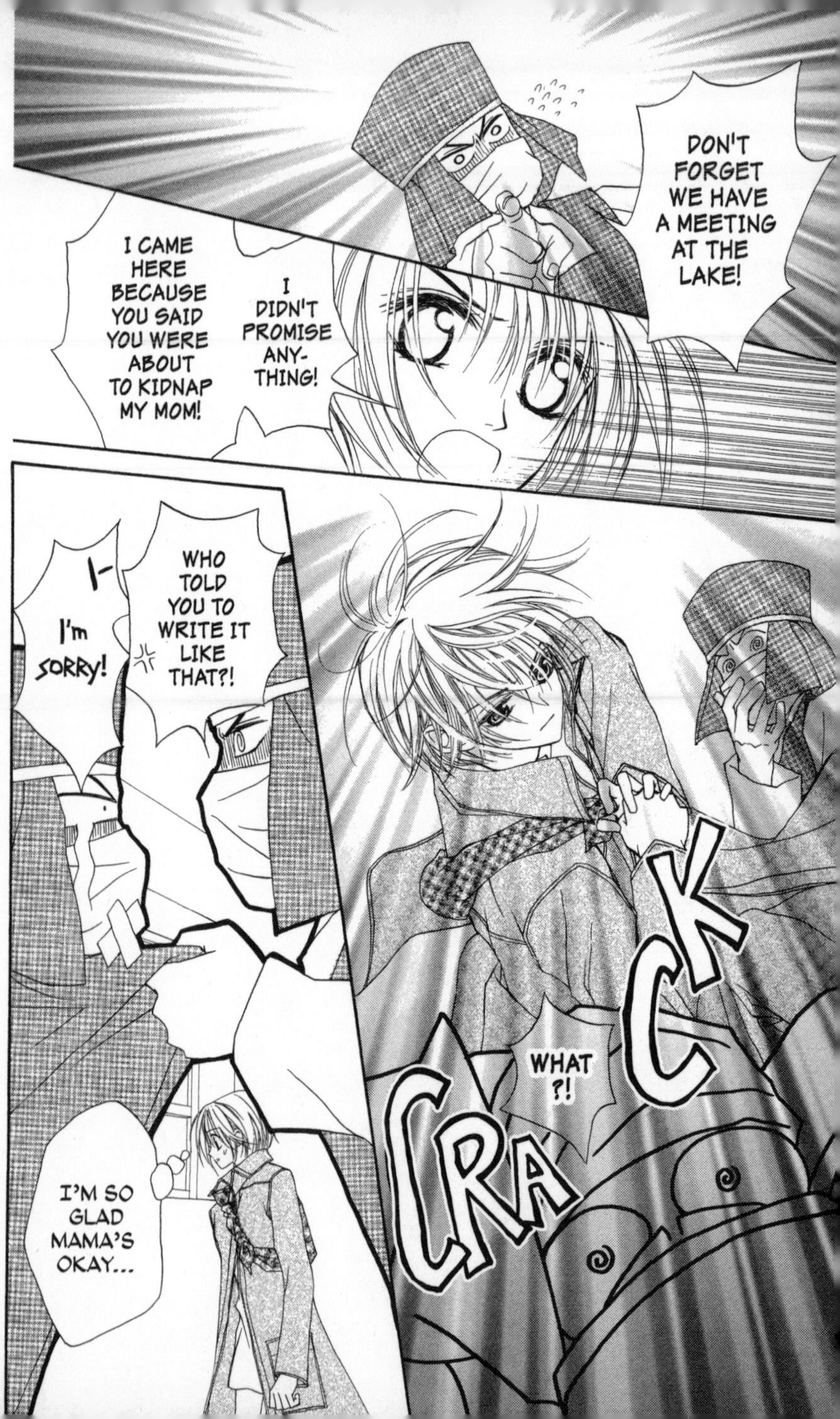
DON'T FORGET WE HAVE A MEETING AT THE LAKE!
I DIDN'T PROMISE ANY-THING!
I CAME HERE BECAUSE YOU SAID YOU WERE ABOUT TO KIDNAP MY MOM!
CRACK
WHAT?!
WHO TOLD YOU TO WRITE IT LIKE THAT?!
I-
I'm SORRY!
I'M SO GLAD MAMA'S OKAY...

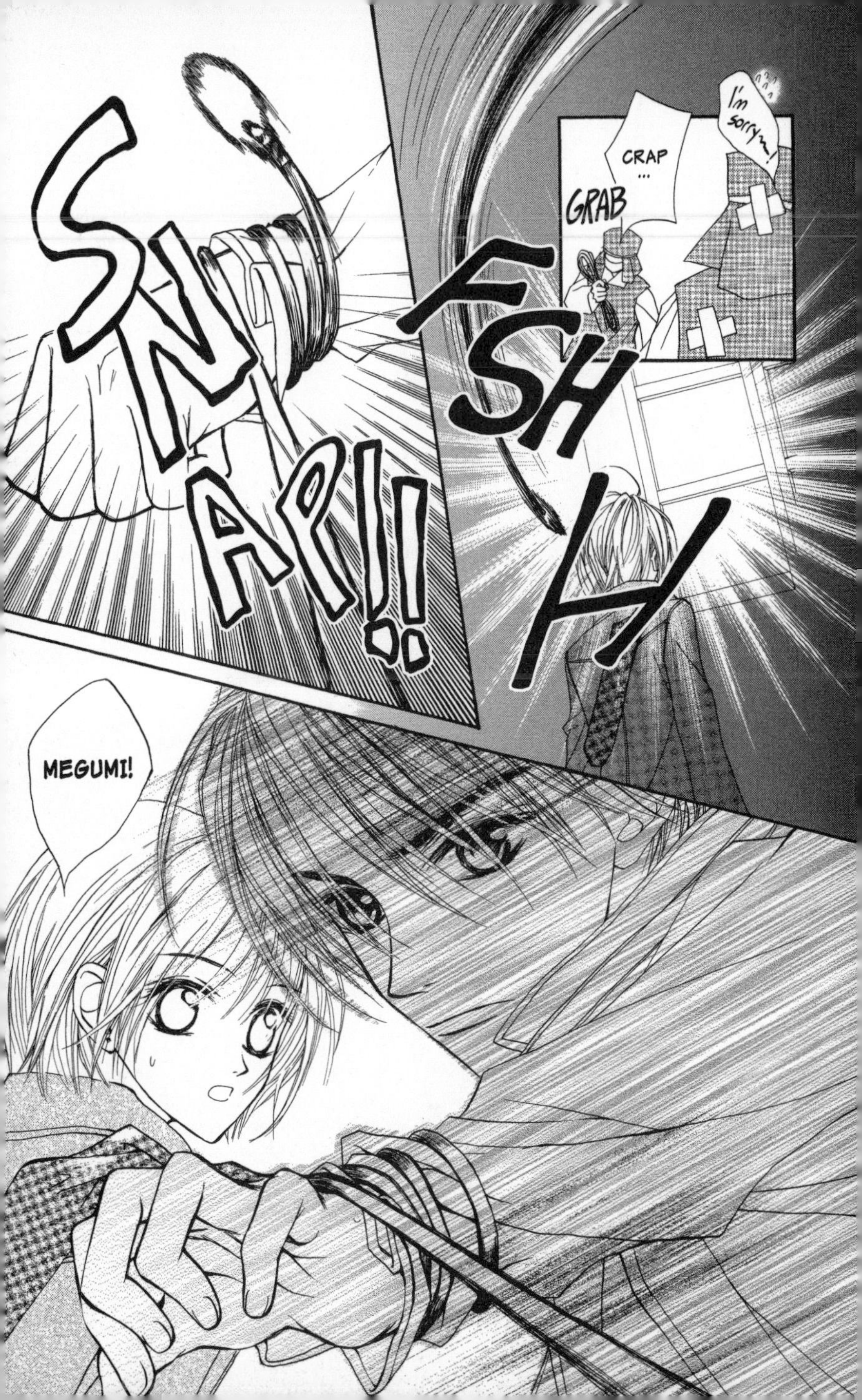
I'm sorry...!
CRAP ...
GRAB
FSHHH
SNAP!!!
MEGUMI!

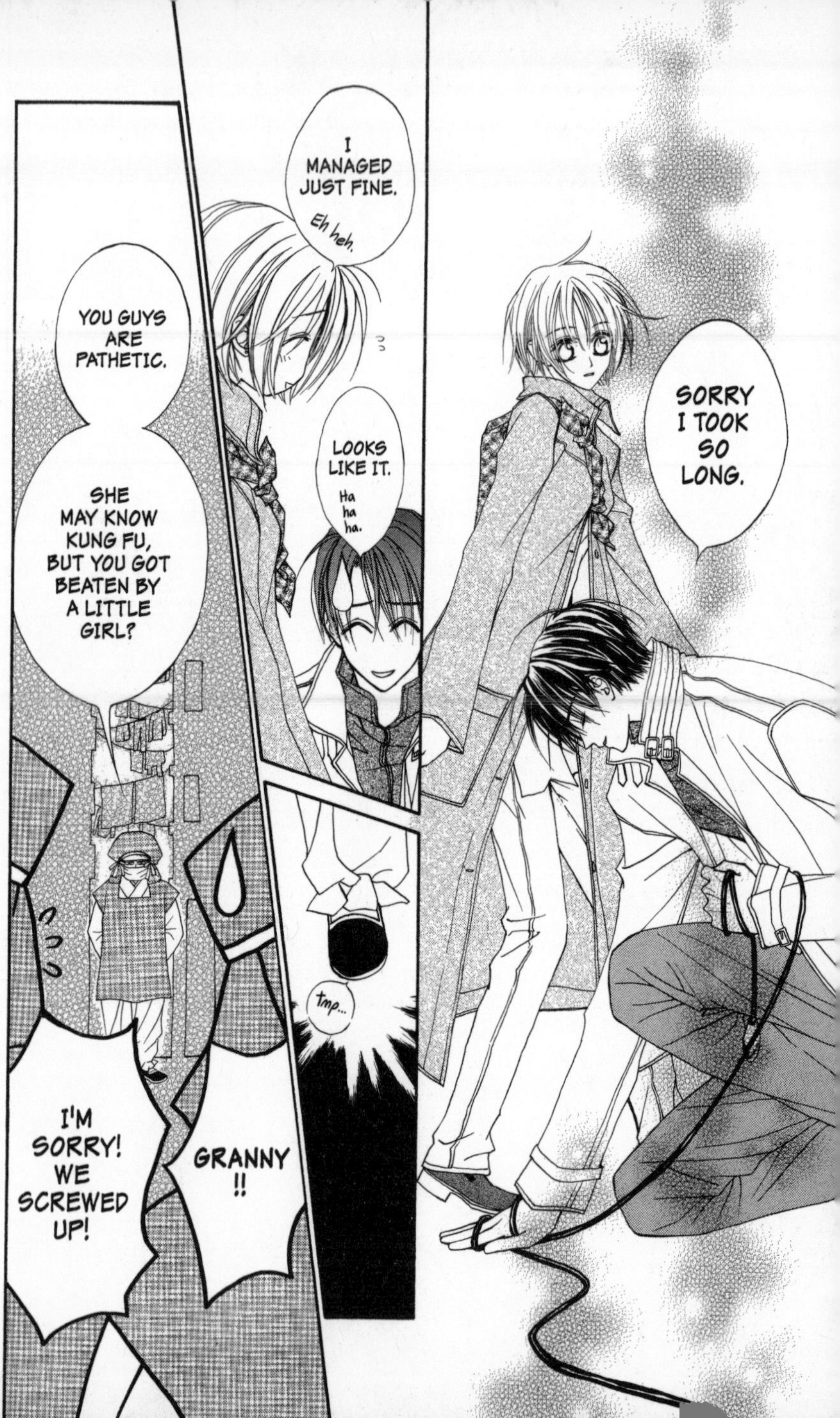
SORRY I TOOK SO LONG.
I MANAGED JUST FINE.
Eh heh.
LOOKS LIKE IT.
Ha ha ha.
tmp...
YOU GUYS ARE PATHETIC.
SHE MAY KNOW KUNG FU, BUT YOU GOT BEATEN BY A LITTLE GIRL?
GRANNY!!
I'M SORRY! WE SCREWED UP!

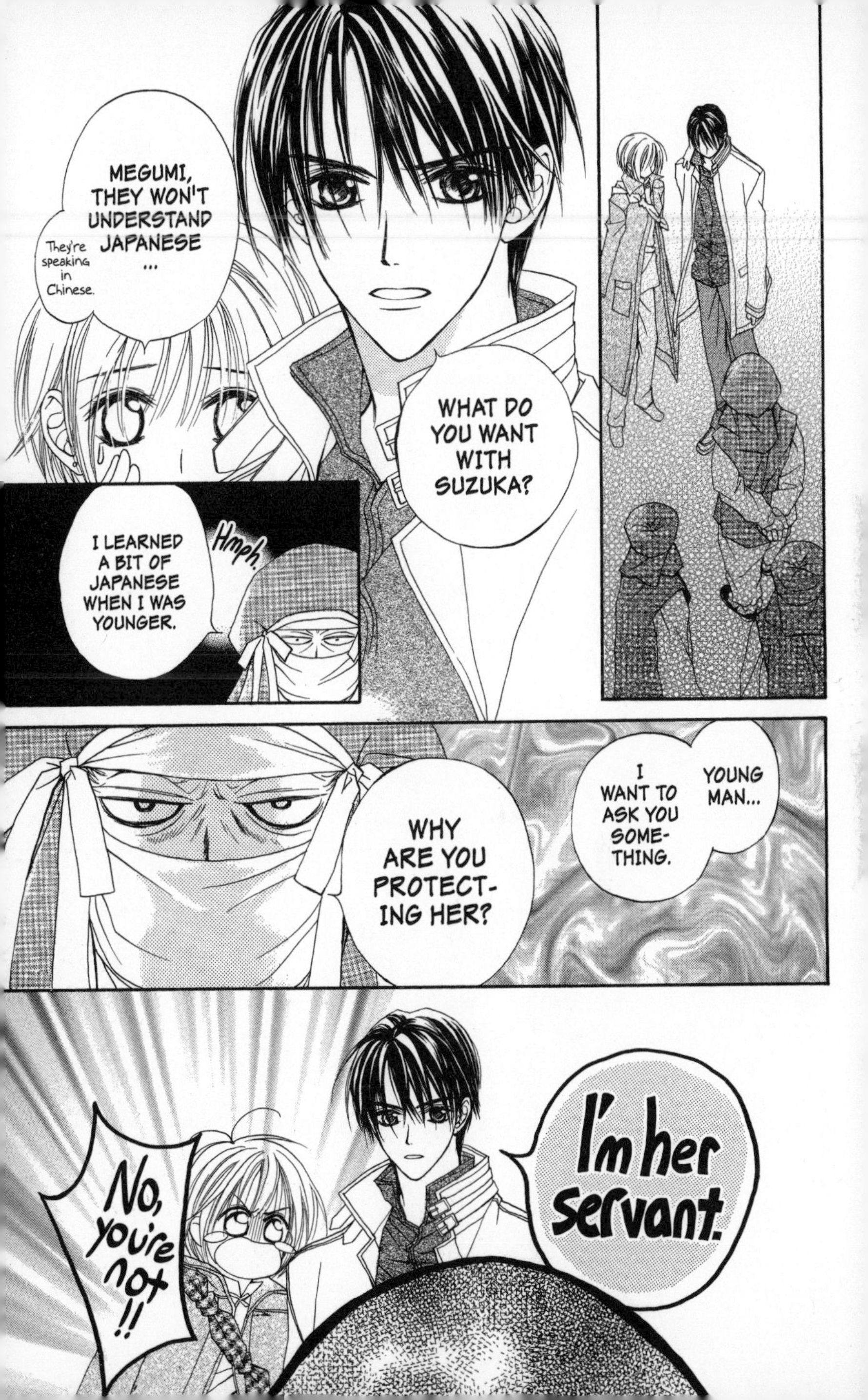
WHAT DO YOU WANT WITH SUZUKA?
MEGUMI, THEY WON'T UNDERSTAND JAPANESE ...
They're speaking in Chinese.
Hmph.
I LEARNED A BIT OF JAPANESE WHEN I WAS YOUNGER.
YOUNG MAN...
I WANT TO ASK YOU SOME-THING.
WHY ARE YOU PROTECT-ING HER?
I'm her servant.
No, you're not!!

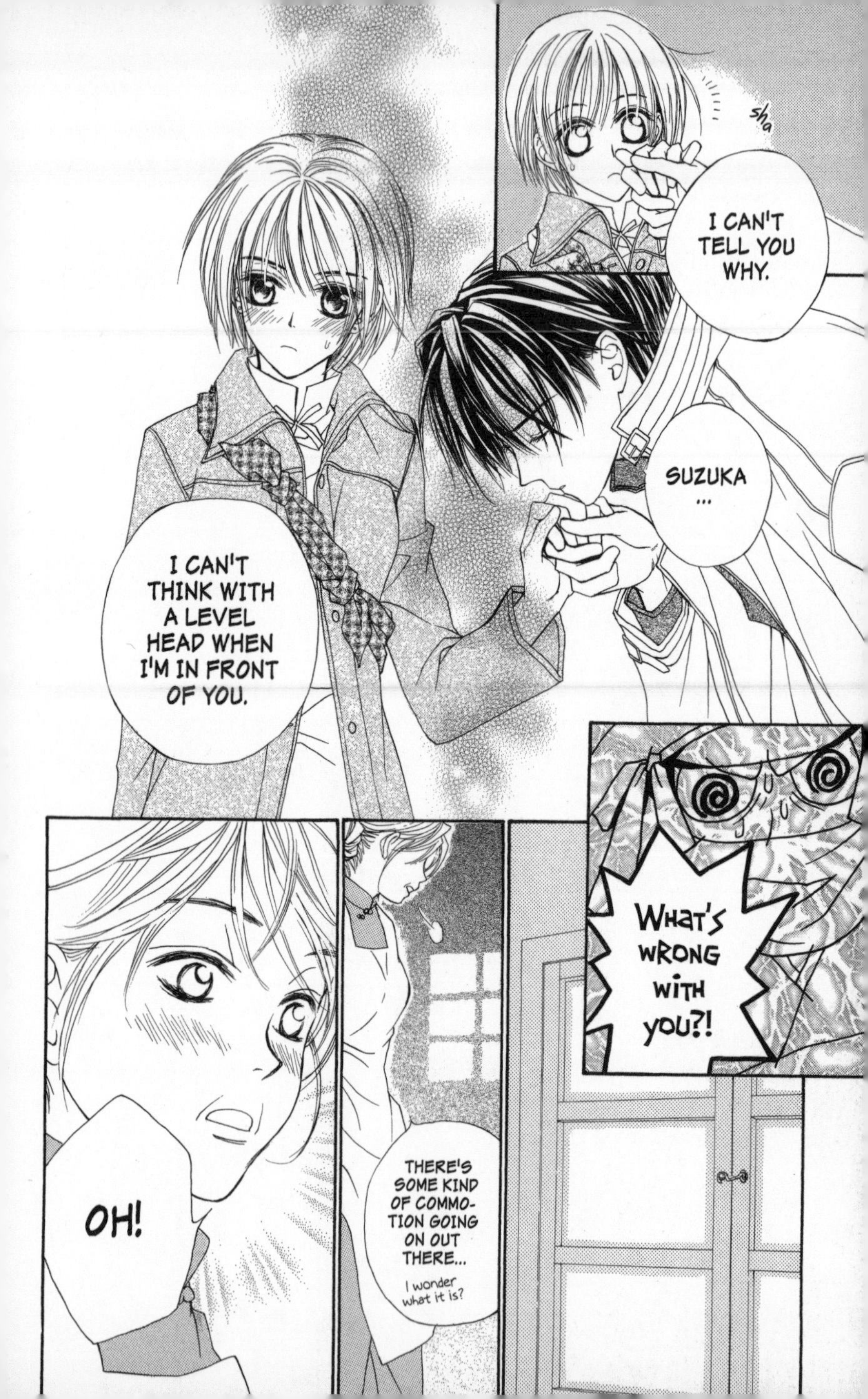
sha
I CAN'T TELL YOU WHY.
SUZUKA ...
I CAN'T THINK WITH A LEVEL HEAD WHEN I'M IN FRONT OF YOU.
WHAT'S WRONG WITH YOU?!
THERE'S SOME KIND OF COMMOTION GOING ON OUT THERE...
I wonder what it is?
OH!

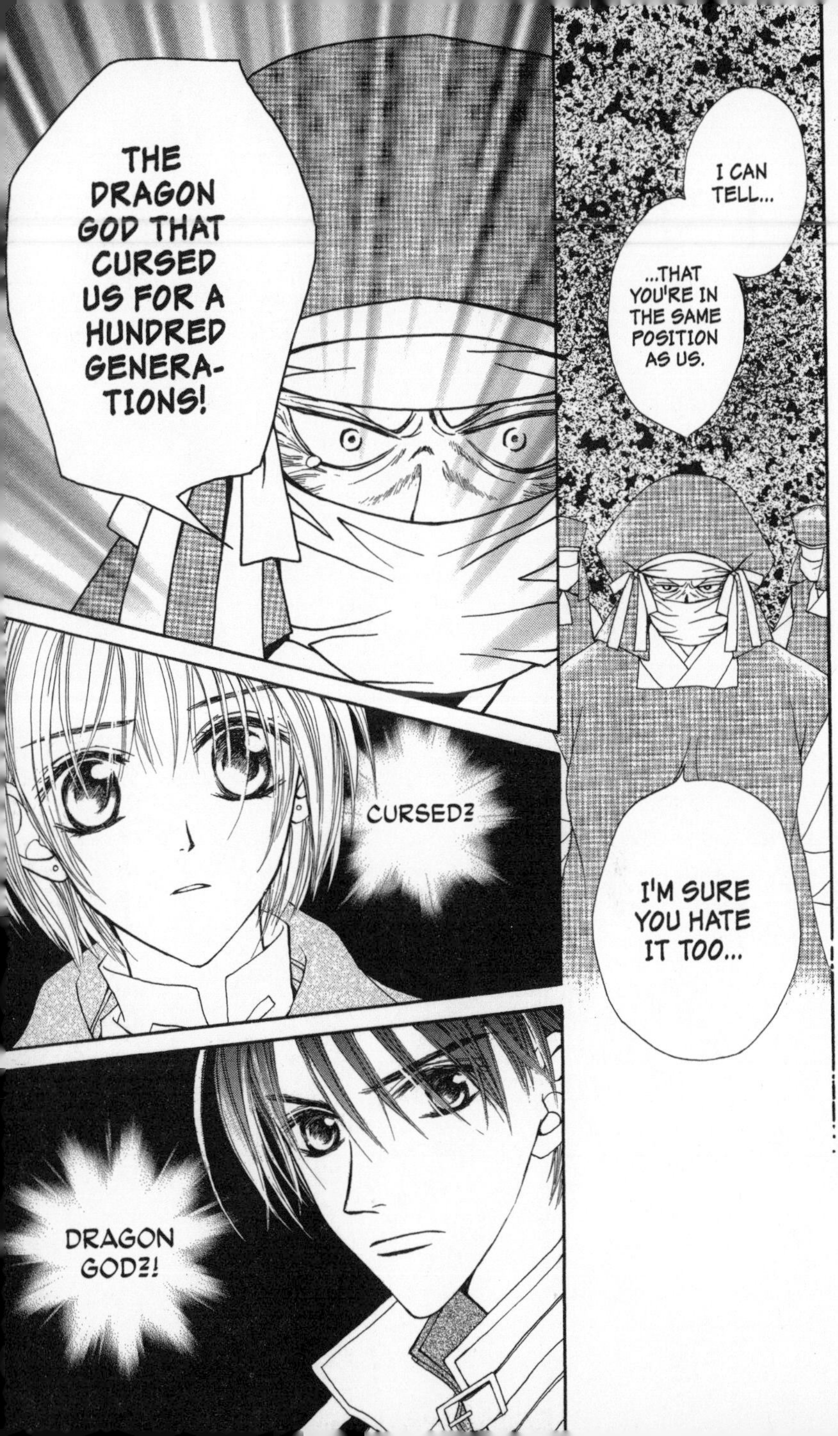
I CAN TELL...
...THAT YOU'RE IN THE SAME POSITION AS US.
I'M SURE YOU HATE IT TOO...
THE DRAGON GOD THAT CURSED US FOR A HUNDRED GENERA-TIONS!
CURSED?
DRAGON GOD?!

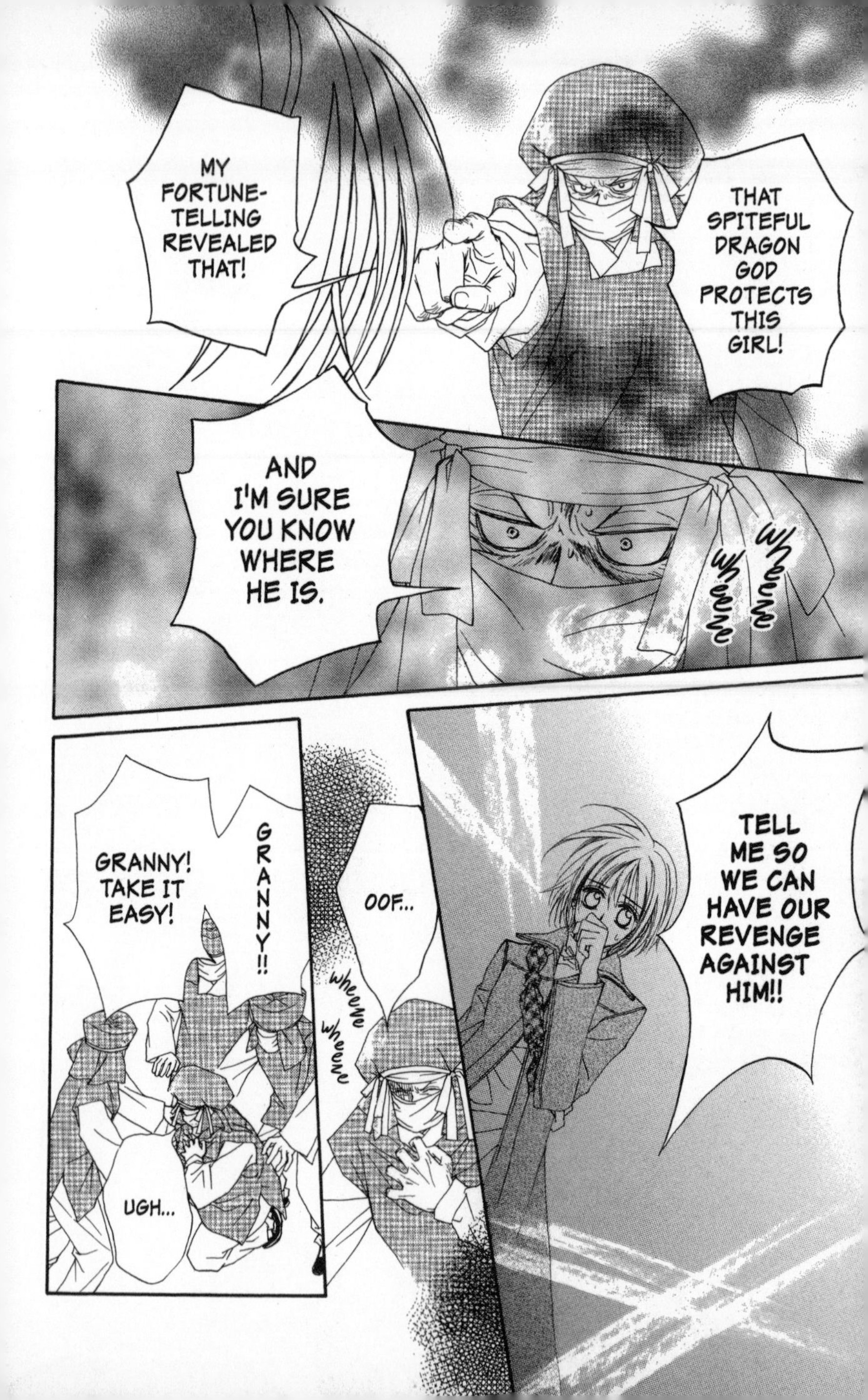
THAT SPITEFUL DRAGON GOD PROTECTS THIS GIRL!
MY FORTUNE-TELLING REVEALED THAT!
AND I'M SURE YOU KNOW WHERE HE IS.
wheeze wheeze
TELL ME SO WE CAN HAVE OUR REVENGE AGAINST HIM!!
OOF...
wheeze wheeze
GRANNY!!
GRANNY! TAKE IT EASY!
UGH...

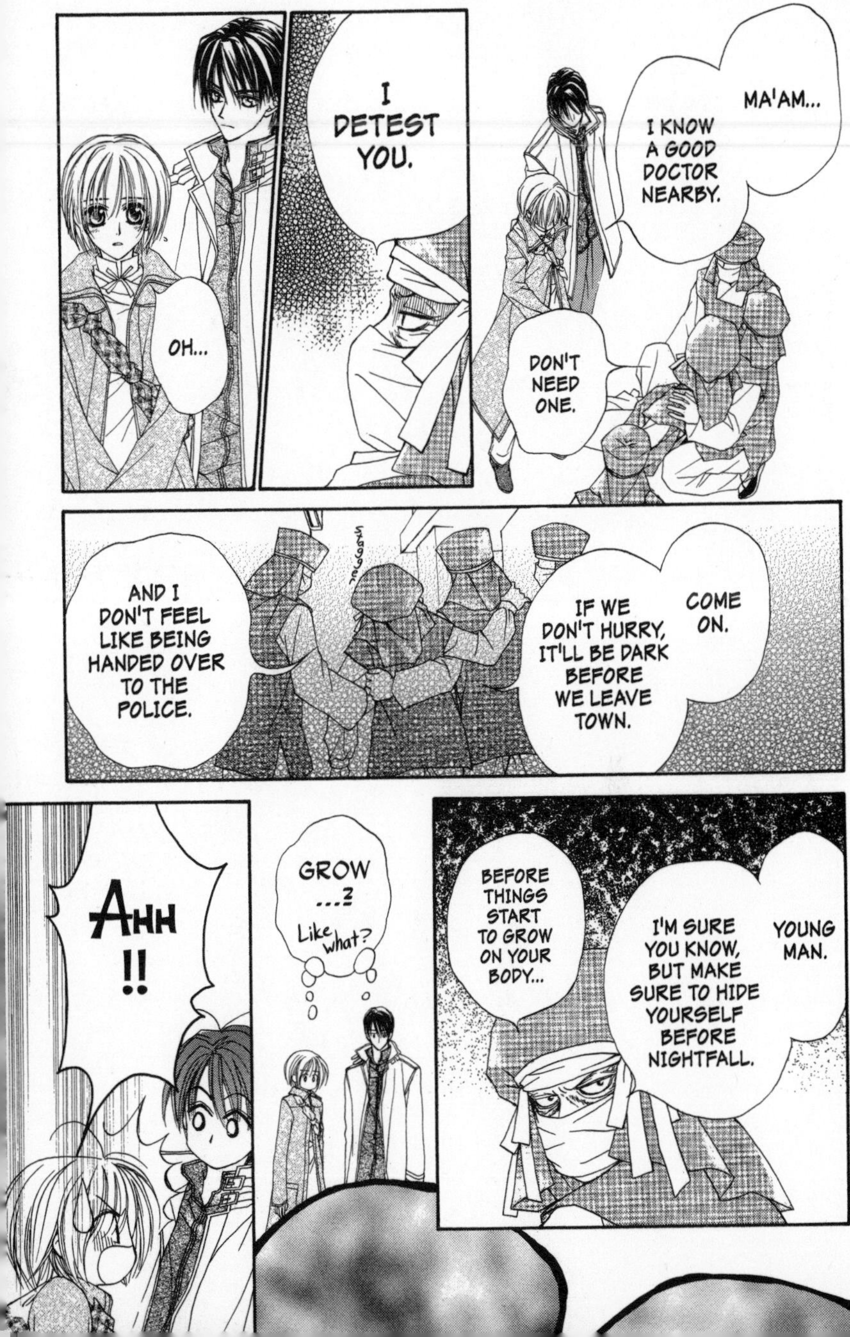
MA'AM...
I KNOW A GOOD DOCTOR NEARBY.
DON'T NEED ONE.
I DETEST YOU.
OH...
COME ON.
IF WE DON'T HURRY, IT'LL BE DARK BEFORE WE LEAVE TOWN.
AND I DON'T FEEL LIKE BEING HANDED OVER TO THE POLICE.
YOUNG MAN.
I'M SURE YOU KNOW, BUT MAKE SURE TO HIDE YOURSELF BEFORE NIGHTFALL.
BEFORE THINGS START TO GROW ON YOUR BODY...
GROW ...?
Like what?
AHH !!

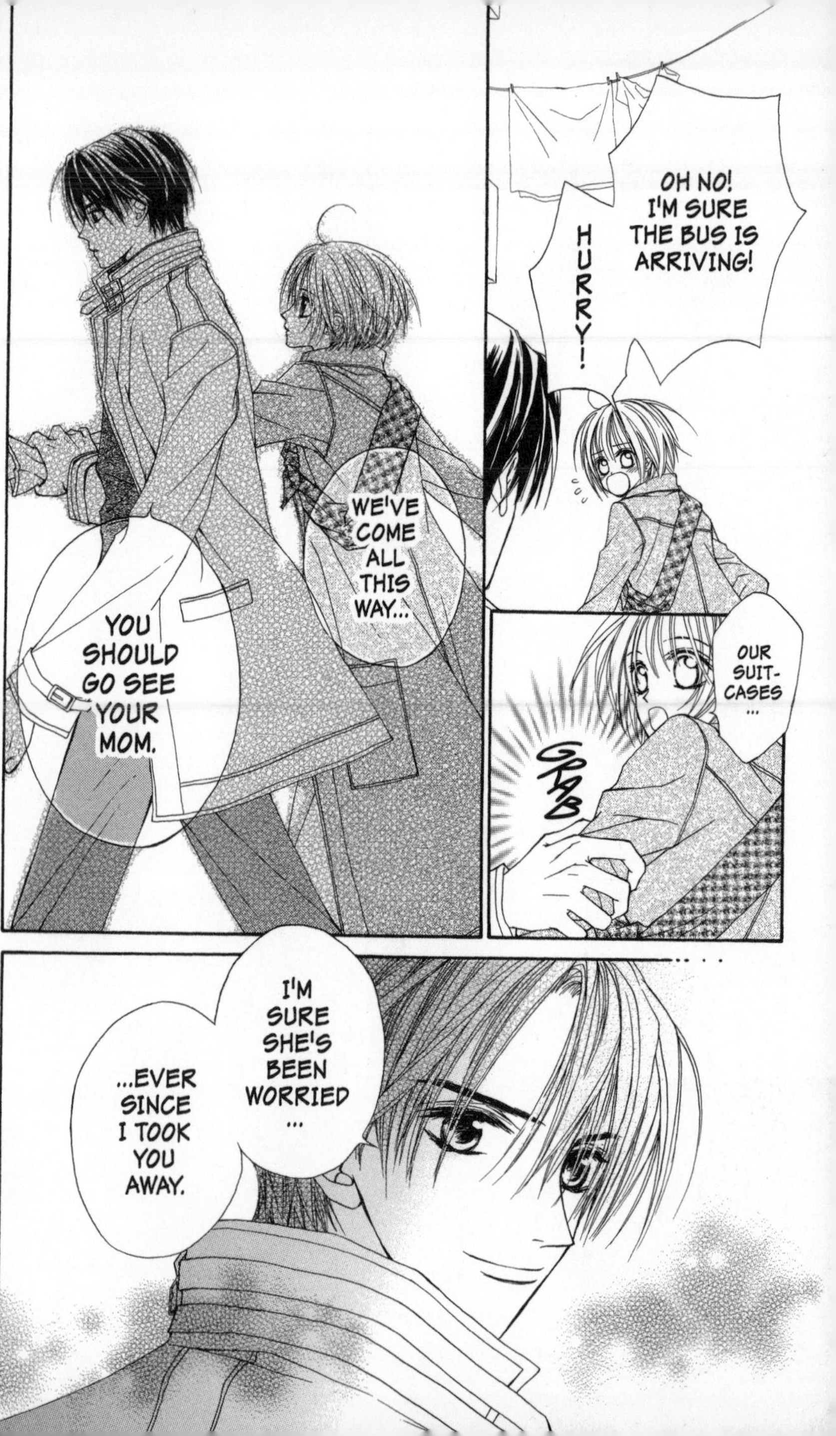
OH NO! I'M SURE THE BUS IS ARRIVING!
HURRY!
OUR SUIT-CASES ...
GRAB
WE'VE COME ALL THIS WAY...
YOU SHOULD GO SEE YOUR MOM.
I'M SURE SHE'S BEEN WORRIED ...
...EVER SINCE I TOOK YOU AWAY.

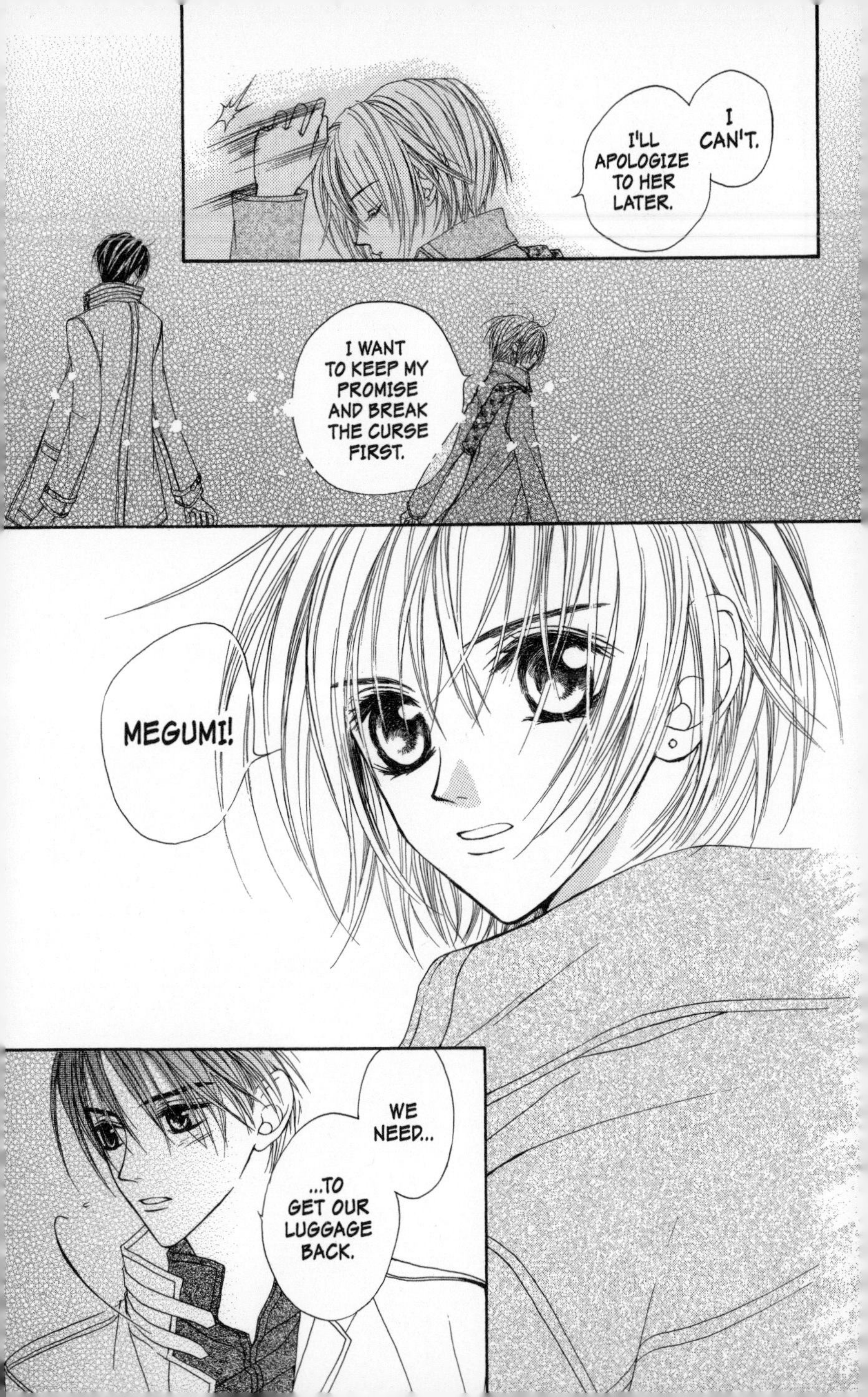
I CAN'T.
I'LL APOLOGIZE TO HER LATER.
I WANT TO KEEP MY PROMISE AND BREAK THE CURSE FIRST.
MEGUMI!
WE NEED...
...TO GET OUR LUGGAGE BACK.

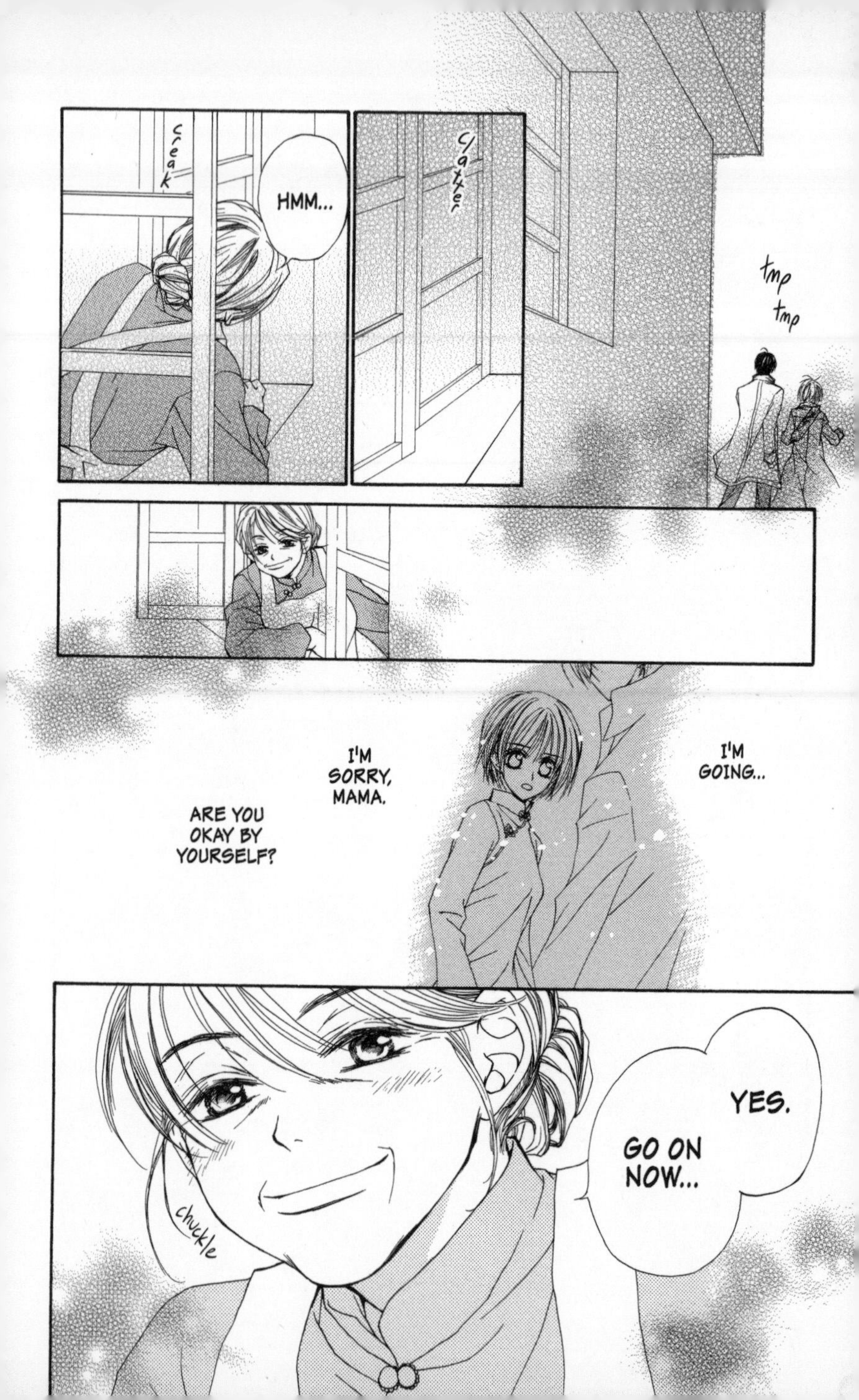
tmp tmp
clatter
creak
HMM...
I'M GOING...
I'M SORRY, MAMA.
ARE YOU OKAY BY YOURSELF?
YES.
GO ON NOW...
chuckle

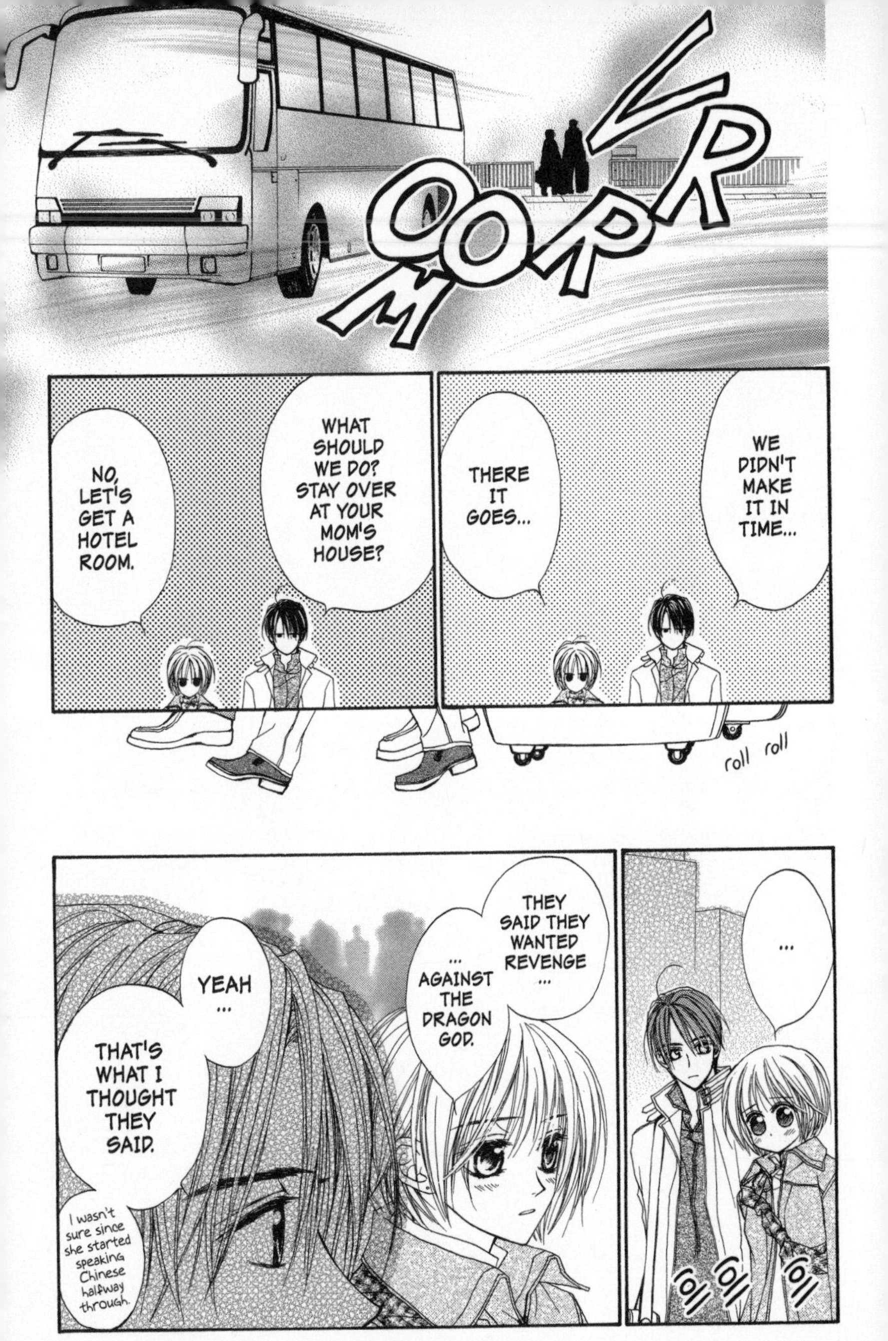
VROOOM
WE DIDN'T MAKE IT IN TIME...
THERE IT GOES...
WHAT SHOULD WE DO? STAY OVER AT YOUR MOM'S HOUSE?
NO, LET'S GET A HOTEL ROOM.
roll roll
...
roll roll roll
THEY SAID THEY WANTED REVENGE ...
... AGAINST THE DRAGON GOD.
YEAH ...
THAT'S WHAT I THOUGHT THEY SAID.
I wasn't sure since she started speaking Chinese halfway through.

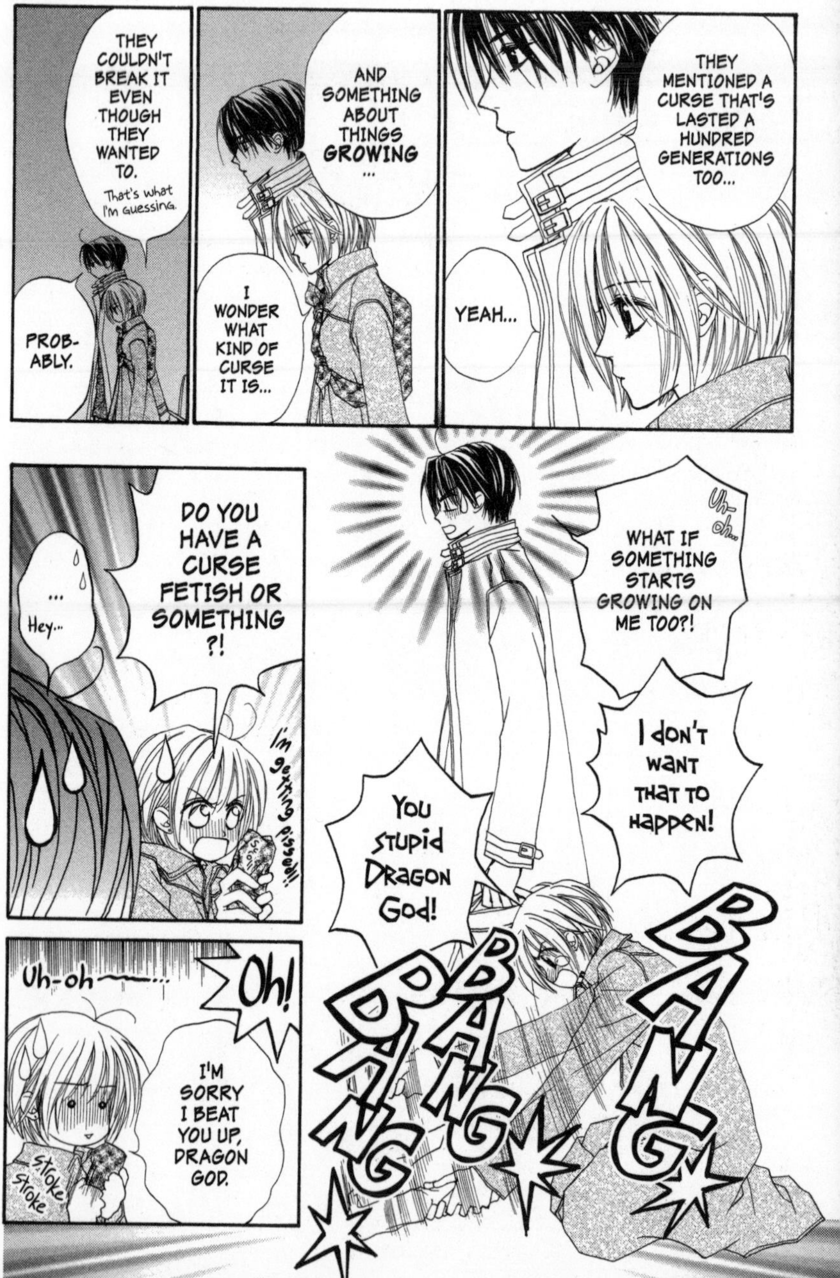
THEY MENTIONED A CURSE THAT'S LASTED A HUNDRED GENERATIONS TOO...
YEAH...
AND SOMETHING ABOUT THINGS GROWING ...
I WONDER WHAT KIND OF CURSE IT IS...
THEY COULDN'T BREAK IT EVEN THOUGH THEY WANTED TO.
That's what I'm guessing.
PROB-ABLY.
Uh-oh...
WHAT IF SOMETHING STARTS GROWING ON ME TOO?!
I don't want that to happen!
You stupid Dragon God!
BANG
BANG
BANG
DO YOU HAVE A CURSE FETISH OR SOMETHING ?!
... Hey...
I'm getting pissed!!
Oh!
Uh-oh———...
I'M SORRY I BEAT YOU UP, DRAGON GOD.
stroke stroke

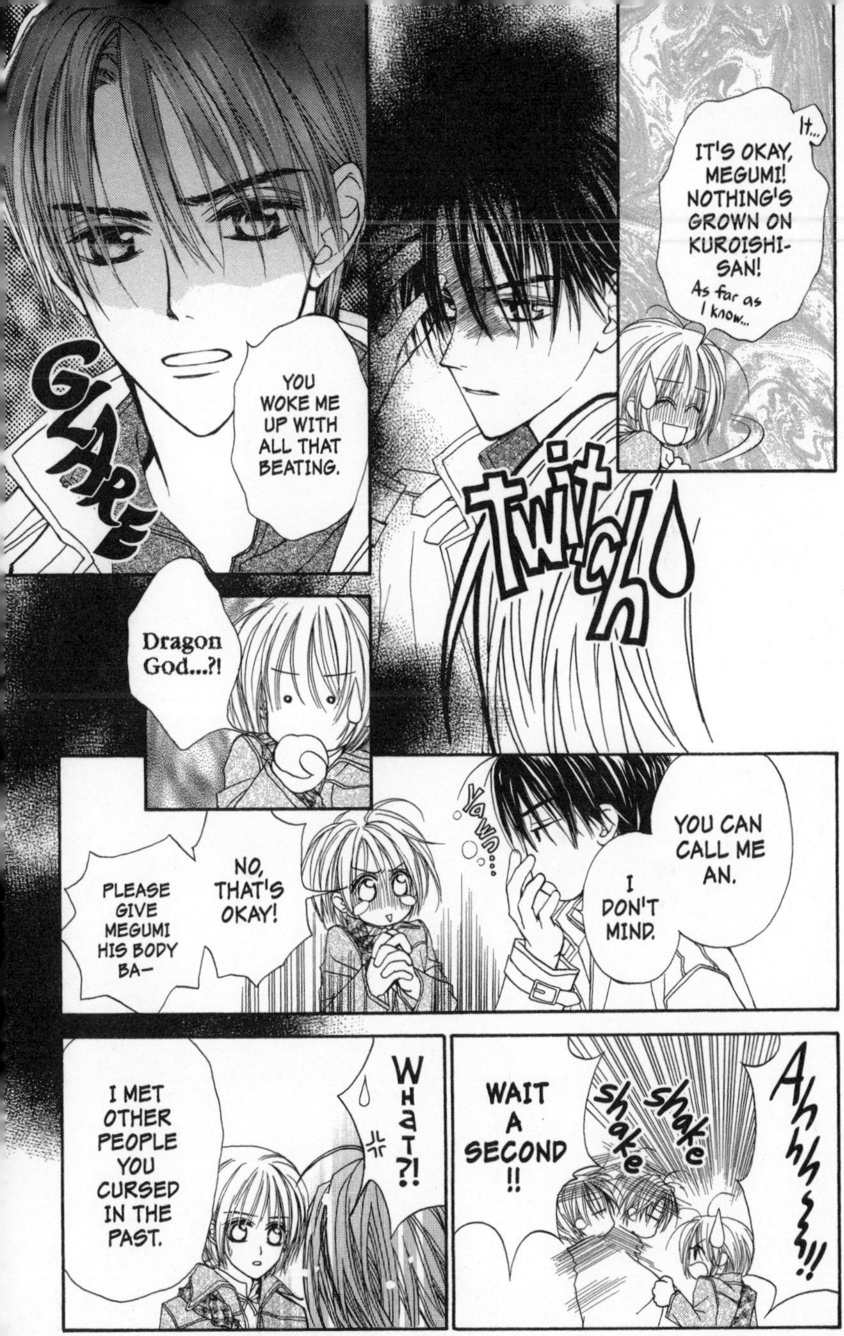
It...
IT'S OKAY, MEGUMI! NOTHING'S GROWN ON KUROISHI-SAN!
As far as I know...
twitch
GLARE
YOU WOKE ME UP WITH ALL THAT BEATING.
Dragon God...?!
YOU CAN CALL ME AN.
I DON'T MIND.
Yawn...
NO, THAT'S OKAY!
PLEASE GIVE MEGUMI HIS BODY BA–
Ahhhh!!
shake
shake
WAIT A SECOND!!
WHAT?!
I MET OTHER PEOPLE YOU CURSED IN THE PAST.

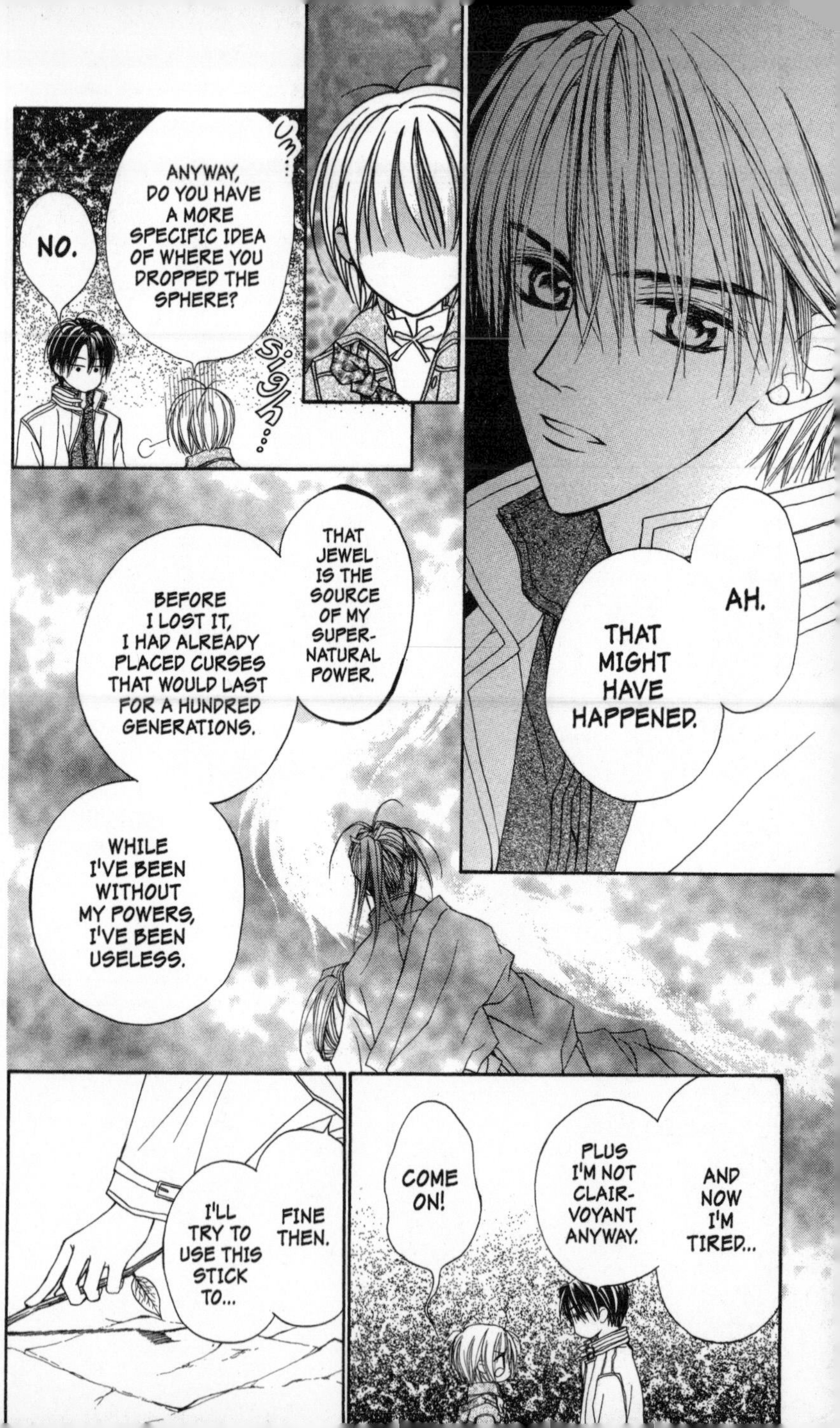
AH.
THAT MIGHT HAVE HAPPENED.
UM...
SIGH...
ANYWAY, DO YOU HAVE A MORE SPECIFIC IDEA OF WHERE YOU DROPPED THE SPHERE?
NO.
THAT JEWEL IS THE SOURCE OF MY SUPER-NATURAL POWER.
BEFORE I LOST IT, I HAD ALREADY PLACED CURSES THAT WOULD LAST FOR A HUNDRED GENERATIONS.
WHILE I'VE BEEN WITHOUT MY POWERS, I'VE BEEN USELESS.
AND NOW I'M TIRED...
PLUS I'M NOT CLAIR-VOYANT ANYWAY.
COME ON!
FINE THEN.
I'LL TRY TO USE THIS STICK TO...

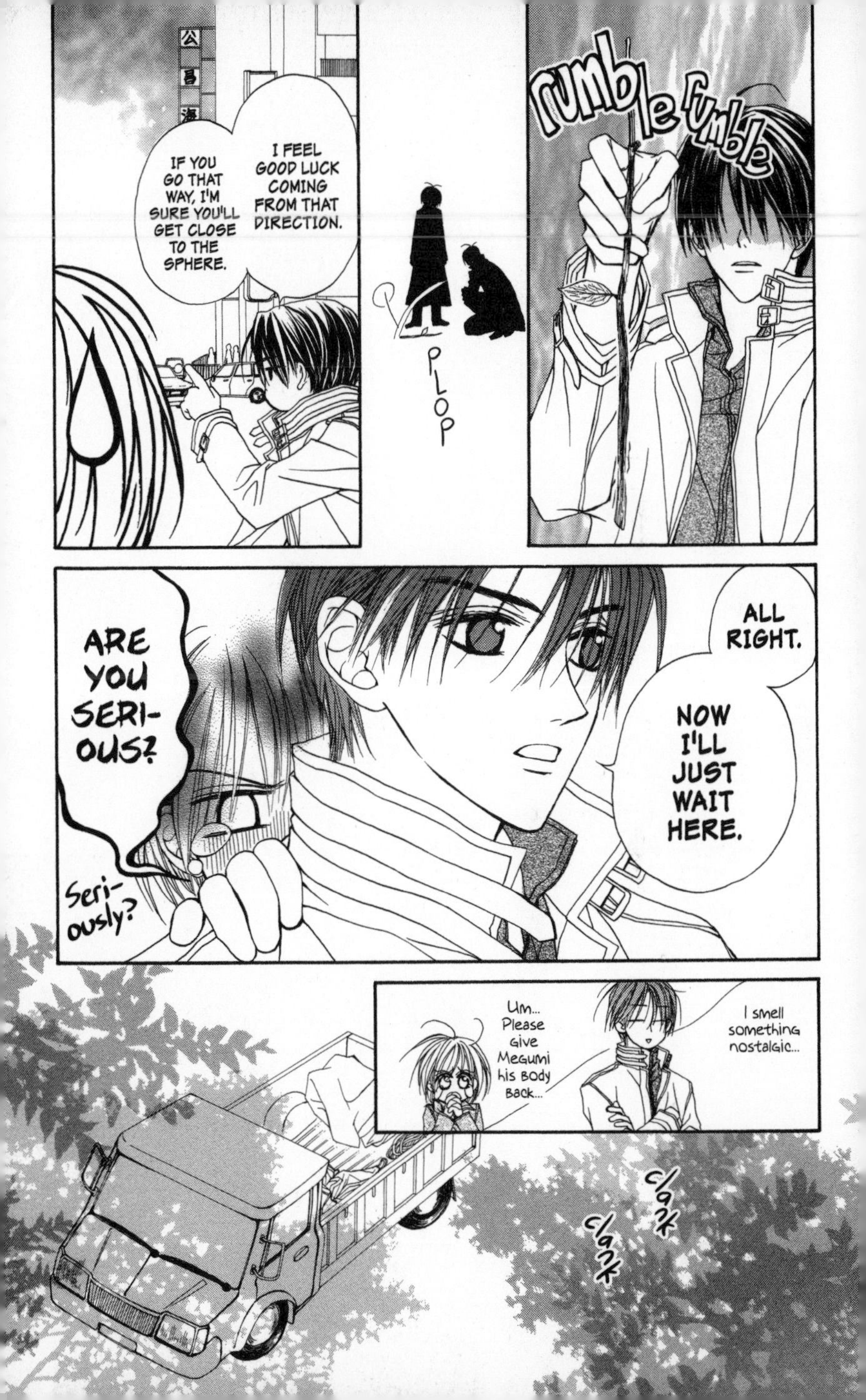
rumble rumble
PLOP
I FEEL GOOD LUCK COMING FROM THAT DIRECTION.
IF YOU GO THAT WAY, I'M SURE YOU'LL GET CLOSE TO THE SPHERE.
ALL RIGHT.
NOW I'LL JUST WAIT HERE.
ARE YOU SERI-OUS?
Seri-ously?
I smell something nostalgic...
Um... Please give Megumi his body back...
clank
clank

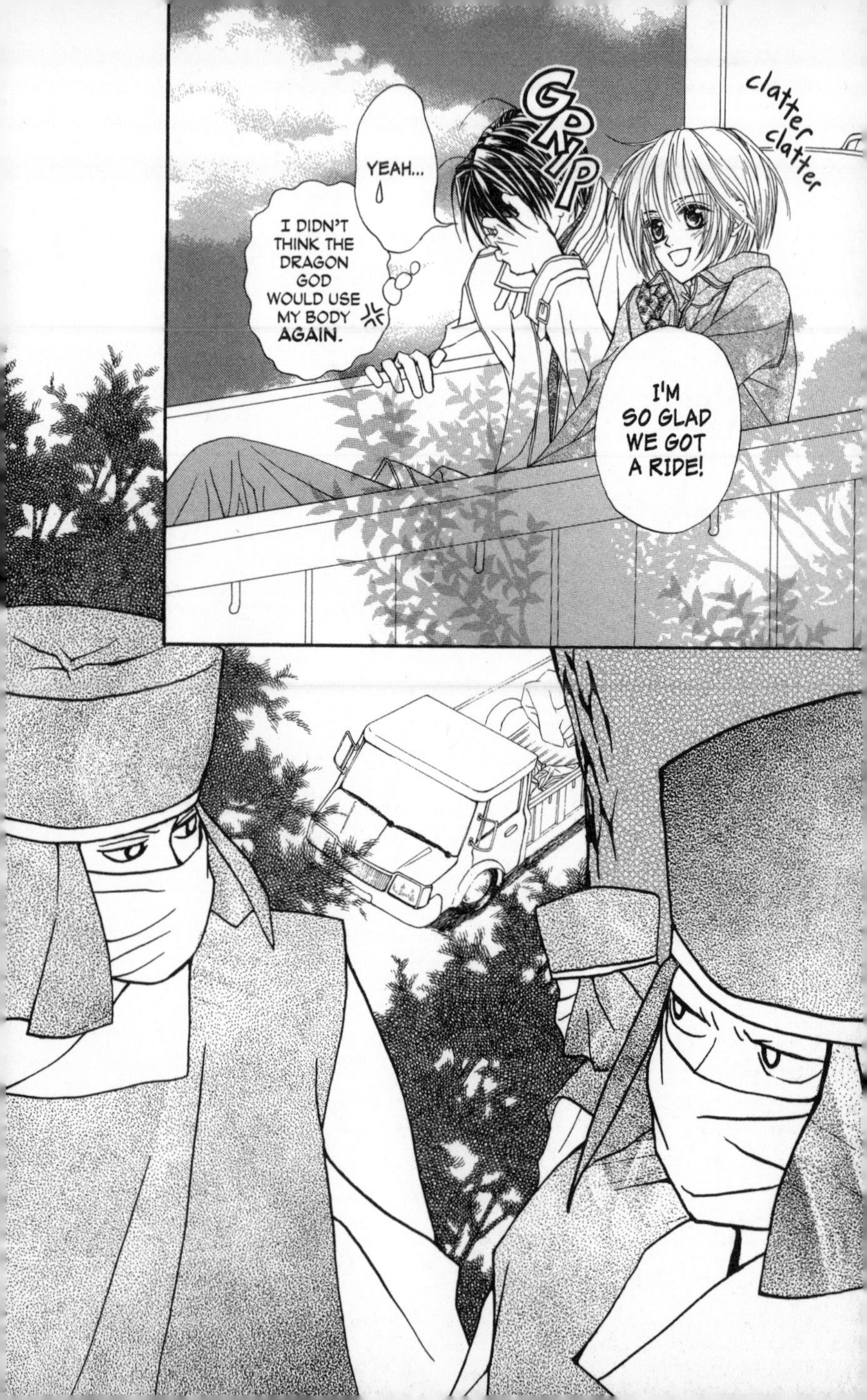
clatter clatter
I'M SO GLAD WE GOT A RIDE!
GRIP
YEAH...
I DIDN'T THINK THE DRAGON GOD WOULD USE MY BODY AGAIN.

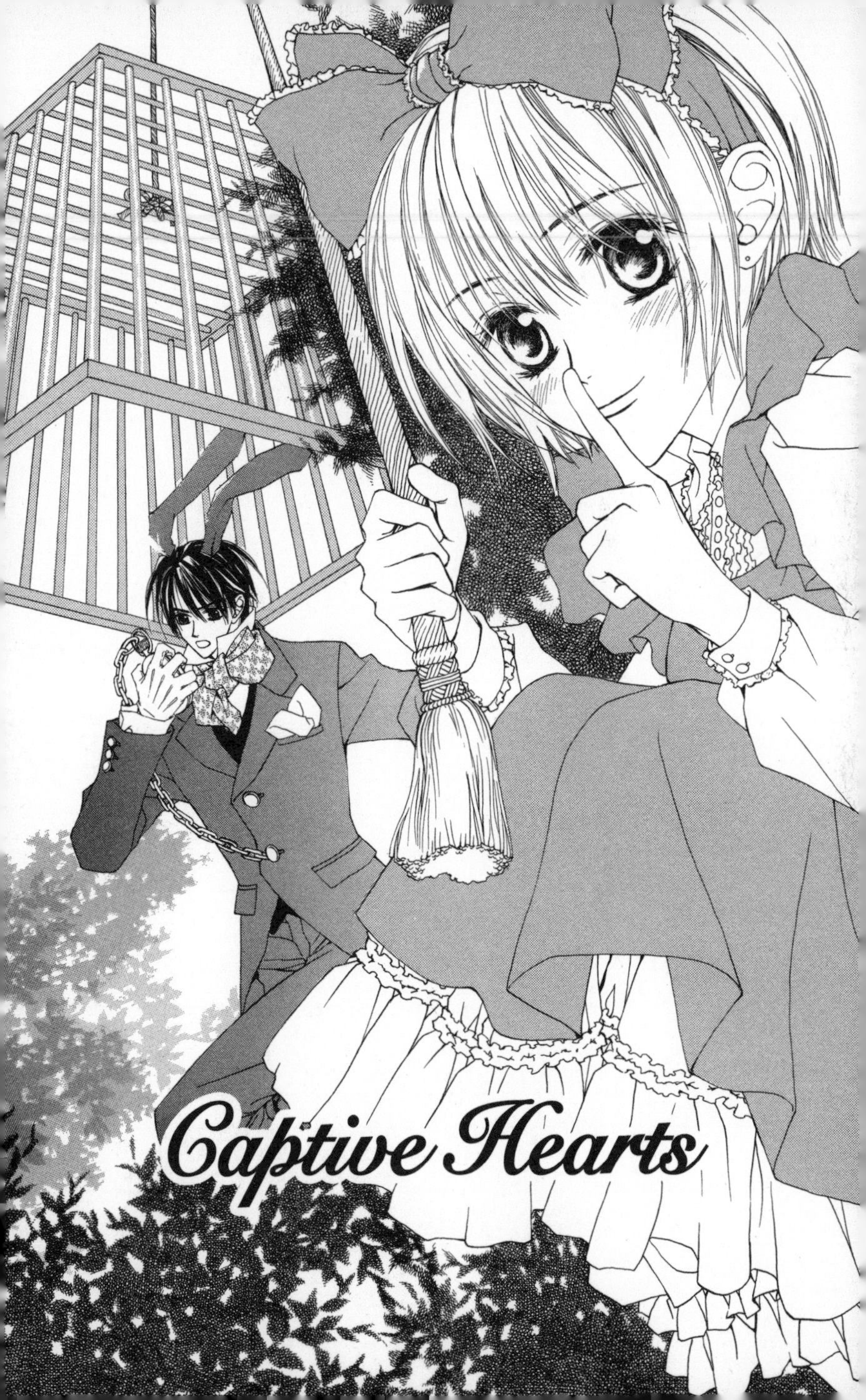
Captive Hearts

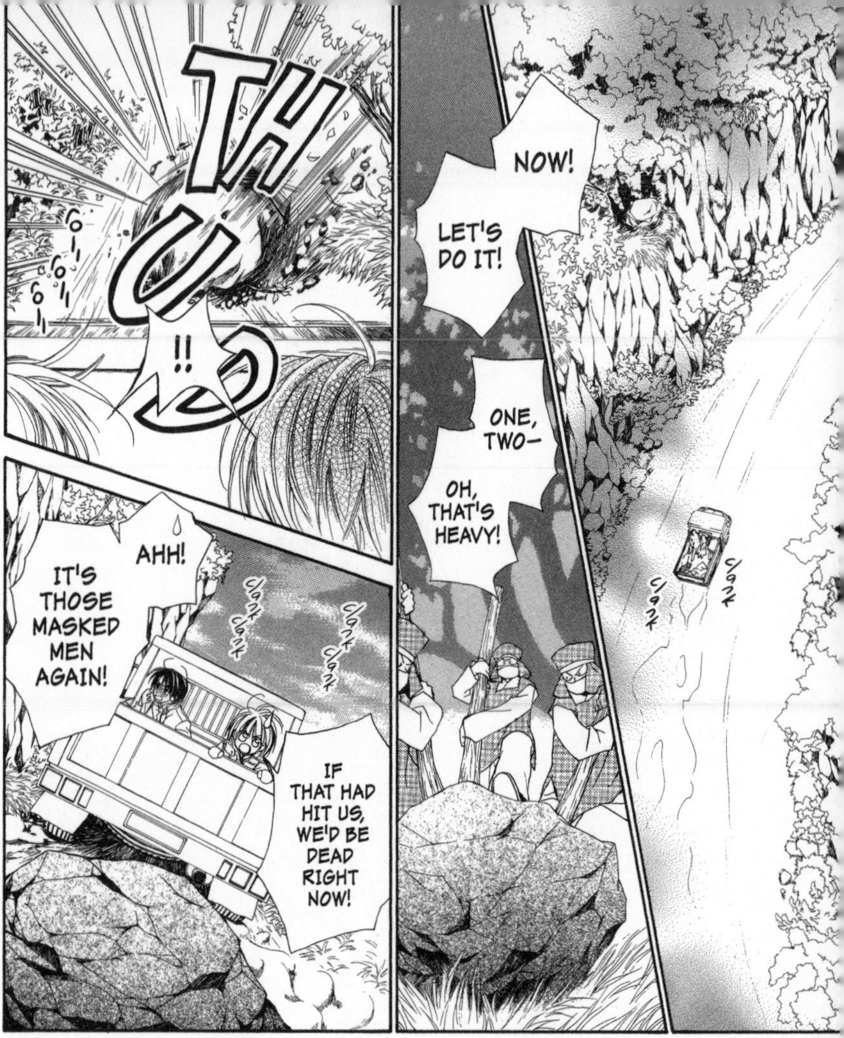
NOW!
LET'S DO IT!
ONE, TWO—
OH, THAT'S HEAVY!
clank
clank
THUD!!
roll
roll
roll
AHH!
IT'S THOSE MASKED MEN AGAIN!
clank clank
clank clank
IF THAT HAD HIT US, WE'D BE DEAD RIGHT NOW!

Backstory② For the cover of this volume of *Captive Hearts*, I used color ink for the first time in a while. Ninety percent of *Captive Hearts* is done in Copic (alcohol-based) markers. It felt like I was falling in love for the first time! For each chapter title page in this volume, I had a specific theme in mind—that of "leaves." ...? I'm not sure why I chose leaves as a theme, either. Probably influence from my trip to China. The forests in China are huge and endless. A lot of it feels like undeveloped land.

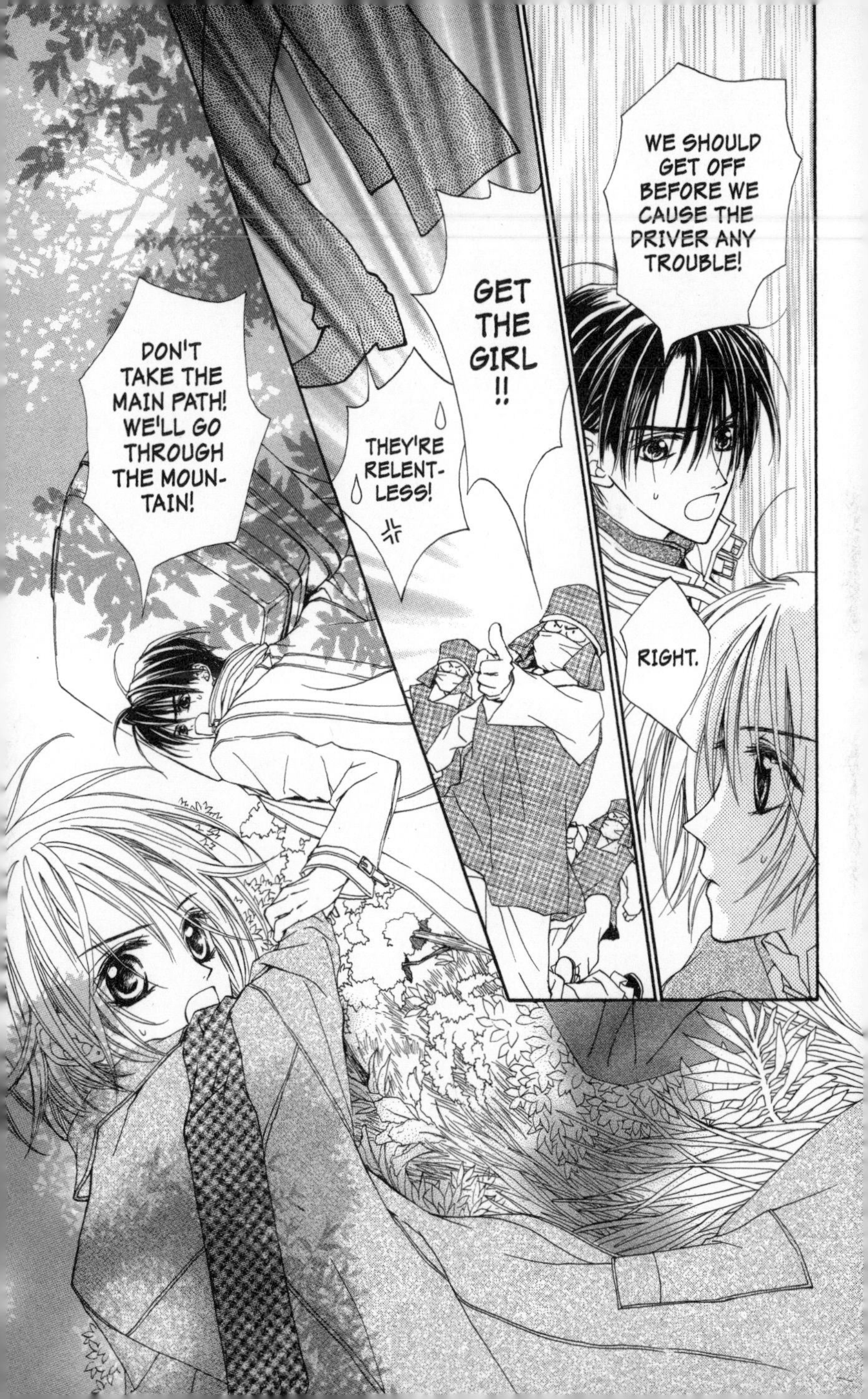
WE SHOULD GET OFF BEFORE WE CAUSE THE DRIVER ANY TROUBLE!
RIGHT.
GET THE GIRL !!
THEY'RE RELENT-LESS!
DON'T TAKE THE MAIN PATH! WE'LL GO THROUGH THE MOUN-TAIN!

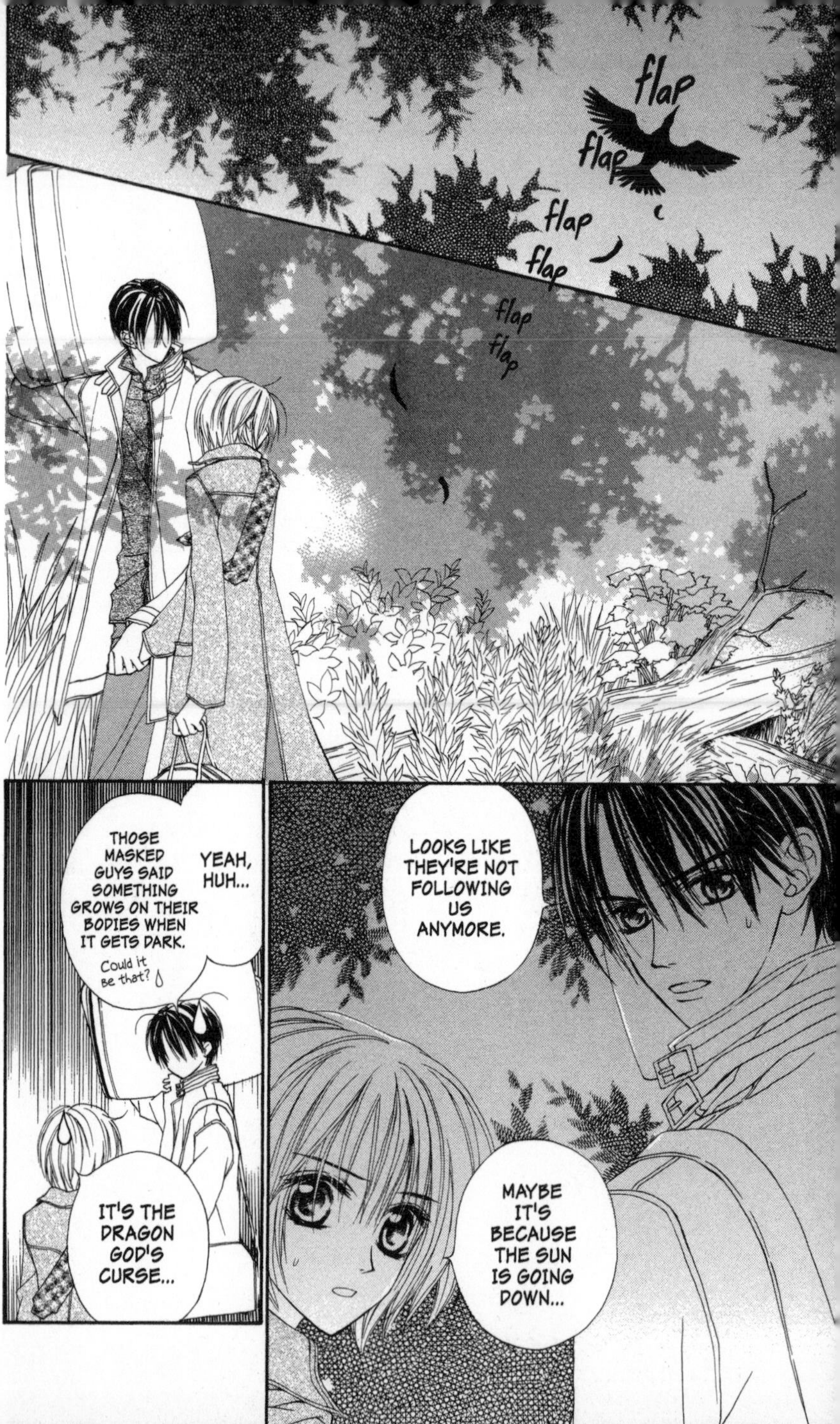
flap
flap
flap
flap
flap
flap
LOOKS LIKE THEY'RE NOT FOLLOWING US ANYMORE.
MAYBE IT'S BECAUSE THE SUN IS GOING DOWN...
THOSE MASKED GUYS SAID SOMETHING GROWS ON THEIR BODIES WHEN IT GETS DARK.
Could it be that?
YEAH, HUH...
IT'S THE DRAGON GOD'S CURSE...

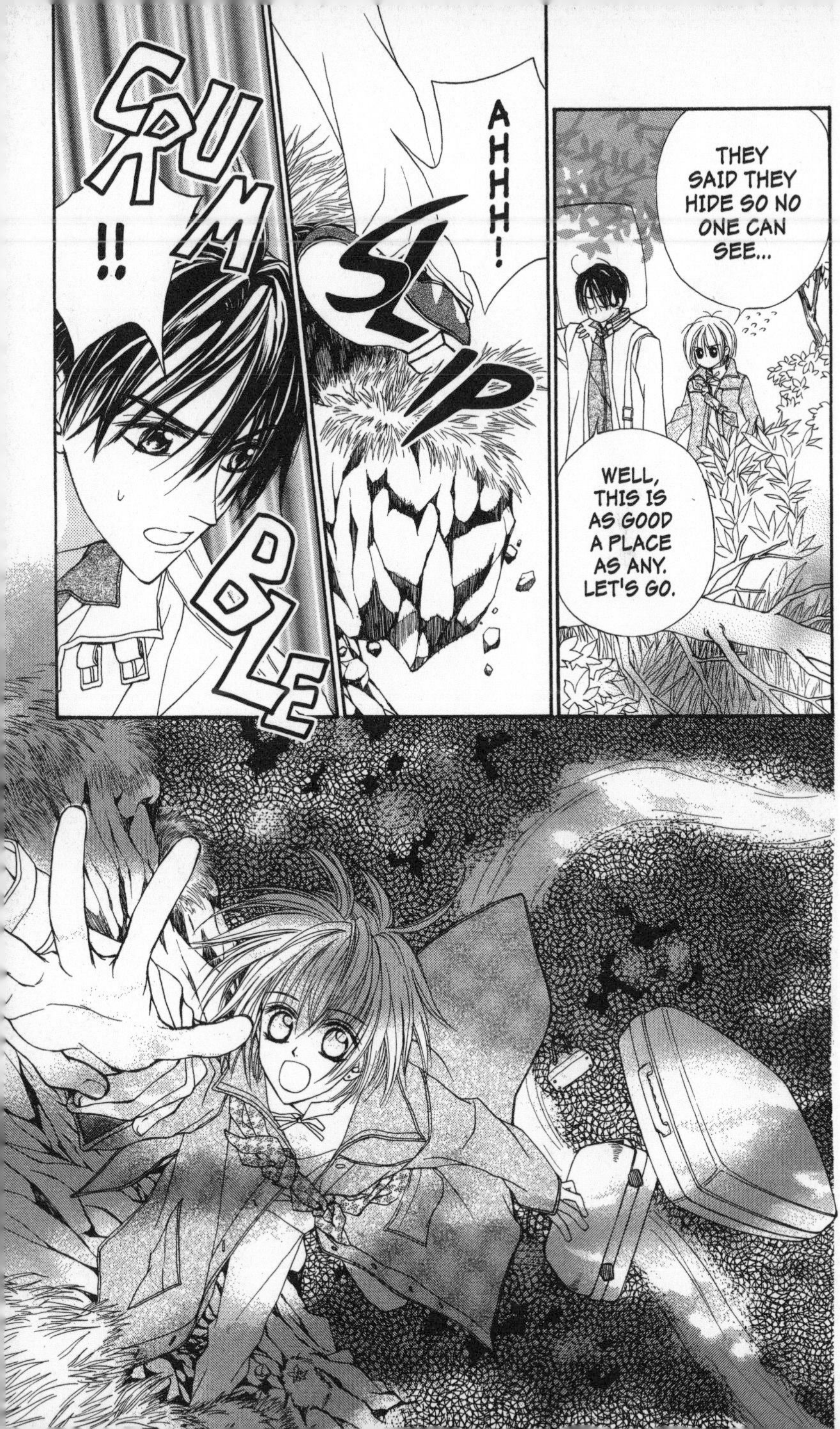
THEY SAID THEY HIDE SO NO ONE CAN SEE...
WELL, THIS IS AS GOOD A PLACE AS ANY. LET'S GO.
AHHHH!
SLIP
CRUMBLE!!

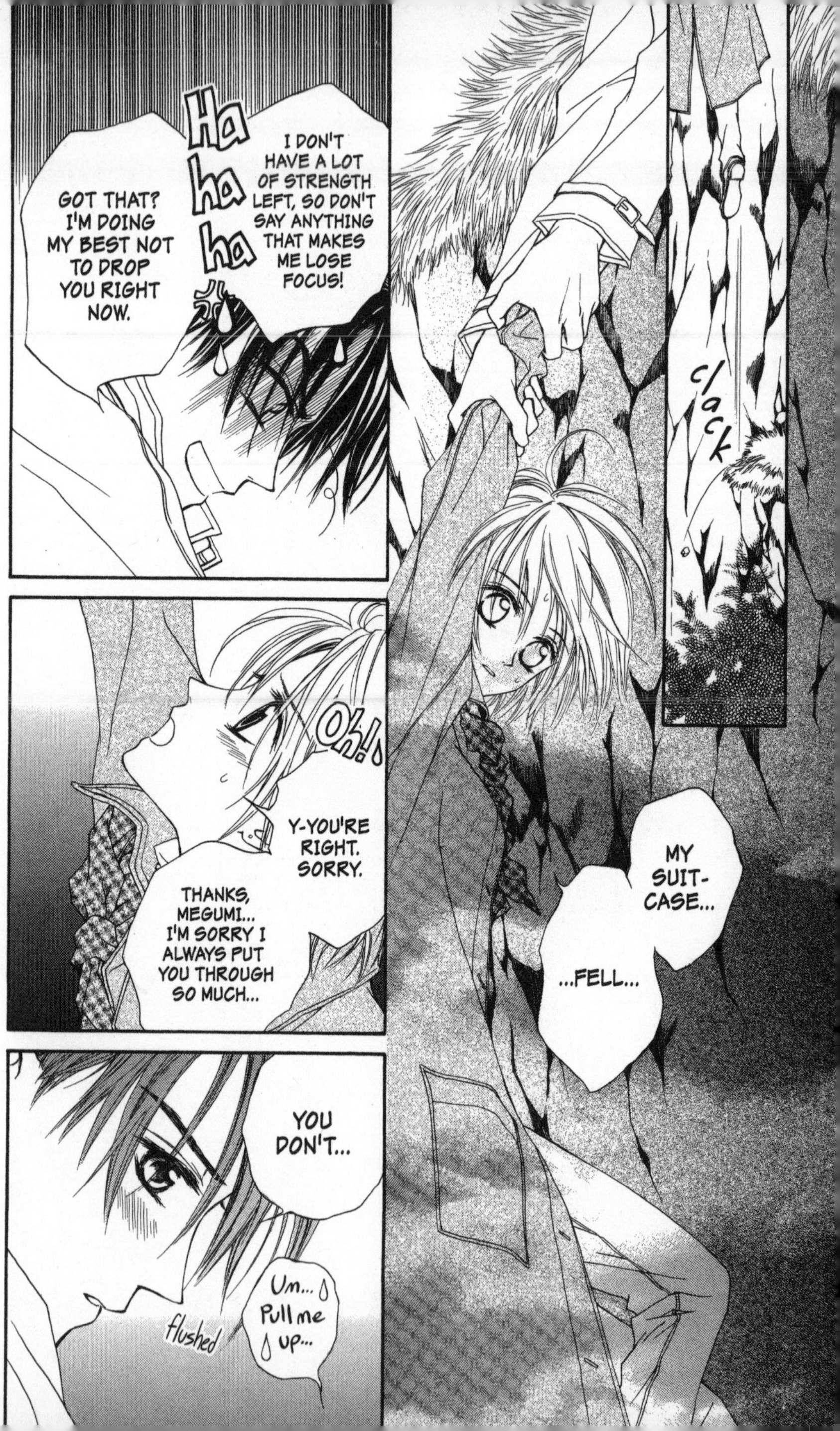
clack
MY SUIT-CASE...
...FELL...
I DON'T HAVE A LOT OF STRENGTH LEFT, SO DON'T SAY ANYTHING THAT MAKES ME LOSE FOCUS!
Ha ha ha
GOT THAT? I'M DOING MY BEST NOT TO DROP YOU RIGHT NOW.
Oh!
Y-YOU'RE RIGHT. SORRY.
THANKS, MEGUMI... I'M SORRY I ALWAYS PUT YOU THROUGH SO MUCH...
YOU DON'T...
Un... Pull me up...
flushed

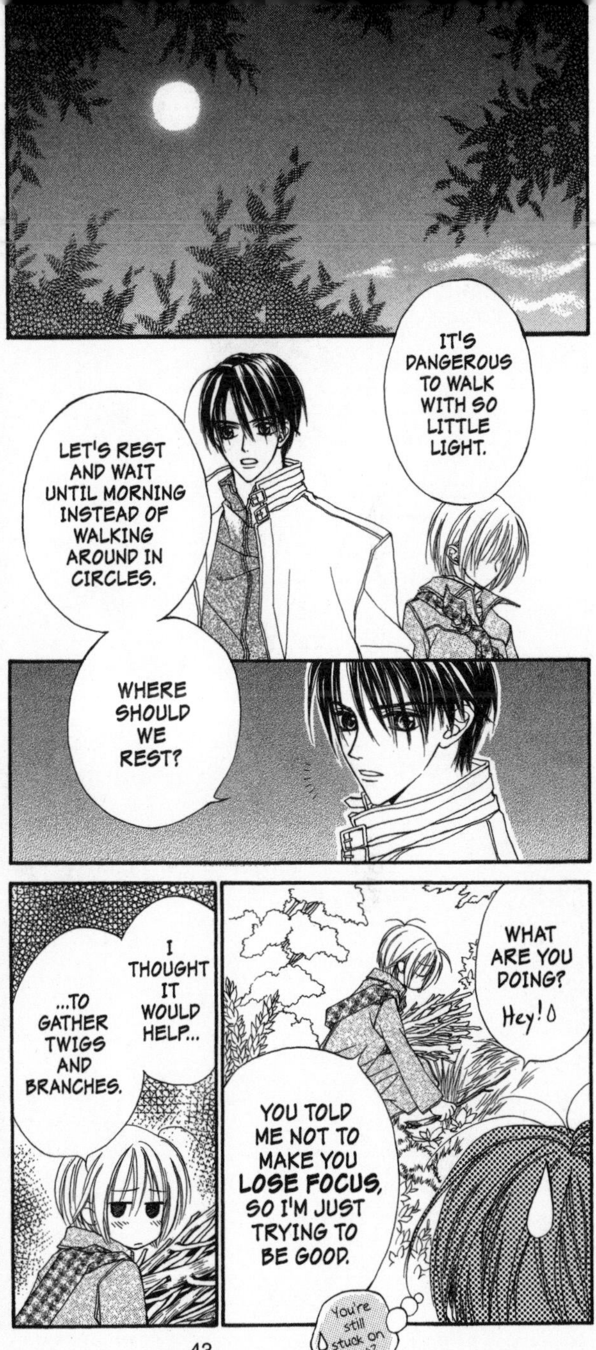
IT'S DANGEROUS TO WALK WITH SO LITTLE LIGHT.
LET'S REST AND WAIT UNTIL MORNING INSTEAD OF WALKING AROUND IN CIRCLES.
WHERE SHOULD WE REST?
WHAT ARE YOU DOING?
Hey!
YOU TOLD ME NOT TO MAKE YOU LOSE FOCUS, SO I'M JUST TRYING TO BE GOOD.
You're still stuck on that?
I THOUGHT IT WOULD HELP...
...TO GATHER TWIGS AND BRANCHES.

About goods

Guess what! Movic will be producing some Captive Hearts GOODS!! Around the time this volume is published, the plans should be with the animators!! I'm soooo happy!!! They're going to make shitajiki [pencil boards], cell phone straps, laminated cards, stationery and envelopes, postcard sets and doorplates! ♥ I think they're going to be awesome. Eh heh heh.♥

Once they go on sale, I'm gonna go to the store and buy some! I guess that's kind of narcissistic.

Right now I'm praying for them to go on sale soon! (Laughs) And for them to sell a lot!

Everyone, please get some too!!!

In the past, LaLa made mugs, perfume, pocketwatches, cushions, stamps, hand mirrors, telephone cards and bookmarks for promotional goods.♥ I think I might put the new goods next to all of those up in my room! ♥♥

Narcissism...

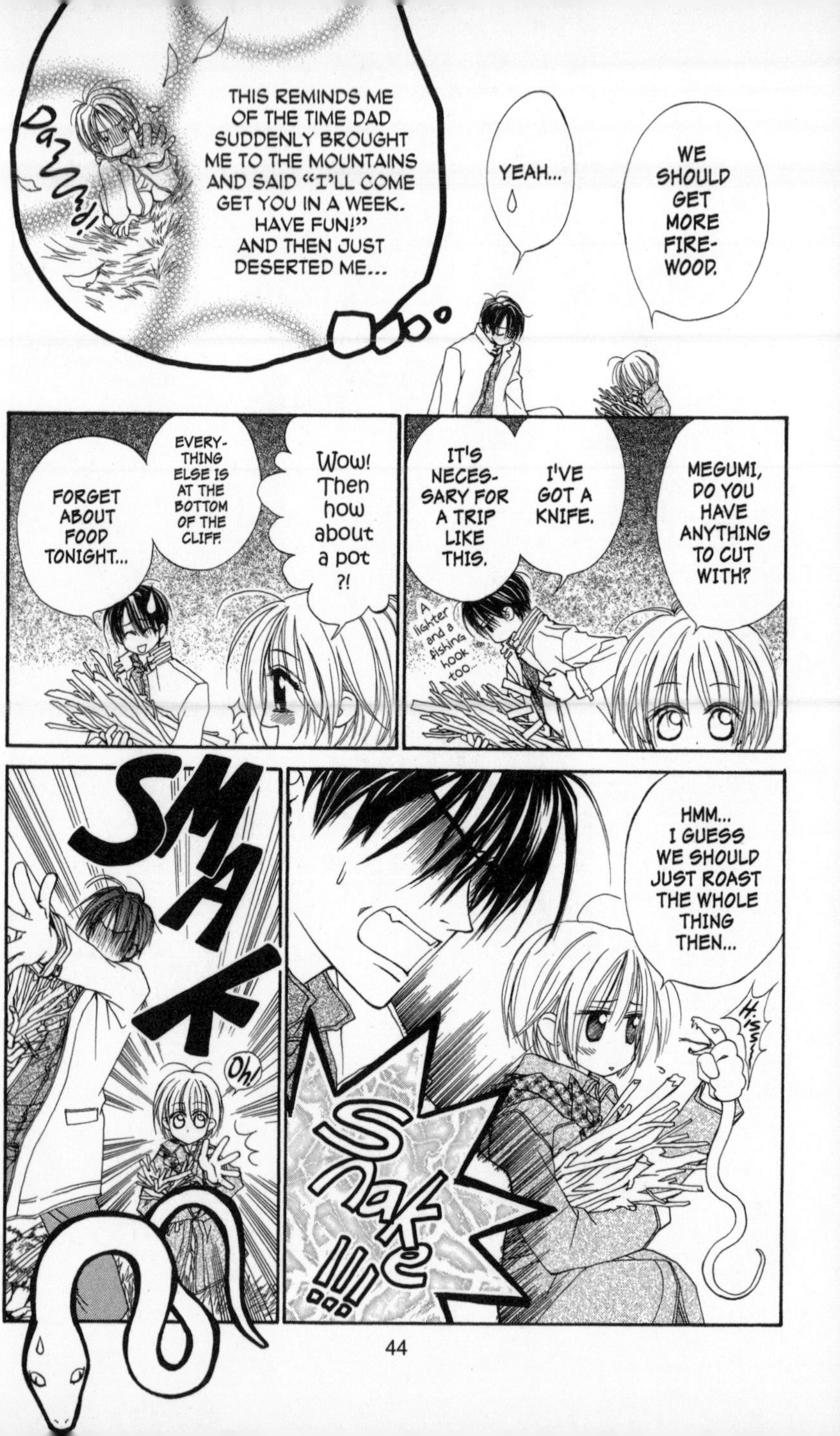
WE SHOULD GET MORE FIRE-WOOD.
YEAH...
THIS REMINDS ME OF THE TIME DAD SUDDENLY BROUGHT ME TO THE MOUNTAINS AND SAID "I'LL COME GET YOU IN A WEEK. HAVE FUN!" AND THEN JUST DESERTED ME...
MEGUMI, DO YOU HAVE ANYTHING TO CUT WITH?
I'VE GOT A KNIFE.
IT'S NECES-SARY FOR A TRIP LIKE THIS.
A lighter and a fishing hook too...
Wow! Then how about a pot ?!
EVERY-THING ELSE IS AT THE BOTTOM OF THE CLIFF.
FORGET ABOUT FOOD TONIGHT...
HMM... I GUESS WE SHOULD JUST ROAST THE WHOLE THING THEN...
Hiss
Snake!!!
SMAK
Oh!

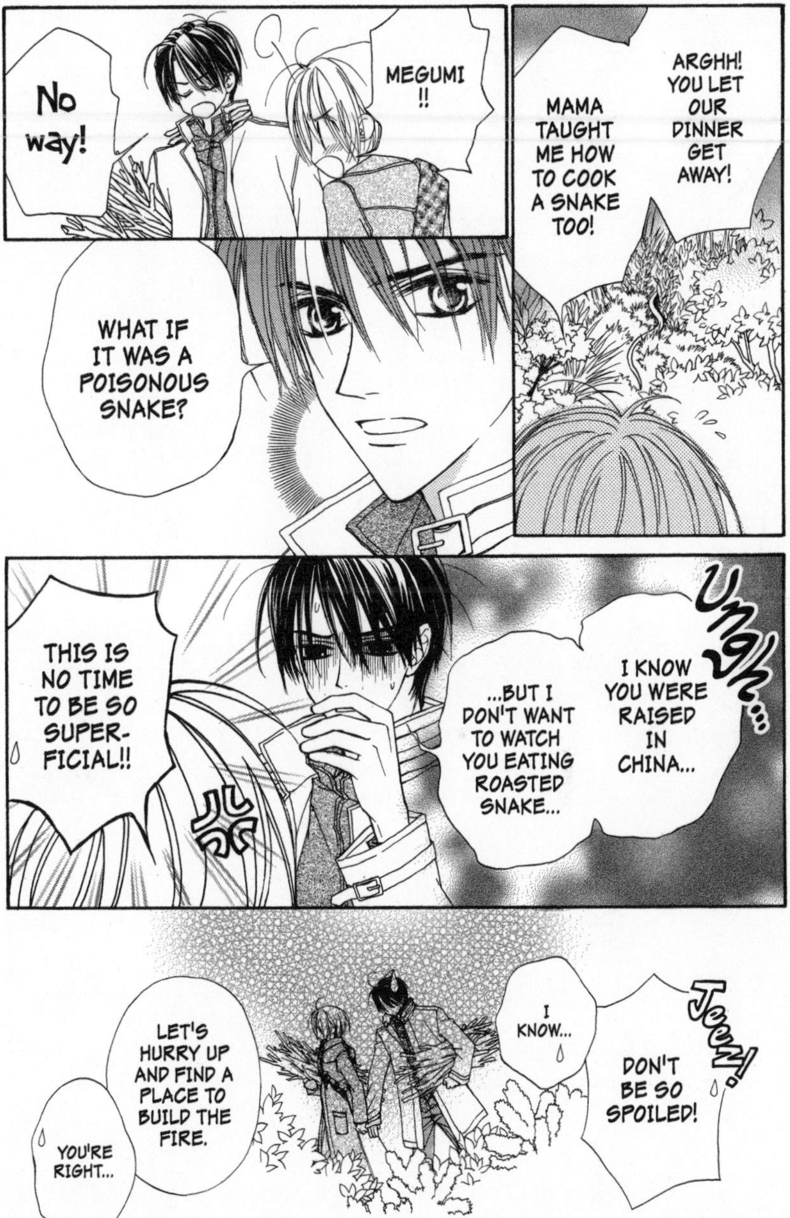
ARGHH! YOU LET OUR DINNER GET AWAY!
MAMA TAUGHT ME HOW TO COOK A SNAKE TOO!
MEGUMI !!
No way!
WHAT IF IT WAS A POISONOUS SNAKE?
Ungh...
I KNOW YOU WERE RAISED IN CHINA...
...BUT I DON'T WANT TO WATCH YOU EATING ROASTED SNAKE...
THIS IS NO TIME TO BE SO SUPER-FICIAL!!
Jeez!
DON'T BE SO SPOILED!
I KNOW...
LET'S HURRY UP AND FIND A PLACE TO BUILD THE FIRE.
YOU'RE RIGHT...

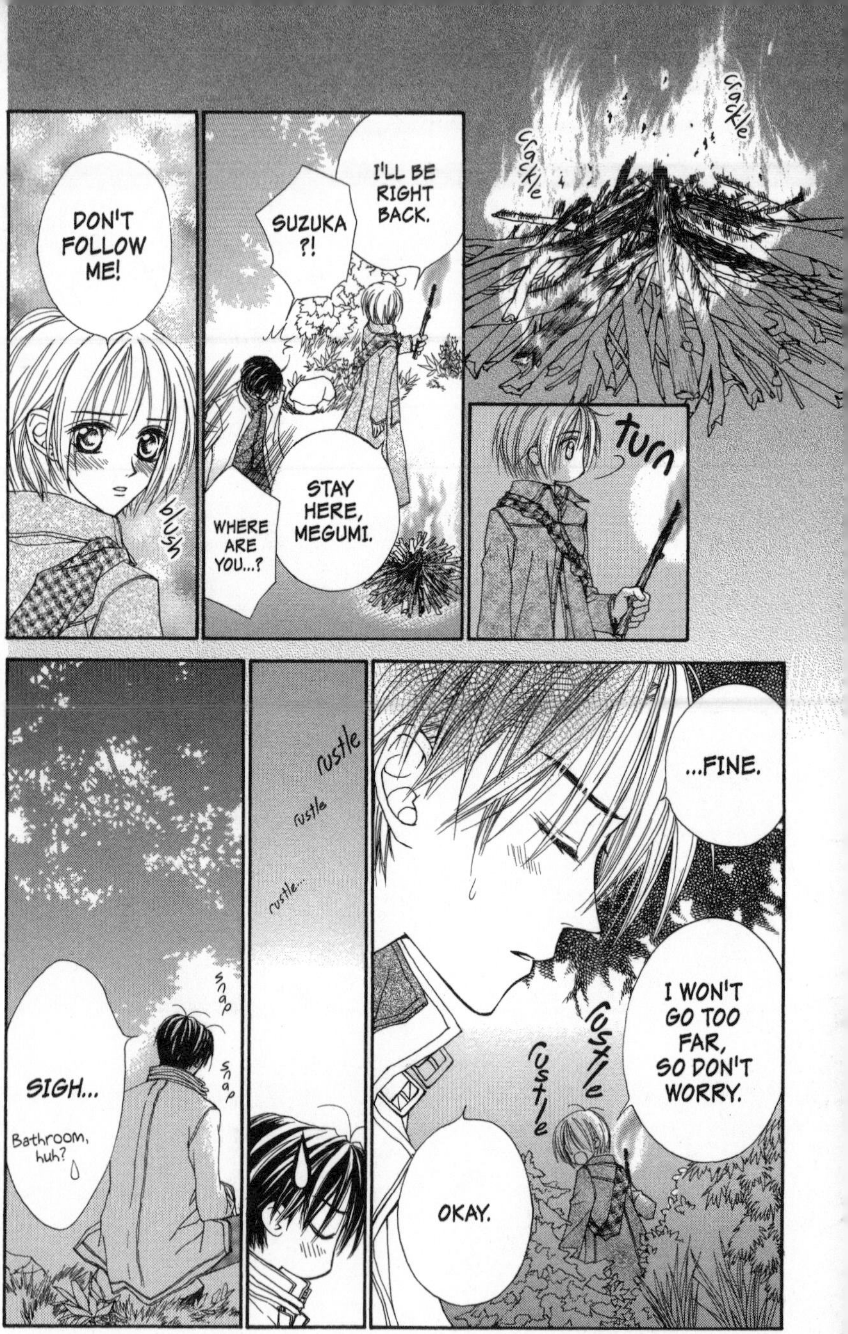
crackle
crackle
turn
I'LL BE RIGHT BACK.
SUZUKA?!
STAY HERE, MEGUMI.
WHERE ARE YOU...?
DON'T FOLLOW ME!
blush
...FINE.
I WON'T GO TOO FAR, SO DON'T WORRY.
rustle
rustle
OKAY.
rustle
rustle
rustle...
snap
snap
SIGH...
Bathroom, huh?

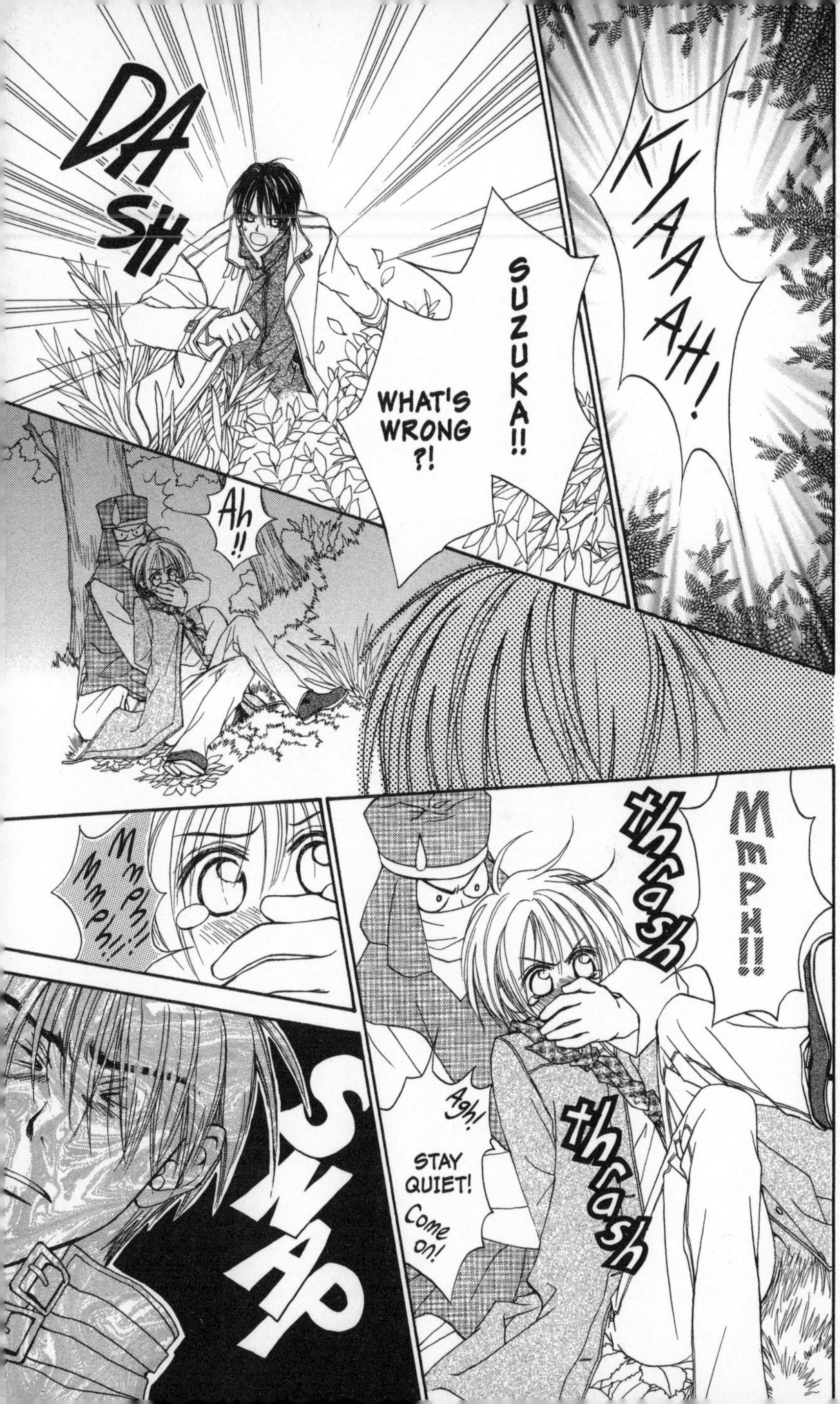
KYAAAAH!
SUZUKA!!
WHAT'S WRONG?!
DASH
Ah!!
MMPH!!
thrash
Agh!
STAY QUIET!
Come on!
thrash
Mmph!! Mmph!!
SNAP

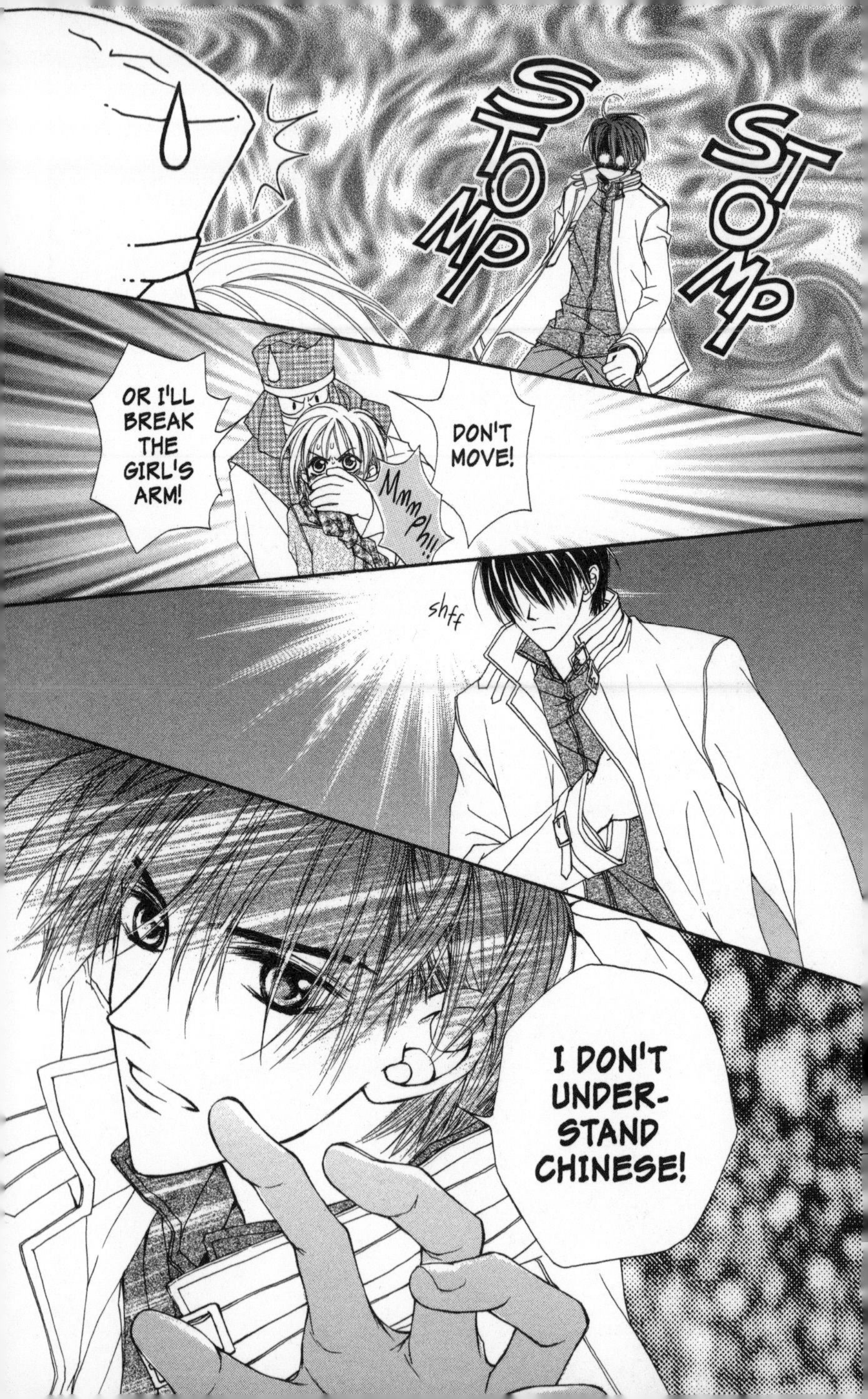
STOMP
STOMP
DON'T MOVE!
Mmmph!!
OR I'LL BREAK THE GIRL'S ARM!
shff
I DON'T UNDER-STAND CHINESE!

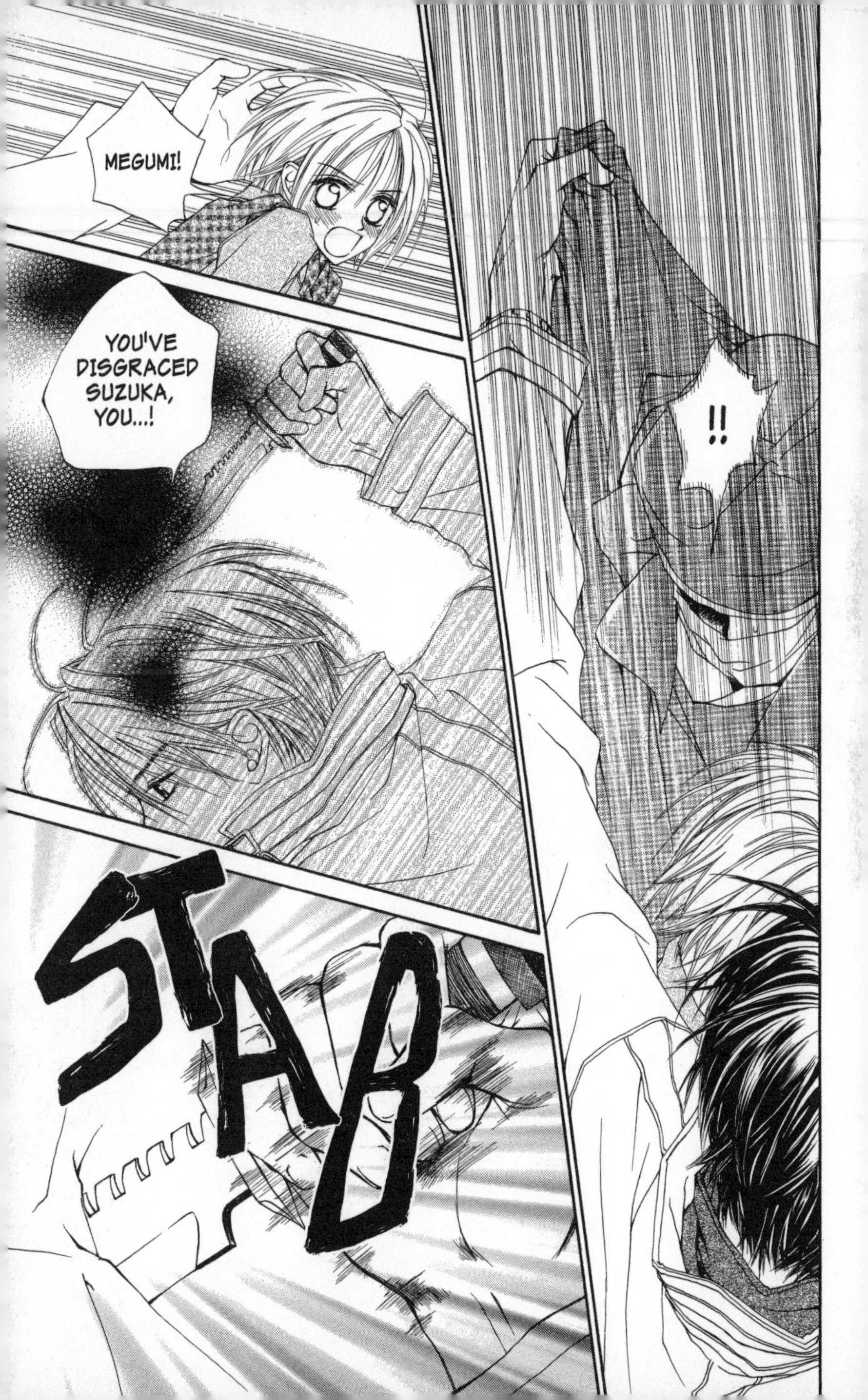
!!
MEGUMI!
YOU'VE DISGRACED SUZUKA, YOU...!
STAB

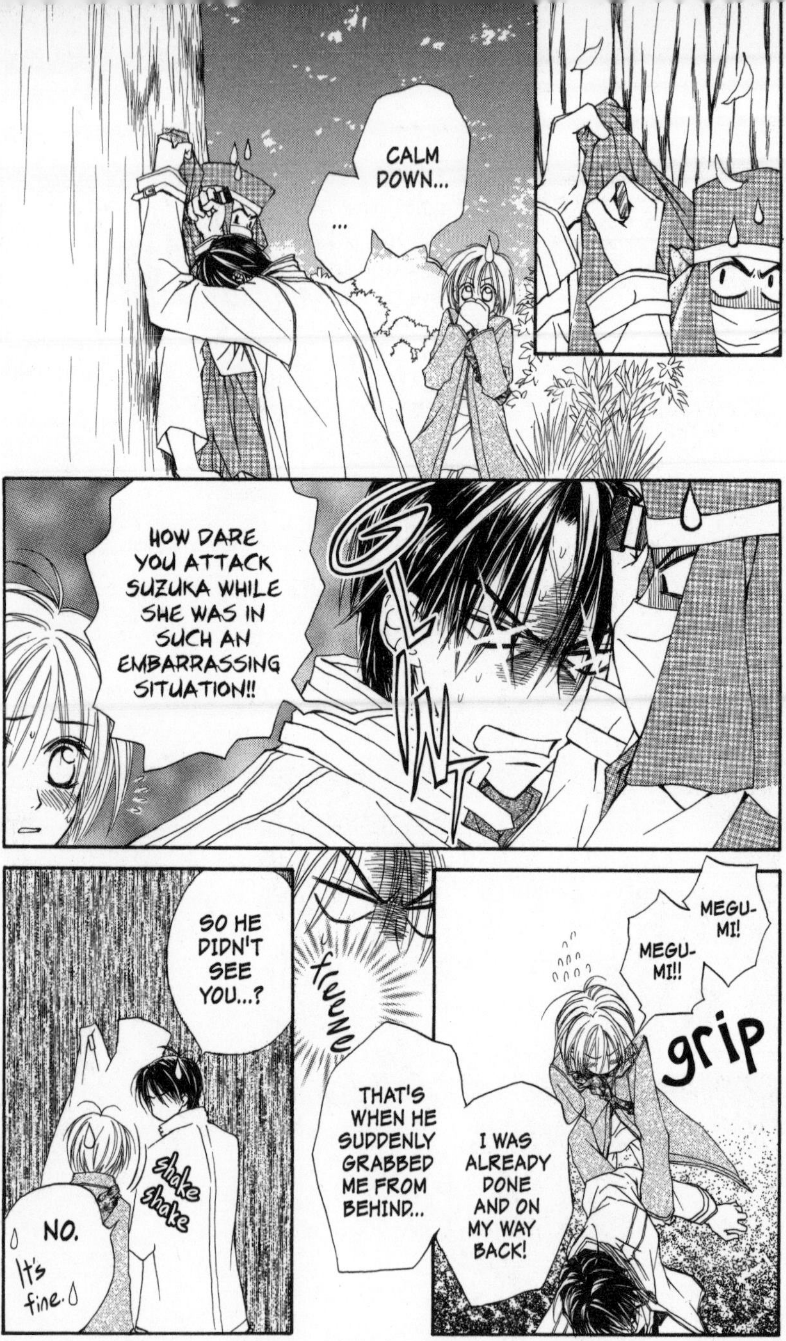
CALM DOWN...
...
HOW DARE YOU ATTACK SUZUKA WHILE SHE WAS IN SUCH AN EMBARRASSING SITUATION!!
GLINT
MEGU-MI!
MEGU-MI!!
grip
I WAS ALREADY DONE AND ON MY WAY BACK!
THAT'S WHEN HE SUDDENLY GRABBED ME FROM BEHIND...
freeze
SO HE DIDN'T SEE YOU...?
shake shake
NO.
It's fine.

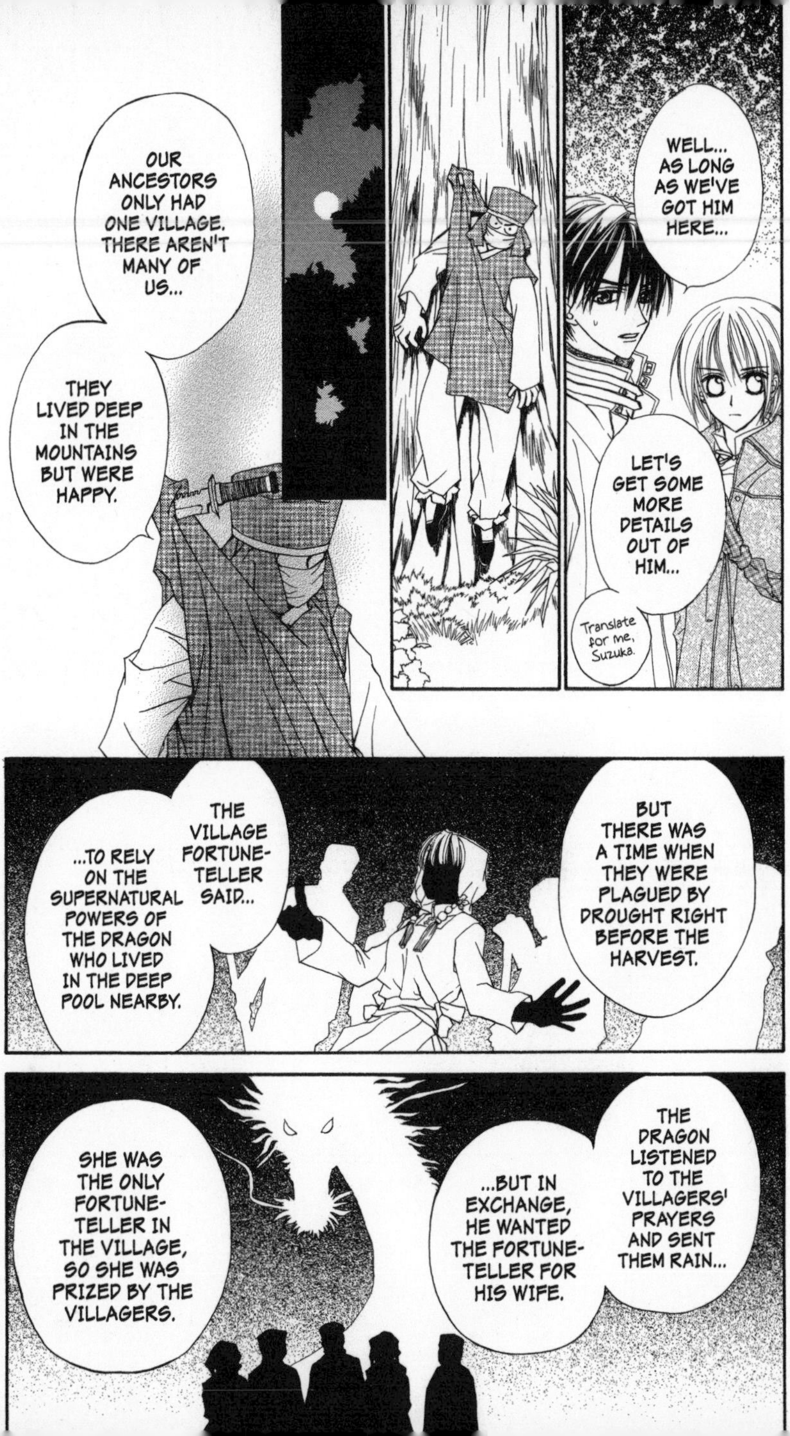
WELL... AS LONG AS WE'VE GOT HIM HERE...
LET'S GET SOME MORE DETAILS OUT OF HIM...
Translate for me, Suzuka.
OUR ANCESTORS ONLY HAD ONE VILLAGE. THERE AREN'T MANY OF US...
THEY LIVED DEEP IN THE MOUNTAINS BUT WERE HAPPY.
BUT THERE WAS A TIME WHEN THEY WERE PLAGUED BY DROUGHT RIGHT BEFORE THE HARVEST.
THE VILLAGE FORTUNE-TELLER SAID...
...TO RELY ON THE SUPERNATURAL POWERS OF THE DRAGON WHO LIVED IN THE DEEP POOL NEARBY.
THE DRAGON LISTENED TO THE VILLAGERS' PRAYERS AND SENT THEM RAIN...
...BUT IN EXCHANGE, HE WANTED THE FORTUNE-TELLER FOR HIS WIFE.
SHE WAS THE ONLY FORTUNE-TELLER IN THE VILLAGE, SO SHE WAS PRIZED BY THE VILLAGERS.

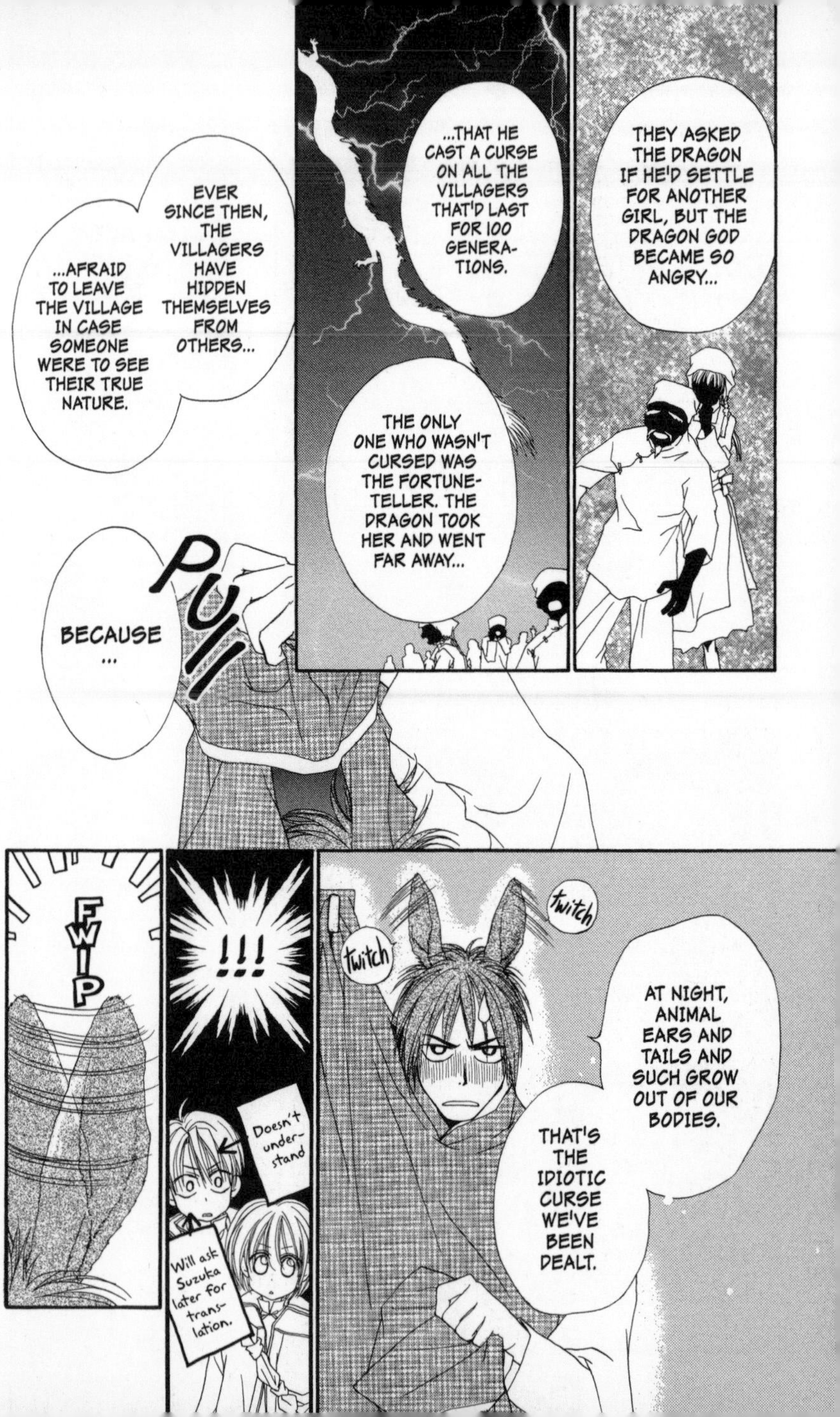
THEY ASKED THE DRAGON IF HE'D SETTLE FOR ANOTHER GIRL, BUT THE DRAGON GOD BECAME SO ANGRY...
...THAT HE CAST A CURSE ON ALL THE VILLAGERS THAT'D LAST FOR 100 GENERATIONS.
THE ONLY ONE WHO WASN'T CURSED WAS THE FORTUNE-TELLER. THE DRAGON TOOK HER AND WENT FAR AWAY...
EVER SINCE THEN, THE VILLAGERS HAVE HIDDEN THEMSELVES FROM OTHERS...
...AFRAID TO LEAVE THE VILLAGE IN CASE SOMEONE WERE TO SEE THEIR TRUE NATURE.
PULL
BECAUSE ...
twitch
twitch
AT NIGHT, ANIMAL EARS AND TAILS AND SUCH GROW OUT OF OUR BODIES.
THAT'S THE IDIOTIC CURSE WE'VE BEEN DEALT.
!!!
Doesn't understand
Will ask Suzuka later for translation.
FWIP

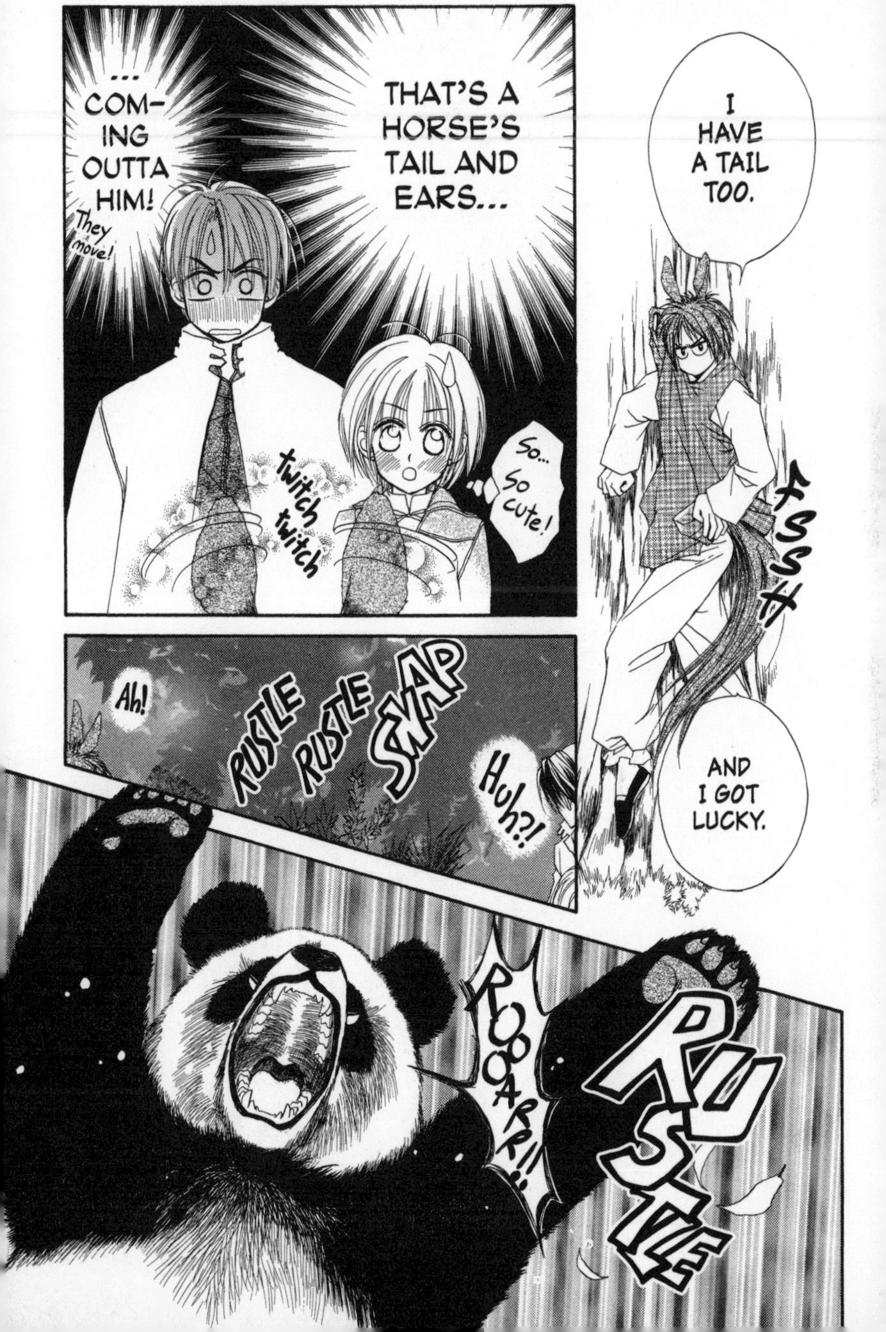
I HAVE A TAIL TOO.
FSSH!
AND I GOT LUCKY.
THAT'S A HORSE'S TAIL AND EARS...
...COMING OUTTA HIM!
They move!
So... So cute!
twitch twitch
Huh?!
SNAP
RUSTLE RUSTLE
Ah!
ROOOARR!!
RUSTLE

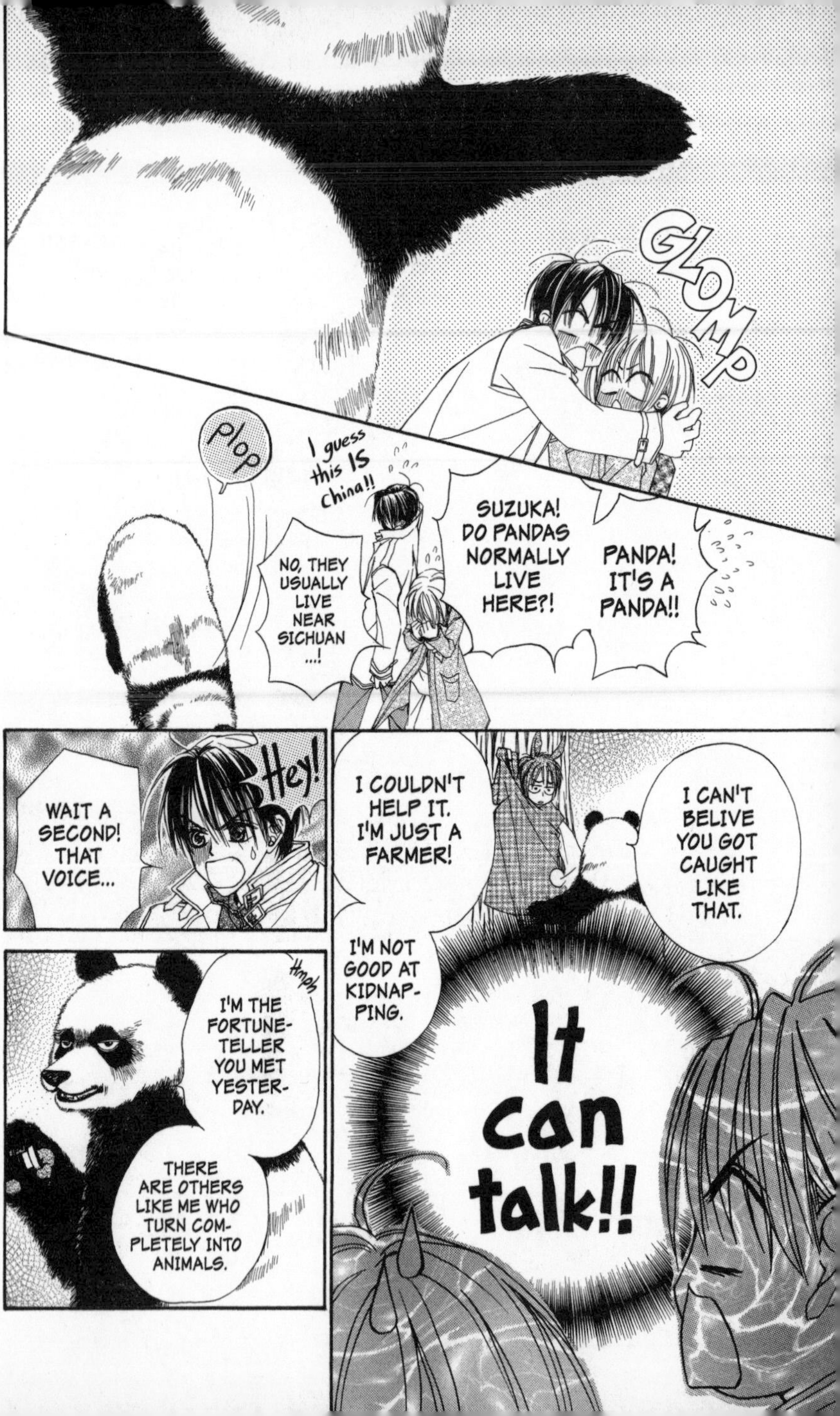
GLOMP
PANDA! IT'S A PANDA!!
SUZUKA! DO PANDAS NORMALLY LIVE HERE?!
I guess this IS China!!
NO, THEY USUALLY LIVE NEAR SICHUAN ...!
plop
I CAN'T BELIVE YOU GOT CAUGHT LIKE THAT.
I COULDN'T HELP IT. I'M JUST A FARMER!
I'M NOT GOOD AT KIDNAPPING.
It can talk!!
Hey!
WAIT A SECOND! THAT VOICE...
Hmph
I'M THE FORTUNE-TELLER YOU MET YESTERDAY.
THERE ARE OTHERS LIKE ME WHO TURN COMPLETELY INTO ANIMALS.

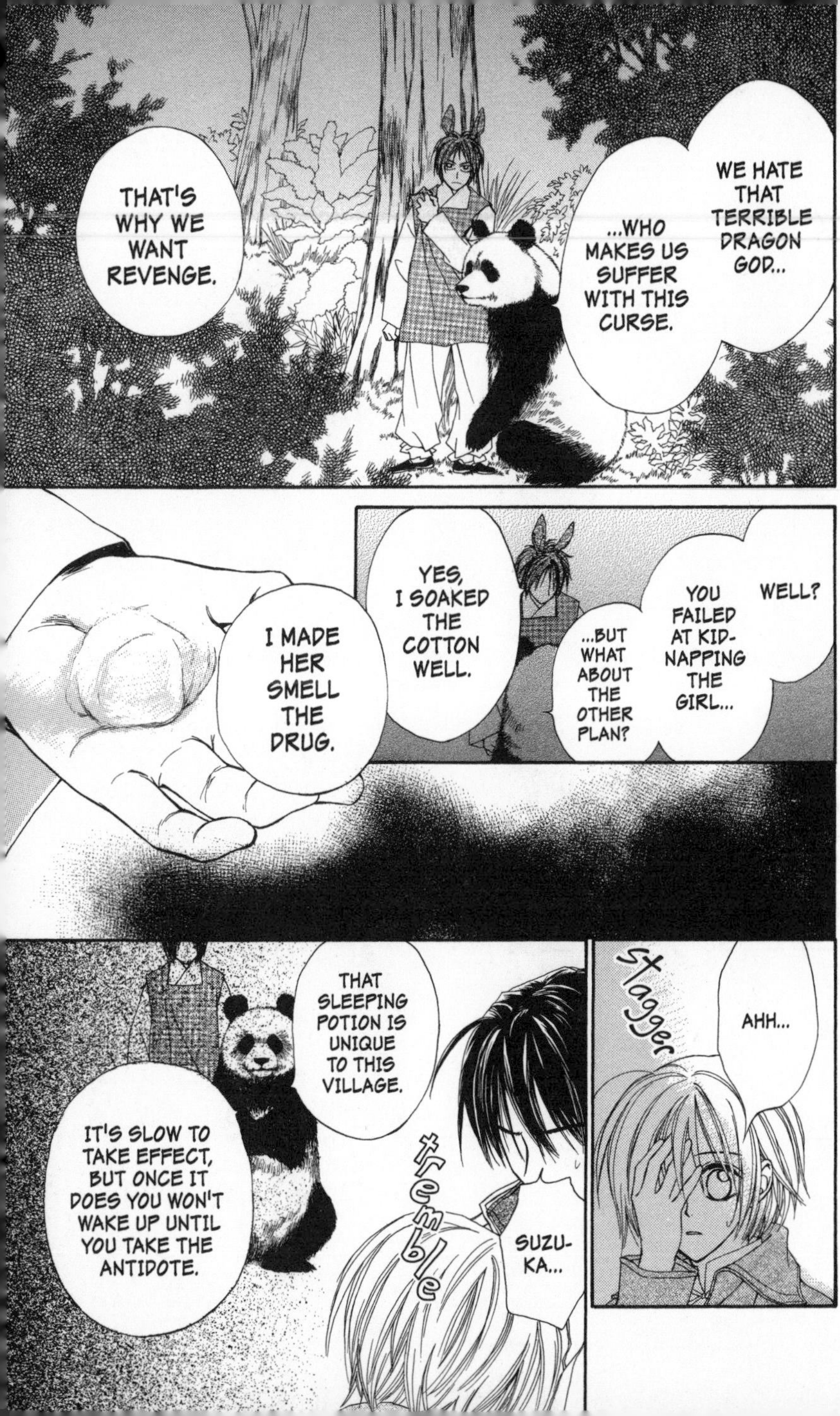
WE HATE THAT TERRIBLE DRAGON GOD...
...WHO MAKES US SUFFER WITH THIS CURSE.
THAT'S WHY WE WANT REVENGE.
WELL?
YOU FAILED AT KID-NAPPING THE GIRL...
...BUT WHAT ABOUT THE OTHER PLAN?
YES, I SOAKED THE COTTON WELL.
I MADE HER SMELL THE DRUG.
stagger
AHH...
THAT SLEEPING POTION IS UNIQUE TO THIS VILLAGE.
tremble
SUZU-KA...
IT'S SLOW TO TAKE EFFECT, BUT ONCE IT DOES YOU WON'T WAKE UP UNTIL YOU TAKE THE ANTIDOTE.

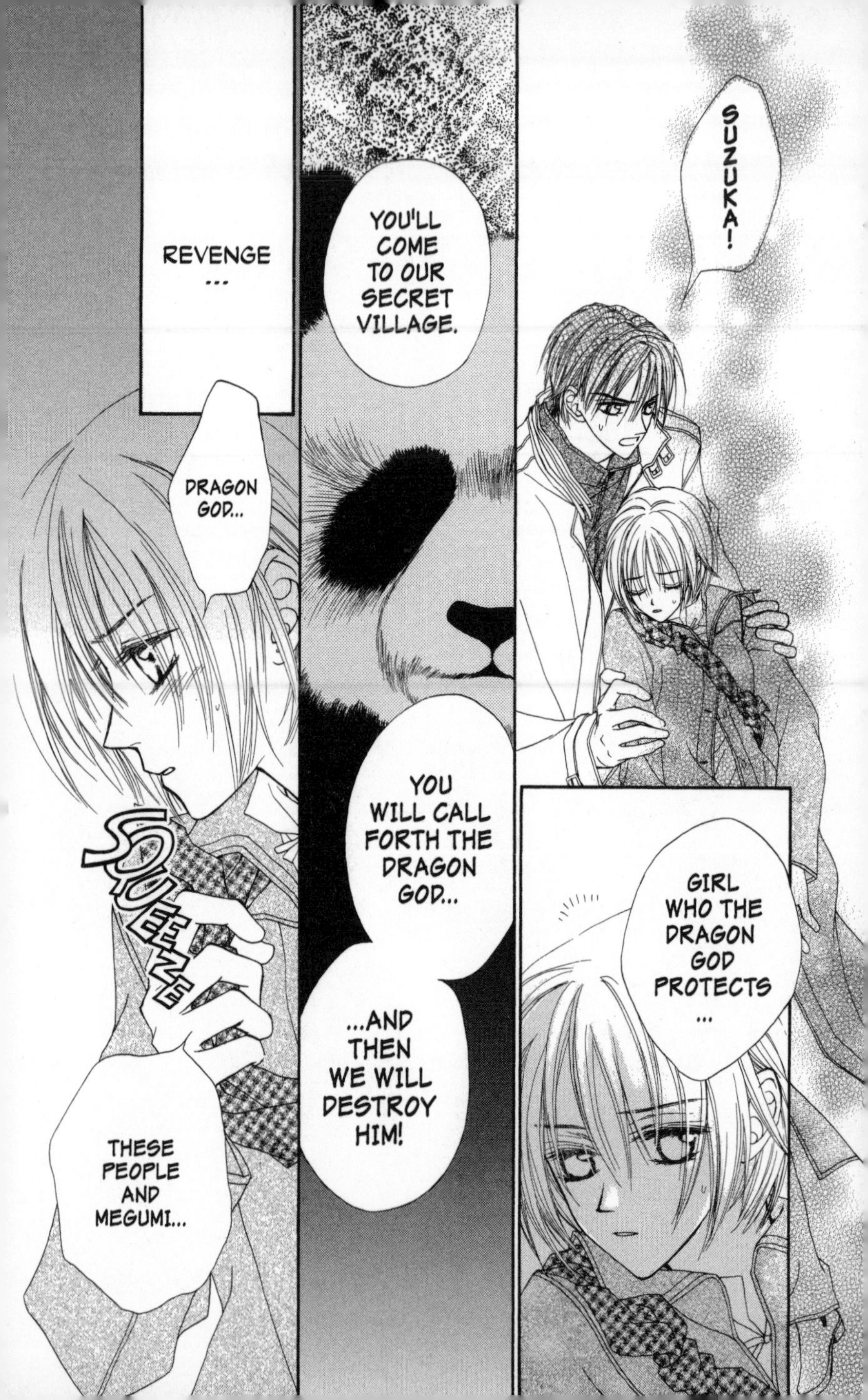
SUZUKA!
GIRL WHO THE DRAGON GOD PROTECTS...
YOU'LL COME TO OUR SECRET VILLAGE.
YOU WILL CALL FORTH THE DRAGON GOD...
...AND THEN WE WILL DESTROY HIM!
REVENGE...
DRAGON GOD...
SQUEEZE
THESE PEOPLE AND MEGUMI...

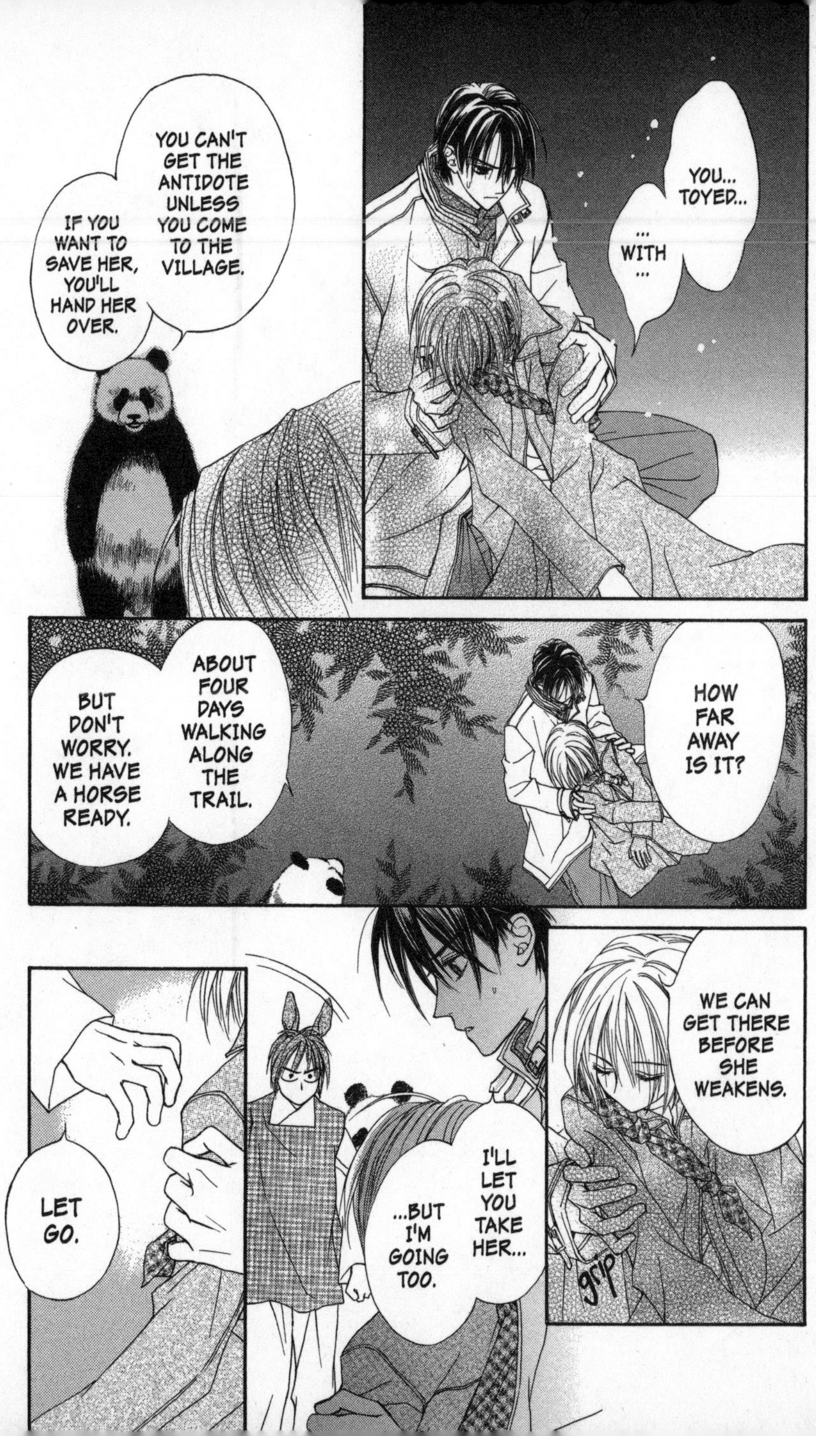
YOU... TOYED...
...WITH...
YOU CAN'T GET THE ANTIDOTE UNLESS YOU COME TO THE VILLAGE.
IF YOU WANT TO SAVE HER, YOU'LL HAND HER OVER.
HOW FAR AWAY IS IT?
ABOUT FOUR DAYS WALKING ALONG THE TRAIL.
BUT DON'T WORRY. WE HAVE A HORSE READY.
WE CAN GET THERE BEFORE SHE WEAKENS.
grip
I'LL LET YOU TAKE HER...
...BUT I'M GOING TOO.
LET GO.

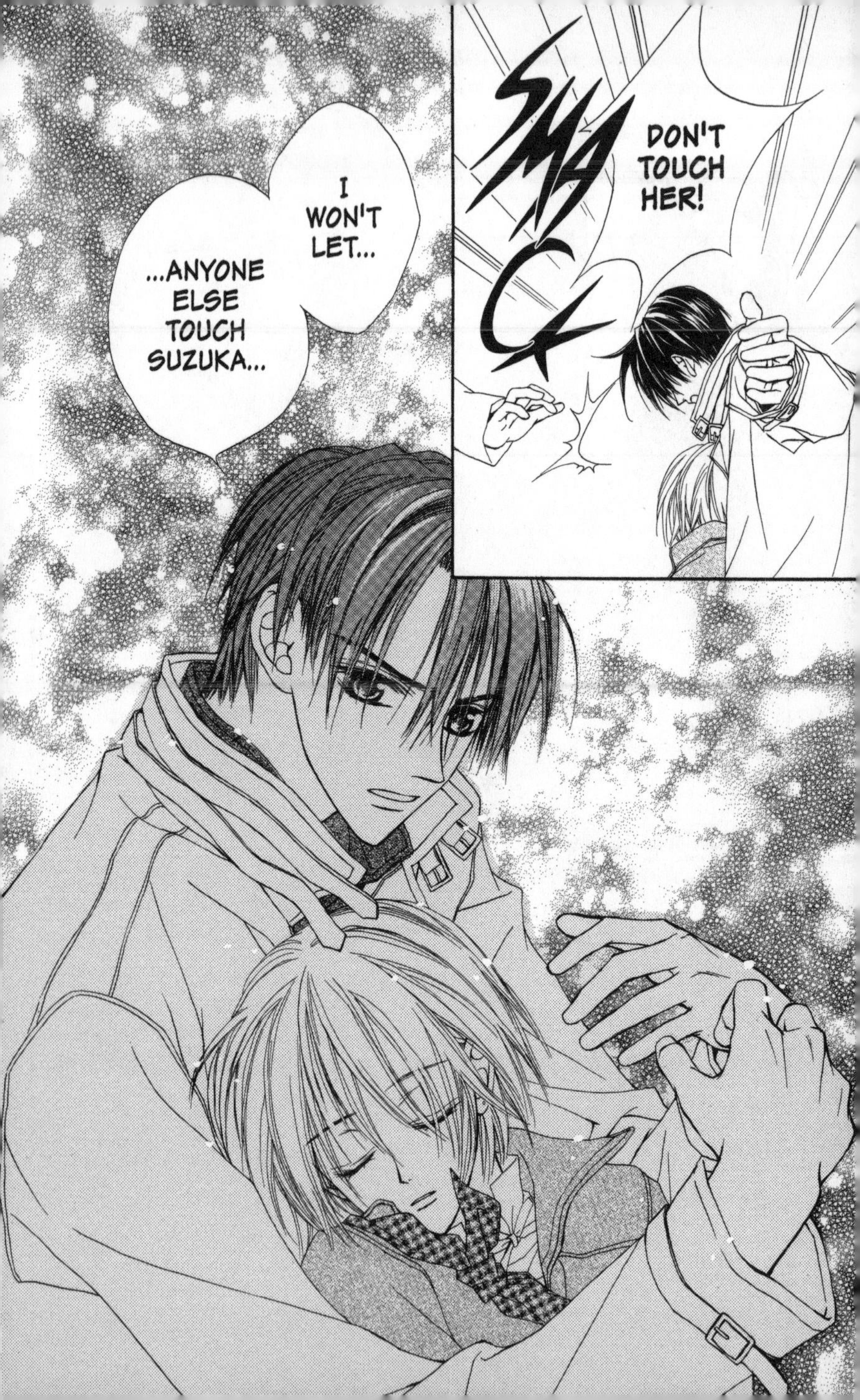
DON'T TOUCH HER!
SMACK
I WON'T LET...
...ANYONE ELSE TOUCH SUZUKA...

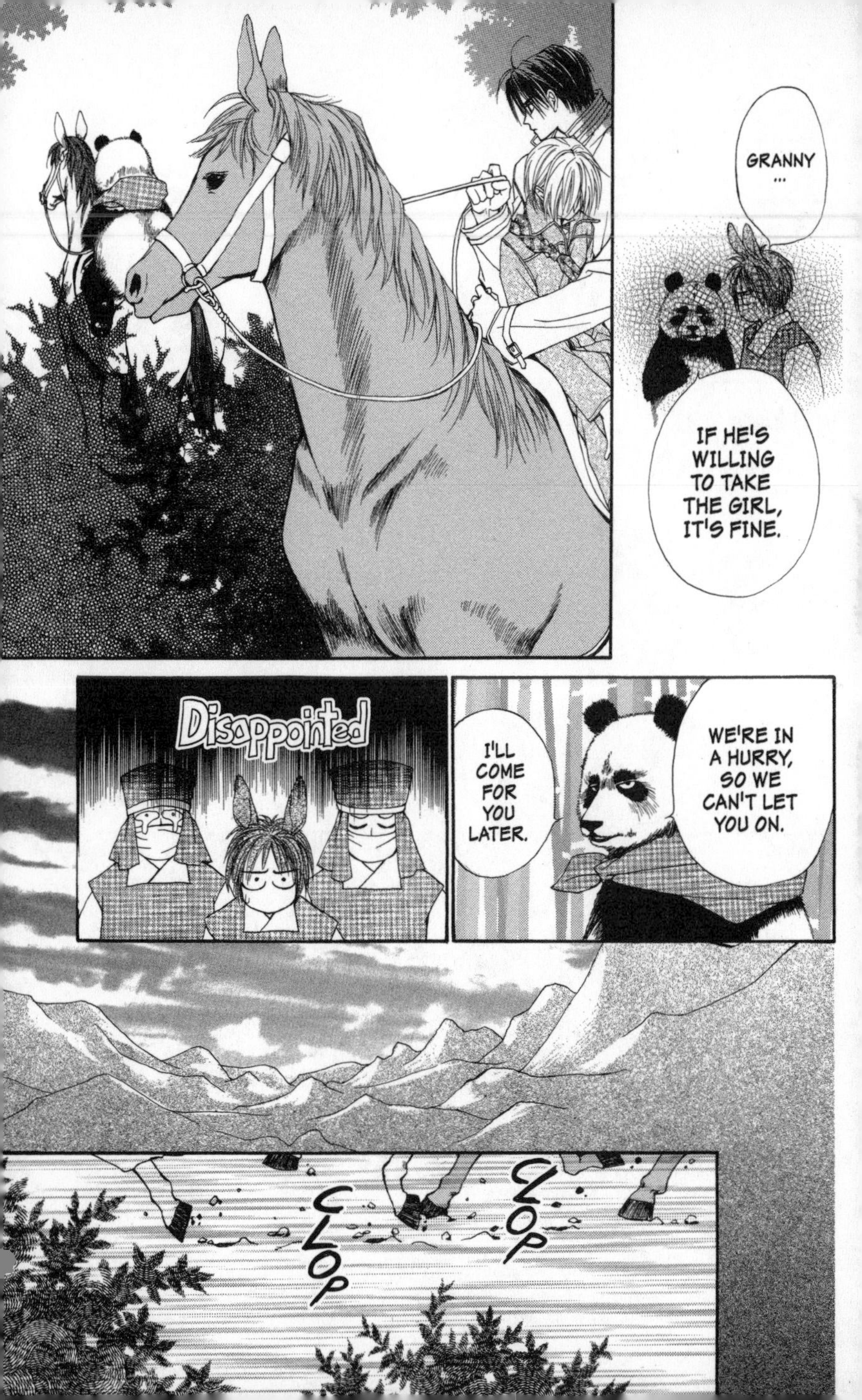
GRANNY ...
IF HE'S WILLING TO TAKE THE GIRL, IT'S FINE.
WE'RE IN A HURRY, SO WE CAN'T LET YOU ON.
I'LL COME FOR YOU LATER.
Disappointed
CLOP
CLOP

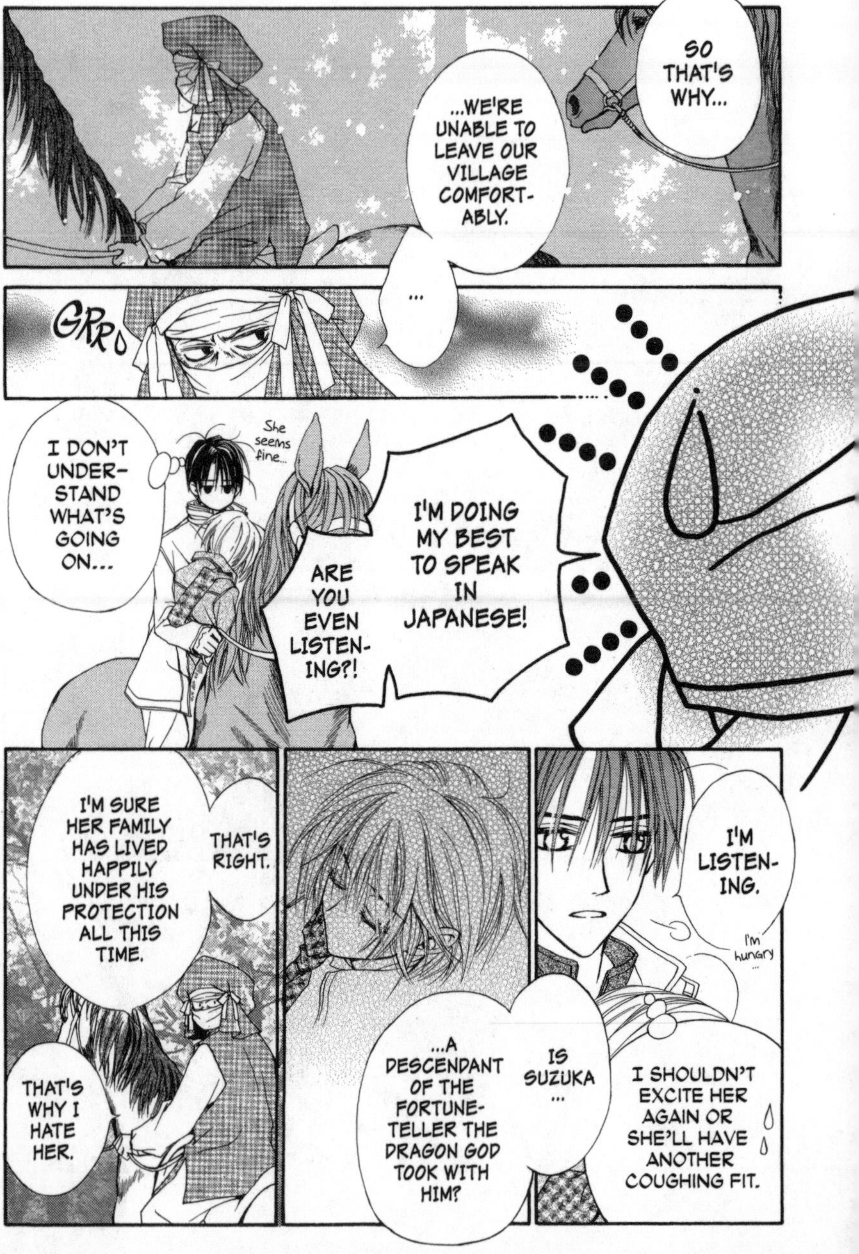

SO THAT'S WHY...
...WE'RE UNABLE TO LEAVE OUR VILLAGE COMFORTABLY.
...
GRR
I'M DOING MY BEST TO SPEAK IN JAPANESE!
ARE YOU EVEN LISTENING?!
She seems fine...
I DON'T UNDERSTAND WHAT'S GOING ON...
I'M LISTENING.
I'm hungry...
I SHOULDN'T EXCITE HER AGAIN OR SHE'LL HAVE ANOTHER COUGHING FIT.
IS SUZUKA...
...A DESCENDANT OF THE FORTUNE-TELLER THE DRAGON GOD TOOK WITH HIM?
THAT'S RIGHT.
I'M SURE HER FAMILY HAS LIVED HAPPILY UNDER HIS PROTECTION ALL THIS TIME.
THAT'S WHY I HATE HER.

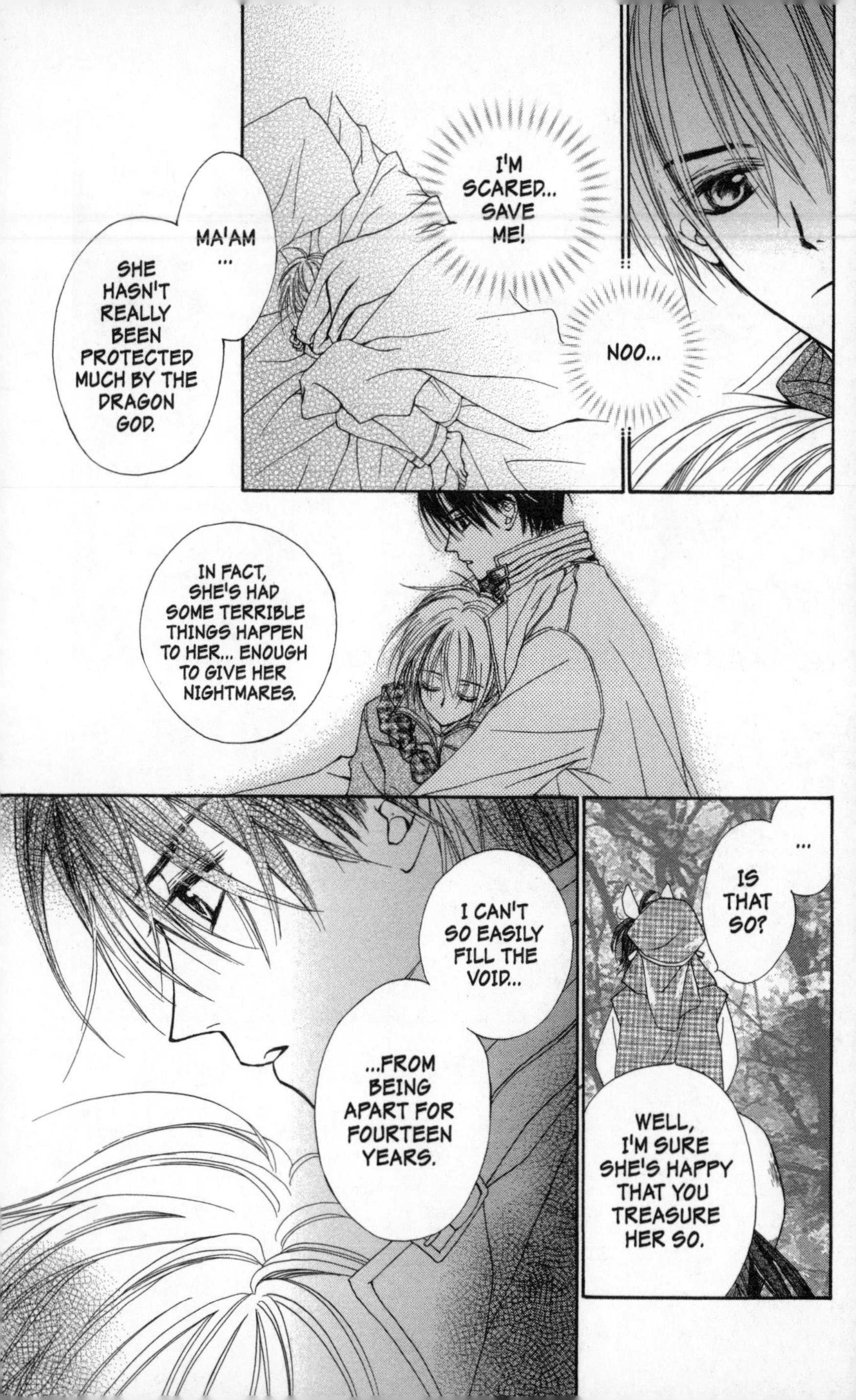
NOO...
I'M SCARED... SAVE ME!
MA'AM ... SHE HASN'T REALLY BEEN PROTECTED MUCH BY THE DRAGON GOD.
IN FACT, SHE'S HAD SOME TERRIBLE THINGS HAPPEN TO HER... ENOUGH TO GIVE HER NIGHTMARES.
... IS THAT SO?
WELL, I'M SURE SHE'S HAPPY THAT YOU TREASURE HER SO.
I CAN'T SO EASILY FILL THE VOID...
...FROM BEING APART FOR FOURTEEN YEARS.

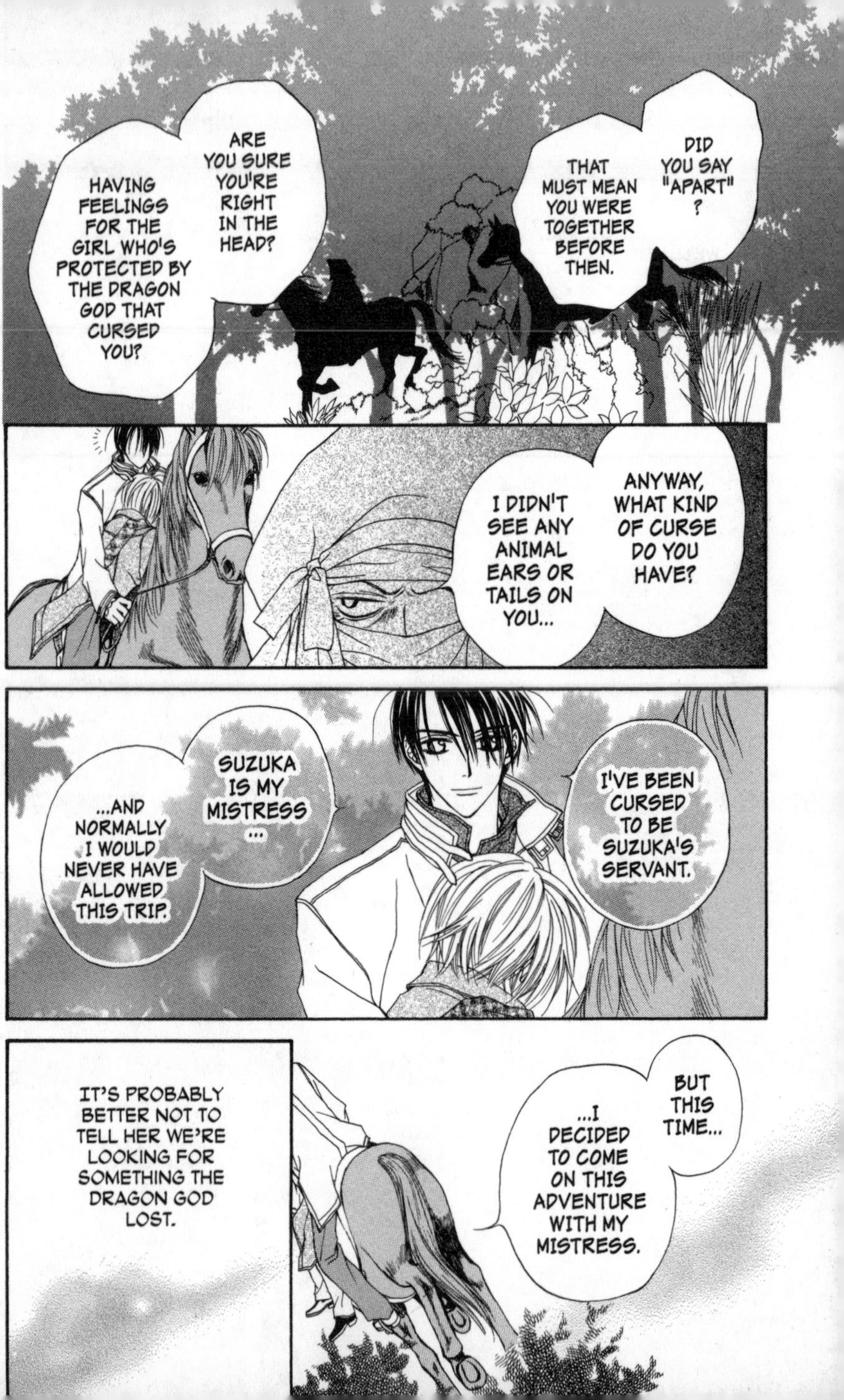
DID YOU SAY "APART"?
THAT MUST MEAN YOU WERE TOGETHER BEFORE THEN.
ARE YOU SURE YOU'RE RIGHT IN THE HEAD?
HAVING FEELINGS FOR THE GIRL WHO'S PROTECTED BY THE DRAGON GOD THAT CURSED YOU?
ANYWAY, WHAT KIND OF CURSE DO YOU HAVE?
I DIDN'T SEE ANY ANIMAL EARS OR TAILS ON YOU...
I'VE BEEN CURSED TO BE SUZUKA'S SERVANT.
SUZUKA IS MY MISTRESS...
...AND NORMALLY I WOULD NEVER HAVE ALLOWED THIS TRIP.
BUT THIS TIME...
...I DECIDED TO COME ON THIS ADVENTURE WITH MY MISTRESS.
IT'S PROBABLY BETTER NOT TO TELL HER WE'RE LOOKING FOR SOMETHING THE DRAGON GOD LOST.

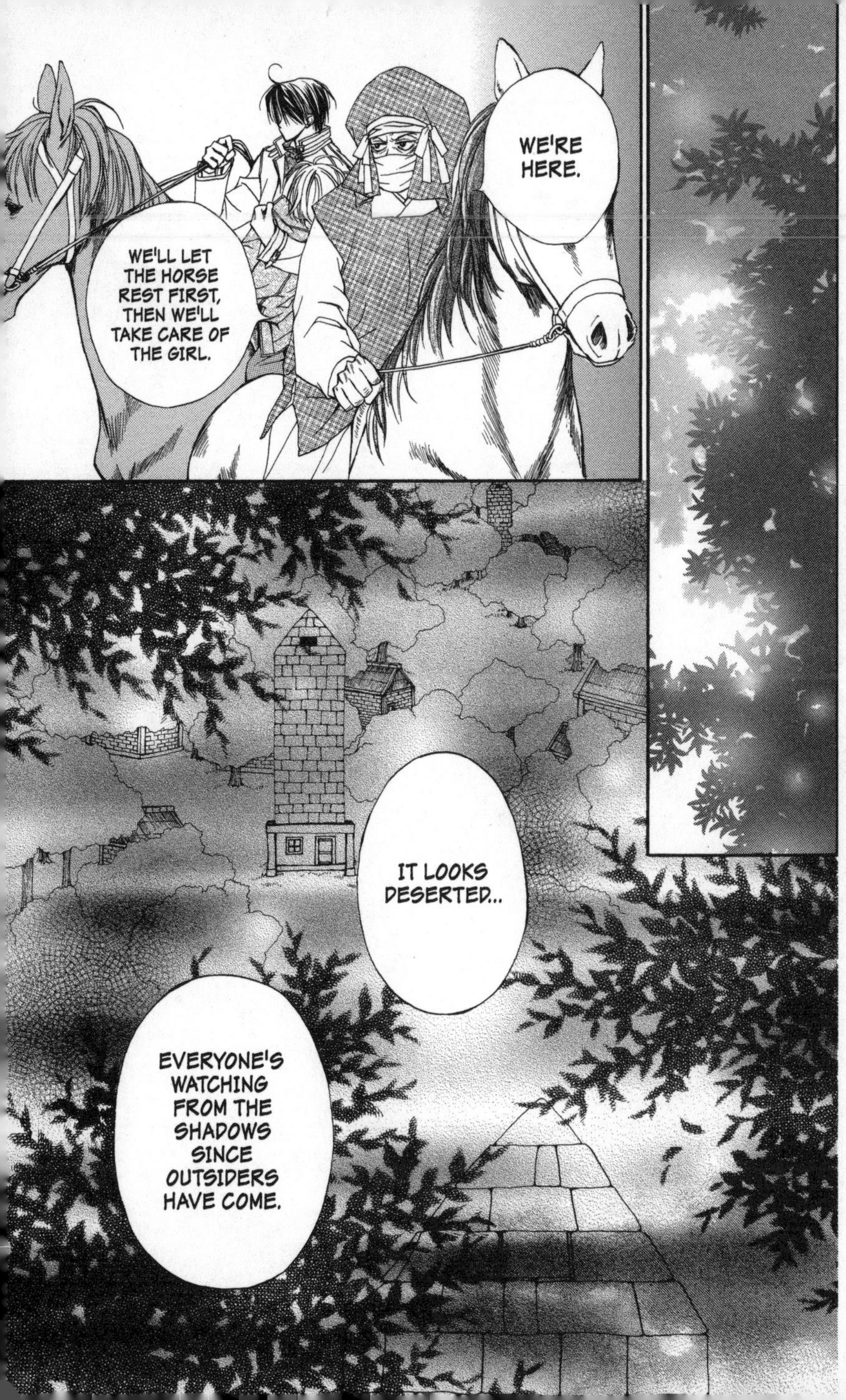
WE'RE HERE.
WE'LL LET THE HORSE REST FIRST, THEN WE'LL TAKE CARE OF THE GIRL.
IT LOOKS DESERTED...
EVERYONE'S WATCHING FROM THE SHADOWS SINCE OUTSIDERS HAVE COME.

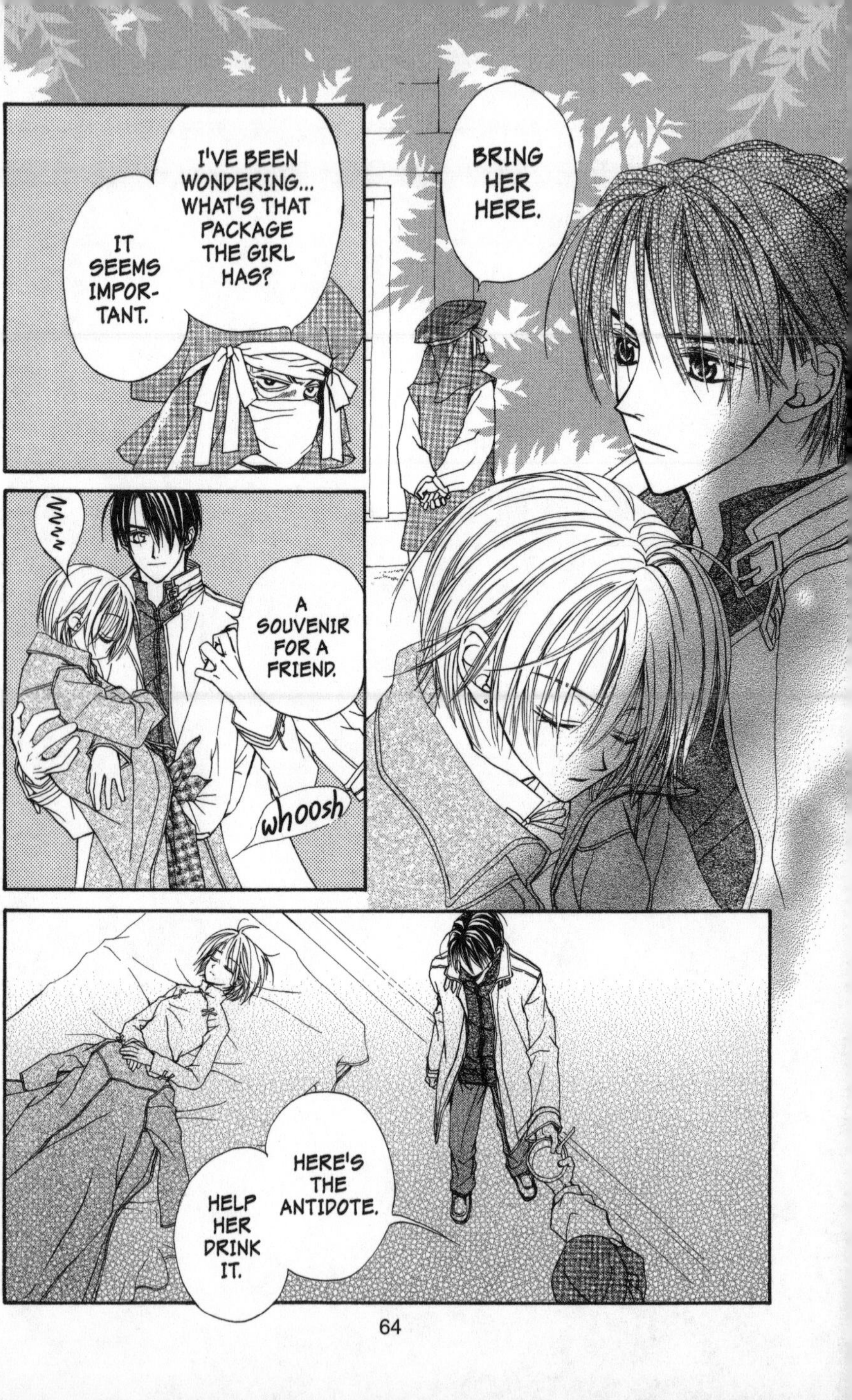
BRING HER HERE.
I'VE BEEN WONDERING... WHAT'S THAT PACKAGE THE GIRL HAS?
IT SEEMS IMPOR-TANT.
Nnn
A SOUVENIR FOR A FRIEND.
whoosh
HERE'S THE ANTIDOTE.
HELP HER DRINK IT.

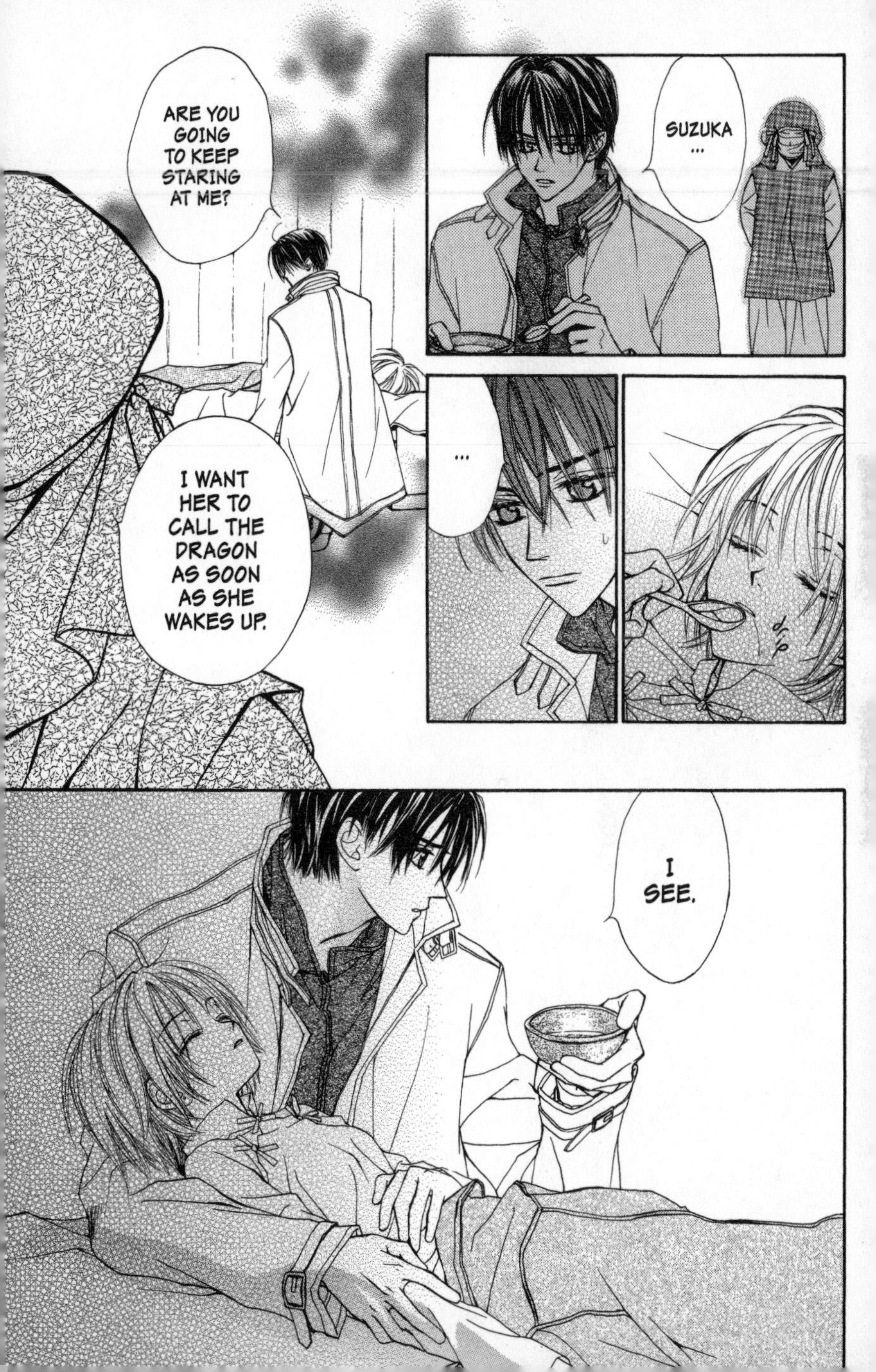
SUZUKA ...
drip
...
ARE YOU GOING TO KEEP STARING AT ME?
I WANT HER TO CALL THE DRAGON AS SOON AS SHE WAKES UP.
I SEE.

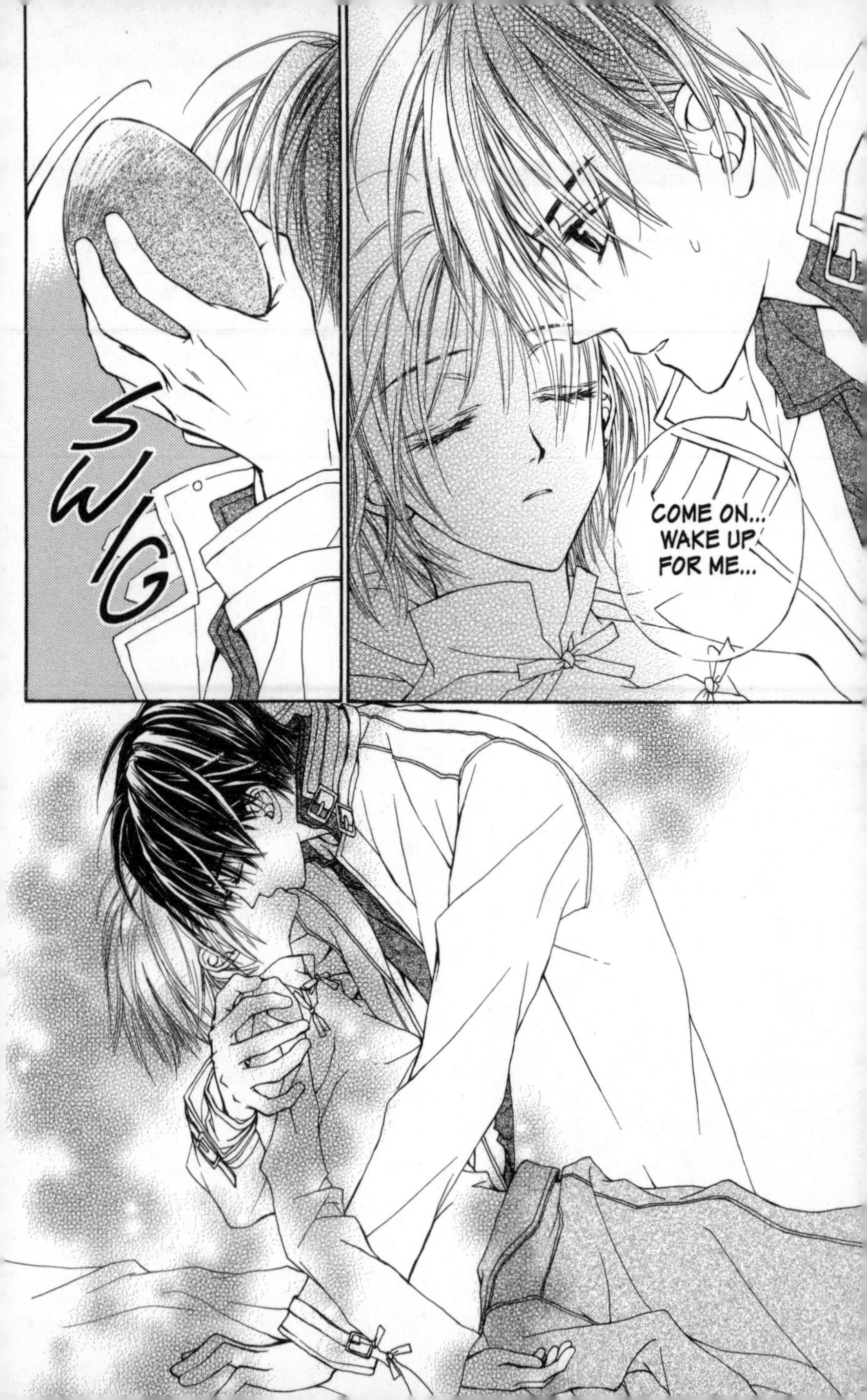
COME ON... WAKE UP FOR ME...
SWIG

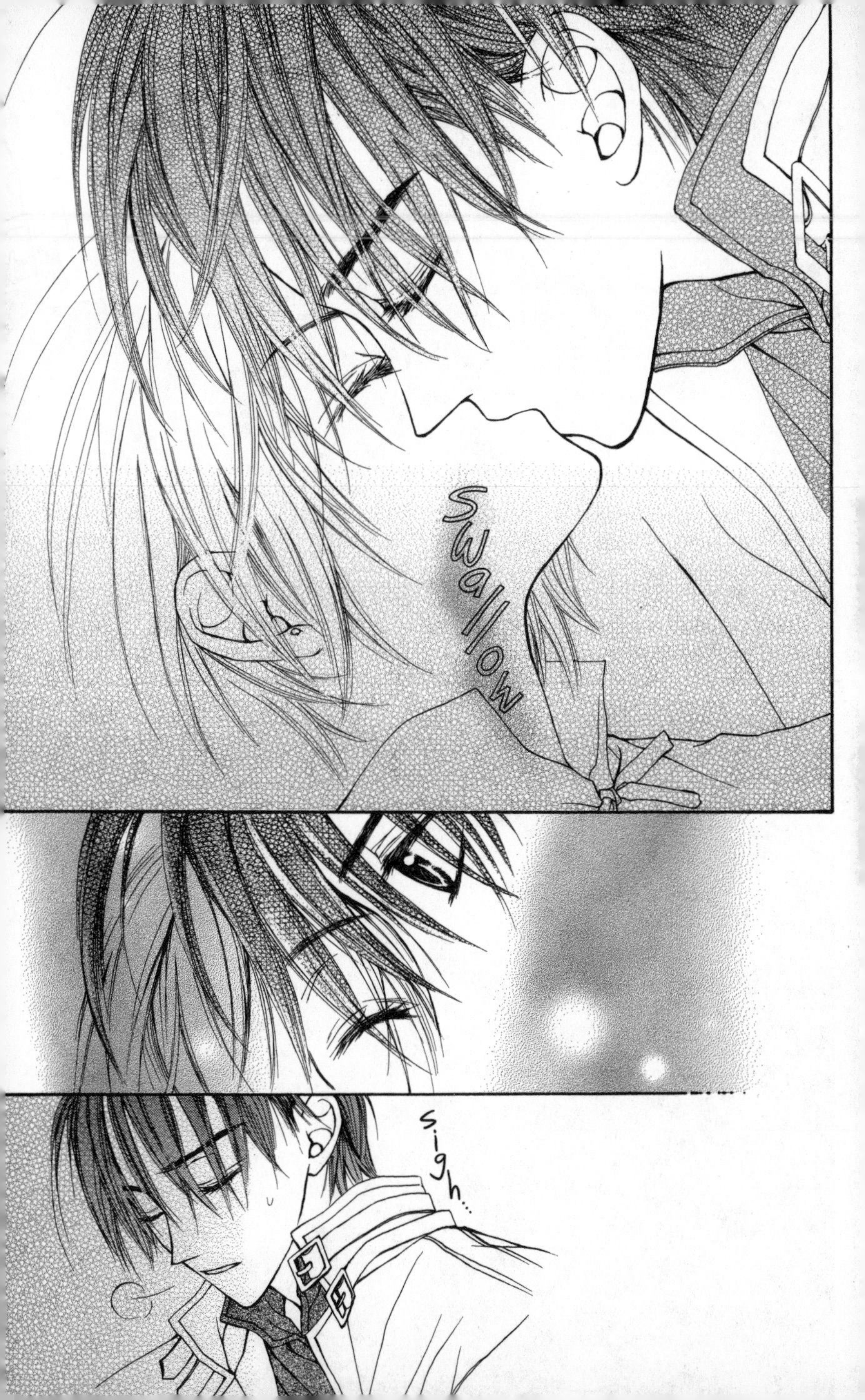
swallow
sigh...

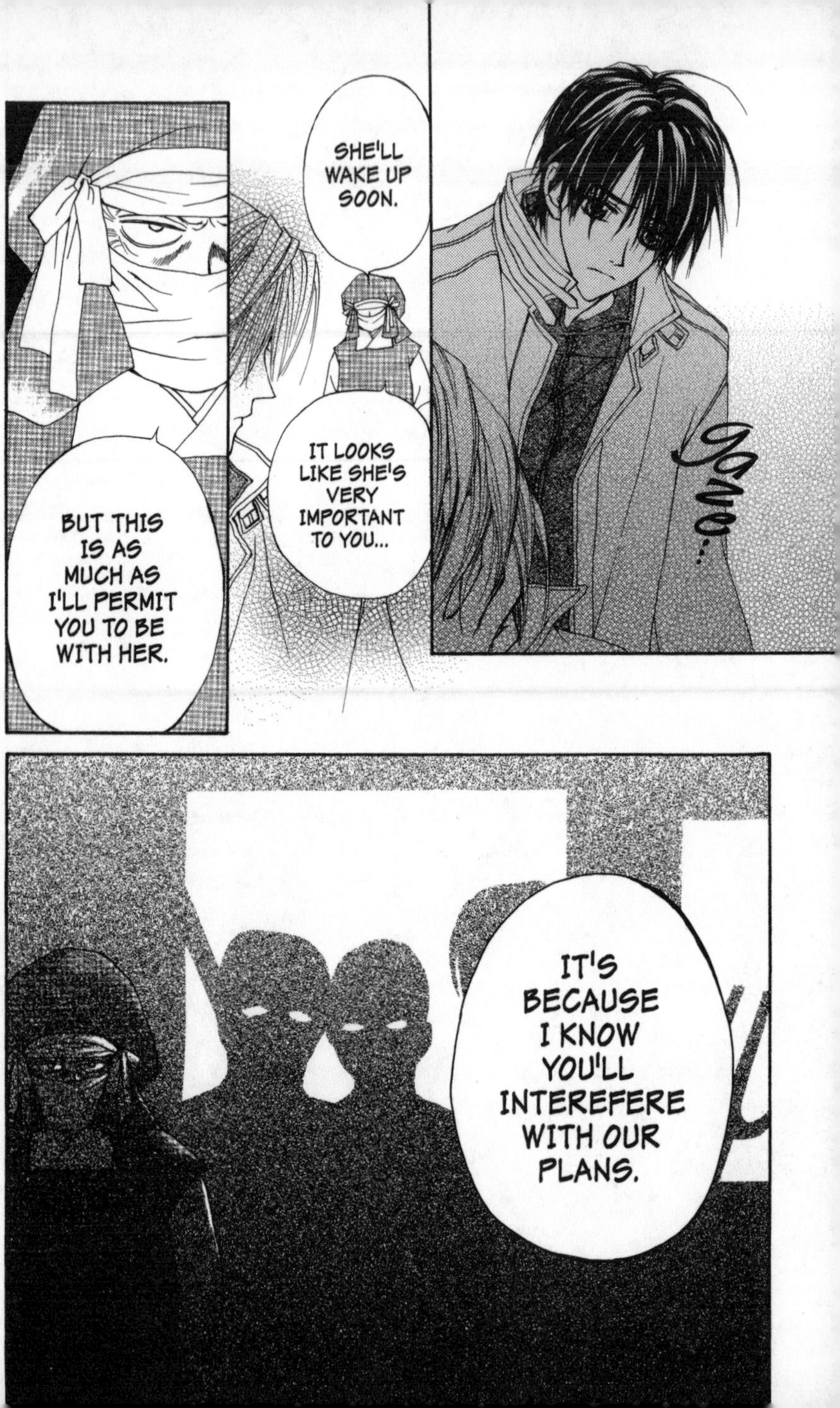
gaze...
SHE'LL WAKE UP SOON.
IT LOOKS LIKE SHE'S VERY IMPORTANT TO YOU...
BUT THIS IS AS MUCH AS I'LL PERMIT YOU TO BE WITH HER.
IT'S BECAUSE I KNOW YOU'LL INTEREFERE WITH OUR PLANS.

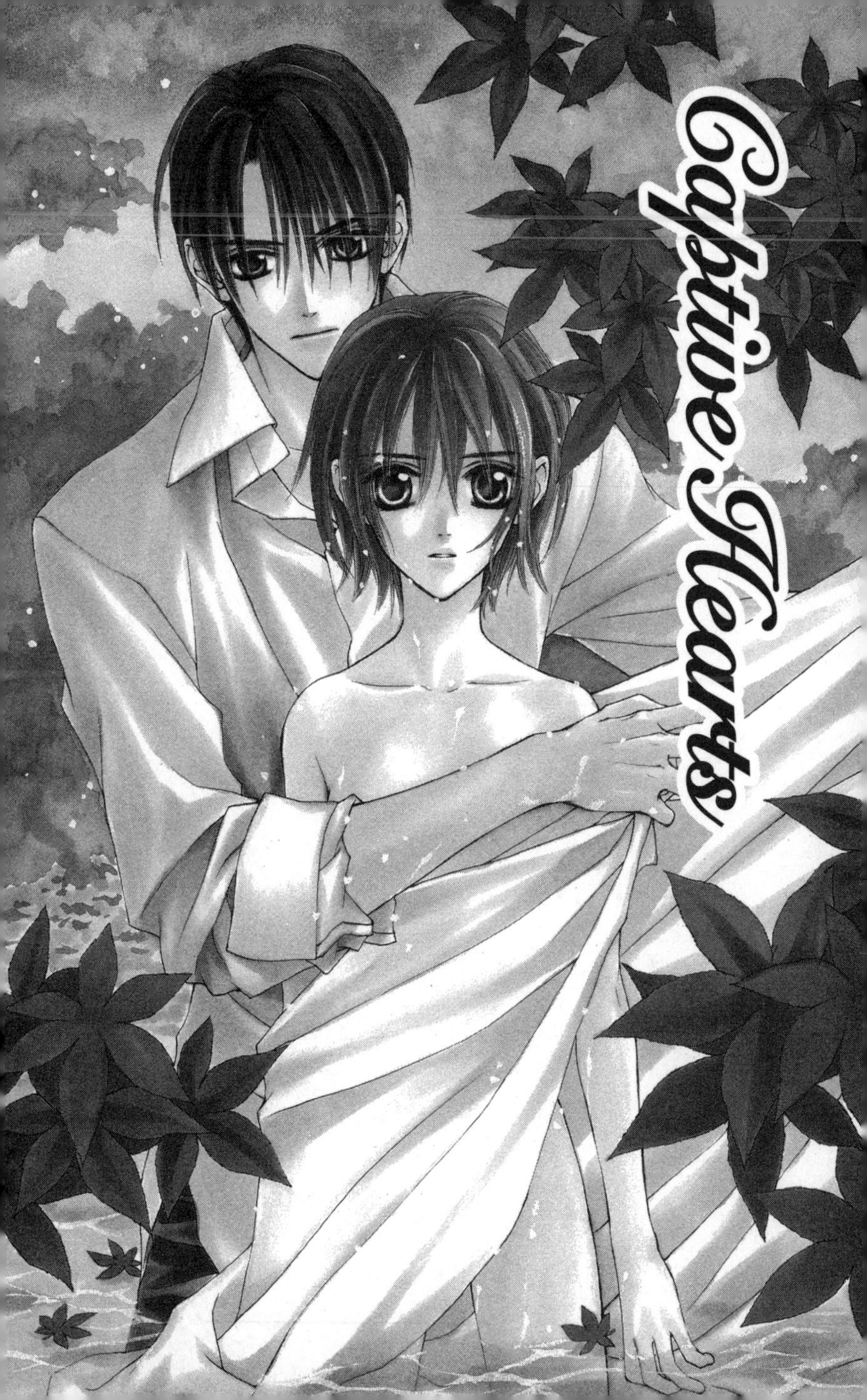
Captive Hearts

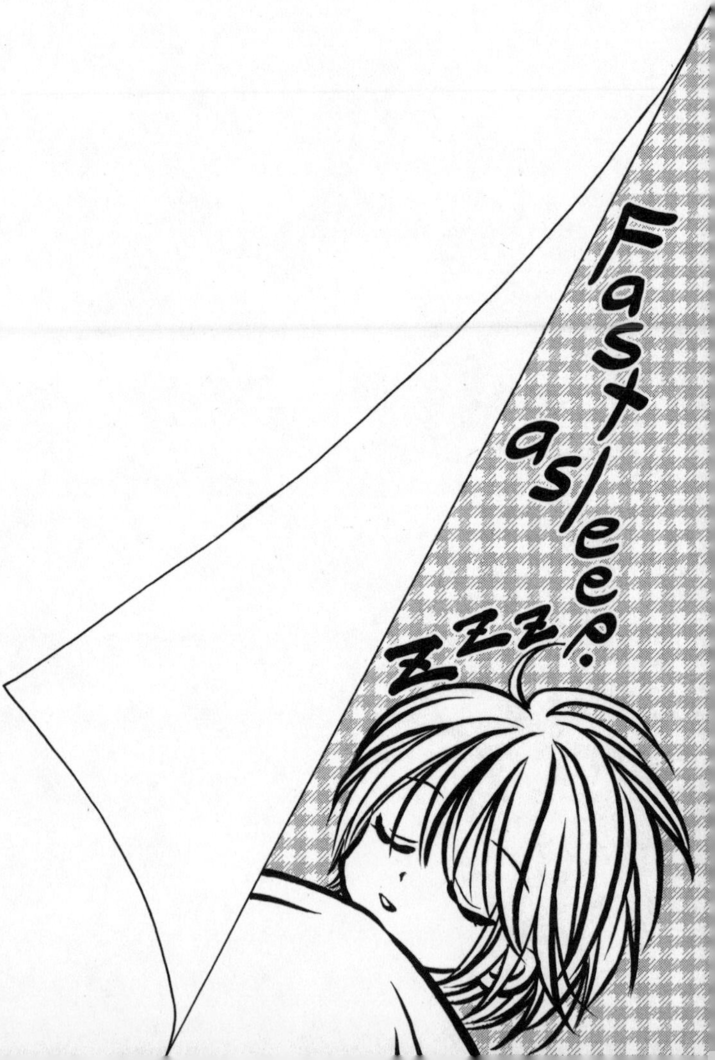

Fast asleep.
ZZZ

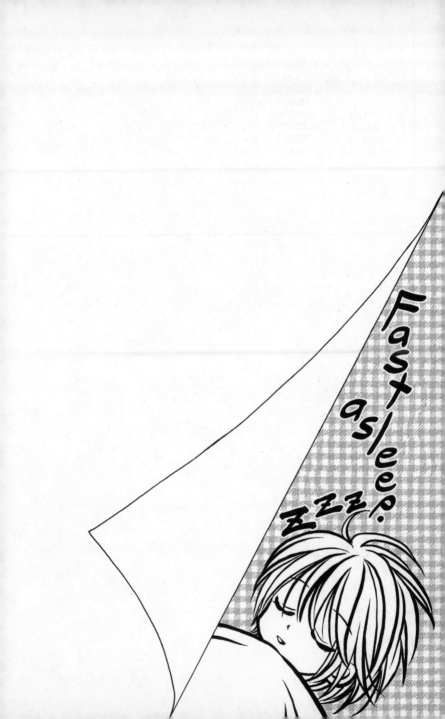

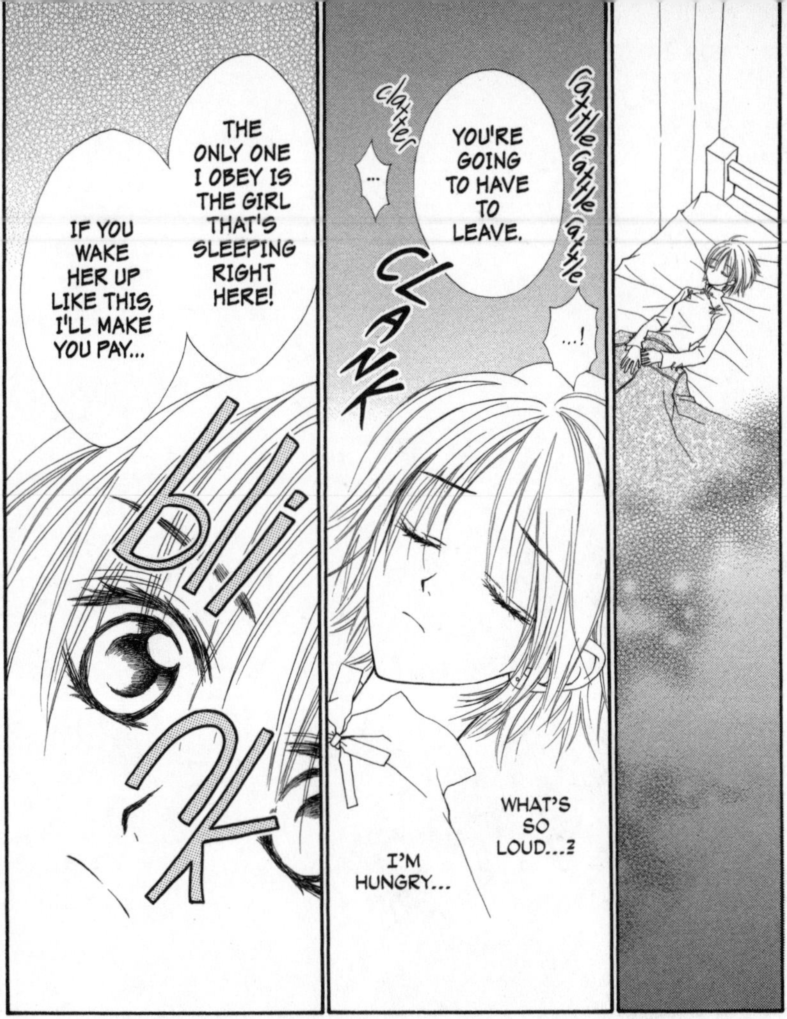
rattle rattle rattle
YOU'RE GOING TO HAVE TO LEAVE.
clatter
...
CLANK
...!
WHAT'S SO LOUD...?
I'M HUNGRY...
THE ONLY ONE I OBEY IS THE GIRL THAT'S SLEEPING RIGHT HERE!
IF YOU WAKE HER UP LIKE THIS, I'LL MAKE YOU PAY...
blink

Backstory ③ I always have to be careful before I draw Megumi. I draw him like a loyal German Shepherd (mix?) who's loved by his owner. In that way, Megumi is a dog. I think of an Abyssinian cat for Suzuka, but she always ends up looking like a chick! For Kuroishi, I think of a black panther that has the aura of a very well-trained Doberman. I guess this means I wish the characters were big dogs and cats! Like a pure white Pomeranian and a giant Maine Coon! But since I know how great mixed breeds can be, my favorite pets are mongrels. ♡

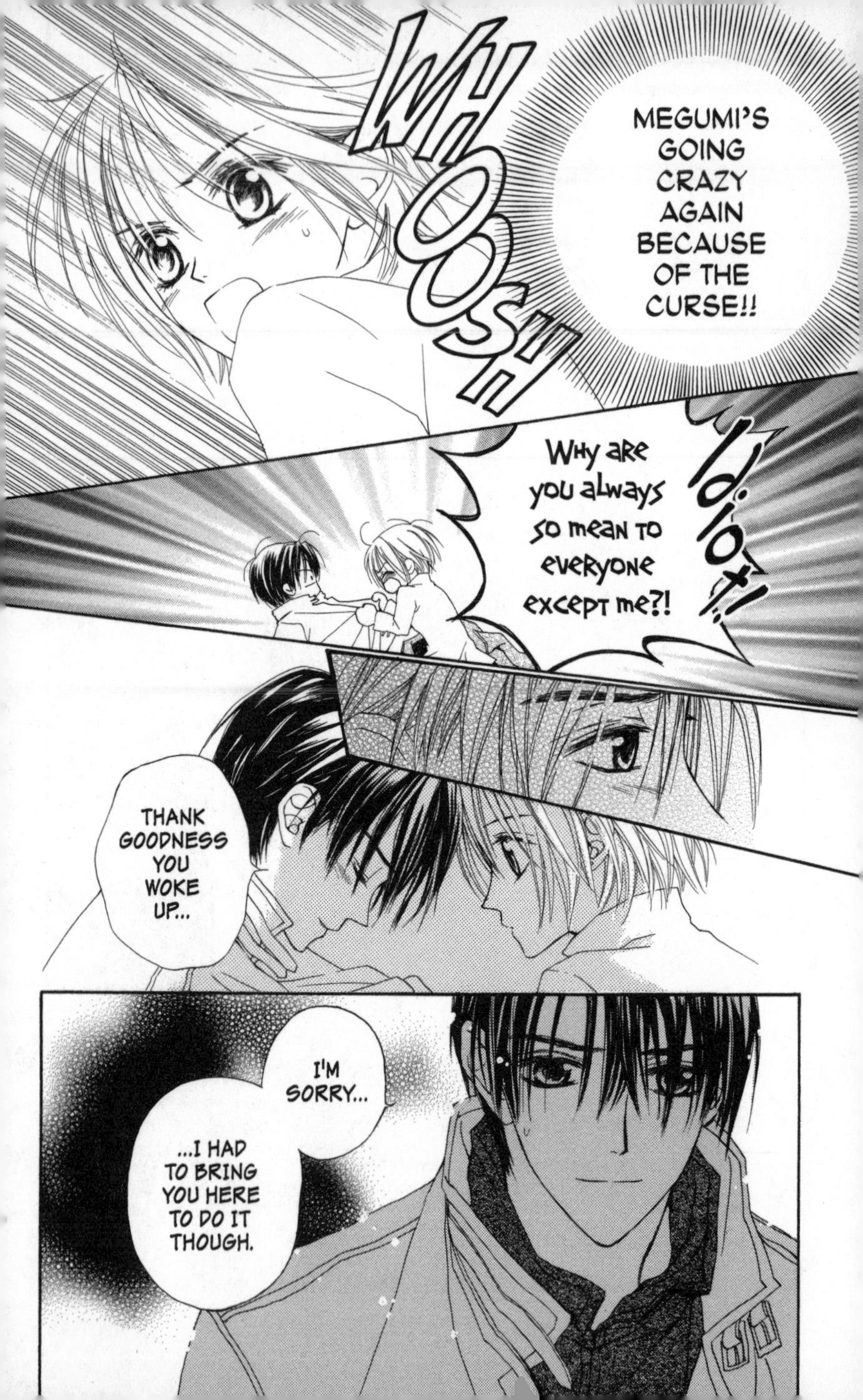
MEGUMI'S GOING CRAZY AGAIN BECAUSE OF THE CURSE!!
WHOOSH!!
Idiot!!
Why are you always so mean to everyone except me?!
THANK GOODNESS YOU WOKE UP...
I'M SORRY...
...I HAD TO BRING YOU HERE TO DO IT THOUGH.

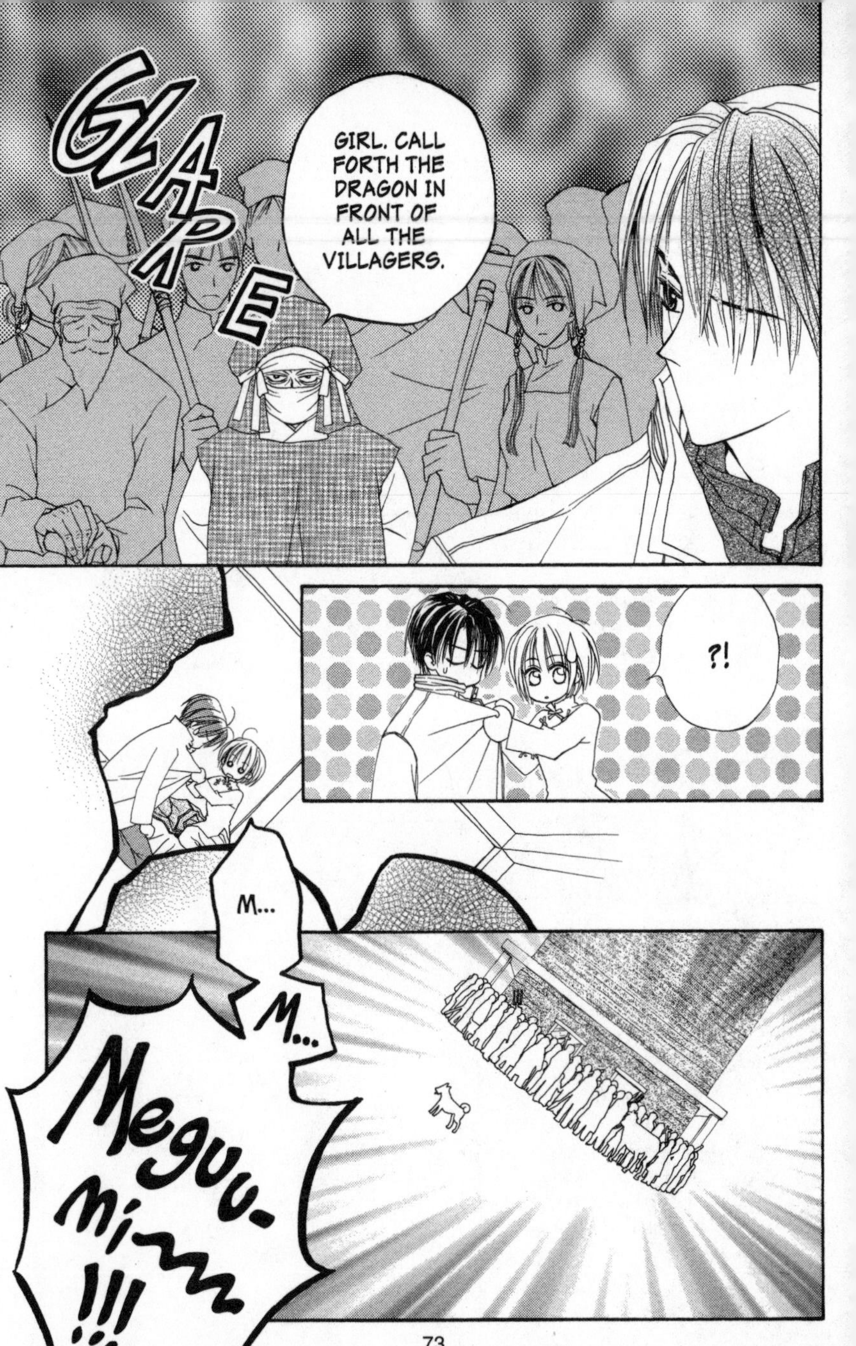
GIRL. CALL FORTH THE DRAGON IN FRONT OF ALL THE VILLAGERS.
GLARE
?!
M...
M...
Meguu-mi~~!!!

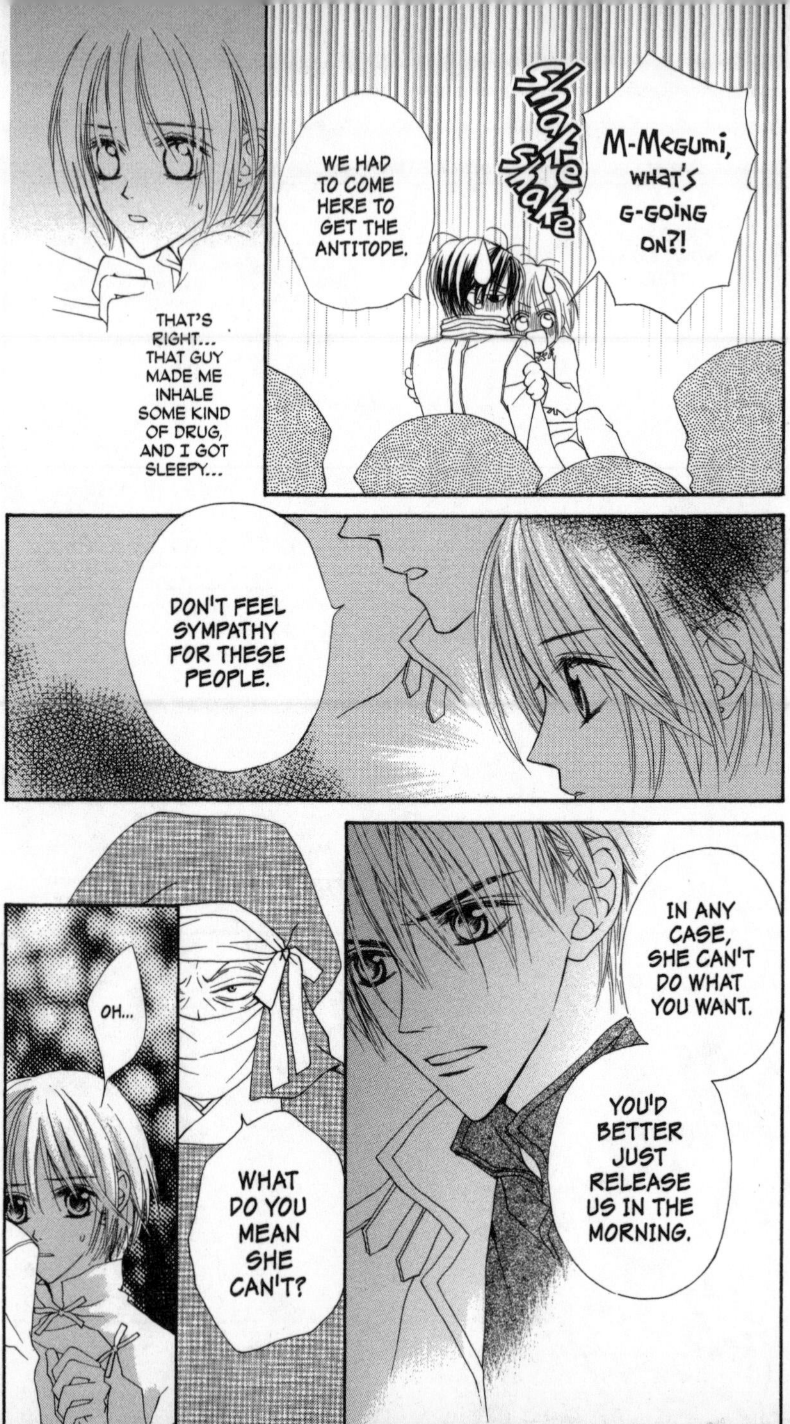
M-Megumi, what's g-going on?!
Shake Shake
We had to come here to get the antitode.
That's right... that guy made me inhale some kind of drug, and I got sleepy...
Don't feel sympathy for these people.
In any case, she can't do what you want.
You'd better just release us in the morning.
Oh...
What do you mean she can't?

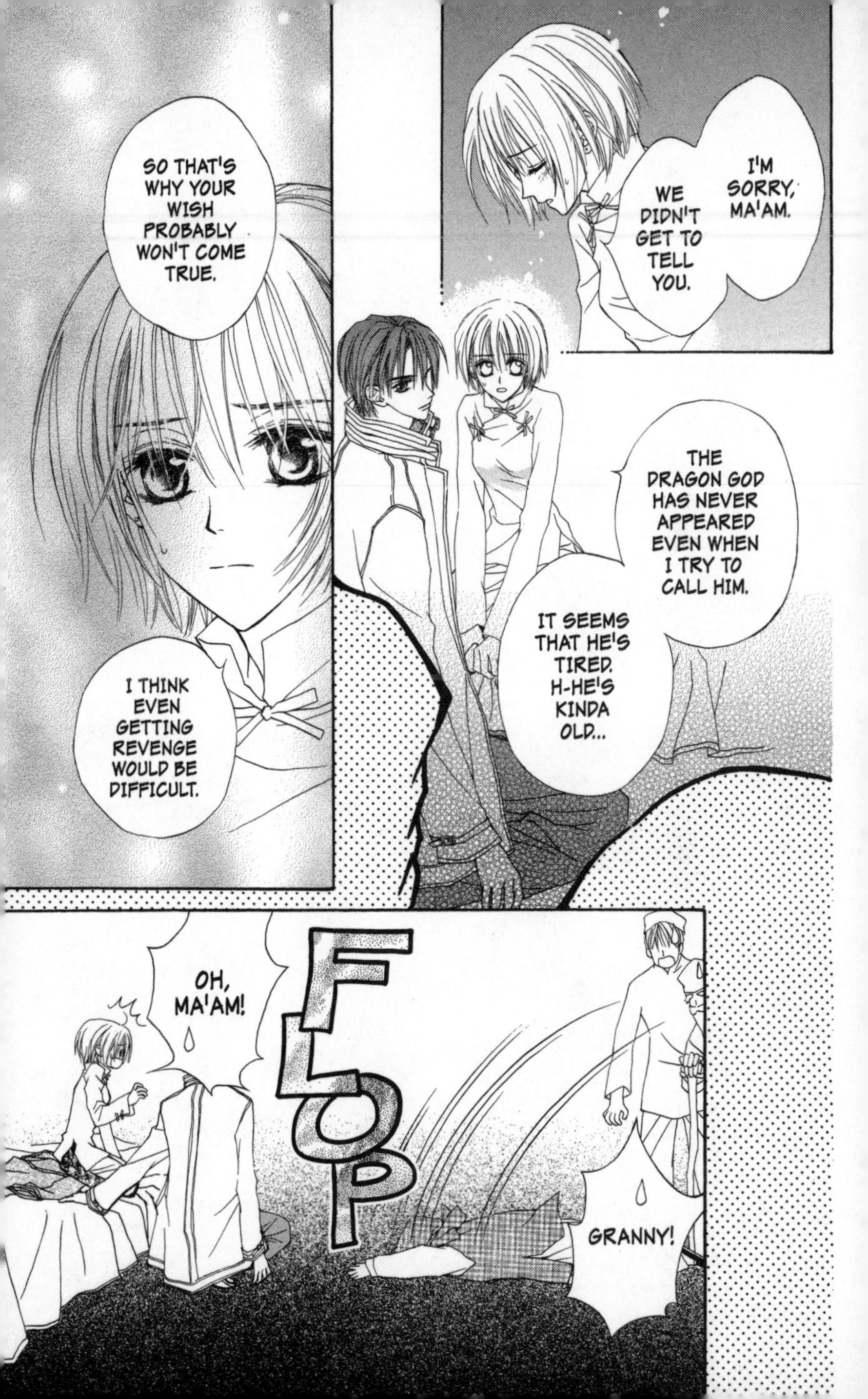
I'M SORRY, MA'AM.
WE DIDN'T GET TO TELL YOU.
THE DRAGON GOD HAS NEVER APPEARED EVEN WHEN I TRY TO CALL HIM.
IT SEEMS THAT HE'S TIRED. H-HE'S KINDA OLD...
SO THAT'S WHY YOUR WISH PROBABLY WON'T COME TRUE.
I THINK EVEN GETTING REVENGE WOULD BE DIFFICULT.
GRANNY!
FLOP
OH, MA'AM!

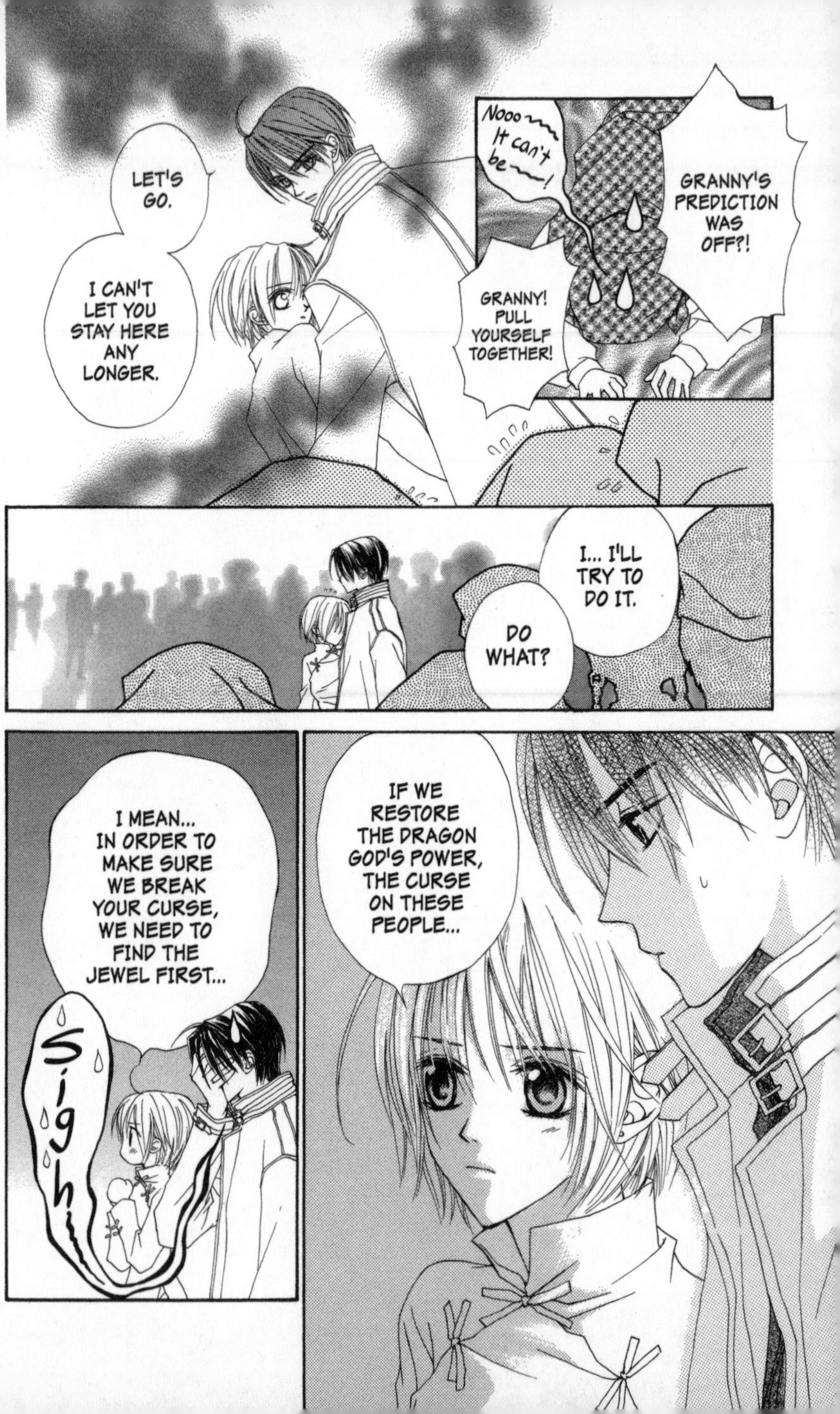
GRANNY'S PREDICTION WAS OFF?!
Nooo~ It can't be~!
GRANNY! PULL YOURSELF TOGETHER!
LET'S GO.
I CAN'T LET YOU STAY HERE ANY LONGER.
I... I'LL TRY TO DO IT.
DO WHAT?
IF WE RESTORE THE DRAGON GOD'S POWER, THE CURSE ON THESE PEOPLE...
I MEAN... IN ORDER TO MAKE SURE WE BREAK YOUR CURSE, WE NEED TO FIND THE JEWEL FIRST...
Sigh

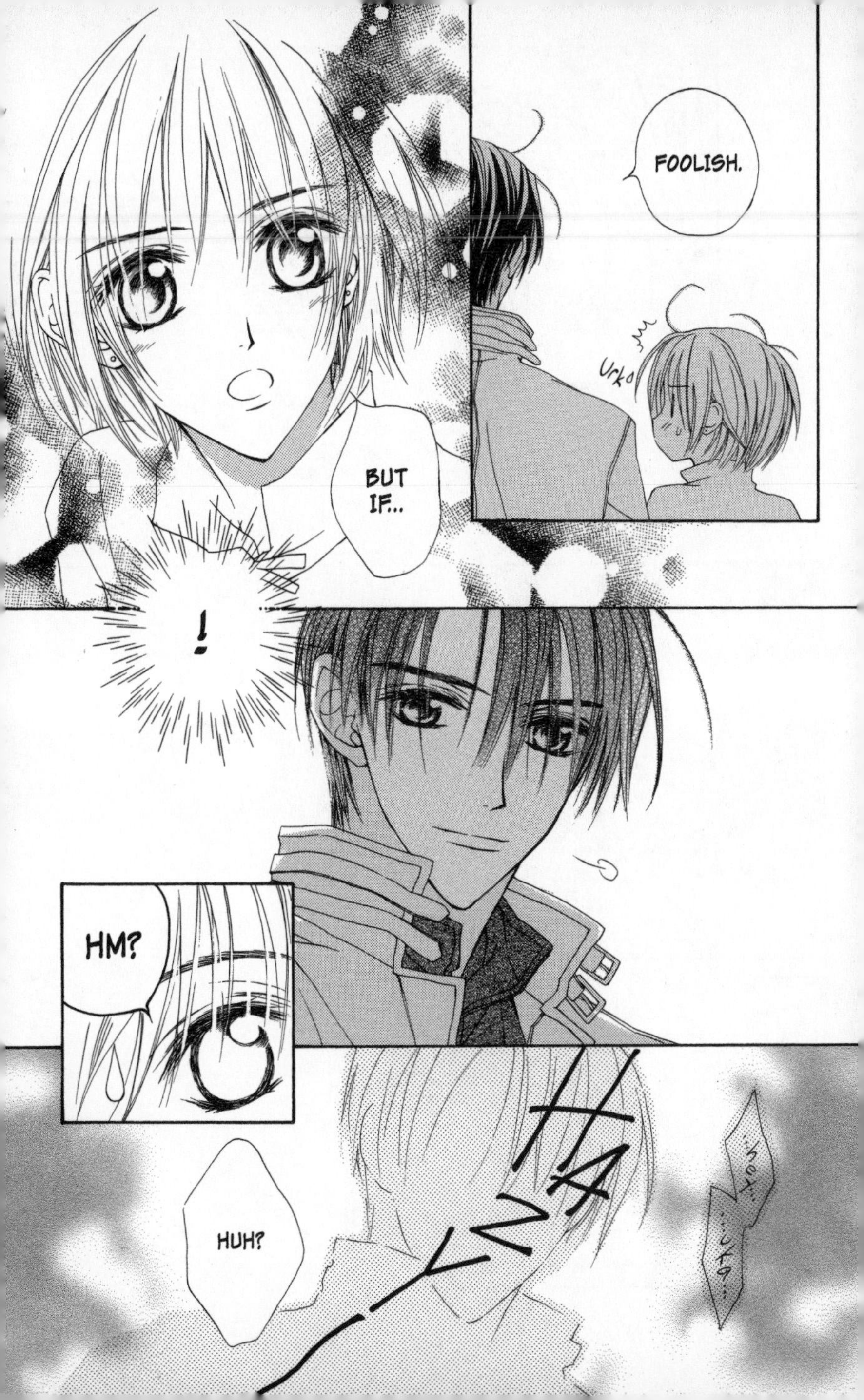
FOOLISH.
Urk
BUT IF...
!
HM?
...hey...
...ukyo...
HAZY
HUH?

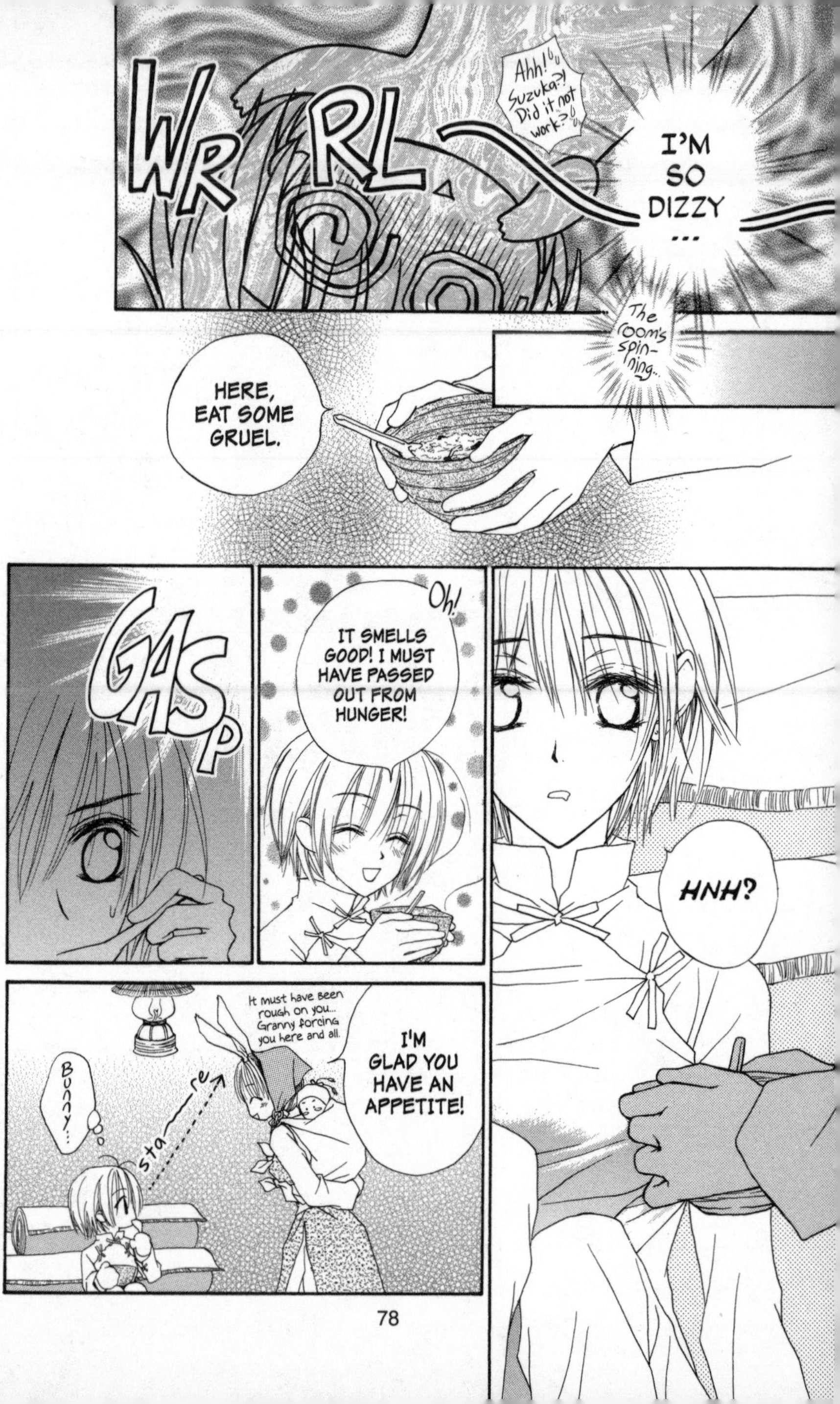
I'M SO DIZZY...
Ahh!? Suzuka?! Did it not work?
WRRL
The room's spinning...
HERE, EAT SOME GRUEL.
HNH?
Oh!
IT SMELLS GOOD! I MUST HAVE PASSED OUT FROM HUNGER!
GASP
I'M GLAD YOU HAVE AN APPETITE!
It must have been rough on you... Granny forcing you here and all.
sta-re
Bunny...

"What?!" Drama CD Backstory, Part 1

Koei released a Captive Hearts **Drama CD** last November!! (I always pictured Koei as a video game company, but this time I found out they deal with drama CDs too. Sorry I didn't know anything!! ∞) (By the way, you can find it at CD stores.) When I first got the proposal, I was wondering how they would express everything just by sound!?? I couldn't even imagine it.

I found the whole process very interesting, from choosing the voice actors to production, so I've decided to write about it here. I never thought the series would get to a point where the characters would be voiced (because at the beginning it was meant as a one-shot story, of course!) so it took an unbelievable amount of time for me to choose the voice actors. I'm sorry!

The exception was Suzuka.

(To be continued...)

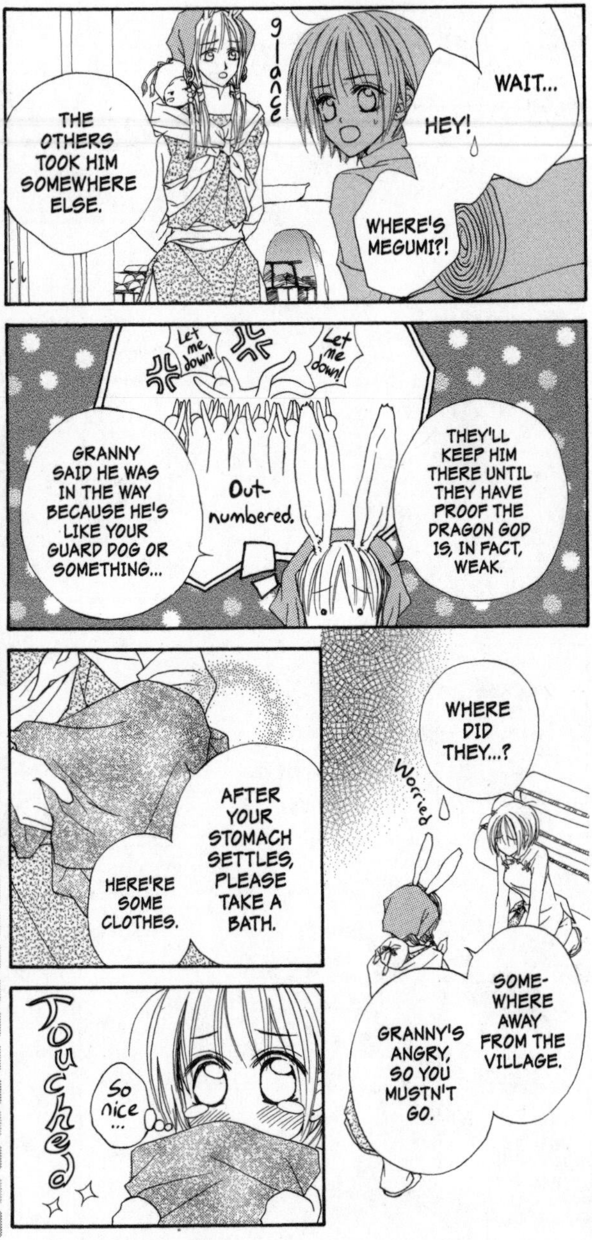

WAIT...
HEY!
WHERE'S MEGUMI?!
glance
THE OTHERS TOOK HIM SOMEWHERE ELSE.
THEY'LL KEEP HIM THERE UNTIL THEY HAVE PROOF THE DRAGON GOD IS, IN FACT, WEAK.
Let me down!
Let me down!
Out-numbered.
GRANNY SAID HE WAS IN THE WAY BECAUSE HE'S LIKE YOUR GUARD DOG OR SOMETHING...
WHERE DID THEY...?
Worried
SOME-WHERE AWAY FROM THE VILLAGE.
GRANNY'S ANGRY, SO YOU MUSTN'T GO.
AFTER YOUR STOMACH SETTLES, PLEASE TAKE A BATH.
HERE'RE SOME CLOTHES.
Touched
So nice...

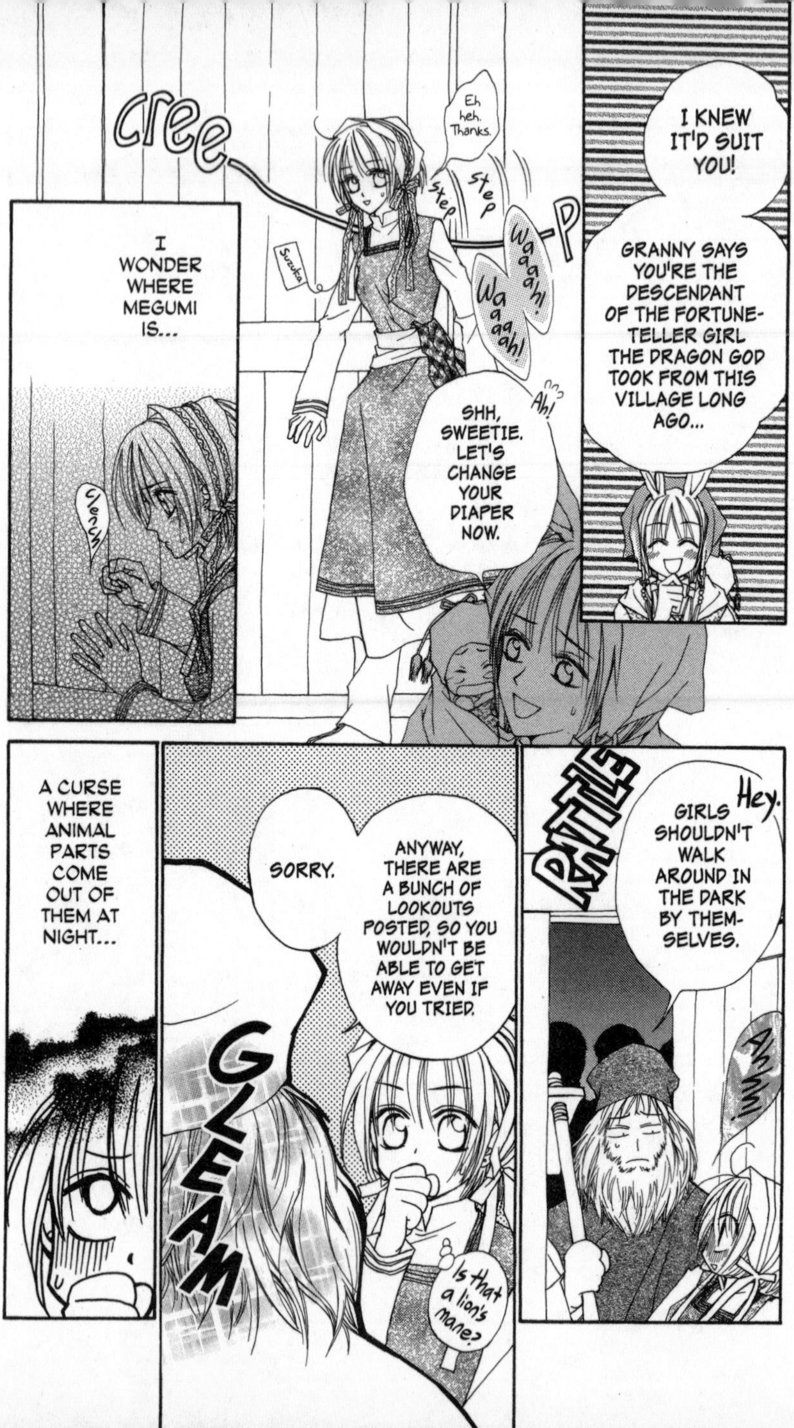
I KNEW IT'D SUIT YOU!
GRANNY SAYS YOU'RE THE DESCENDANT OF THE FORTUNE-TELLER GIRL THE DRAGON GOD TOOK FROM THIS VILLAGE LONG AGO...
cree-p
Eh heh. Thanks.
step step
Suzuka
Waaaah! Waaaah!
Ah!
SHH, SWEETIE. LET'S CHANGE YOUR DIAPER NOW.
I WONDER WHERE MEGUMI IS...
clench
RATTLE
Hey.
GIRLS SHOULDN'T WALK AROUND IN THE DARK BY THEMSELVES.
Ahhh!
SORRY.
ANYWAY, THERE ARE A BUNCH OF LOOKOUTS POSTED, SO YOU WOULDN'T BE ABLE TO GET AWAY EVEN IF YOU TRIED.
GLEAM
Is that a lion's mane?
A CURSE WHERE ANIMAL PARTS COME OUT OF THEM AT NIGHT...

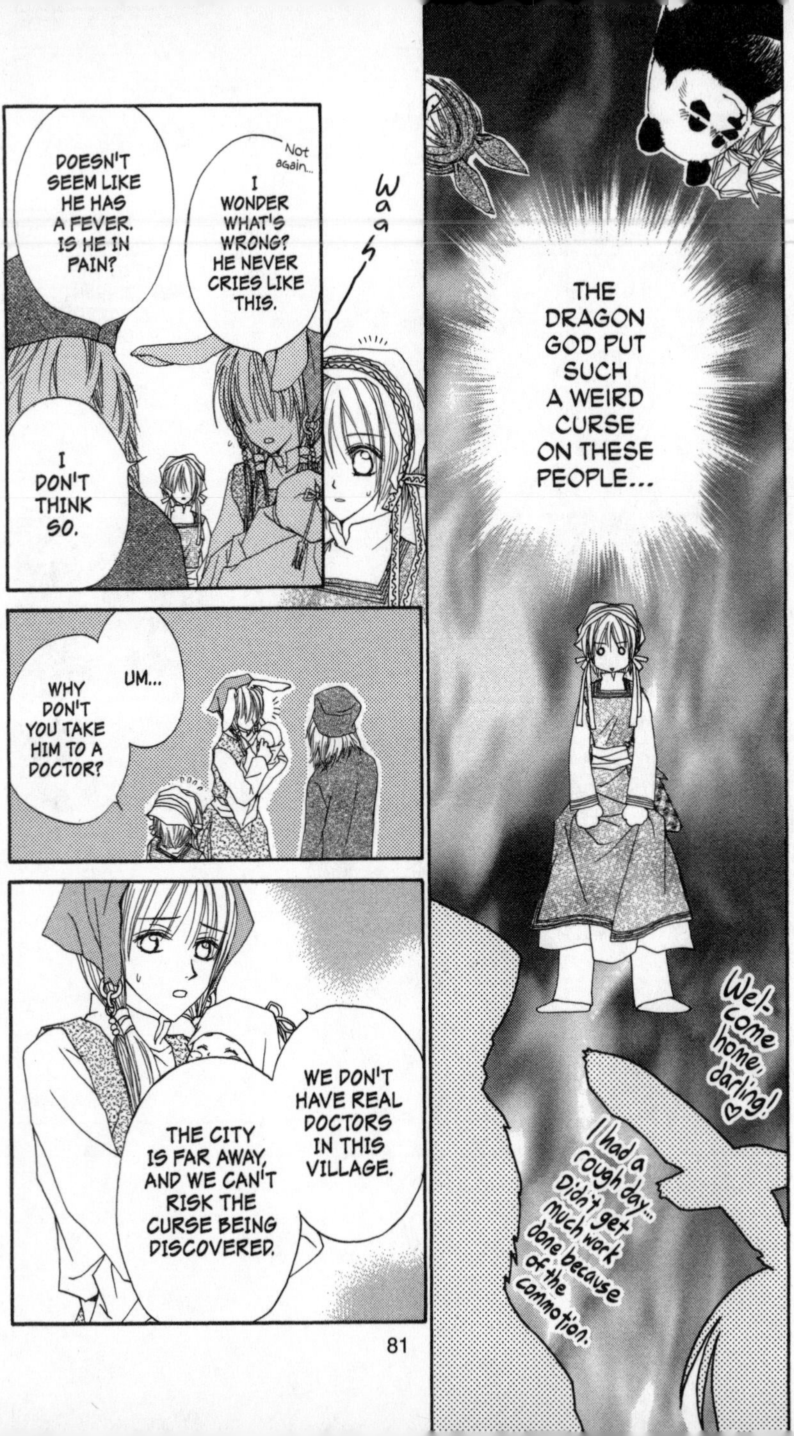
THE DRAGON GOD PUT SUCH A WEIRD CURSE ON THESE PEOPLE...
Wel-come home, darling! ♥
I had a rough day... Didn't get much work done because of the commotion.
Waah
Not again...
I WONDER WHAT'S WRONG? HE NEVER CRIES LIKE THIS.
DOESN'T SEEM LIKE HE HAS A FEVER. IS HE IN PAIN?
I DON'T THINK SO.
UM...
WHY DON'T YOU TAKE HIM TO A DOCTOR?
WE DON'T HAVE REAL DOCTORS IN THIS VILLAGE.
THE CITY IS FAR AWAY, AND WE CAN'T RISK THE CURSE BEING DISCOVERED.

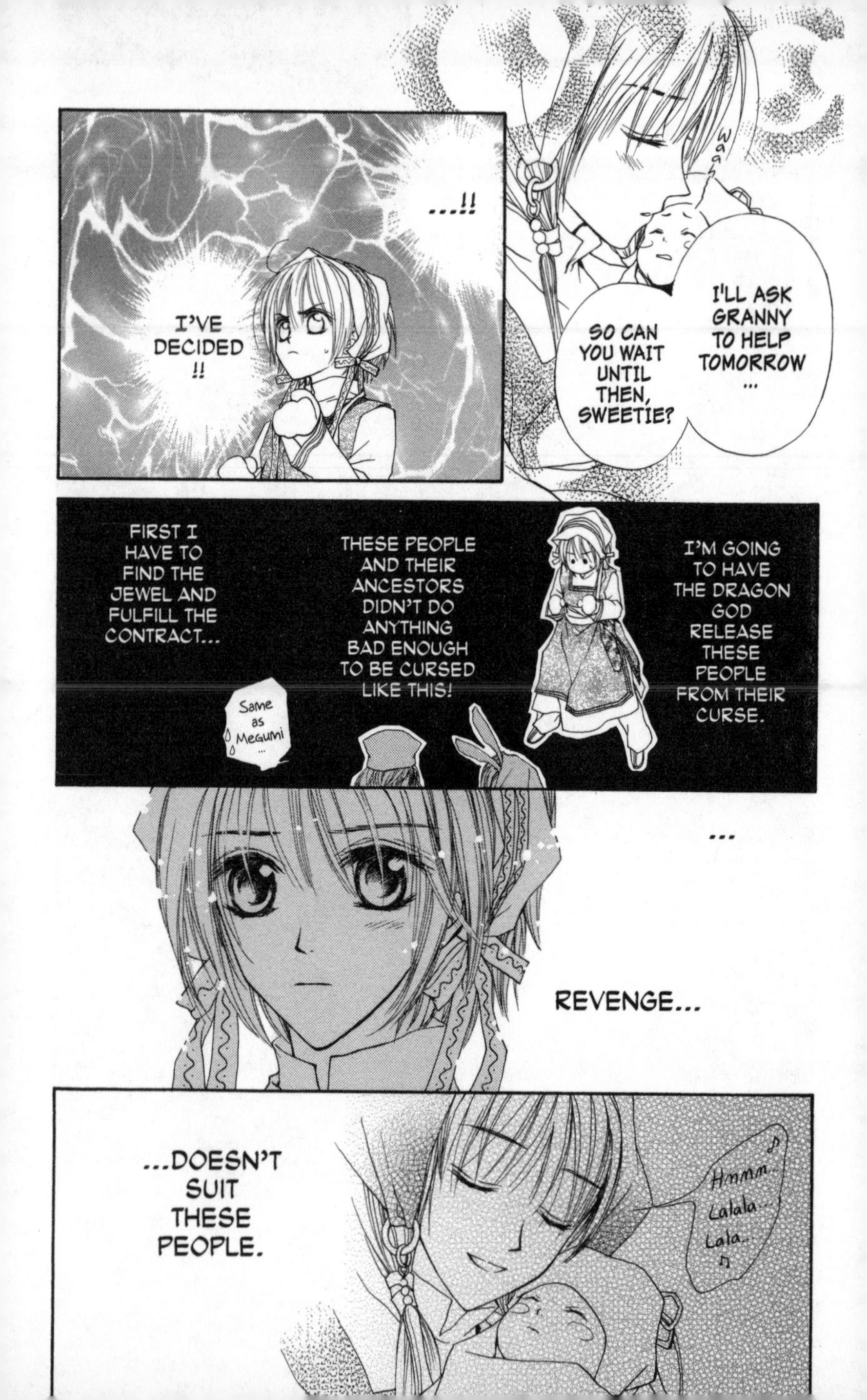
Waaa
I'LL ASK GRANNY TO HELP TOMORROW...
SO CAN YOU WAIT UNTIL THEN, SWEETIE?
...!!
I'VE DECIDED !!
I'M GOING TO HAVE THE DRAGON GOD RELEASE THESE PEOPLE FROM THEIR CURSE.
THESE PEOPLE AND THEIR ANCESTORS DIDN'T DO ANYTHING BAD ENOUGH TO BE CURSED LIKE THIS!
Same as Megumi...
FIRST I HAVE TO FIND THE JEWEL AND FULFILL THE CONTRACT...
...
REVENGE...
Hmmm... Lalala... Lala...
...DOESN'T SUIT THESE PEOPLE.

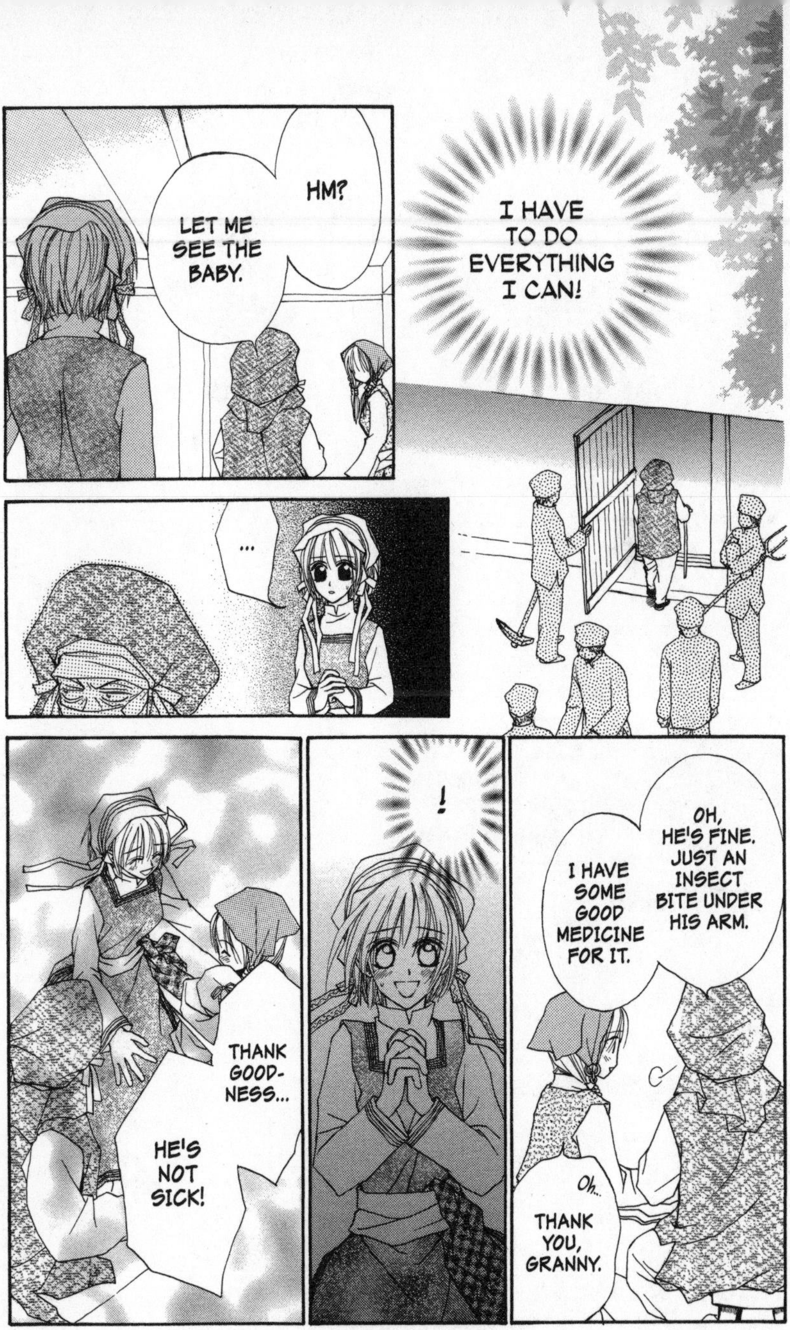
I HAVE TO DO EVERYTHING I CAN!
HM?
LET ME SEE THE BABY.
...
OH, HE'S FINE. JUST AN INSECT BITE UNDER HIS ARM.
I HAVE SOME GOOD MEDICINE FOR IT.
Oh...
THANK YOU, GRANNY.
!
THANK GOODNESS...
HE'S NOT SICK!

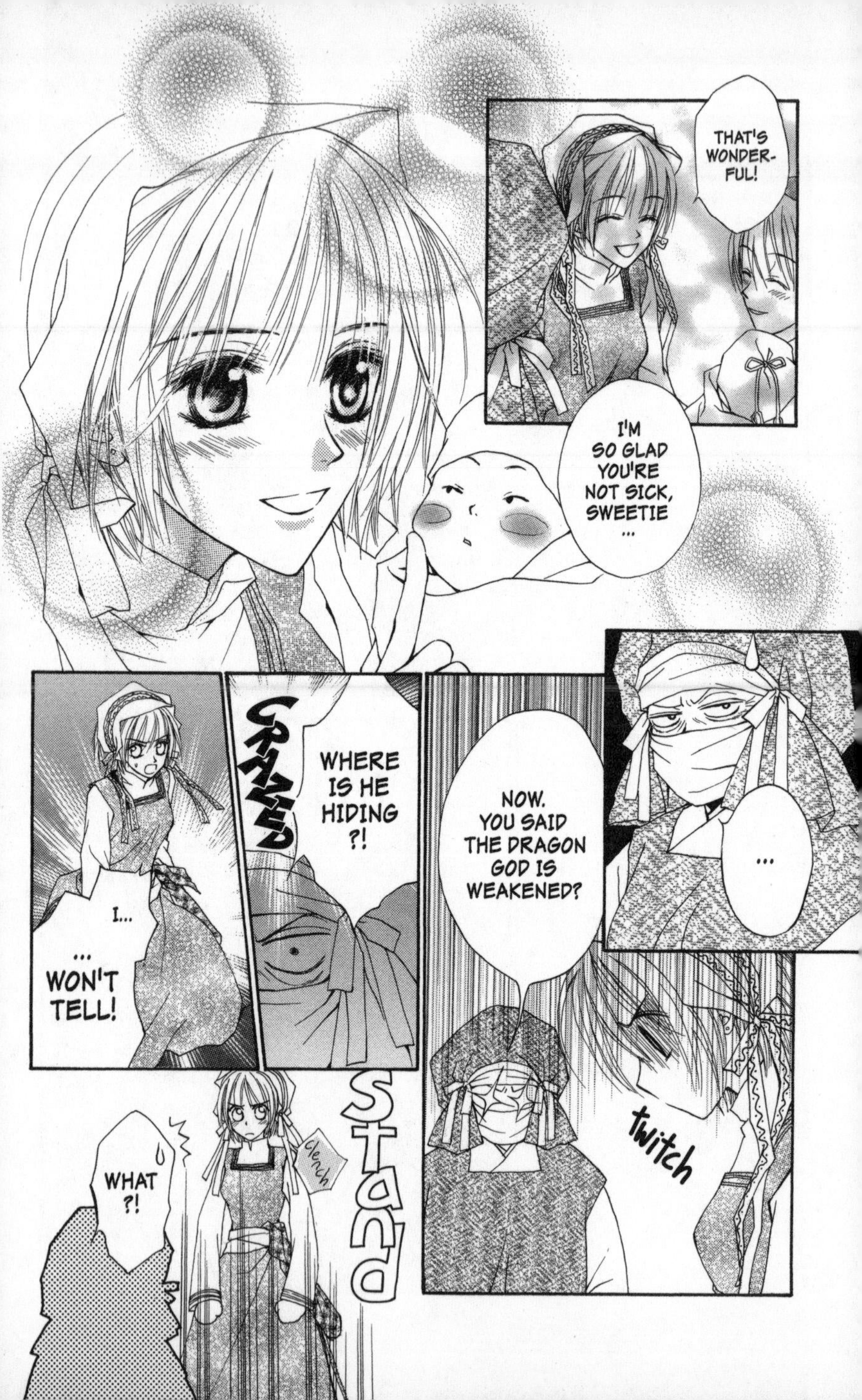
THAT'S WONDER-FUL!
I'M SO GLAD YOU'RE NOT SICK, SWEETIE ...
...
NOW. YOU SAID THE DRAGON GOD IS WEAKENED?
twitch
CRAZED
WHERE IS HE HIDING ?!
I...
... WON'T TELL!
Stand
Clench
WHAT ?!

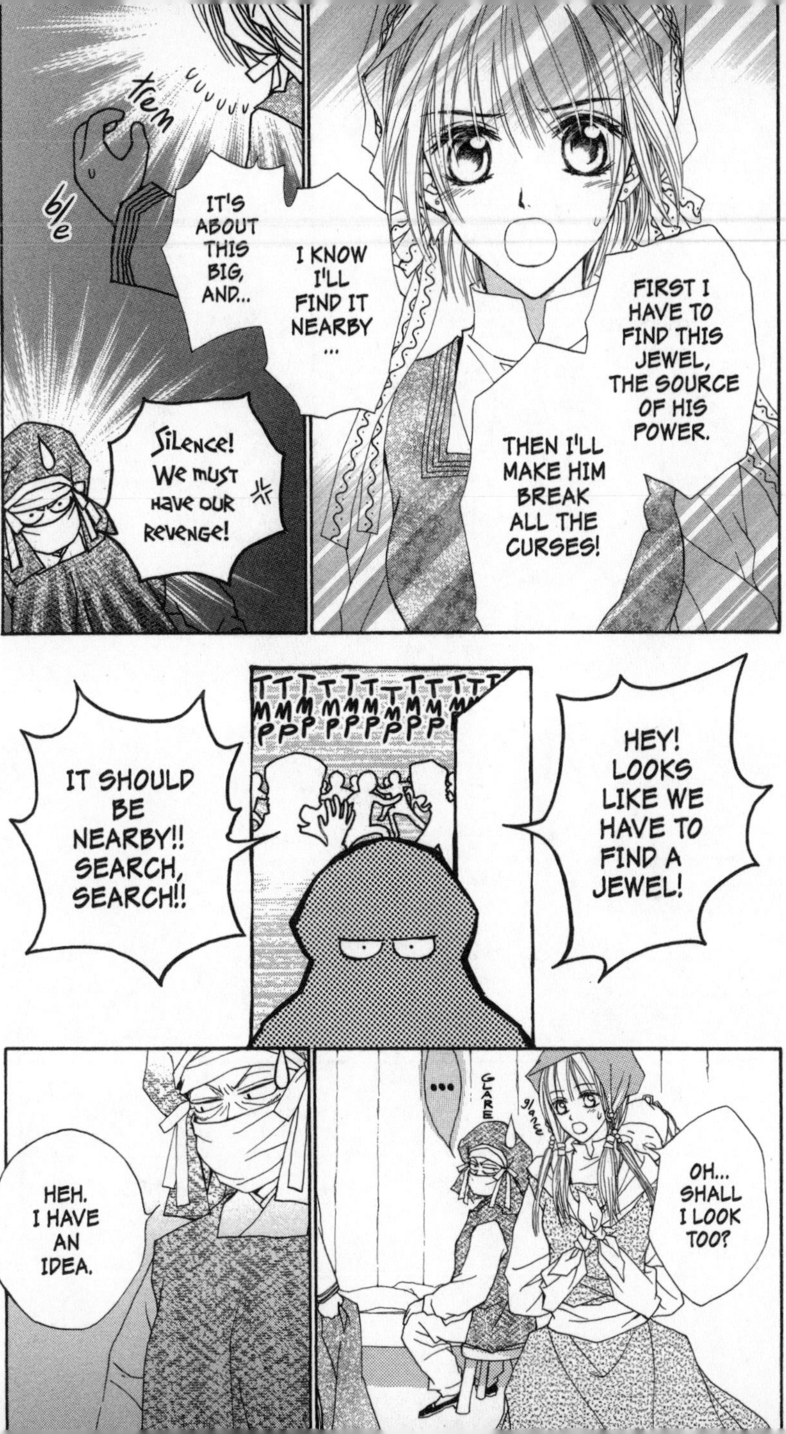
FIRST I HAVE TO FIND THIS JEWEL, THE SOURCE OF HIS POWER.
THEN I'LL MAKE HIM BREAK ALL THE CURSES!
I KNOW I'LL FIND IT NEARBY...
IT'S ABOUT THIS BIG, AND...
trem
ble
Silence! We must have our revenge!
HEY! LOOKS LIKE WE HAVE TO FIND A JEWEL!
TMP TMP TMP TMP TMP TMP TMP TMP TMP TMP
IT SHOULD BE NEARBY!! SEARCH, SEARCH!!
OH... SHALL I LOOK TOO?
glance
GLARE
...
HEH. I HAVE AN IDEA.

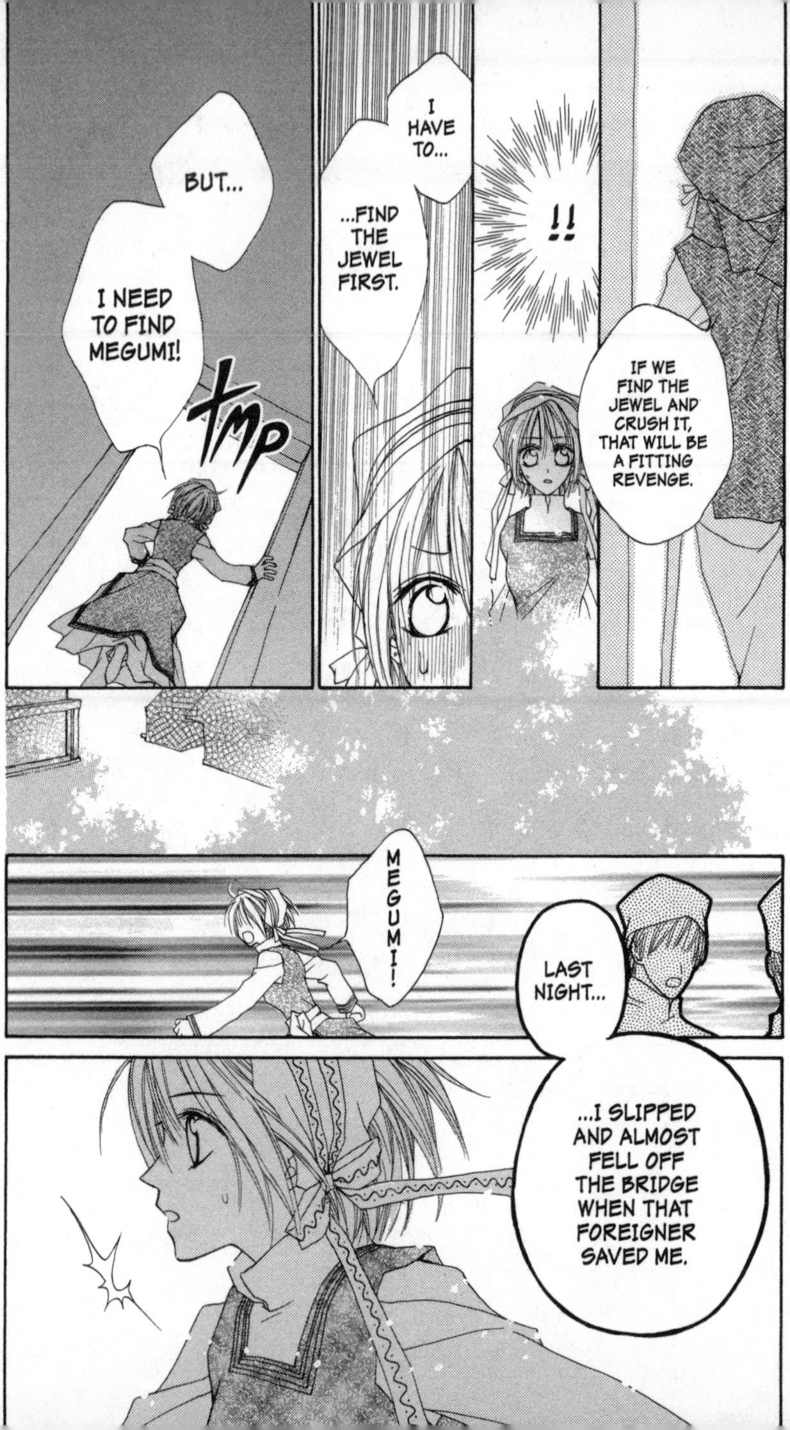
IF WE FIND THE JEWEL AND CRUSH IT, THAT WILL BE A FITTING REVENGE.
!!
I HAVE TO...
...FIND THE JEWEL FIRST.
BUT...
I NEED TO FIND MEGUMI!
TMP
LAST NIGHT...
MEGUMI!
...I SLIPPED AND ALMOST FELL OFF THE BRIDGE WHEN THAT FOREIGNER SAVED ME.

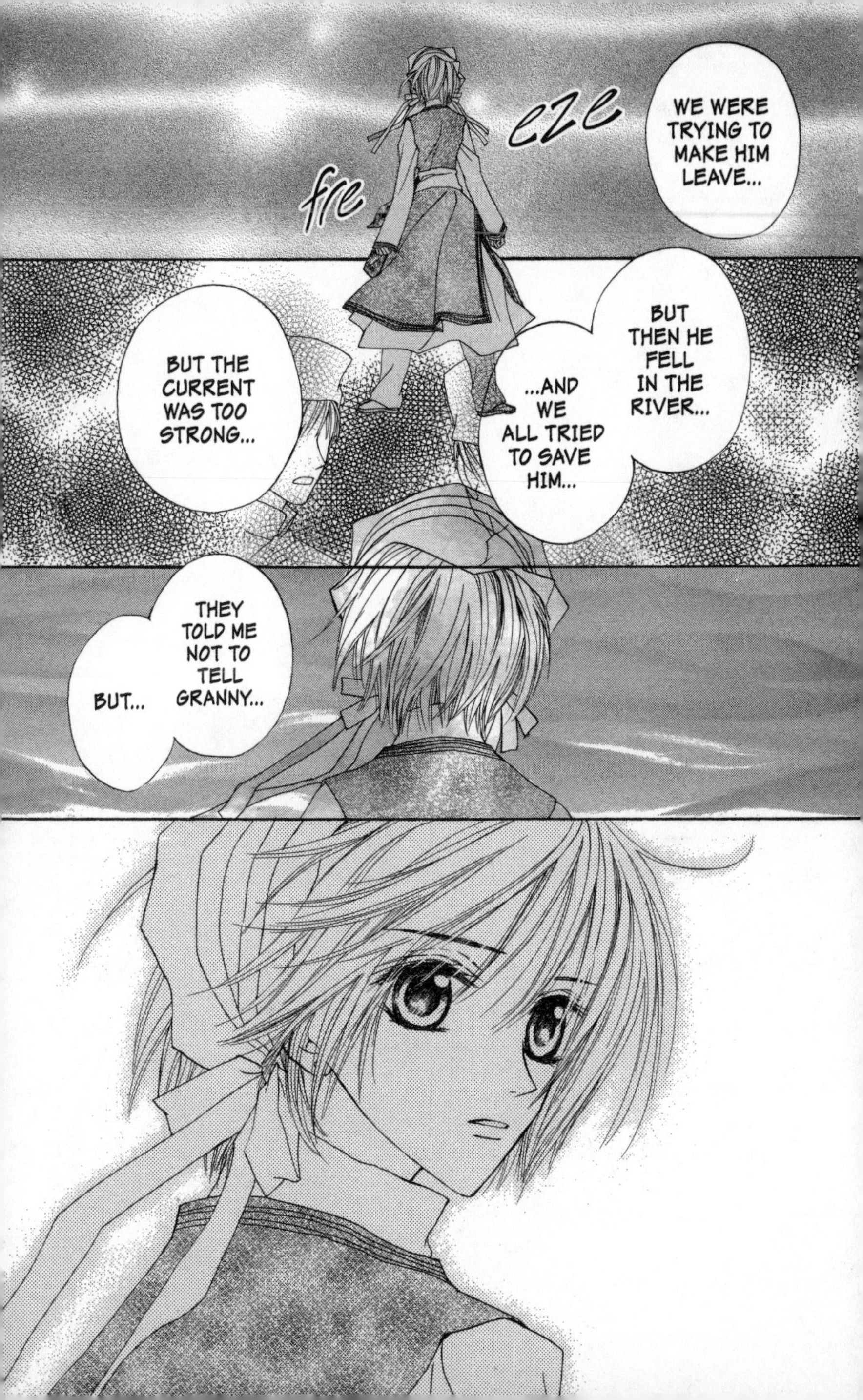
WE WERE TRYING TO MAKE HIM LEAVE...
freeze
BUT THEN HE FELL IN THE RIVER...
...AND WE ALL TRIED TO SAVE HIM...
BUT THE CURRENT WAS TOO STRONG...
THEY TOLD ME NOT TO TELL GRANNY...
BUT...

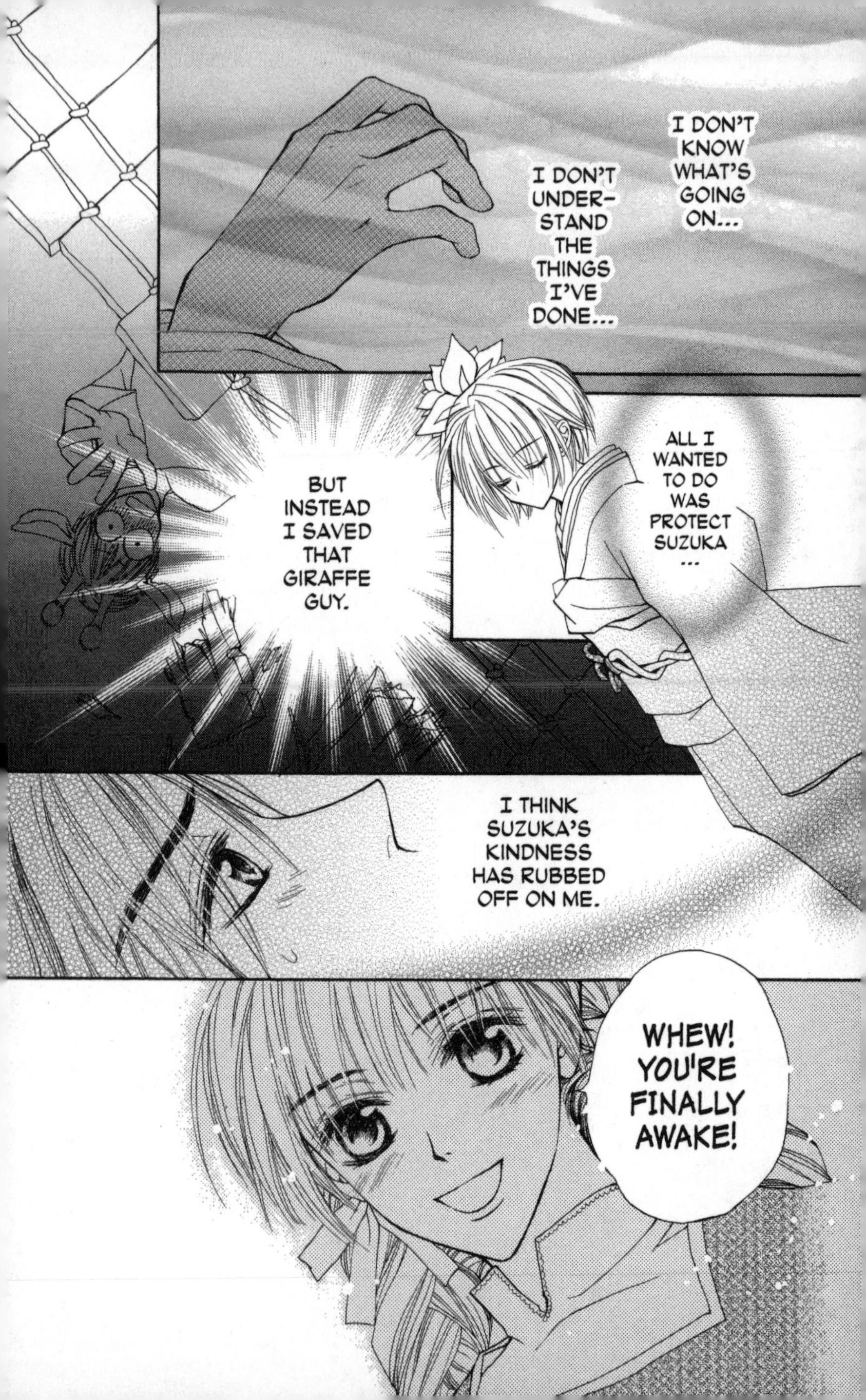
I DON'T KNOW WHAT'S GOING ON...
I DON'T UNDER-STAND THE THINGS I'VE DONE...
ALL I WANTED TO DO WAS PROTECT SUZUKA...
BUT INSTEAD I SAVED THAT GIRAFFE GUY.
I THINK SUZUKA'S KINDNESS HAS RUBBED OFF ON ME.
WHEW! YOU'RE FINALLY AWAKE!

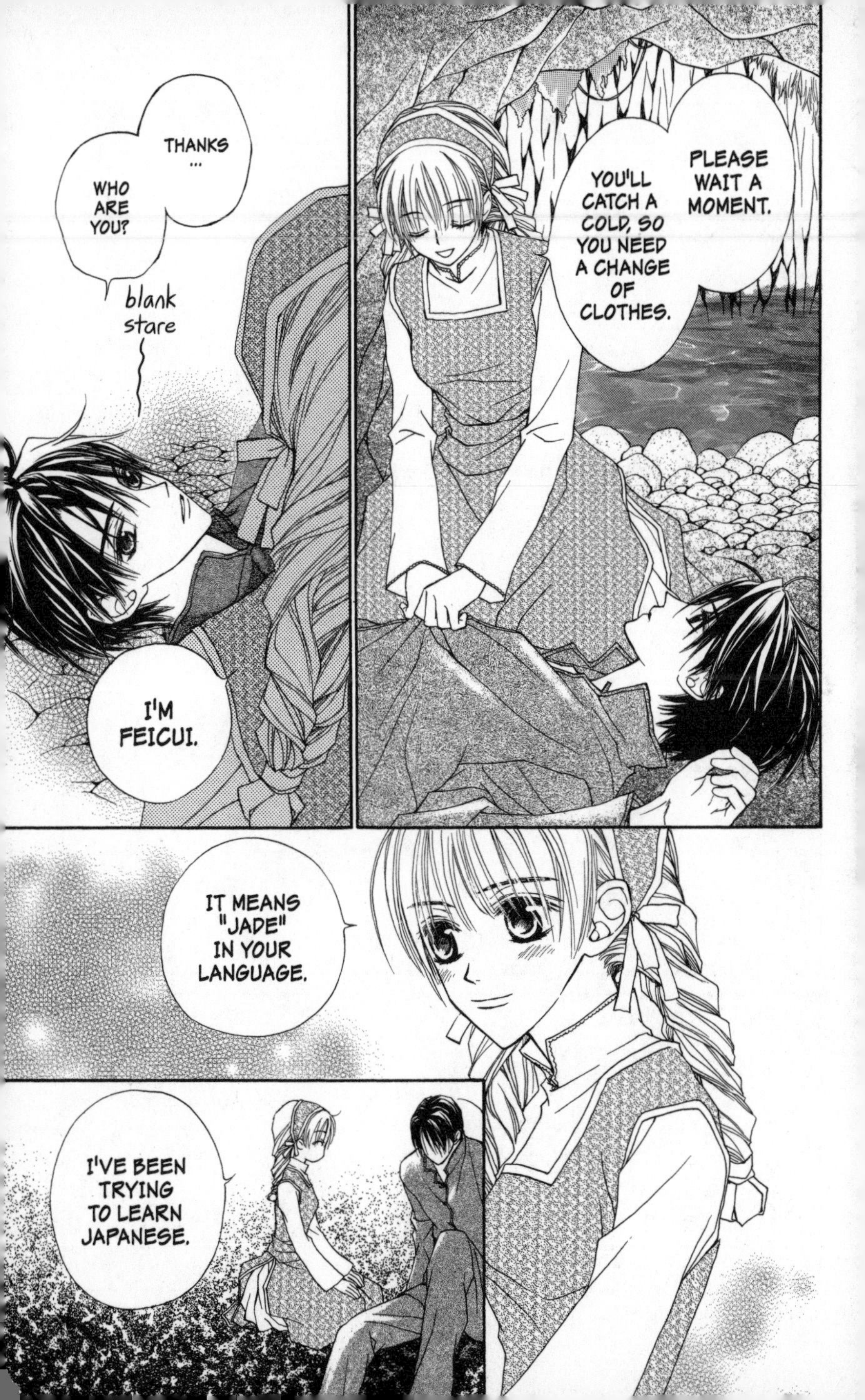
PLEASE WAIT A MOMENT.
YOU'LL CATCH A COLD, SO YOU NEED A CHANGE OF CLOTHES.
THANKS ...
WHO ARE YOU?
blank stare
I'M FEICUI.
IT MEANS "JADE" IN YOUR LANGUAGE.
I'VE BEEN TRYING TO LEARN JAPANESE.

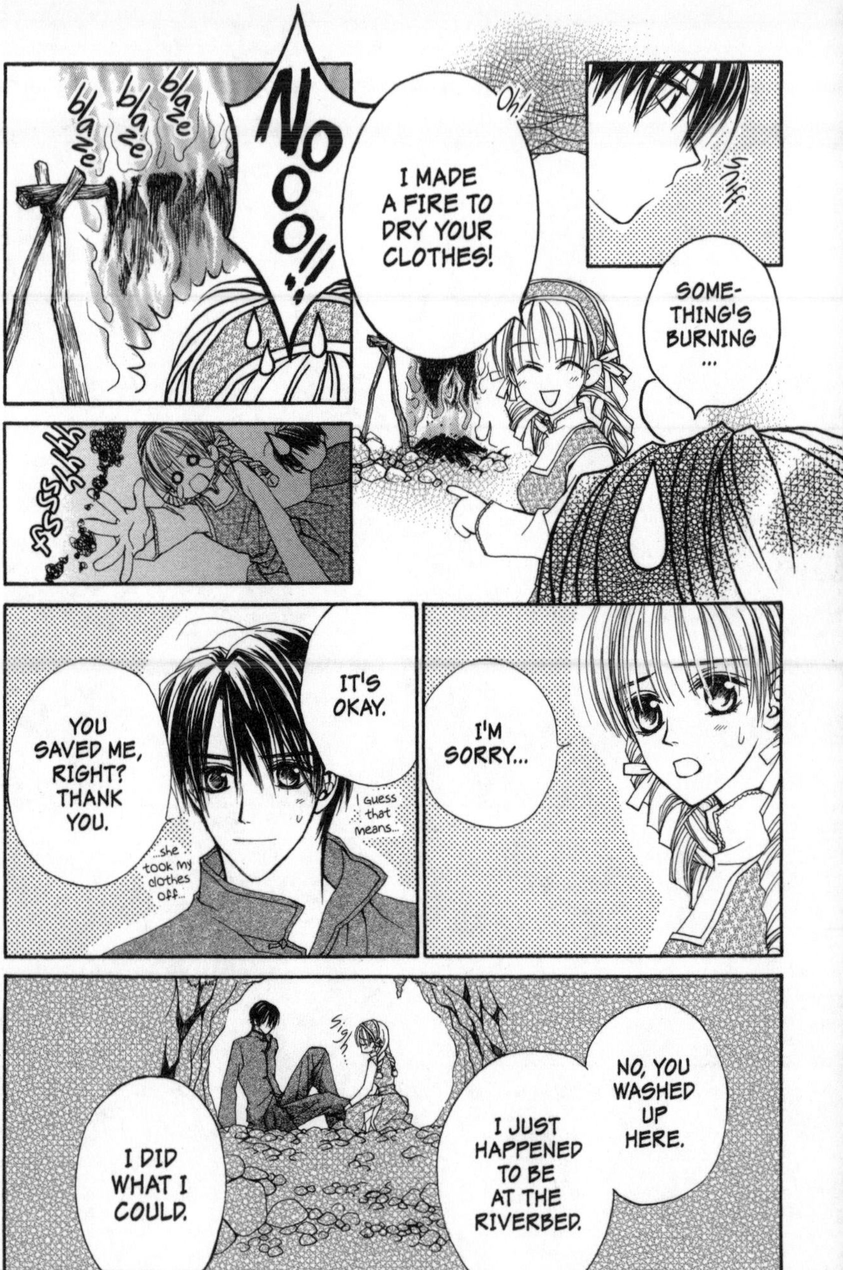
Oh!
Sniff
SOME-THING'S BURNING ...
I MADE A FIRE TO DRY YOUR CLOTHES!
blaze blaze blaze
NOOOO!!
fssss
I'M SORRY...
IT'S OKAY.
I guess that means...
...she took my clothes off...
YOU SAVED ME, RIGHT? THANK YOU.
NO, YOU WASHED UP HERE.
I JUST HAPPENED TO BE AT THE RIVERBED.
Sigh...
I DID WHAT I COULD.

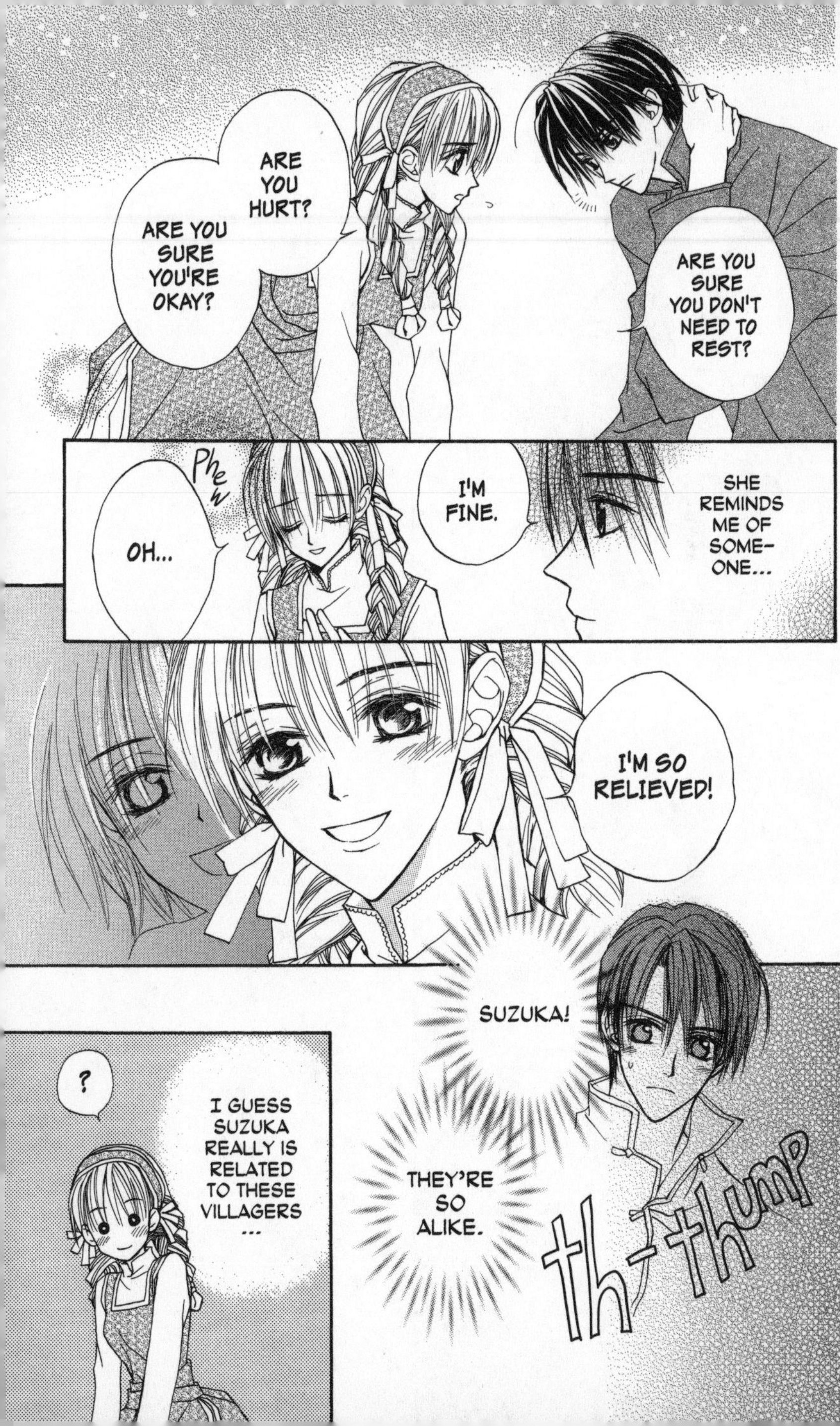
ARE YOU SURE YOU DON'T NEED TO REST?
ARE YOU HURT?
ARE YOU SURE YOU'RE OKAY?
SHE REMINDS ME OF SOME-ONE...
I'M FINE.
Phew
OH...
I'M SO RELIEVED!
SUZUKA!
th-thump
THEY'RE SO ALIKE.
I GUESS SUZUKA REALLY IS RELATED TO THESE VILLAGERS ...
?

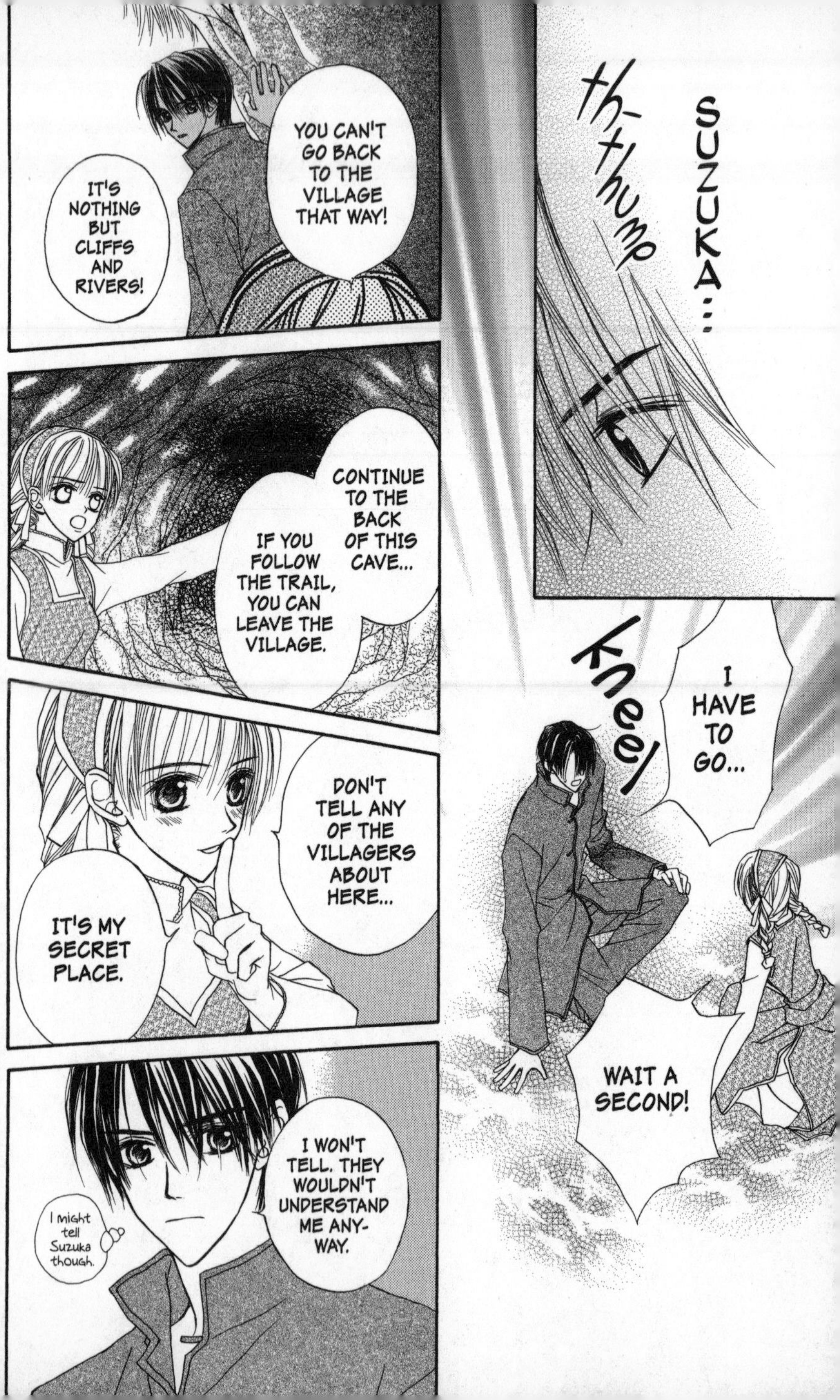
SUZUKA...
th-thump
kneel
I HAVE TO GO...
WAIT A SECOND!
YOU CAN'T GO BACK TO THE VILLAGE THAT WAY!
IT'S NOTHING BUT CLIFFS AND RIVERS!
CONTINUE TO THE BACK OF THIS CAVE...
IF YOU FOLLOW THE TRAIL, YOU CAN LEAVE THE VILLAGE.
DON'T TELL ANY OF THE VILLAGERS ABOUT HERE...
IT'S MY SECRET PLACE.
I WON'T TELL. THEY WOULDN'T UNDERSTAND ME ANYWAY.
I might tell Suzuka though.

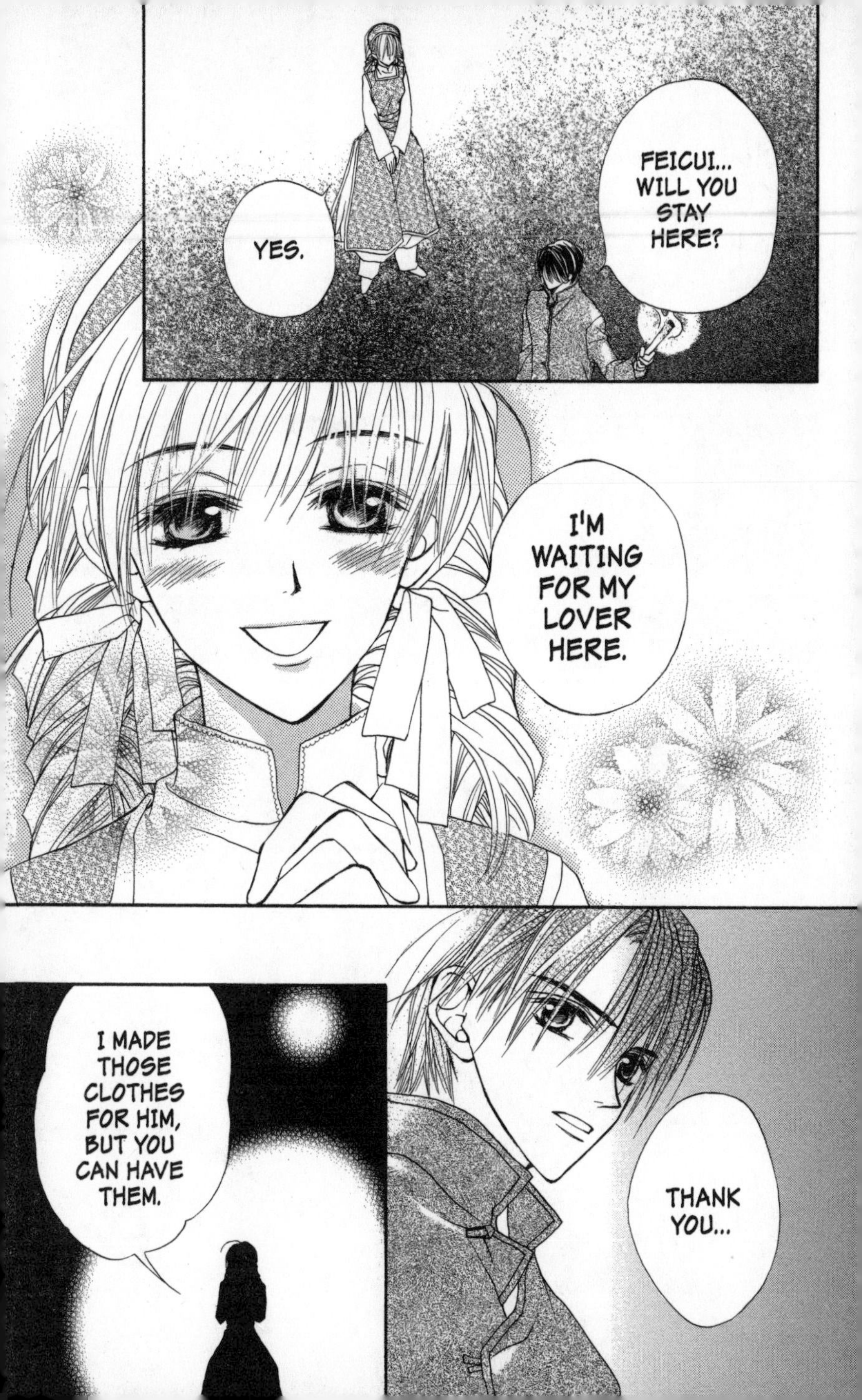
FEICUI... WILL YOU STAY HERE?
YES.
I'M WAITING FOR MY LOVER HERE.
THANK YOU...
I MADE THOSE CLOTHES FOR HIM, BUT YOU CAN HAVE THEM.

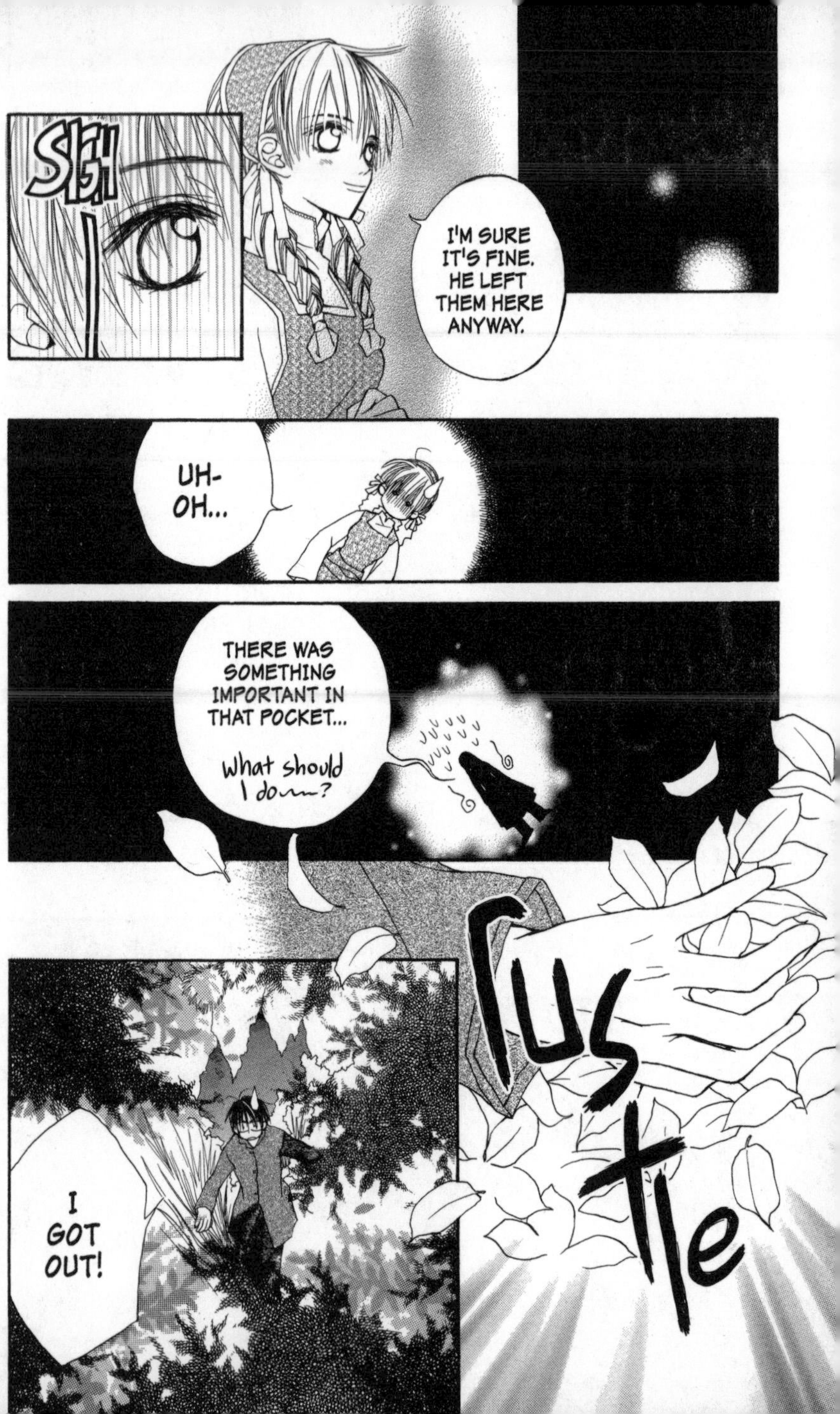
I'M SURE IT'S FINE. HE LEFT THEM HERE ANYWAY.
SIGH
UH-OH...
THERE WAS SOMETHING IMPORTANT IN THAT POCKET...
What should I do~?
rustle
I GOT OUT!

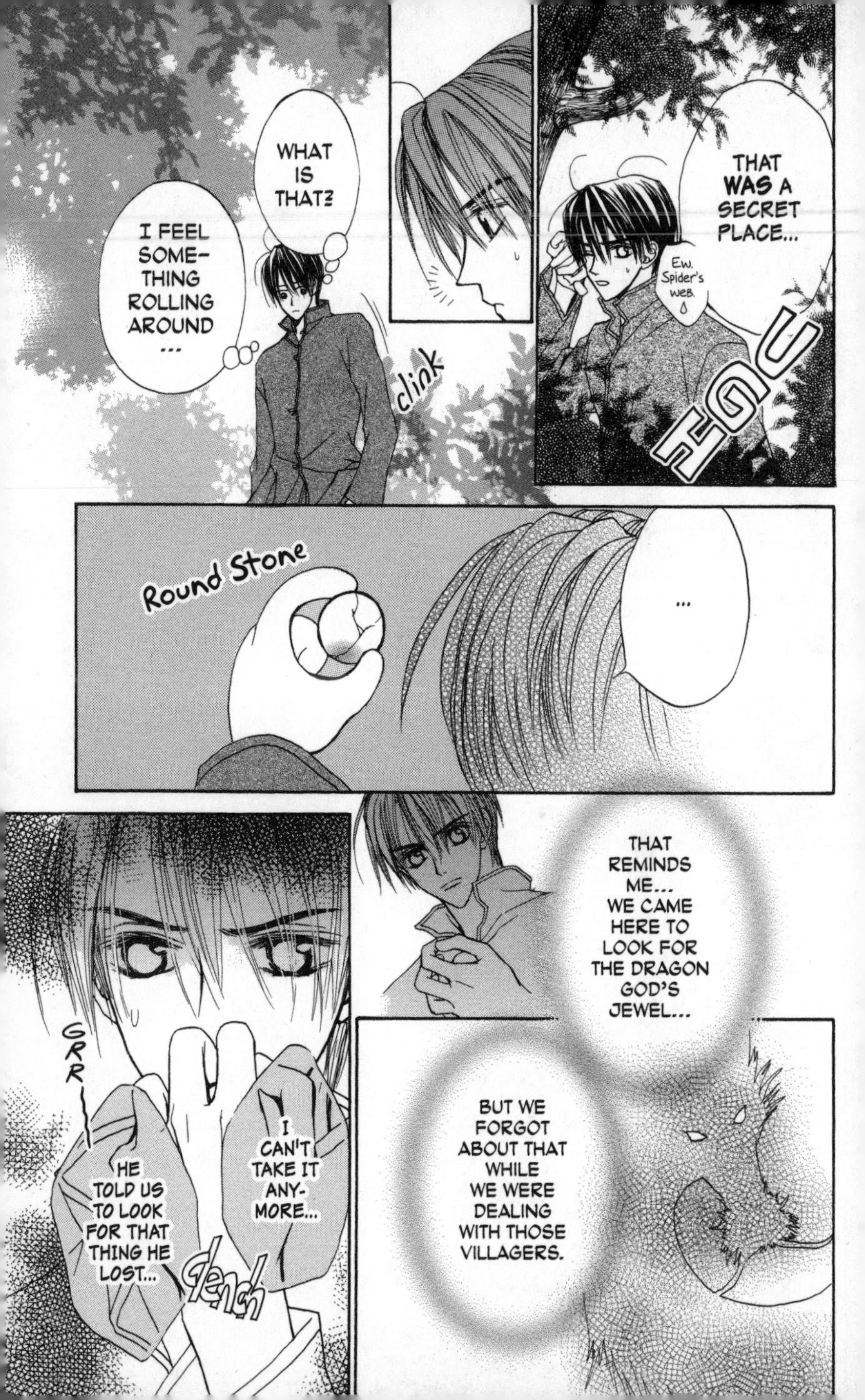

THAT WAS A SECRET PLACE...
Ew. Spider's web.
HGU
WHAT IS THAT?
I FEEL SOME-THING ROLLING AROUND...
clink
...
Round Stone
THAT REMINDS ME... WE CAME HERE TO LOOK FOR THE DRAGON GOD'S JEWEL...
BUT WE FORGOT ABOUT THAT WHILE WE WERE DEALING WITH THOSE VILLAGERS.
I CAN'T TAKE IT ANY-MORE...
HE TOLD US TO LOOK FOR THAT THING HE LOST...
GRR
clench

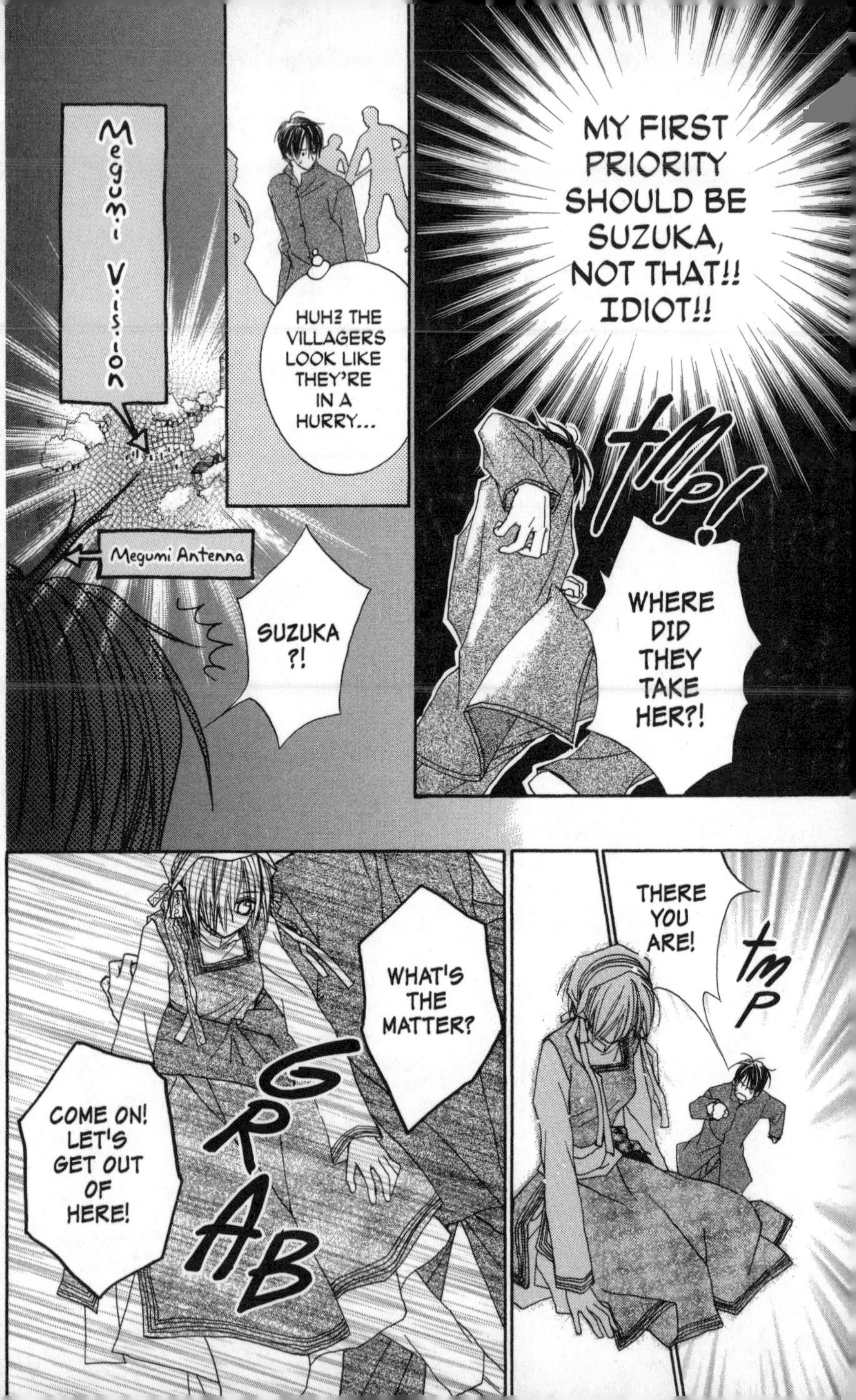
MY FIRST PRIORITY SHOULD BE SUZUKA, NOT THAT!! IDIOT!!
tmp!
WHERE DID THEY TAKE HER?!
HUH? THE VILLAGERS LOOK LIKE THEY'RE IN A HURRY...
Megumi Vision
Megumi Antenna
SUZUKA ?!
THERE YOU ARE!
tmp
WHAT'S THE MATTER?
GRAB
COME ON! LET'S GET OUT OF HERE!

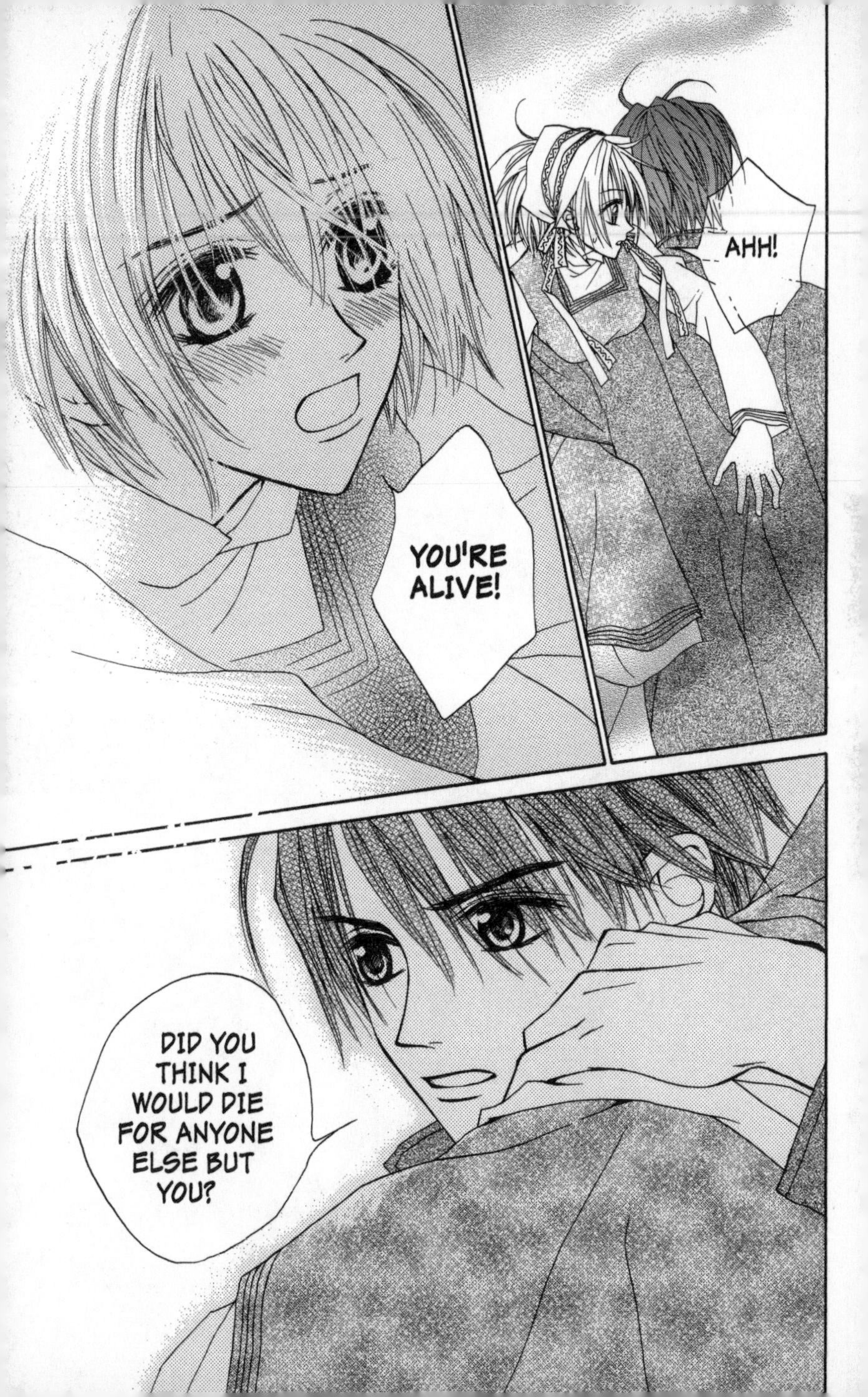
AHH!
YOU'RE ALIVE!
DID YOU THINK I WOULD DIE FOR ANYONE ELSE BUT YOU?

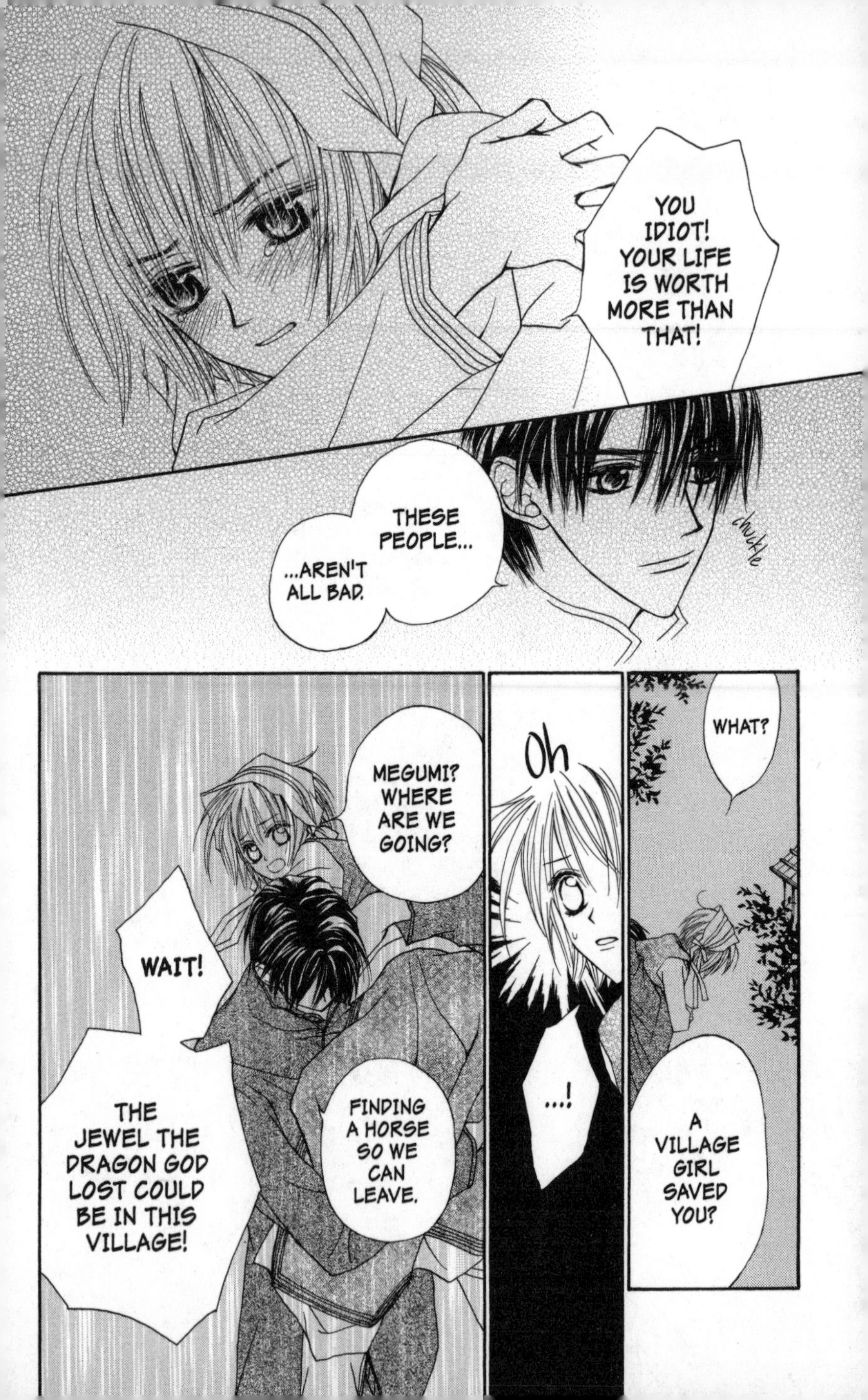
YOU IDIOT! YOUR LIFE IS WORTH MORE THAN THAT!
chuckle
THESE PEOPLE...
...AREN'T ALL BAD.
WHAT?
A VILLAGE GIRL SAVED YOU?
Oh
...!
MEGUMI? WHERE ARE WE GOING?
FINDING A HORSE SO WE CAN LEAVE.
WAIT!
THE JEWEL THE DRAGON GOD LOST COULD BE IN THIS VILLAGE!

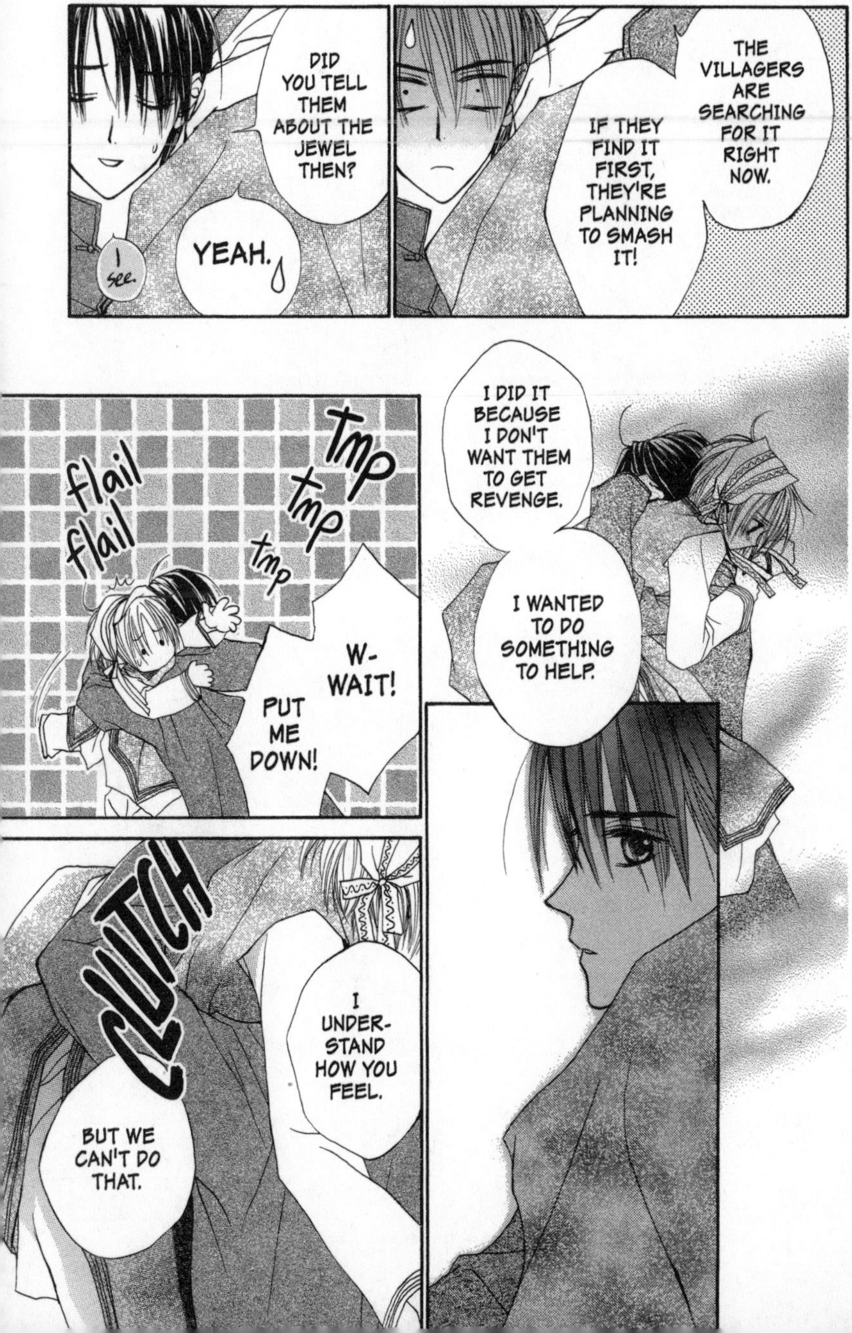
THE VILLAGERS ARE SEARCHING FOR IT RIGHT NOW.
IF THEY FIND IT FIRST, THEY'RE PLANNING TO SMASH IT!
DID YOU TELL THEM ABOUT THE JEWEL THEN?
YEAH.
I see.
I DID IT BECAUSE I DON'T WANT THEM TO GET REVENGE.
I WANTED TO DO SOMETHING TO HELP.
tmp tmp tmp
flail flail
W-WAIT!
PUT ME DOWN!
CLUTCH
I UNDER-STAND HOW YOU FEEL.
BUT WE CAN'T DO THAT.

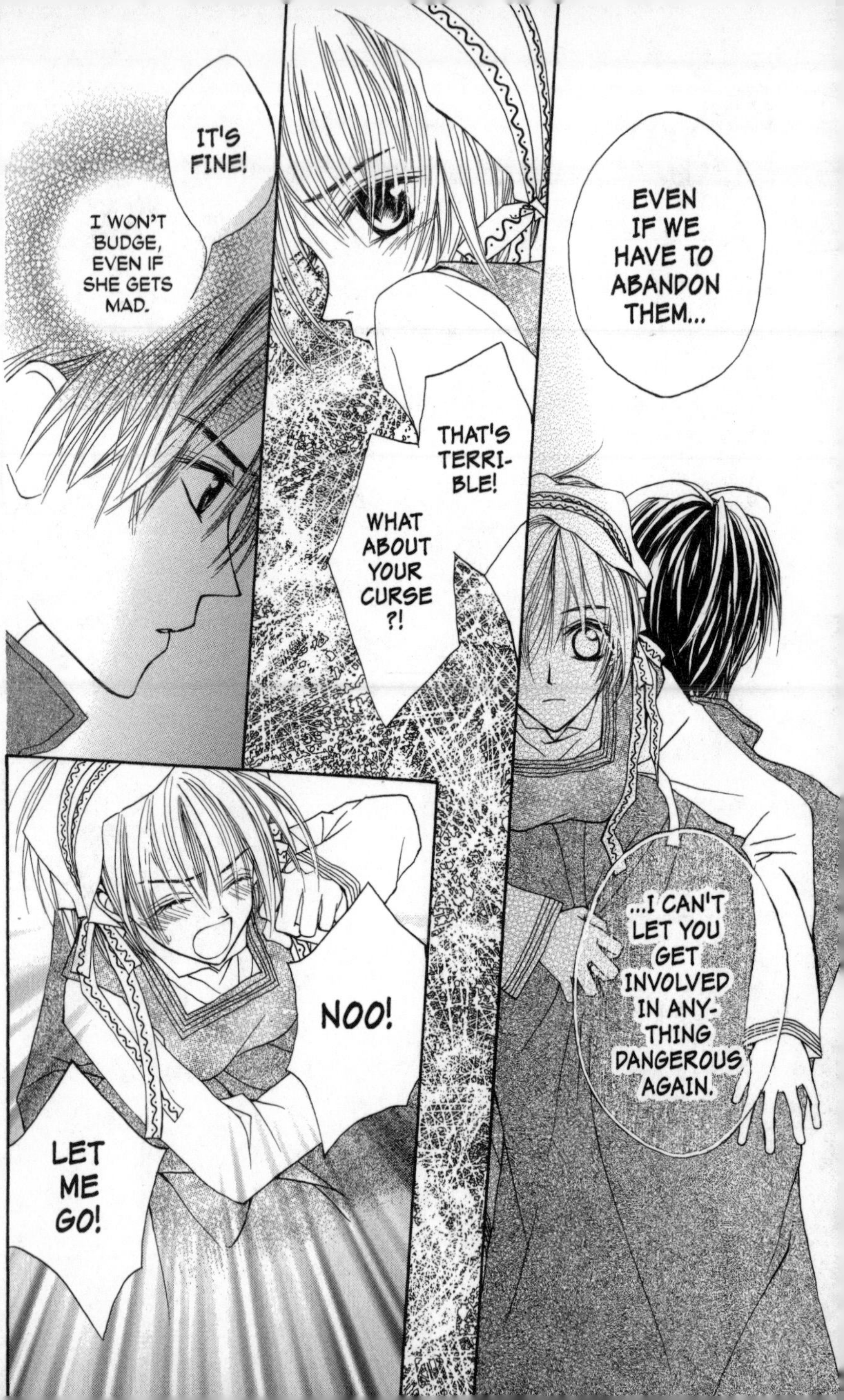
EVEN IF WE HAVE TO ABANDON THEM...
...I CAN'T LET YOU GET INVOLVED IN ANYTHING DANGEROUS AGAIN.
THAT'S TERRIBLE!
WHAT ABOUT YOUR CURSE?!
IT'S FINE!
I WON'T BUDGE, EVEN IF SHE GETS MAD.
NOO!
LET ME GO!

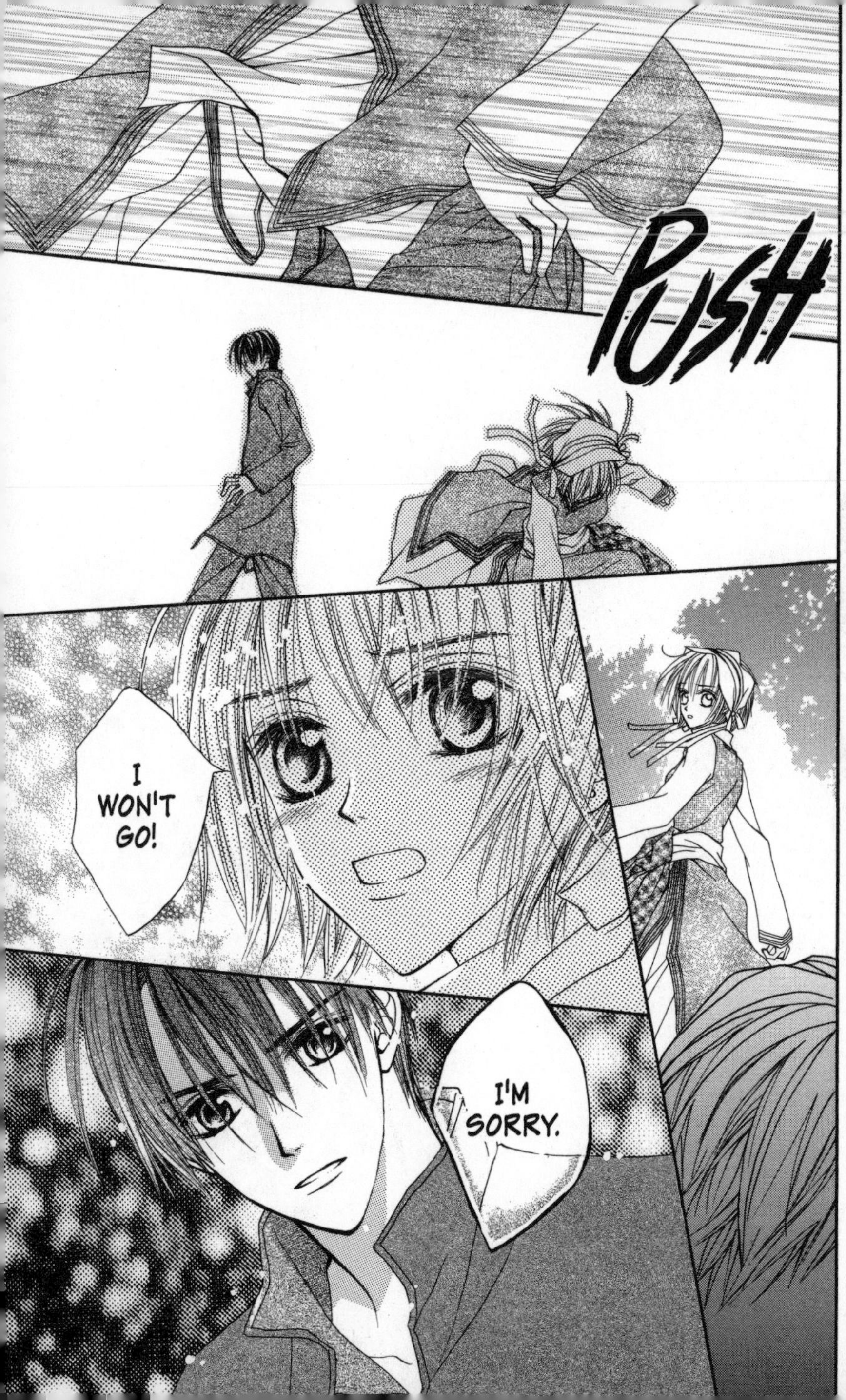
PUSH
I WON'T GO!
I'M SORRY.

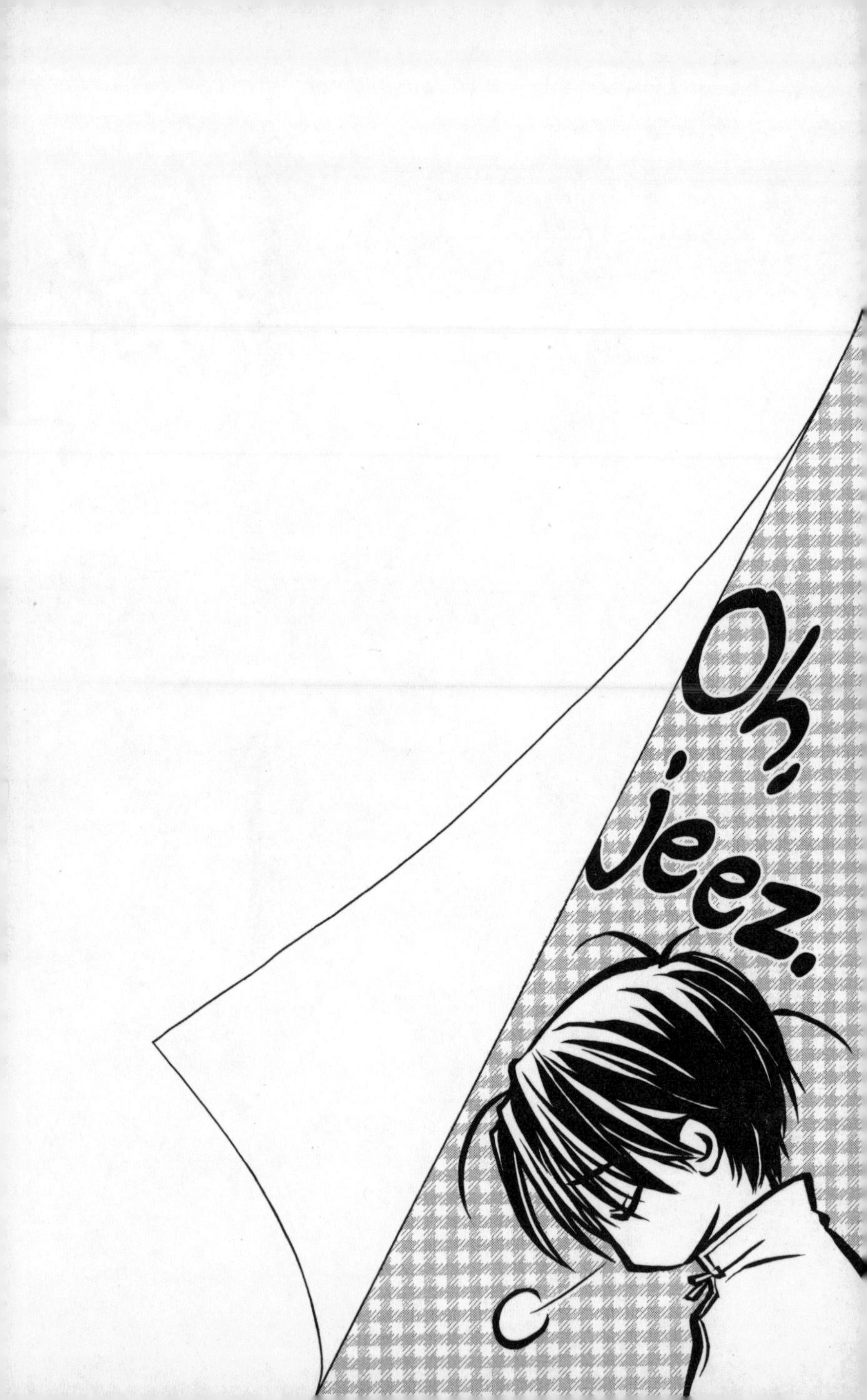
Oh, jeez.

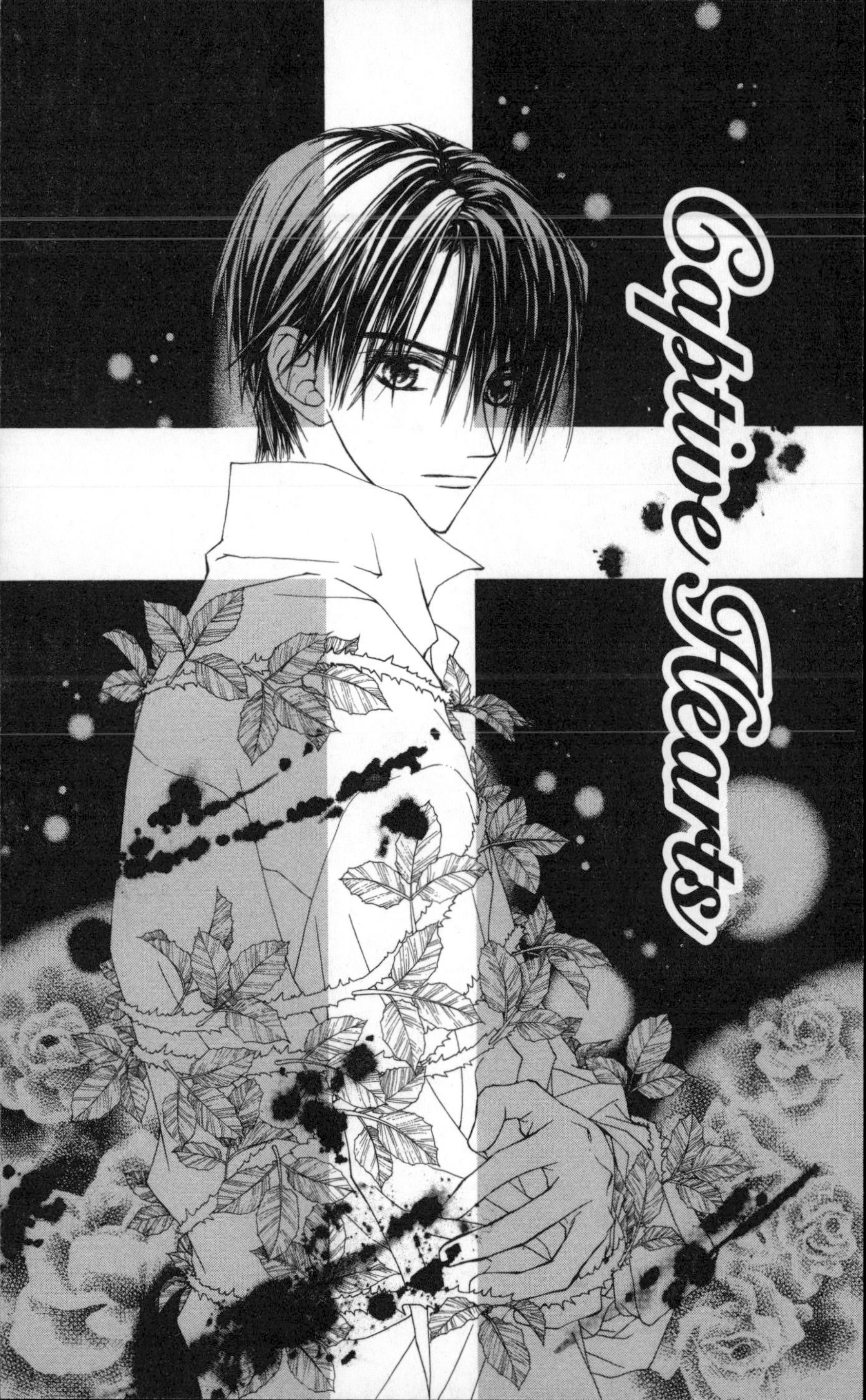
Captive Hearts

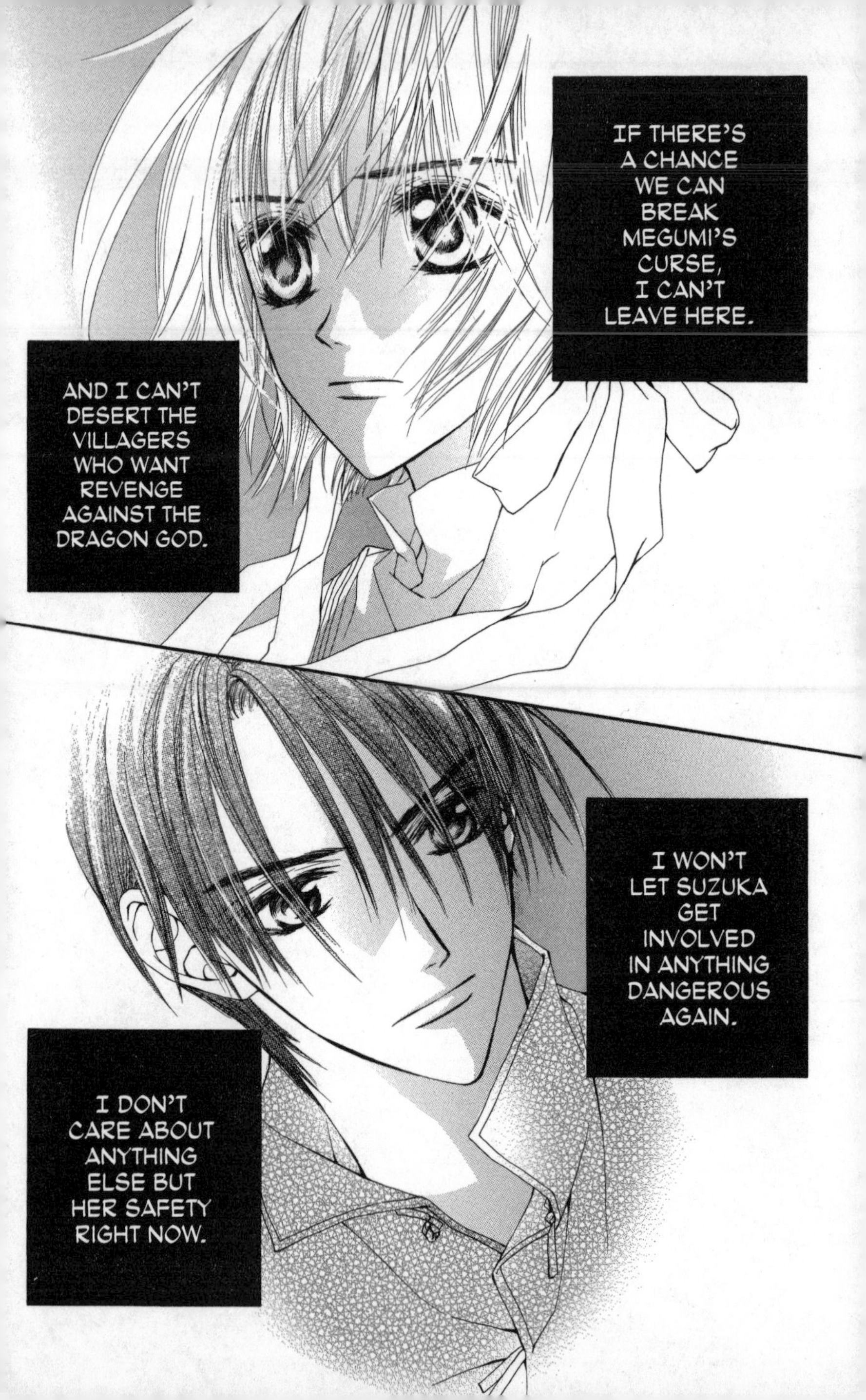
IF THERE'S A CHANCE WE CAN BREAK MEGUMI'S CURSE, I CAN'T LEAVE HERE.
AND I CAN'T DESERT THE VILLAGERS WHO WANT REVENGE AGAINST THE DRAGON GOD.
I WON'T LET SUZUKA GET INVOLVED IN ANYTHING DANGEROUS AGAIN.
I DON'T CARE ABOUT ANYTHING ELSE BUT HER SAFETY RIGHT NOW.

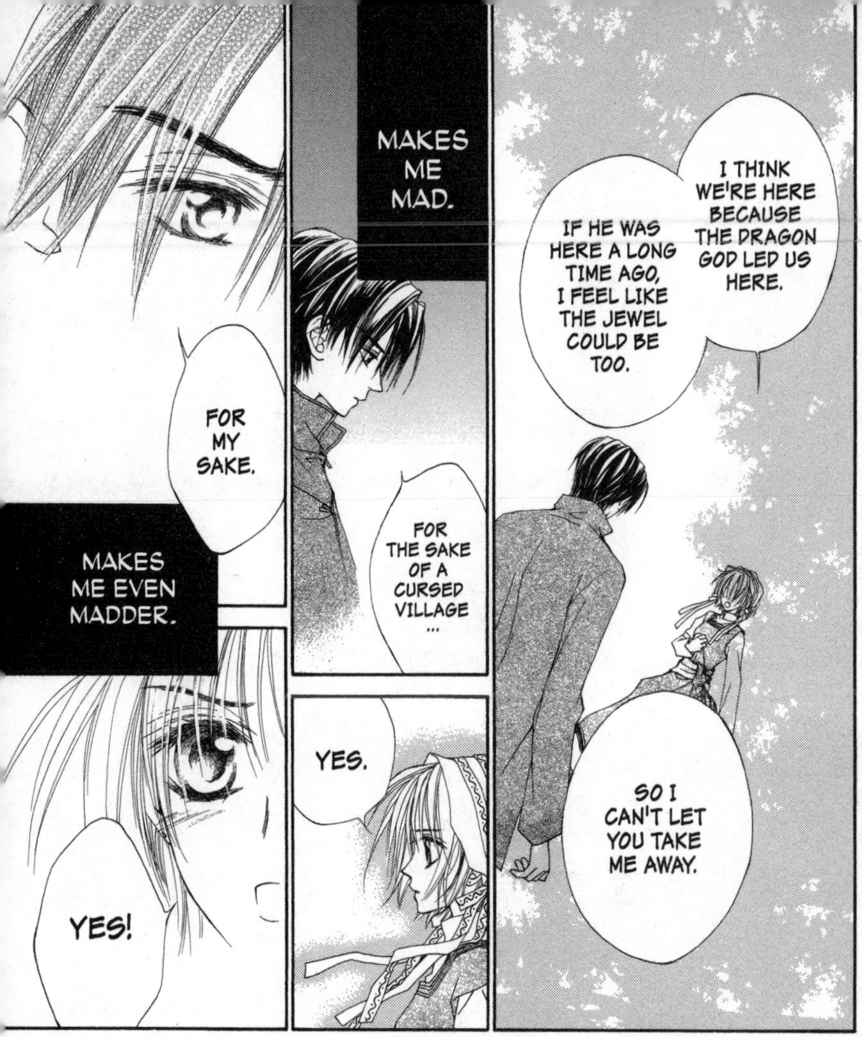
I THINK WE'RE HERE BECAUSE THE DRAGON GOD LED US HERE.
IF HE WAS HERE A LONG TIME AGO, I FEEL LIKE THE JEWEL COULD BE TOO.
SO I CAN'T LET YOU TAKE ME AWAY.
MAKES ME MAD.
FOR THE SAKE OF A CURSED VILLAGE ...
FOR MY SAKE.
MAKES ME EVEN MADDER.
YES.
YES!

Backstory ④ My goal for this China story was "happily ever after." The other keywords I had were "breaking the curse." As soon as I decided on the characters being the witch (Granny Fortune-teller), the bad(?) dragon, the knight (pseudo) and the princess (pseudo), it became a fairy tale-like world. I think the whole concept of *Captive Hearts* is fairy tale-ish. ♥ I think the story progressed like a snowball that kept rolling and getting bigger and heavier. Oh well. I learned a lot.

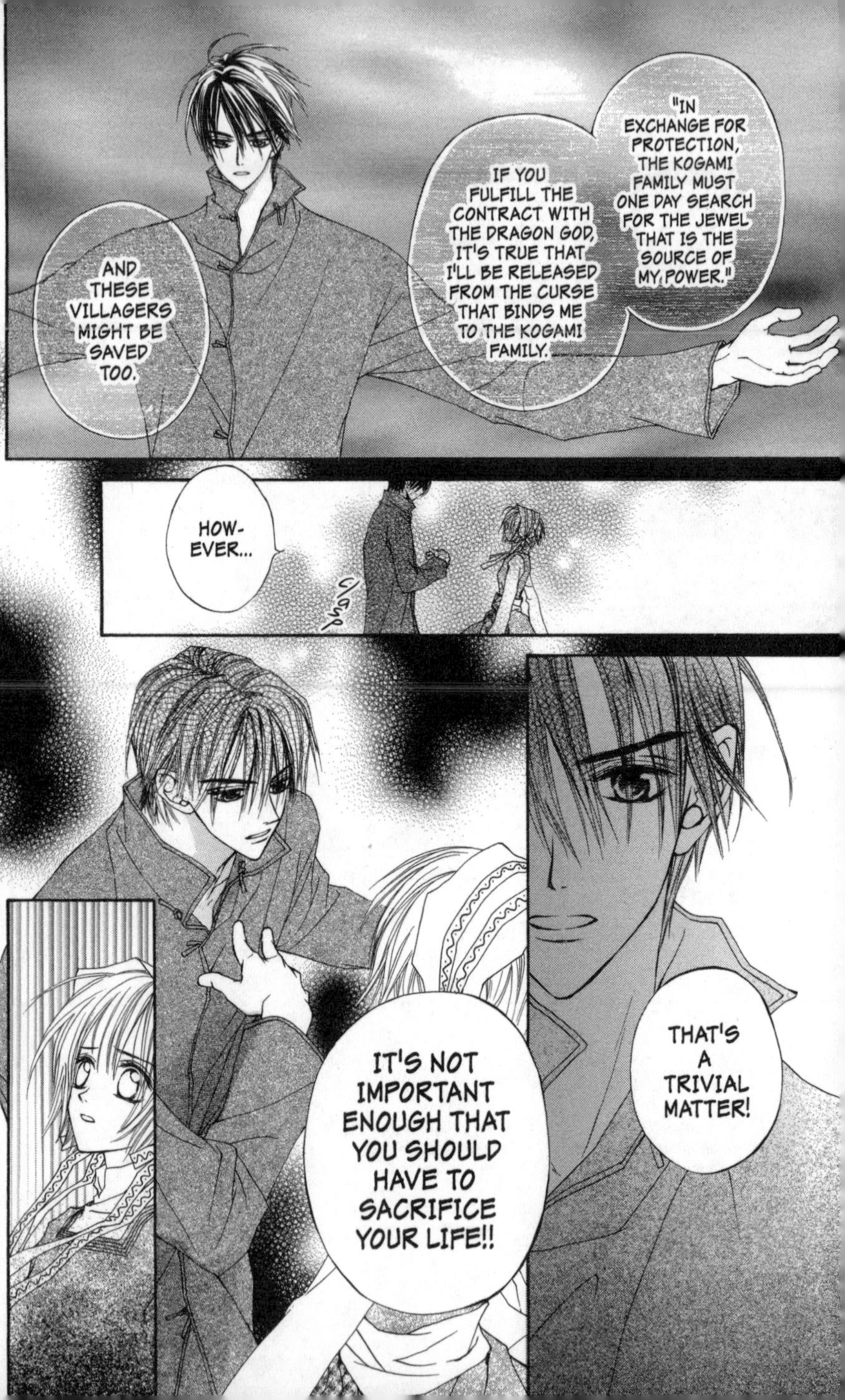
"IN EXCHANGE FOR PROTECTION, THE KOGAMI FAMILY MUST ONE DAY SEARCH FOR THE JEWEL THAT IS THE SOURCE OF MY POWER."
IF YOU FULFILL THE CONTRACT WITH THE DRAGON GOD, IT'S TRUE THAT I'LL BE RELEASED FROM THE CURSE THAT BINDS ME TO THE KOGAMI FAMILY.
AND THESE VILLAGERS MIGHT BE SAVED TOO.
HOW-EVER...
clasp
THAT'S A TRIVIAL MATTER!
IT'S NOT IMPORTANT ENOUGH THAT YOU SHOULD HAVE TO SACRIFICE YOUR LIFE!!

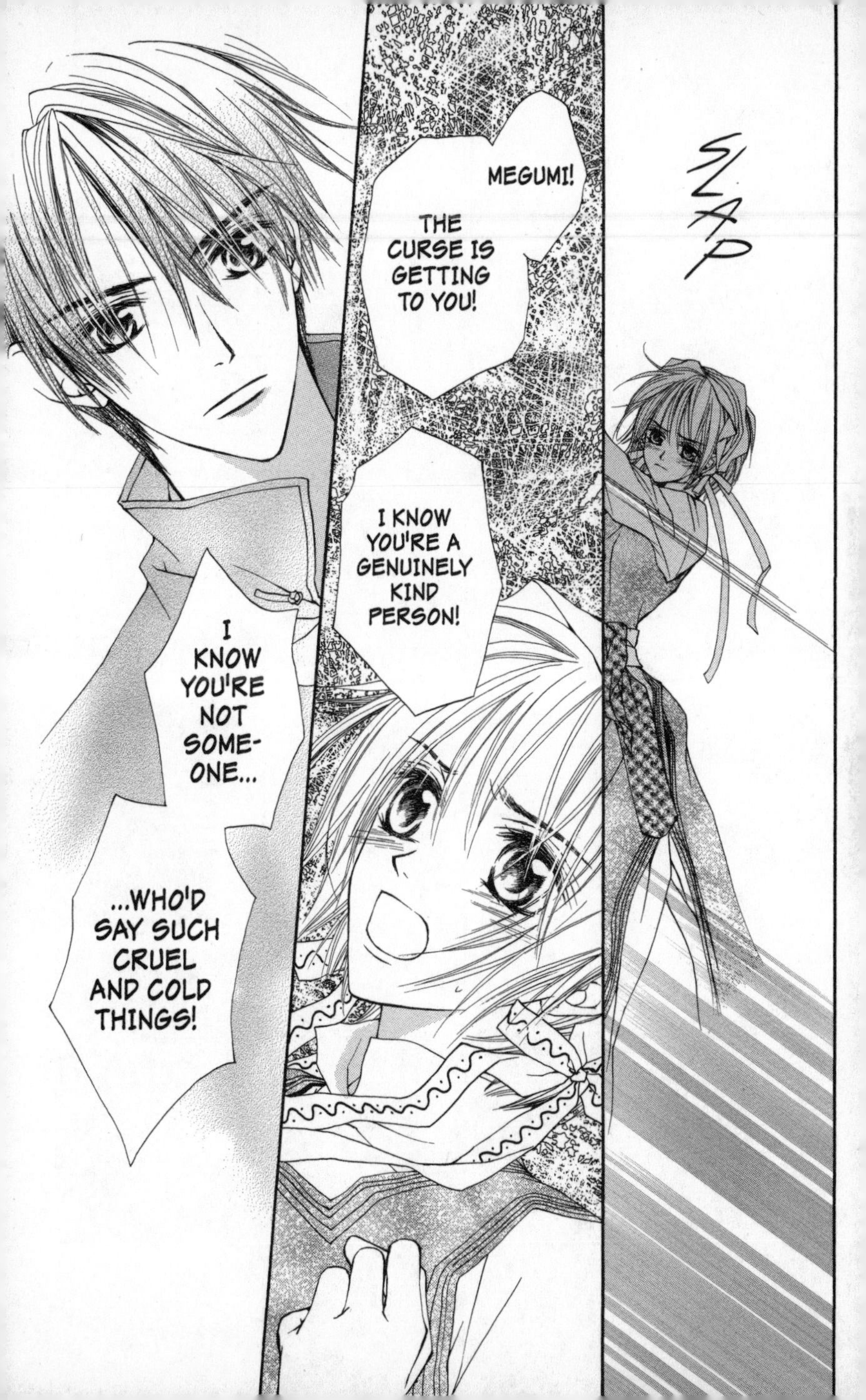
SLAP
MEGUMI!
THE CURSE IS GETTING TO YOU!
I KNOW YOU'RE A GENUINELY KIND PERSON!
I KNOW YOU'RE NOT SOME-ONE...
...WHO'D SAY SUCH CRUEL AND COLD THINGS!

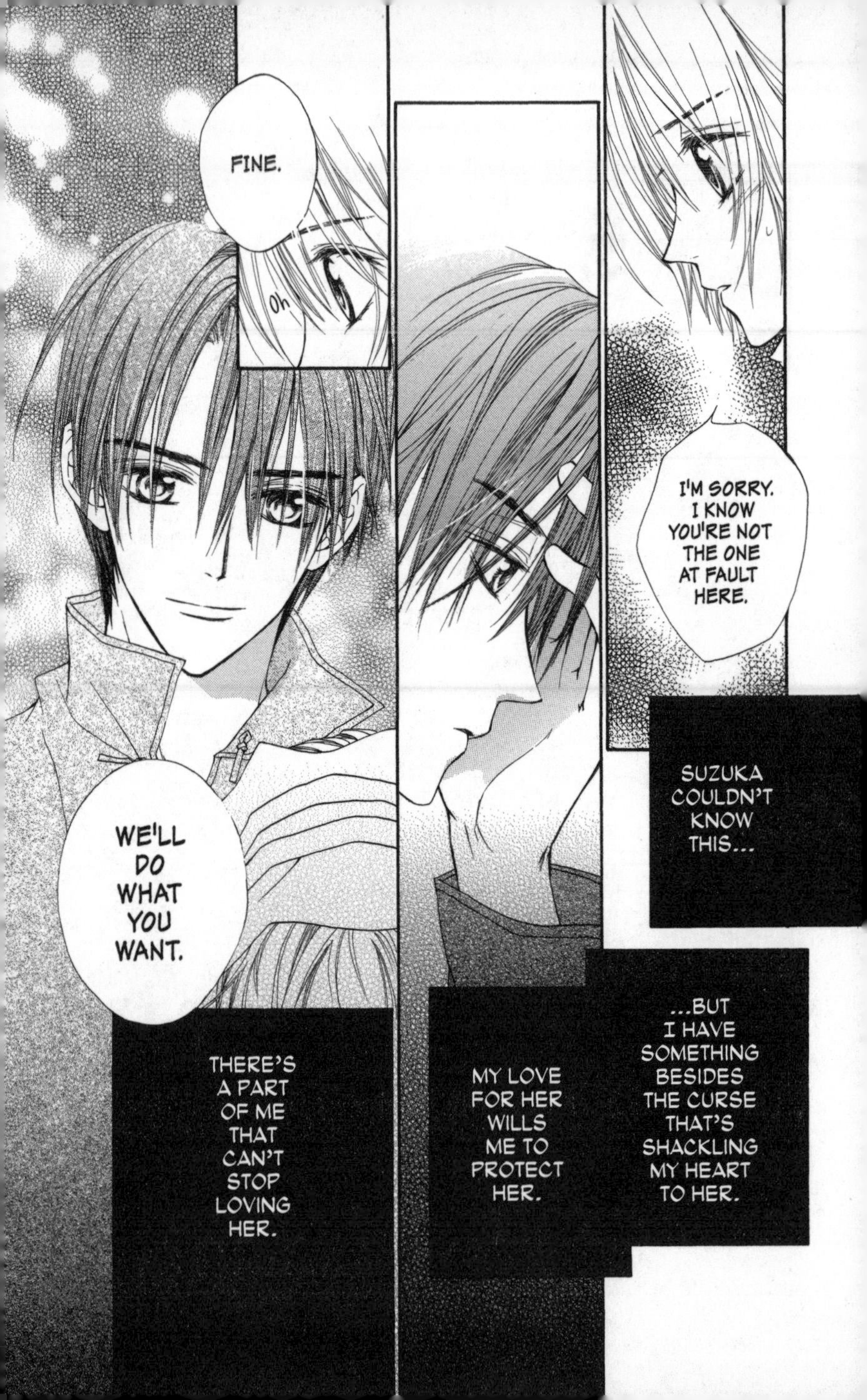

I'M SORRY. I KNOW YOU'RE NOT THE ONE AT FAULT HERE.
SUZUKA COULDN'T KNOW THIS...
...BUT I HAVE SOMETHING BESIDES THE CURSE THAT'S SHACKLING MY HEART TO HER.
MY LOVE FOR HER WILLS ME TO PROTECT HER.
FINE.
Oh
WE'LL DO WHAT YOU WANT.
THERE'S A PART OF ME THAT CAN'T STOP LOVING HER.

...
OKAY.
Granny!
There you are! Granny !!
SLAM
YOU CAN SEE VISIONS, RIGHT?!
Huhh ?!
WHAT IS IT?!
GAAAH! I DON'T EVEN KNOW ANY-MORE AT THIS POINT! I MIGHT HAVE TO START ALL OVER AGAIN!!
GROWL!
SORRY!?

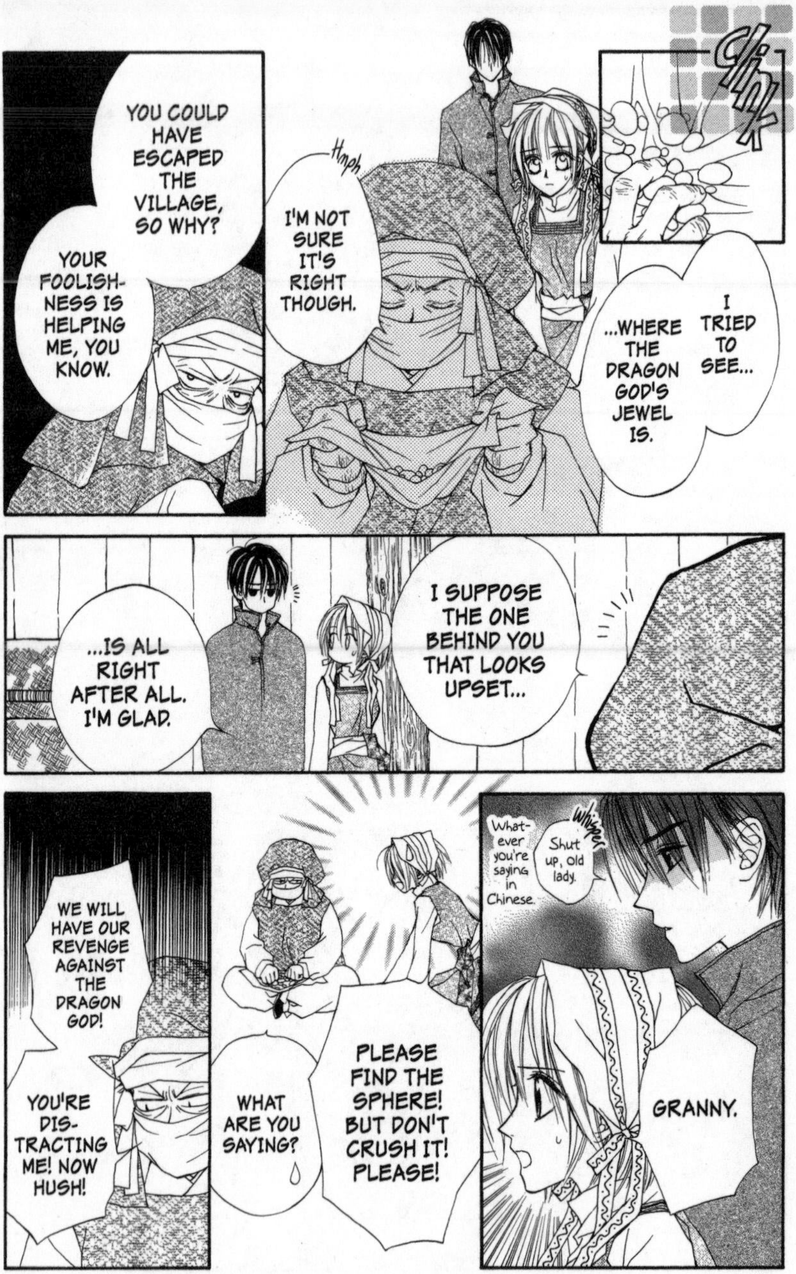
Clink
I TRIED TO SEE...
...WHERE THE DRAGON GOD'S JEWEL IS.
Hmph
I'M NOT SURE IT'S RIGHT THOUGH.
YOU COULD HAVE ESCAPED THE VILLAGE, SO WHY?
YOUR FOOLISHNESS IS HELPING ME, YOU KNOW.
I SUPPOSE THE ONE BEHIND YOU THAT LOOKS UPSET...
...IS ALL RIGHT AFTER ALL. I'M GLAD.
whisper
Shut up, old lady.
Whatever you're saying in Chinese.
GRANNY.
PLEASE FIND THE SPHERE! BUT DON'T CRUSH IT! PLEASE!
WHAT ARE YOU SAYING?
WE WILL HAVE OUR REVENGE AGAINST THE DRAGON GOD!
YOU'RE DISTRACTING ME! NOW HUSH!

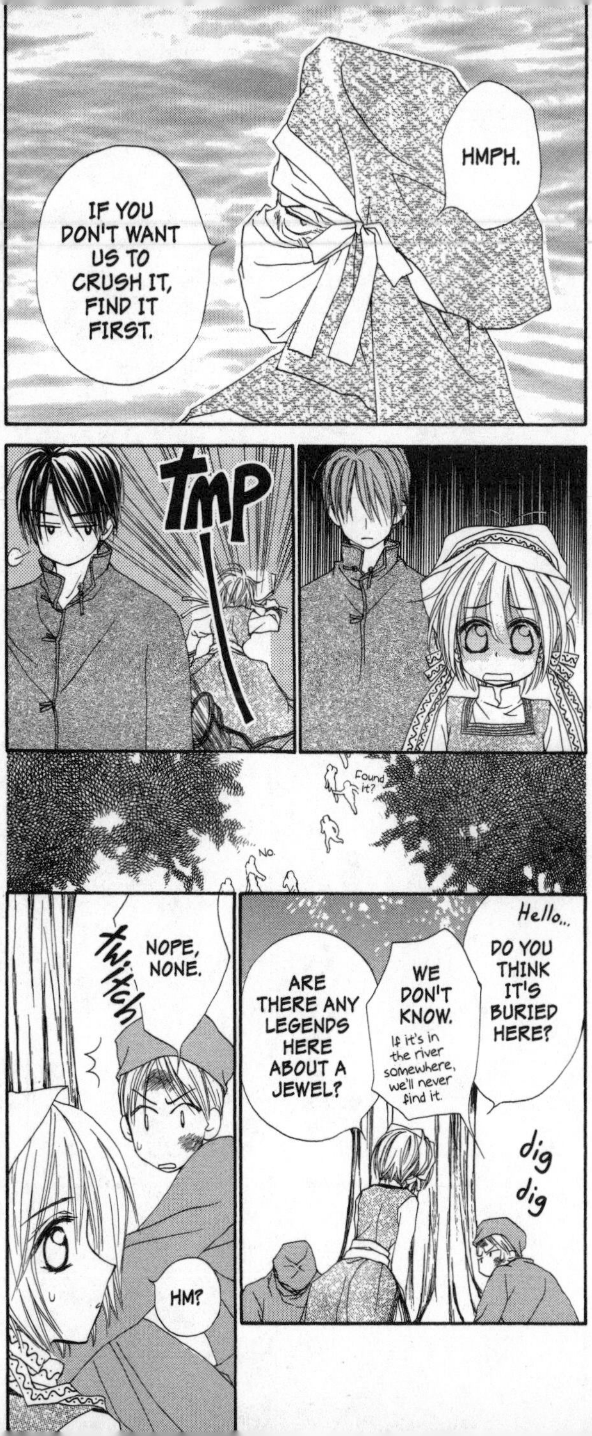
HMPH.
IF YOU DON'T WANT US TO CRUSH IT, FIND IT FIRST.
tmp
Found it?
No.
Hello...
DO YOU THINK IT'S BURIED HERE?
WE DON'T KNOW.
If it's in the river somewhere, we'll never find it.
ARE THERE ANY LEGENDS HERE ABOUT A JEWEL?
dig dig
NOPE, NONE.
twitch
HM?

"Yaaay!" Drama CD Backstory, Part 2

I just happened to be watching anime on TV when I heard this girl who had the prettiest voice. It was the voice of Ayako Kawasumi. I knew she had to be the one to play Suzuka, so her role was decided from the beginning. Sagara's was the next one that was decided. Since she's a boy who became a girl, I knew I wanted a female voice for Sagara. A gentle sexy♡ voice. I felt like it had to sound like one of the Husky Sisters (Pseudonym. Helped with the naming of Kuronekomaru before.♡), so we decided on Minami Takayama-san. I had an idea of what I wanted for Kuroishi's voice, but I had no idea who I wanted to play him.♪ After I received a voice sample, I knew immediately. Hideyuki Tanaka-san!! So that was the order they were decided, but I still had no idea who would play Megumi.

(To be continued...)

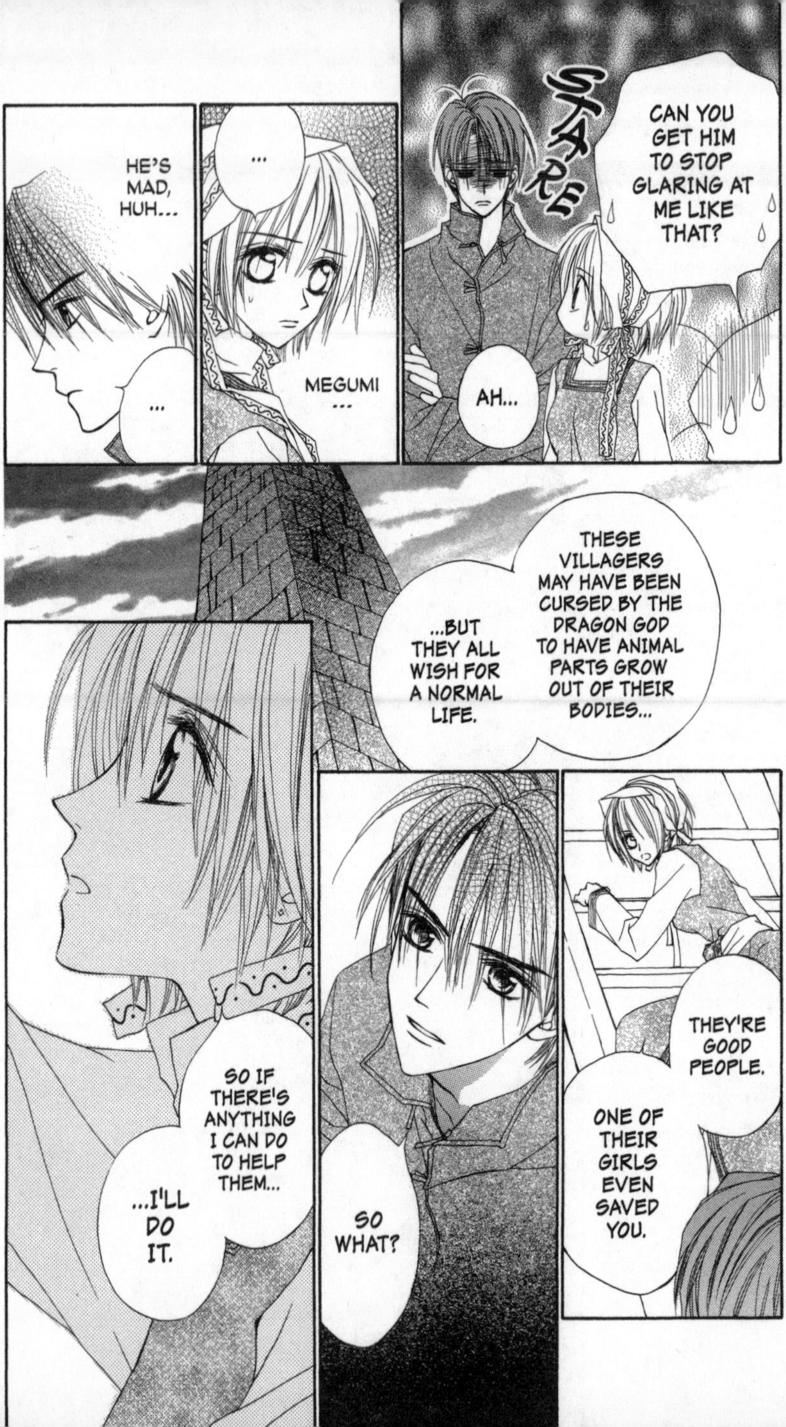
STARE
CAN YOU GET HIM TO STOP GLARING AT ME LIKE THAT?
AH...
...
MEGUMI ...
HE'S MAD, HUH...
...
THESE VILLAGERS MAY HAVE BEEN CURSED BY THE DRAGON GOD TO HAVE ANIMAL PARTS GROW OUT OF THEIR BODIES...
...BUT THEY ALL WISH FOR A NORMAL LIFE.
THEY'RE GOOD PEOPLE.
ONE OF THEIR GIRLS EVEN SAVED YOU.
SO WHAT?
SO IF THERE'S ANYTHING I CAN DO TO HELP THEM...
...I'LL DO IT.

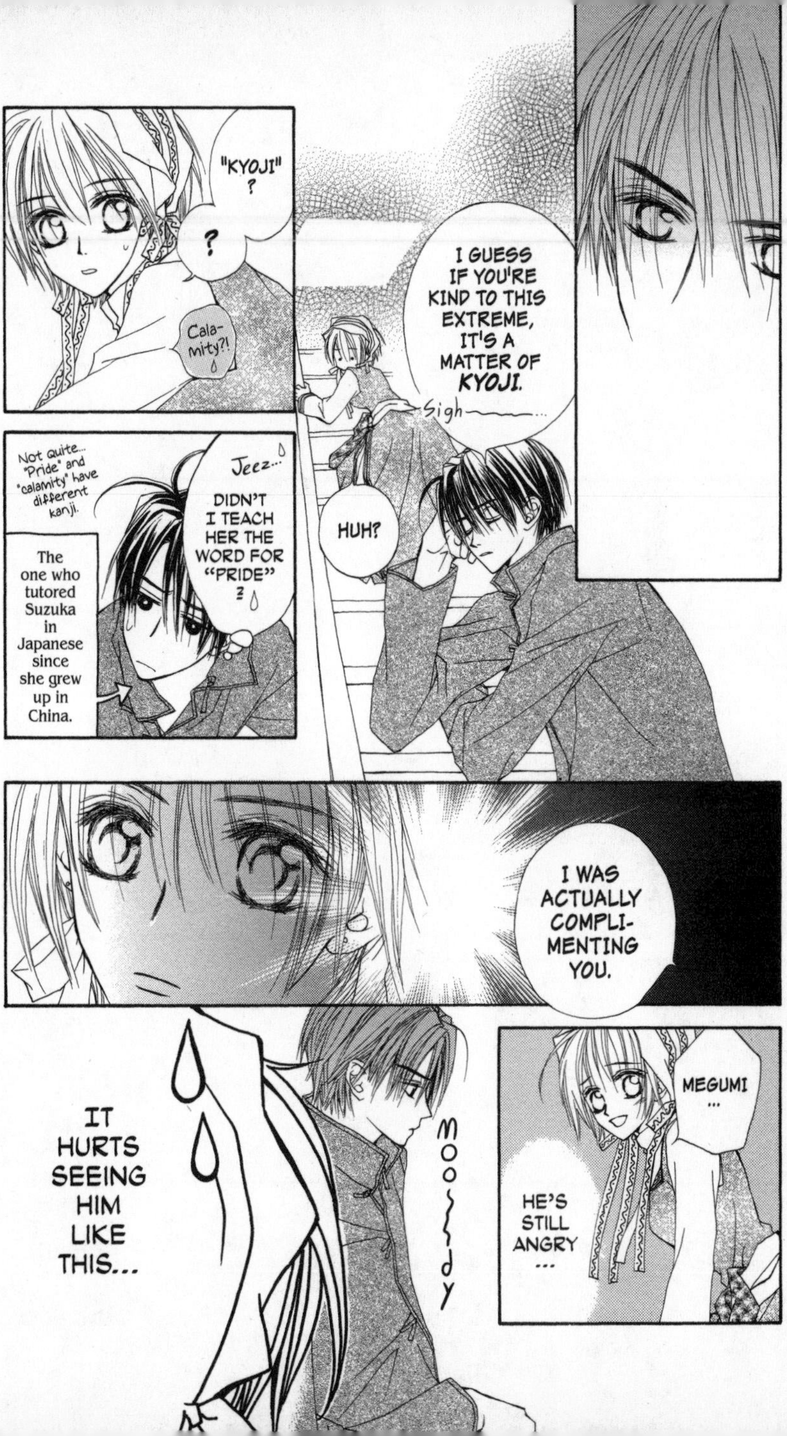
I GUESS IF YOU'RE KIND TO THIS EXTREME, IT'S A MATTER OF **KYOJI**.
Sigh...
HUH?
"KYOJI"?
?
Cala-mity?!
Jeez...
DIDN'T I TEACH HER THE WORD FOR "PRIDE"?
Not quite... "Pride" and "calamity" have different kanji.
The one who tutored Suzuka in Japanese since she grew up in China.
I WAS ACTUALLY COMPLI-MENTING YOU.
MEGUMI...
HE'S STILL ANGRY...
MOO~~DY
IT HURTS SEEING HIM LIKE THIS...

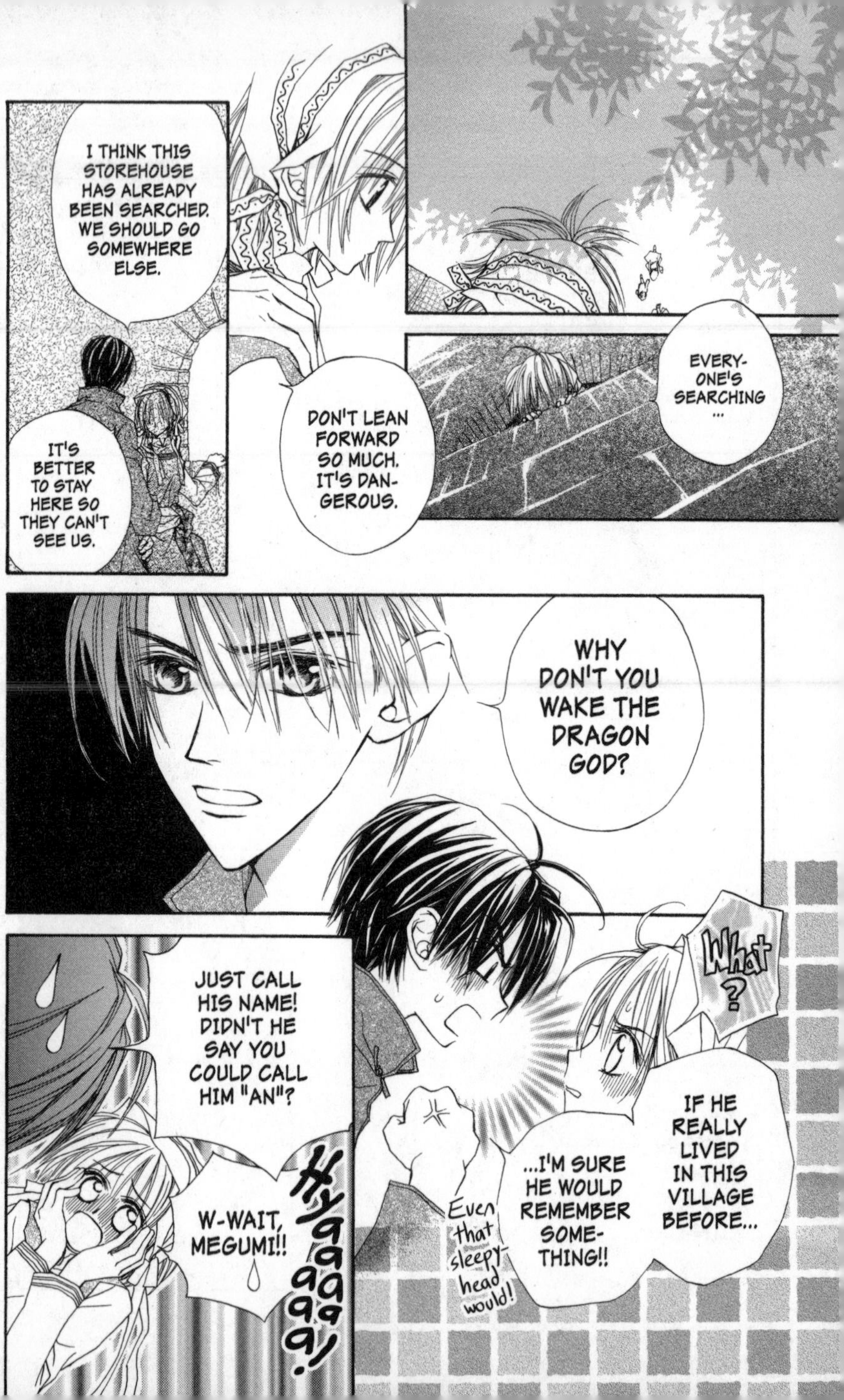
EVERY-ONE'S SEARCHING ...
I THINK THIS STOREHOUSE HAS ALREADY BEEN SEARCHED. WE SHOULD GO SOMEWHERE ELSE.
DON'T LEAN FORWARD SO MUCH. IT'S DAN-GEROUS.
IT'S BETTER TO STAY HERE SO THEY CAN'T SEE US.
WHY DON'T YOU WAKE THE DRAGON GOD?
What?
IF HE REALLY LIVED IN THIS VILLAGE BEFORE...
...I'M SURE HE WOULD REMEMBER SOME-THING!!
Even that sleepy-head would!
JUST CALL HIS NAME! DIDN'T HE SAY YOU COULD CALL HIM "AN"?
W-WAIT, MEGUMI!!
Hyaaaaaaa!

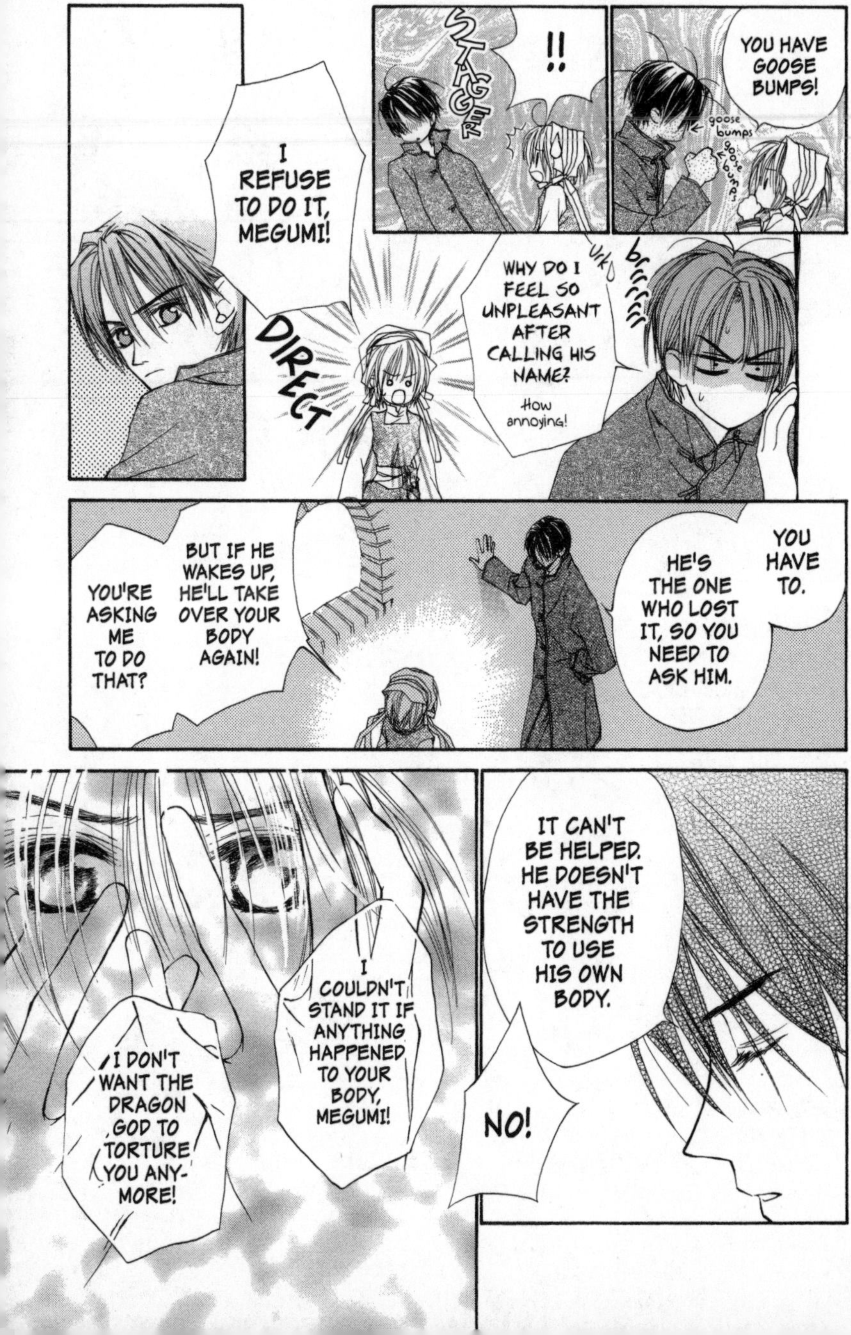
YOU HAVE GOOSE BUMPS!
goose bumps
goose bumps
STAGGER
!!
brrrrrr
urk
WHY DO I FEEL SO UNPLEASANT AFTER CALLING HIS NAME?
How annoying!
DIRECT
I REFUSE TO DO IT, MEGUMI!
YOU HAVE TO.
HE'S THE ONE WHO LOST IT, SO YOU NEED TO ASK HIM.
BUT IF HE WAKES UP, HE'LL TAKE OVER YOUR BODY AGAIN!
YOU'RE ASKING ME TO DO THAT?
IT CAN'T BE HELPED. HE DOESN'T HAVE THE STRENGTH TO USE HIS OWN BODY.
NO!
I COULDN'T STAND IT IF ANYTHING HAPPENED TO YOUR BODY, MEGUMI!
I DON'T WANT THE DRAGON GOD TO TORTURE YOU ANYMORE!

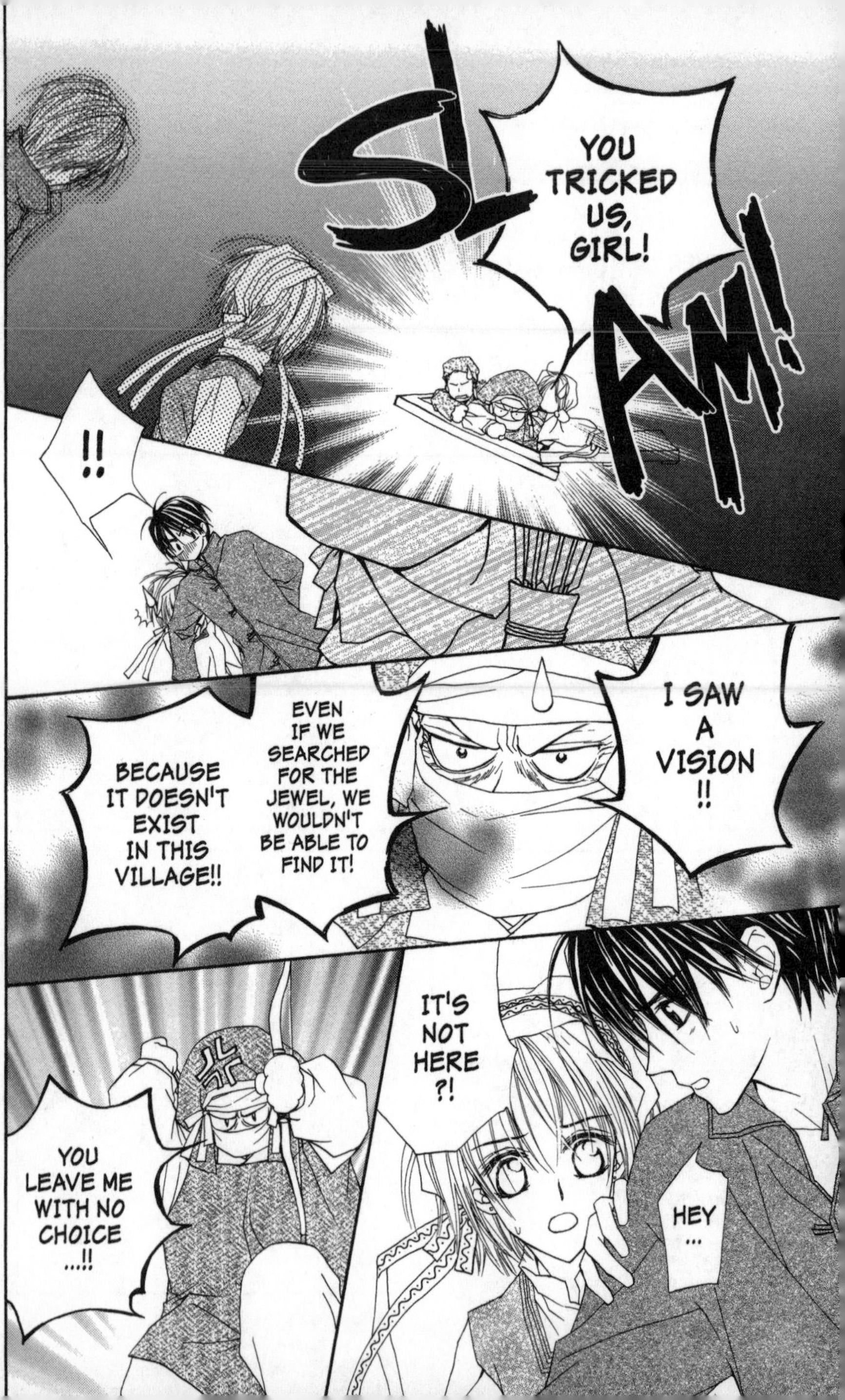
YOU TRICKED US, GIRL!
SLAM!
!!
I SAW A VISION !!
EVEN IF WE SEARCHED FOR THE JEWEL, WE WOULDN'T BE ABLE TO FIND IT!
BECAUSE IT DOESN'T EXIST IN THIS VILLAGE!!
IT'S NOT HERE ?!
HEY ...
YOU LEAVE ME WITH NO CHOICE ...!!

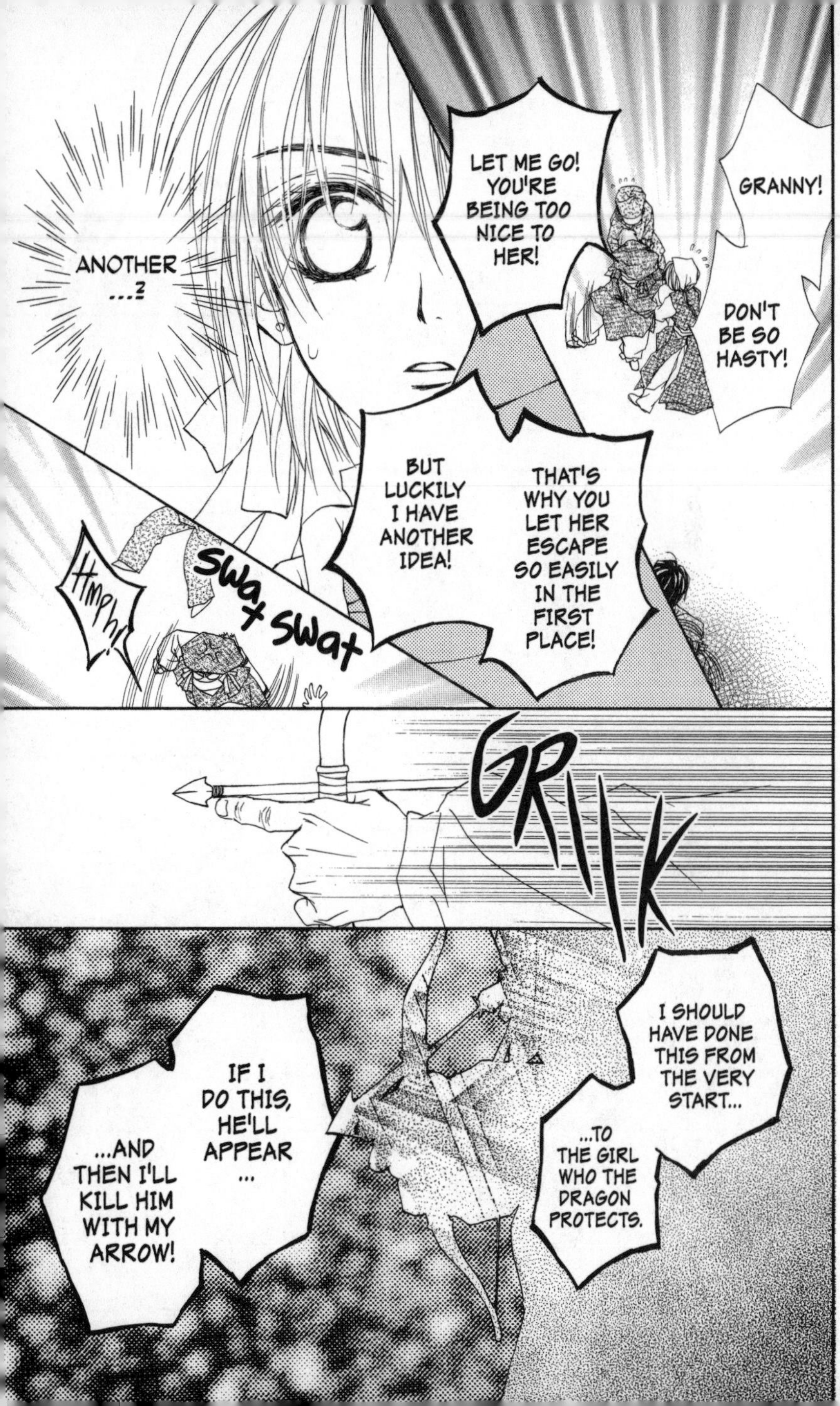
GRANNY!
DON'T BE SO HASTY!
LET ME GO! YOU'RE BEING TOO NICE TO HER!
THAT'S WHY YOU LET HER ESCAPE SO EASILY IN THE FIRST PLACE!
BUT LUCKILY I HAVE ANOTHER IDEA!
ANOTHER ...?
Hmph!
Swat swat
GRIIK
I SHOULD HAVE DONE THIS FROM THE VERY START...
...TO THE GIRL WHO THE DRAGON PROTECTS.
IF I DO THIS, HE'LL APPEAR...
...AND THEN I'LL KILL HIM WITH MY ARROW!

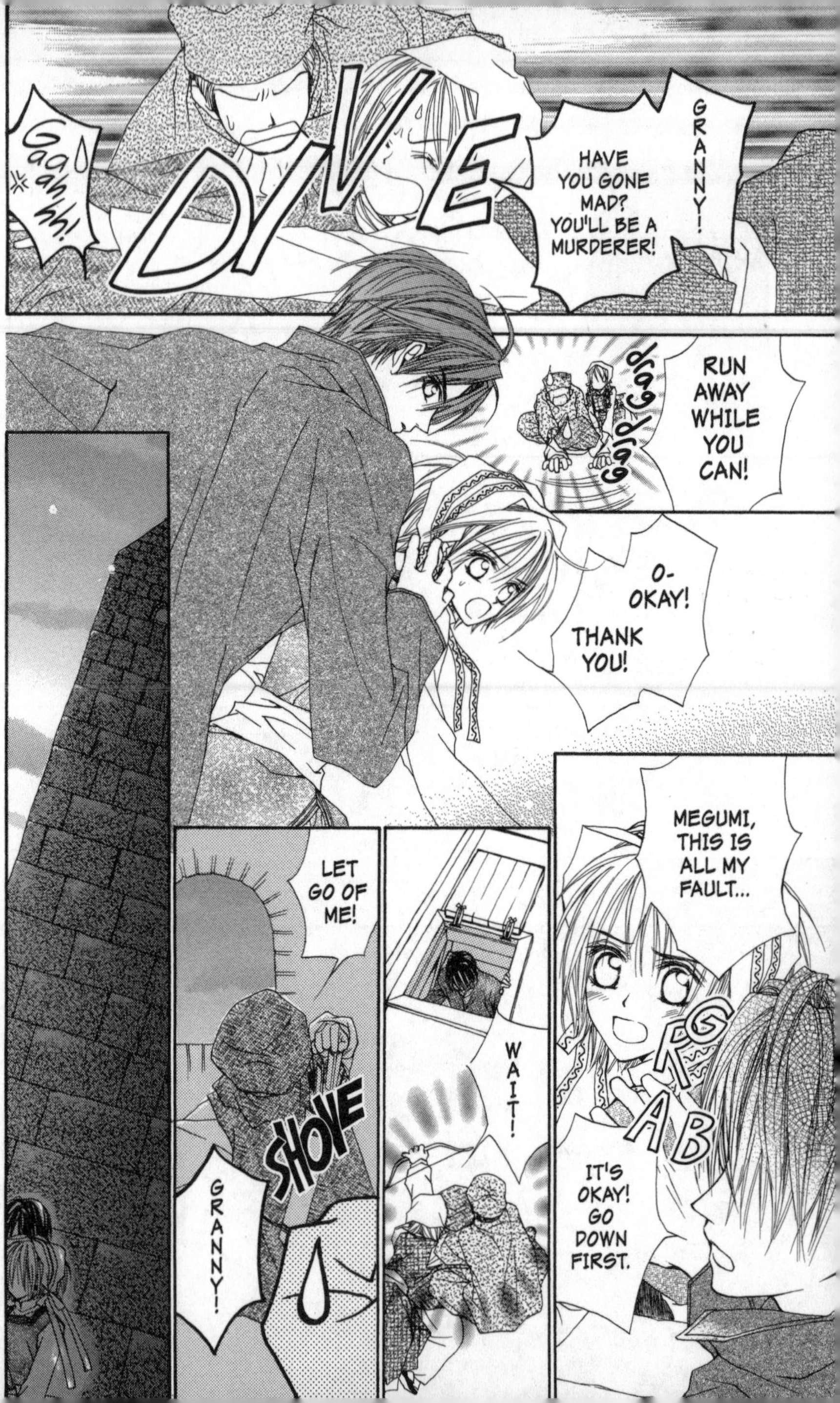
GRANNY!
HAVE YOU GONE MAD? YOU'LL BE A MURDERER!
DIVE
Gaahhh!
RUN AWAY WHILE YOU CAN!
drag drag
O-OKAY!
THANK YOU!
MEGUMI, THIS IS ALL MY FAULT...
GRAB
IT'S OKAY! GO DOWN FIRST.
WAIT!
LET GO OF ME!
SHOVE
GRANNY!

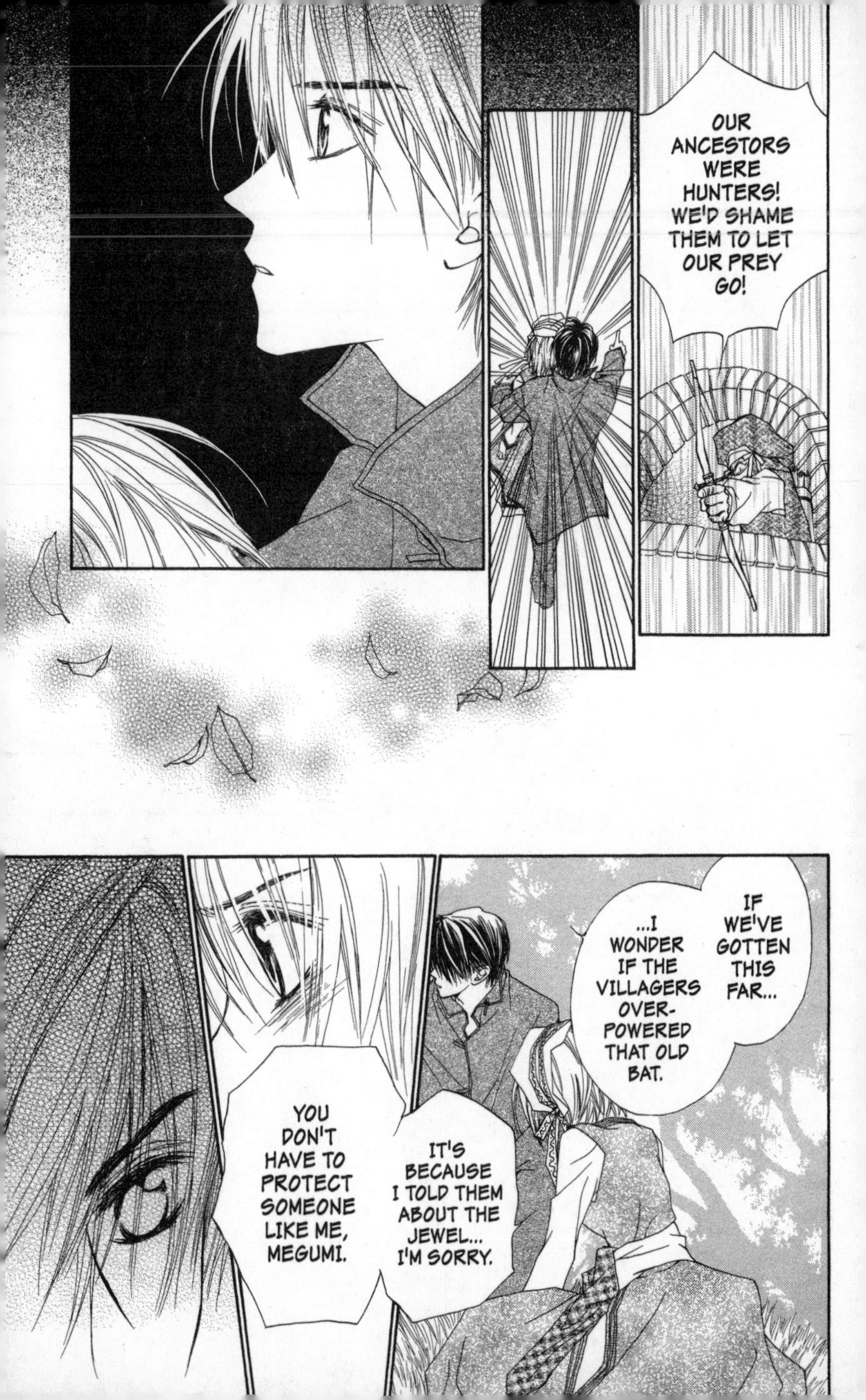
OUR ANCESTORS WERE HUNTERS! WE'D SHAME THEM TO LET OUR PREY GO!
IF WE'VE GOTTEN THIS FAR...
...I WONDER IF THE VILLAGERS OVER-POWERED THAT OLD BAT.
IT'S BECAUSE I TOLD THEM ABOUT THE JEWEL... I'M SORRY.
YOU DON'T HAVE TO PROTECT SOMEONE LIKE ME, MEGUMI.

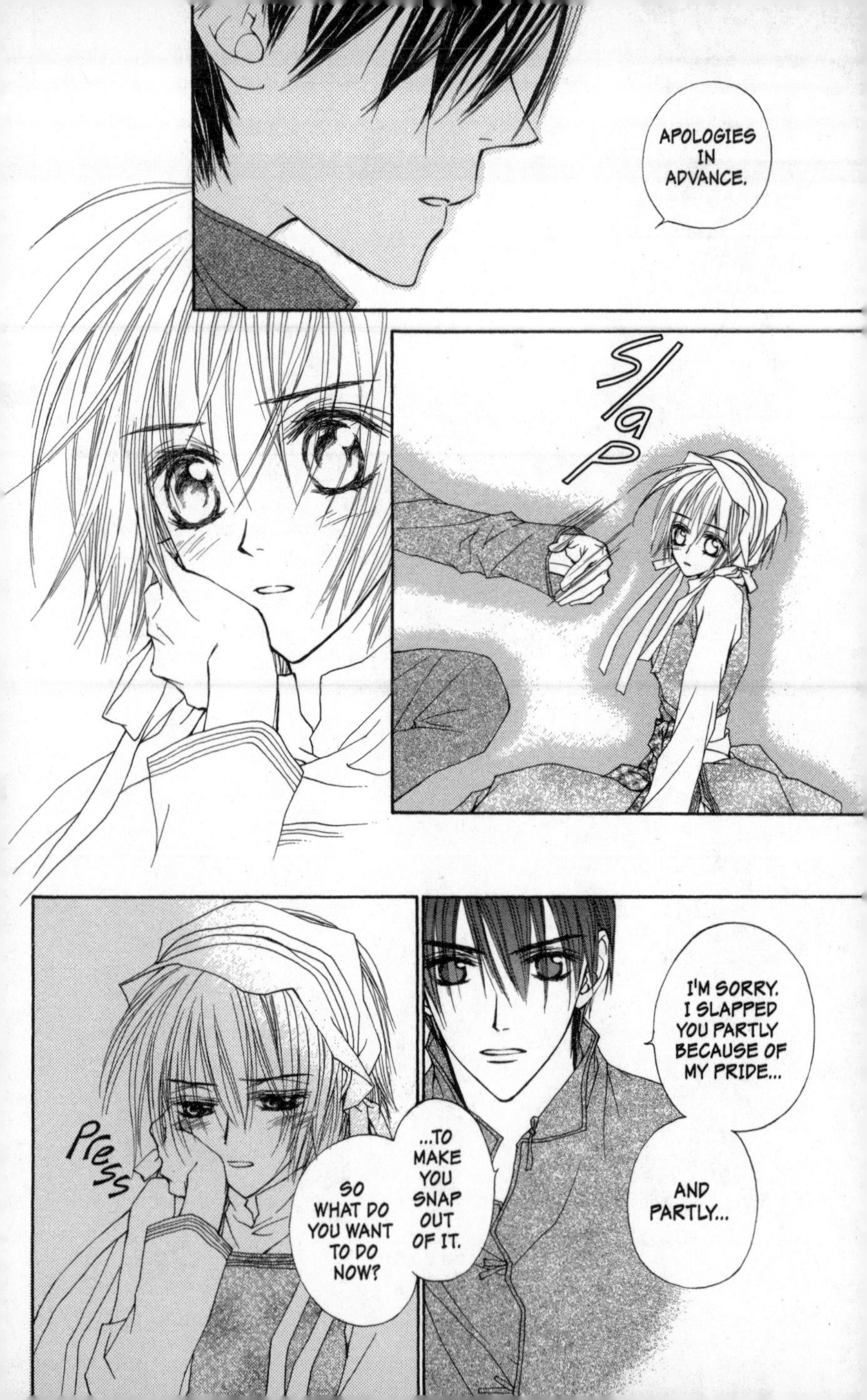
APOLOGIES IN ADVANCE.
Slap
I'M SORRY. I SLAPPED YOU PARTLY BECAUSE OF MY PRIDE...
AND PARTLY...
...TO MAKE YOU SNAP OUT OF IT.
Press
SO WHAT DO YOU WANT TO DO NOW?

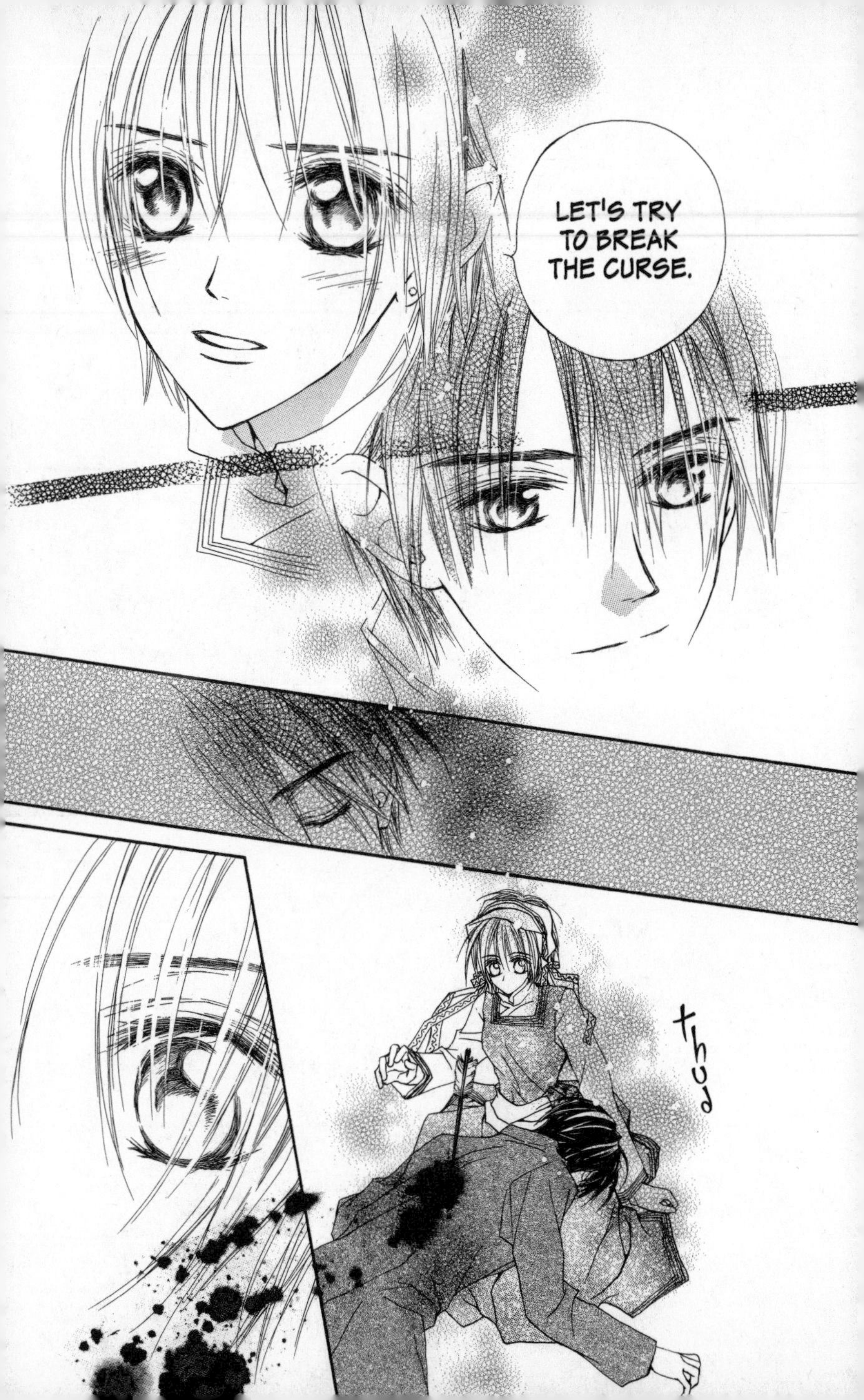
LET'S TRY TO BREAK THE CURSE.
thud

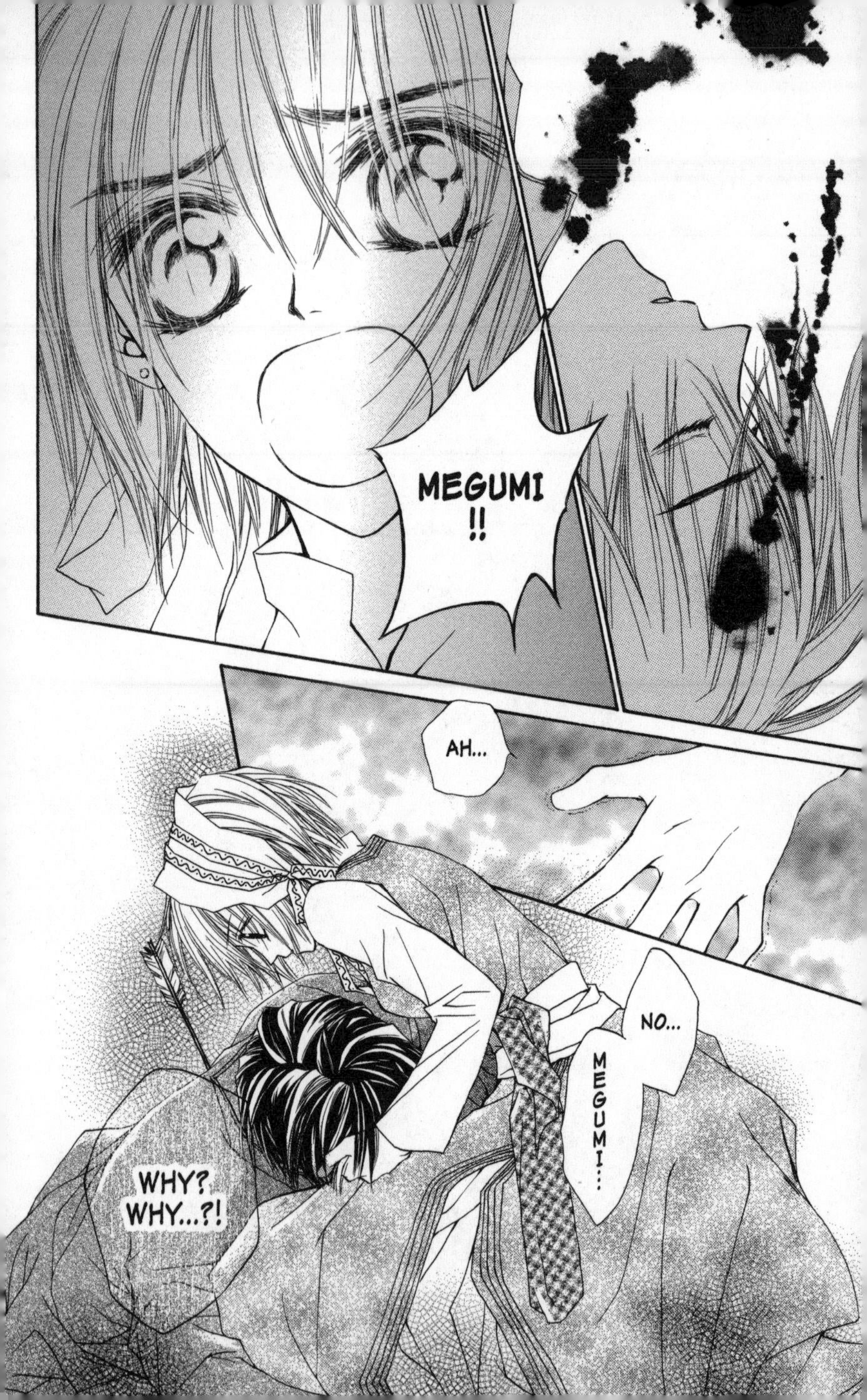
MEGUMI !!
AH...
NO...
MEGUMI...
WHY? WHY...?!

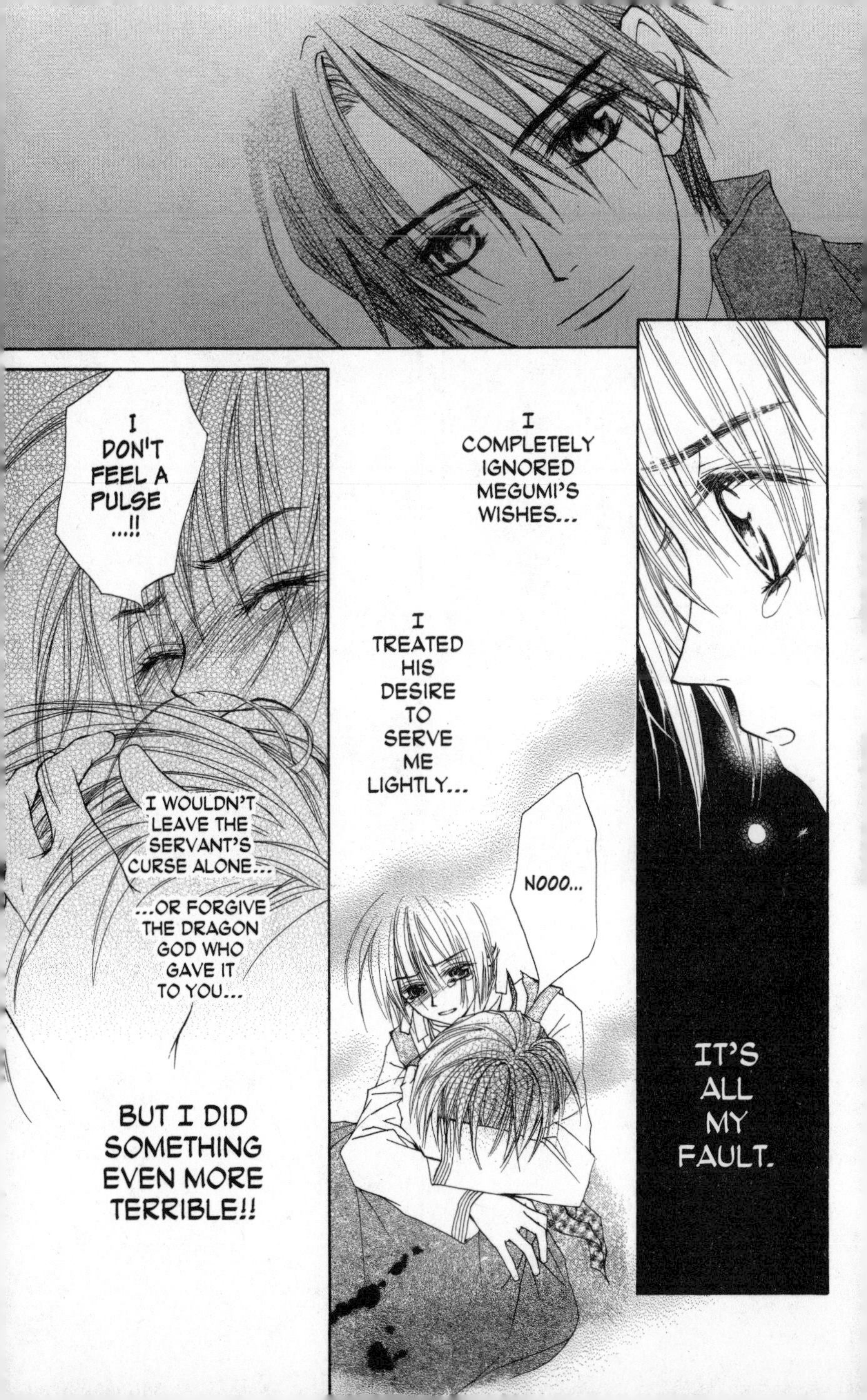
I COMPLETELY IGNORED MEGUMI'S WISHES...
I TREATED HIS DESIRE TO SERVE ME LIGHTLY...
IT'S ALL MY FAULT.
NOOO...
I DON'T FEEL A PULSE ...!!
I WOULDN'T LEAVE THE SERVANT'S CURSE ALONE...
...OR FORGIVE THE DRAGON GOD WHO GAVE IT TO YOU...
BUT I DID SOMETHING EVEN MORE TERRIBLE!!

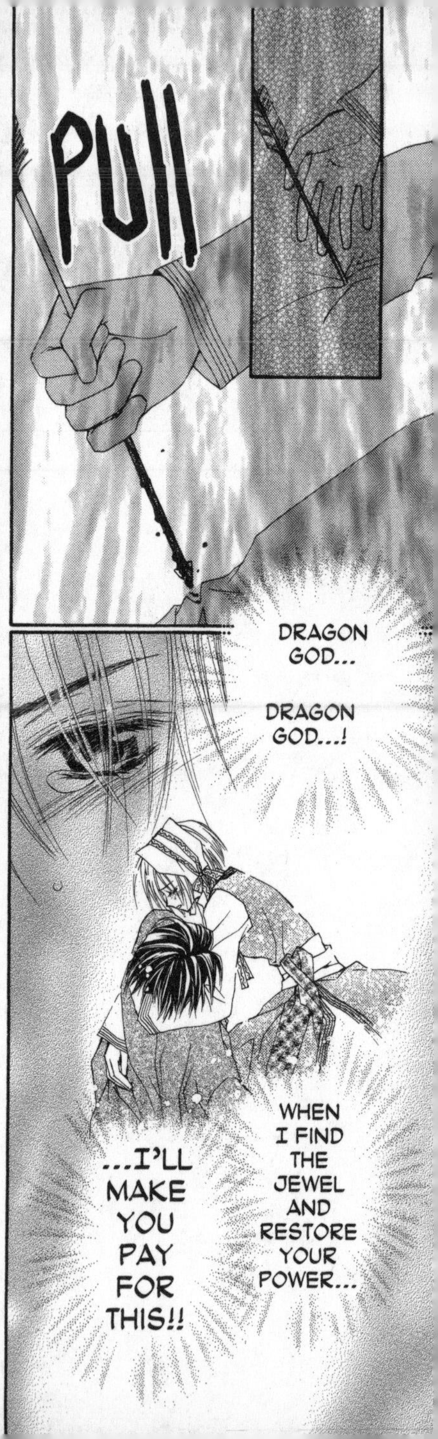
PULL
DRAGON GOD...
DRAGON GOD...!
WHEN I FIND THE JEWEL AND RESTORE YOUR POWER...
...I'LL MAKE YOU PAY FOR THIS!!
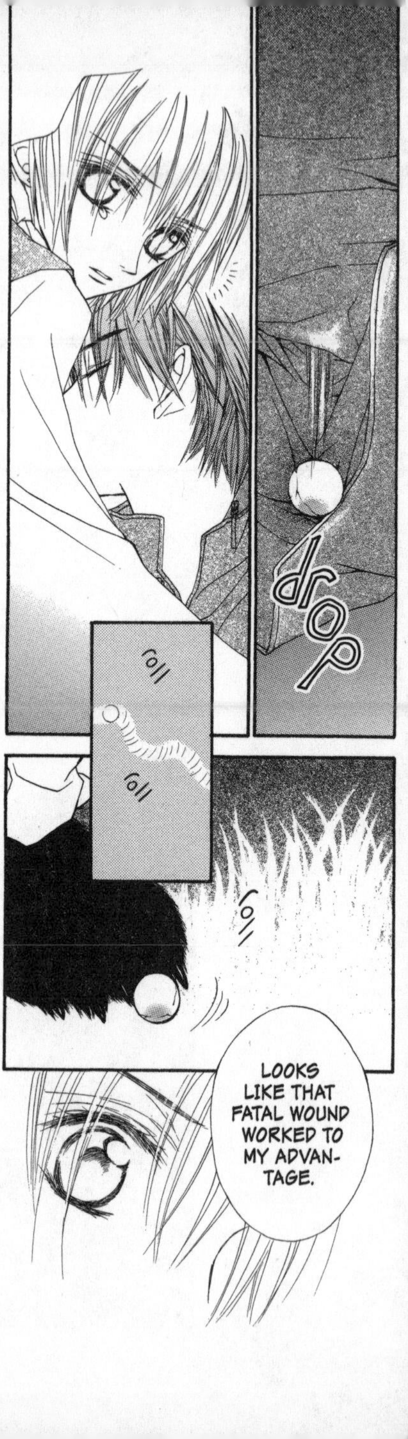
drop
roll
roll
roll
LOOKS LIKE THAT FATAL WOUND WORKED TO MY ADVANTAGE.

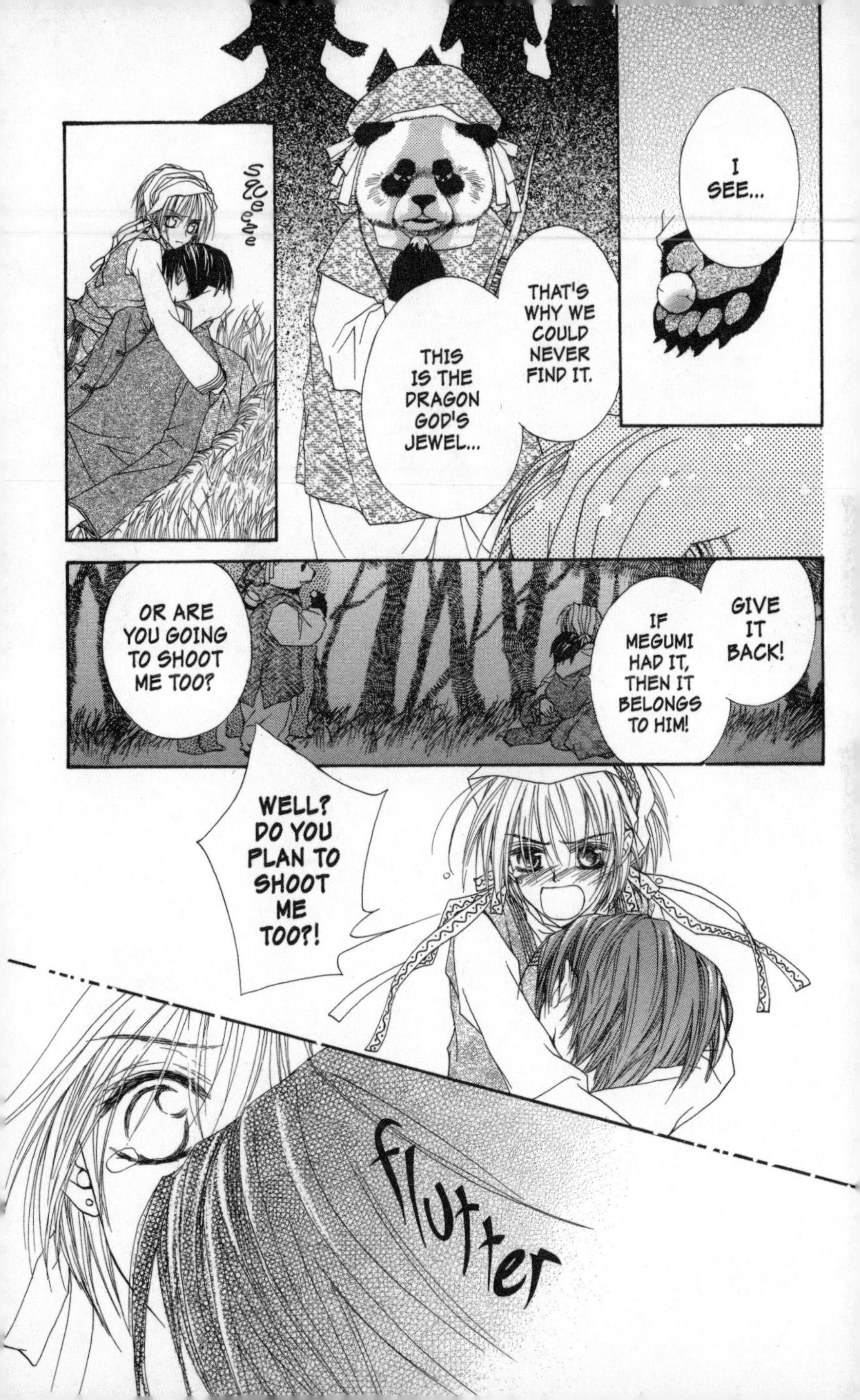

I SEE...
THAT'S WHY WE COULD NEVER FIND IT.
THIS IS THE DRAGON GOD'S JEWEL...
squeeze
GIVE IT BACK!
IF MEGUMI HAD IT, THEN IT BELONGS TO HIM!
OR ARE YOU GOING TO SHOOT ME TOO?
WELL? DO YOU PLAN TO SHOOT ME TOO?!
flutter

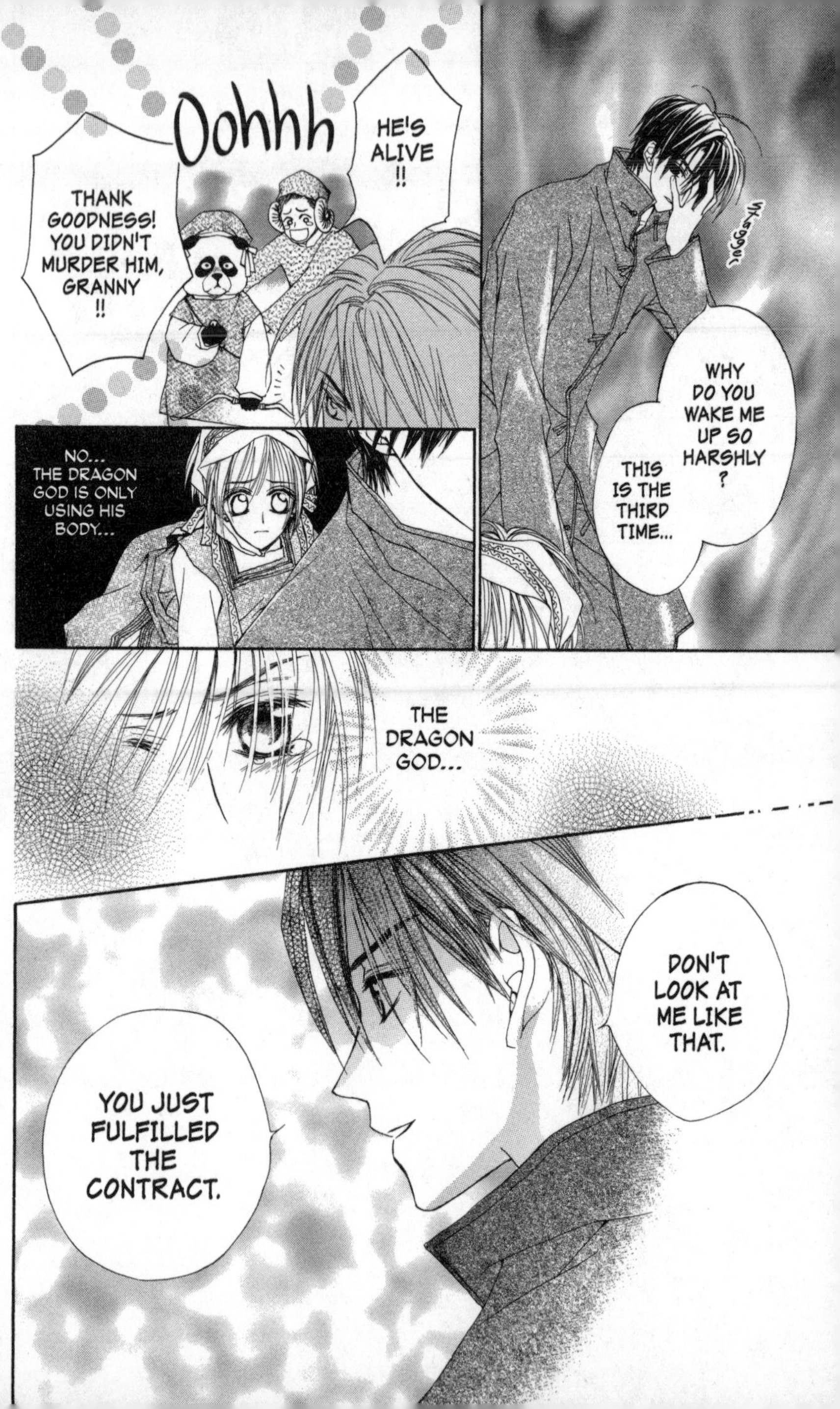
stagger
WHY DO YOU WAKE ME UP SO HARSHLY?
THIS IS THE THIRD TIME...
HE'S ALIVE !!
Oohhh
THANK GOODNESS! YOU DIDN'T MURDER HIM, GRANNY !!
NO... THE DRAGON GOD IS ONLY USING HIS BODY...
THE DRAGON GOD...
DON'T LOOK AT ME LIKE THAT.
YOU JUST FULFILLED THE CONTRACT.

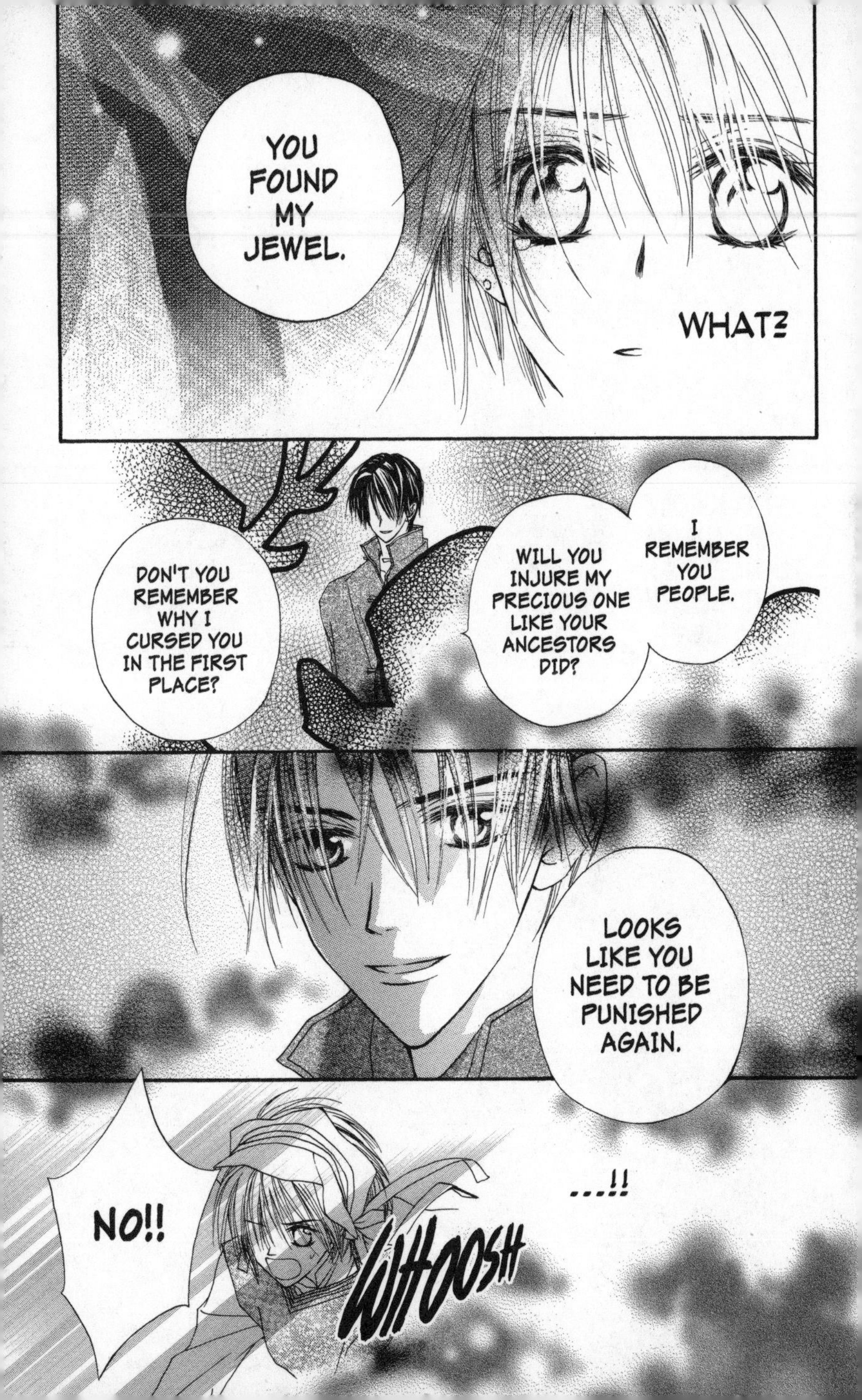
YOU FOUND MY JEWEL.
WHAT?
I REMEMBER YOU PEOPLE.
WILL YOU INJURE MY PRECIOUS ONE LIKE YOUR ANCESTORS DID?
DON'T YOU REMEMBER WHY I CURSED YOU IN THE FIRST PLACE?
LOOKS LIKE YOU NEED TO BE PUNISHED AGAIN.
...!!
NO!!
WHOOSH

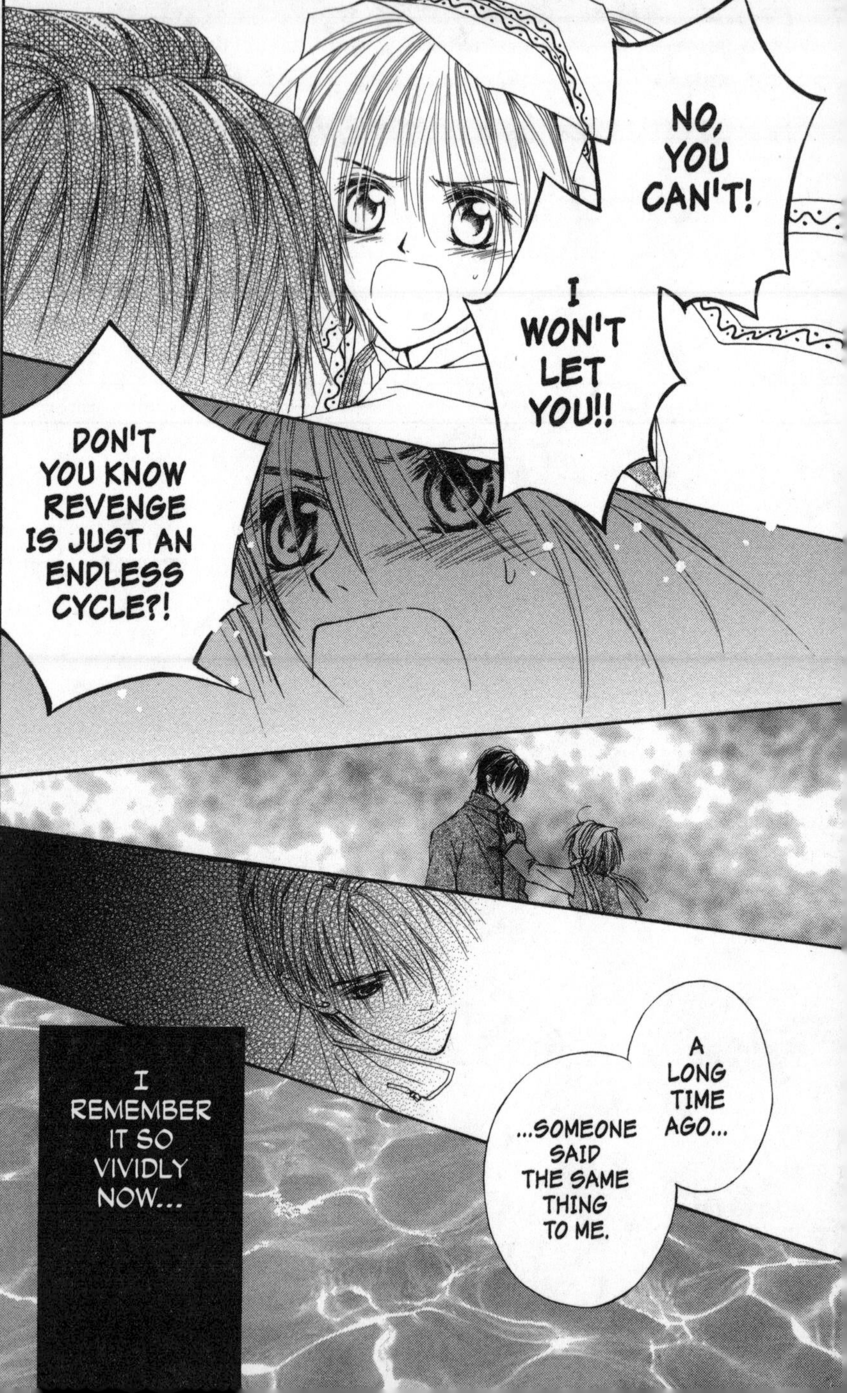
NO, YOU CAN'T!
I WON'T LET YOU!!
DON'T YOU KNOW REVENGE IS JUST AN ENDLESS CYCLE?!
A LONG TIME AGO...
...SOMEONE SAID THE SAME THING TO ME.
I REMEMBER IT SO VIVIDLY NOW...

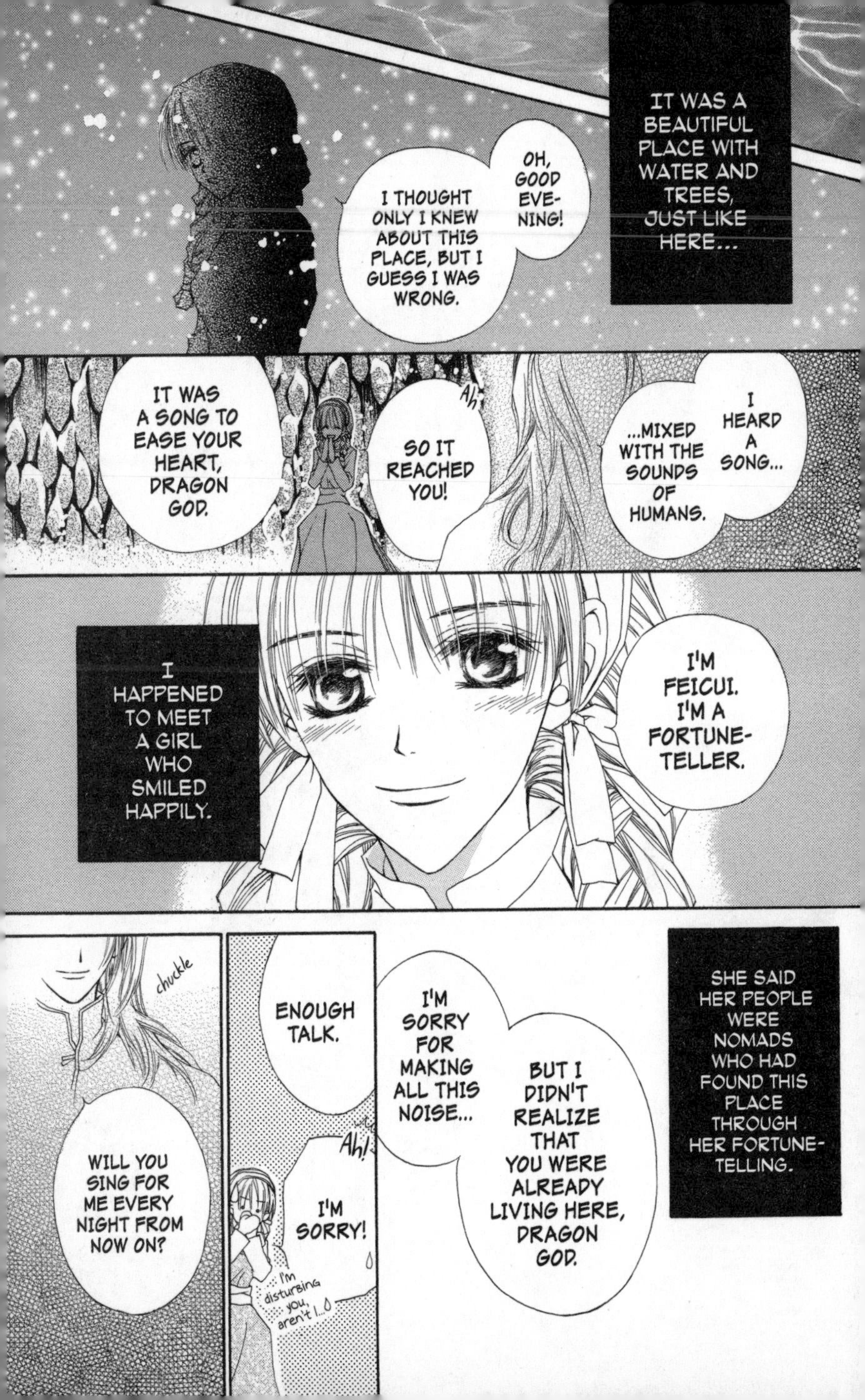
IT WAS A BEAUTIFUL PLACE WITH WATER AND TREES, JUST LIKE HERE...
OH, GOOD EVE-NING!
I THOUGHT ONLY I KNEW ABOUT THIS PLACE, BUT I GUESS I WAS WRONG.
I HEARD A SONG...
...MIXED WITH THE SOUNDS OF HUMANS.
Ah
SO IT REACHED YOU!
IT WAS A SONG TO EASE YOUR HEART, DRAGON GOD.
I'M FEICUI. I'M A FORTUNE-TELLER.
I HAPPENED TO MEET A GIRL WHO SMILED HAPPILY.
SHE SAID HER PEOPLE WERE NOMADS WHO HAD FOUND THIS PLACE THROUGH HER FORTUNE-TELLING.
I'M SORRY FOR MAKING ALL THIS NOISE...
BUT I DIDN'T REALIZE THAT YOU WERE ALREADY LIVING HERE, DRAGON GOD.
ENOUGH TALK.
Ah!
I'M SORRY!
I'm disturbing you, aren't I...
chuckle
WILL YOU SING FOR ME EVERY NIGHT FROM NOW ON?

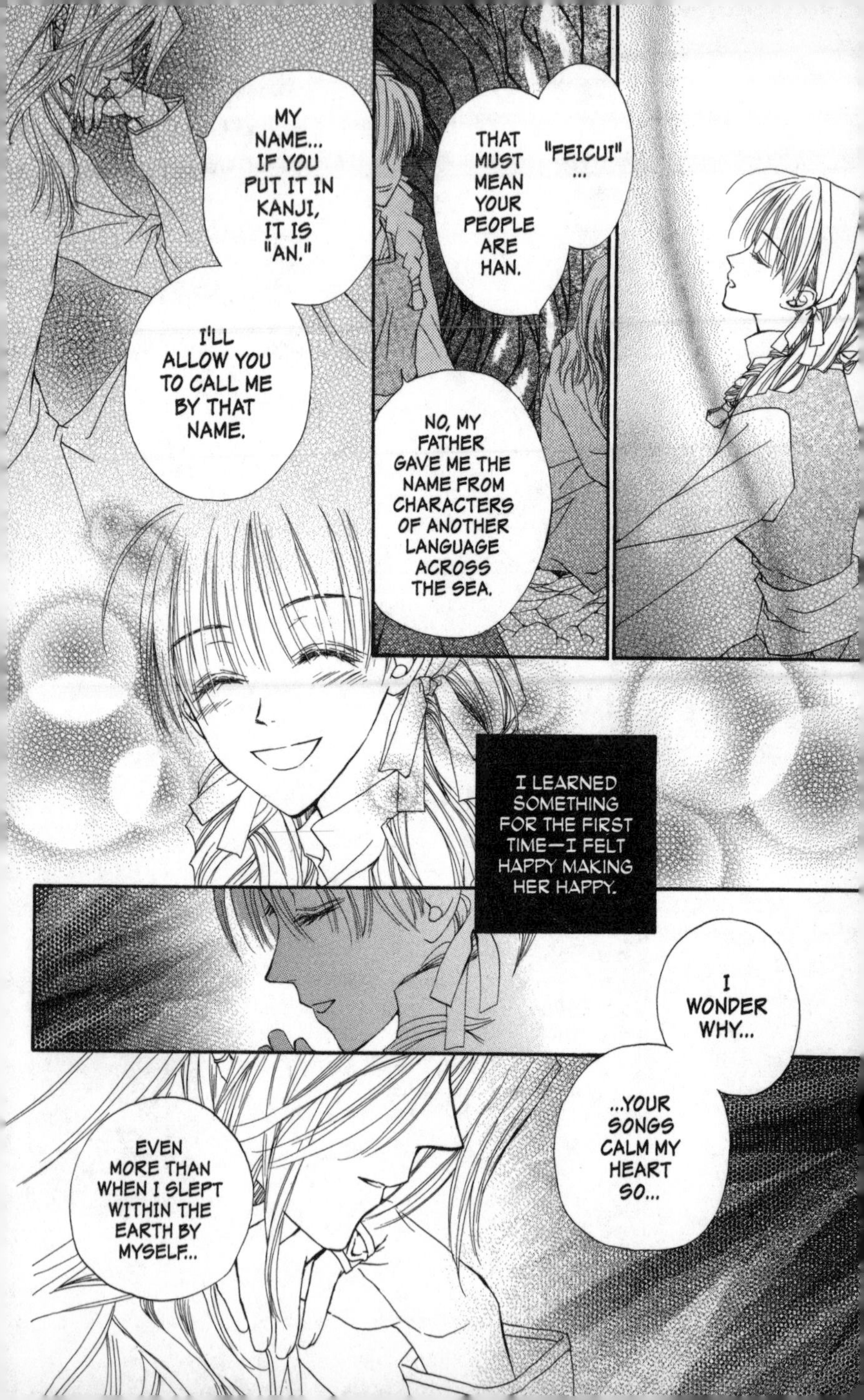
"FEICUI" ...
THAT MUST MEAN YOUR PEOPLE ARE HAN.
NO, MY FATHER GAVE ME THE NAME FROM CHARACTERS OF ANOTHER LANGUAGE ACROSS THE SEA.
MY NAME... IF YOU PUT IT IN KANJI, IT IS "AN."
I'LL ALLOW YOU TO CALL ME BY THAT NAME.
I LEARNED SOMETHING FOR THE FIRST TIME—I FELT HAPPY MAKING HER HAPPY.
I WONDER WHY...
...YOUR SONGS CALM MY HEART SO...
EVEN MORE THAN WHEN I SLEPT WITHIN THE EARTH BY MYSELF...

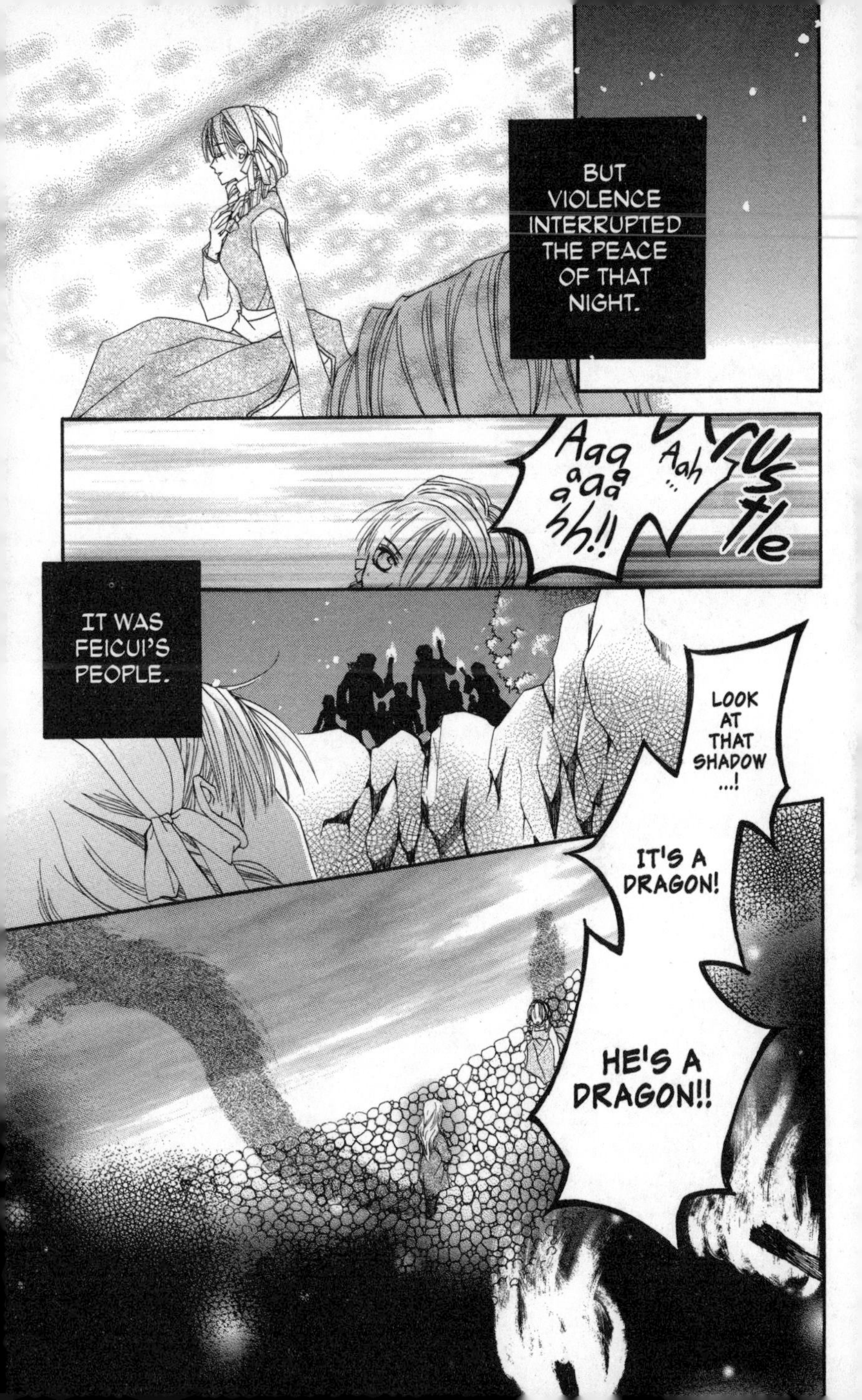
BUT VIOLENCE INTERRUPTED THE PEACE OF THAT NIGHT.
RUSTLE
Aah...
Aaaaaaaaahh!!
IT WAS FEICUI'S PEOPLE.
LOOK AT THAT SHADOW...!
IT'S A DRAGON!
HE'S A DRAGON!!

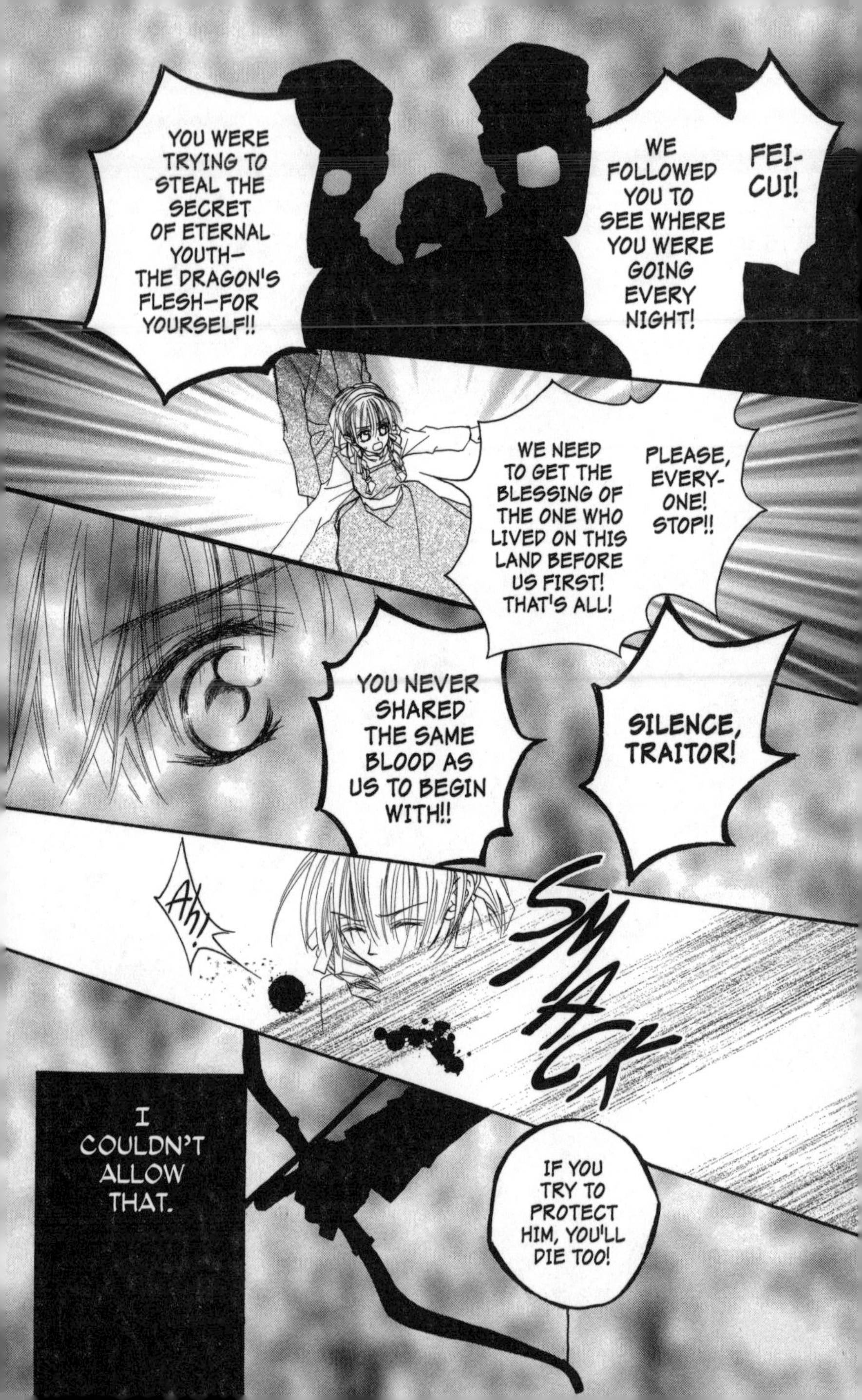
FEI-CUI!
WE FOLLOWED YOU TO SEE WHERE YOU WERE GOING EVERY NIGHT!
YOU WERE TRYING TO STEAL THE SECRET OF ETERNAL YOUTH— THE DRAGON'S FLESH—FOR YOURSELF!!
PLEASE, EVERYONE! STOP!!
WE NEED TO GET THE BLESSING OF THE ONE WHO LIVED ON THIS LAND BEFORE US FIRST! THAT'S ALL!
SILENCE, TRAITOR!
YOU NEVER SHARED THE SAME BLOOD AS US TO BEGIN WITH!!
SMACK
Ah!
IF YOU TRY TO PROTECT HIM, YOU'LL DIE TOO!
I COULDN'T ALLOW THAT.

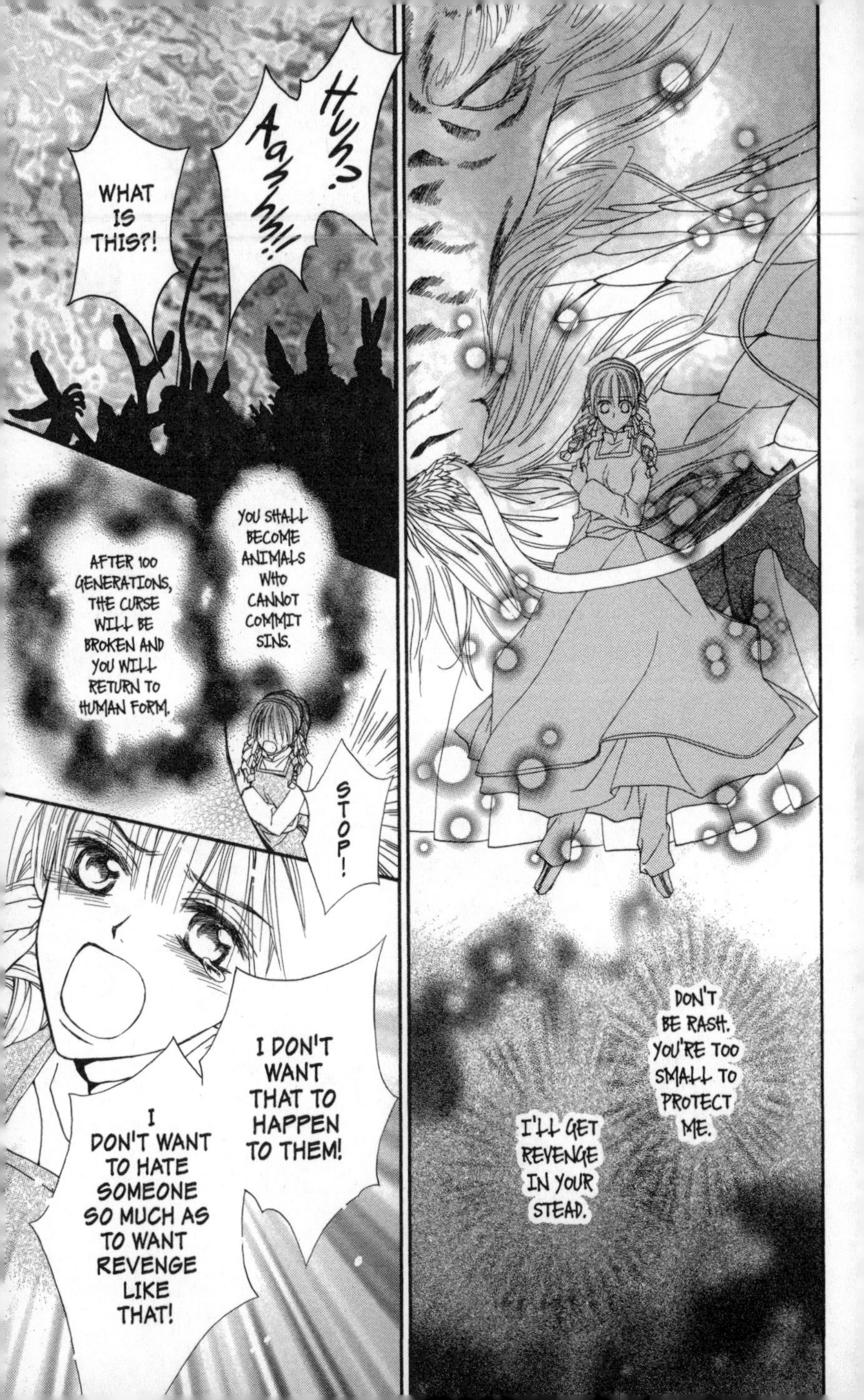
DON'T BE RASH. YOU'RE TOO SMALL TO PROTECT ME.
I'LL GET REVENGE IN YOUR STEAD.
Huh? Aahhhh!!
WHAT IS THIS?!
YOU SHALL BECOME ANIMALS WHO CANNOT COMMIT SINS.
AFTER 100 GENERATIONS, THE CURSE WILL BE BROKEN AND YOU WILL RETURN TO HUMAN FORM.
STOP!
I DON'T WANT THAT TO HAPPEN TO THEM!
I DON'T WANT TO HATE SOMEONE SO MUCH AS TO WANT REVENGE LIKE THAT!

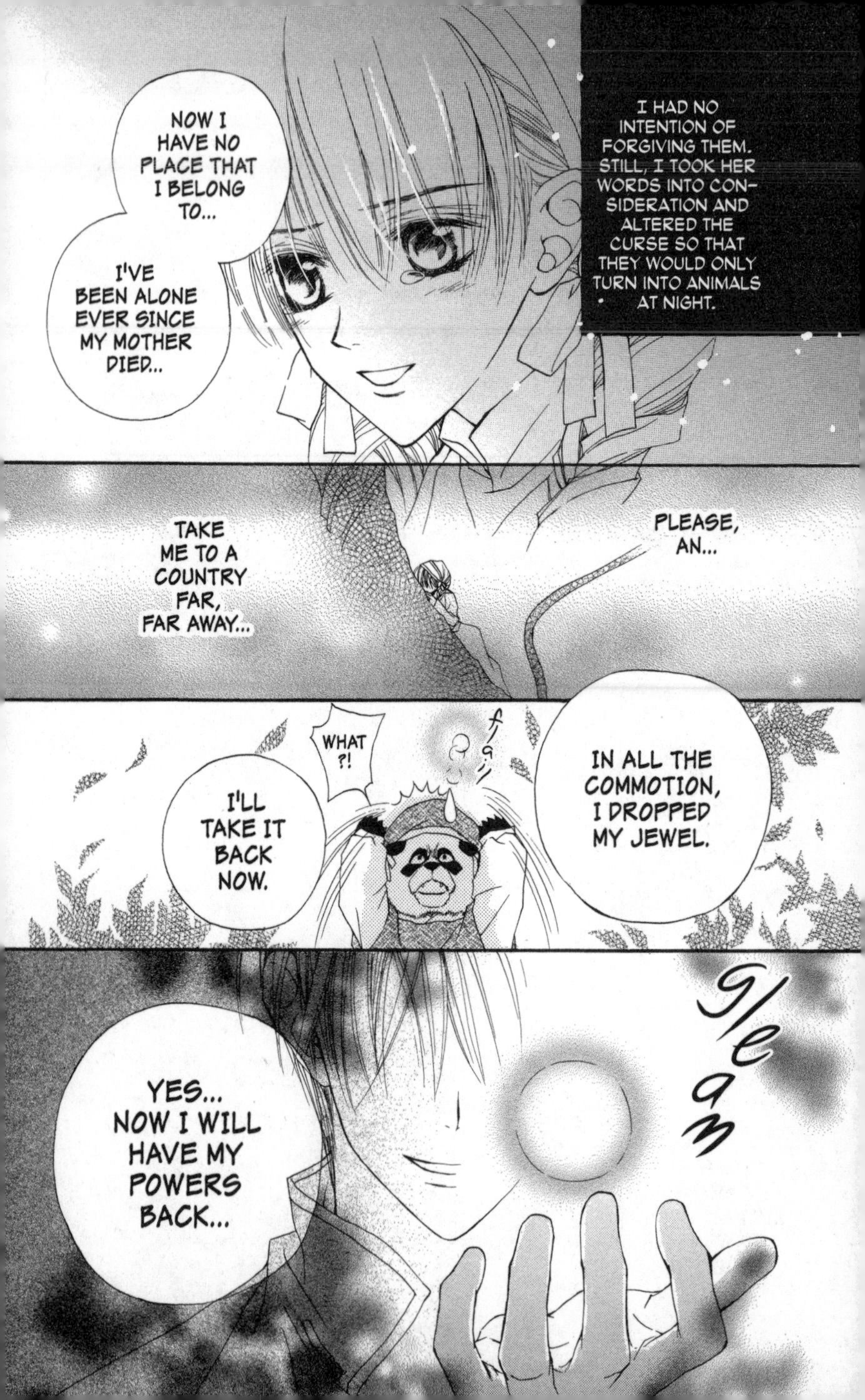
I HAD NO INTENTION OF FORGIVING THEM. STILL, I TOOK HER WORDS INTO CONSIDERATION AND ALTERED THE CURSE SO THAT THEY WOULD ONLY TURN INTO ANIMALS AT NIGHT.
NOW I HAVE NO PLACE THAT I BELONG TO...
I'VE BEEN ALONE EVER SINCE MY MOTHER DIED...
PLEASE, AN...
TAKE ME TO A COUNTRY FAR, FAR AWAY...
IN ALL THE COMMOTION, I DROPPED MY JEWEL.
WHAT ?!
I'LL TAKE IT BACK NOW.
gleam
YES... NOW I WILL HAVE MY POWERS BACK...

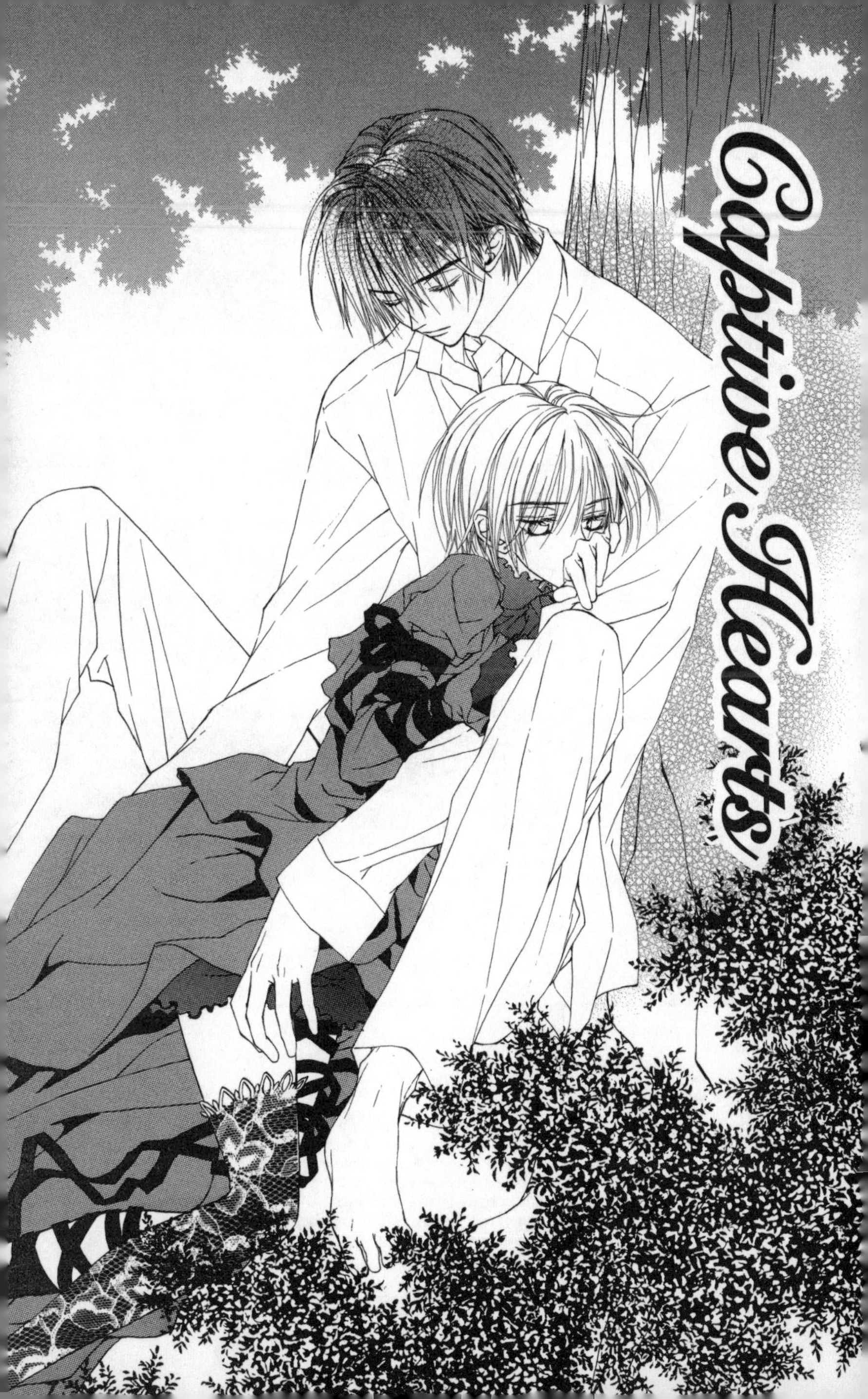
Captive Hearts

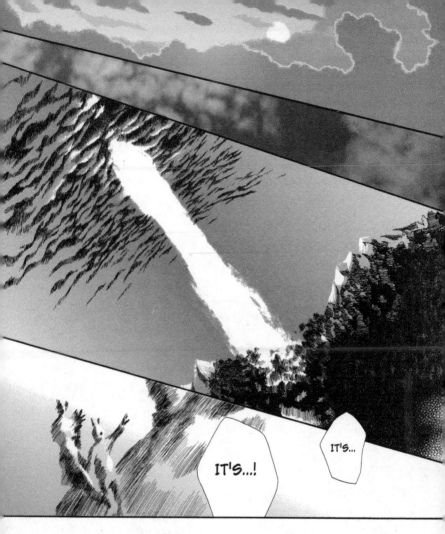

IT'S...!

IT'S...

Backstory ⑤ Captive Hearts was originally a one-shot story, and I thought it was just going to be the first silly manga I did. I didn't hold anything back and drew everything I wanted to draw and decided to worry about the details later. ♭ But because of that decision, it created a lot of obstacles and regrets later. ♭♭ It started out as a comedy but grew into something more serious (while still retaining all the gags). It's a strange combination. ♭ I found out it's really difficult to give it my all while still staying levelheaded. I really learned a lot!

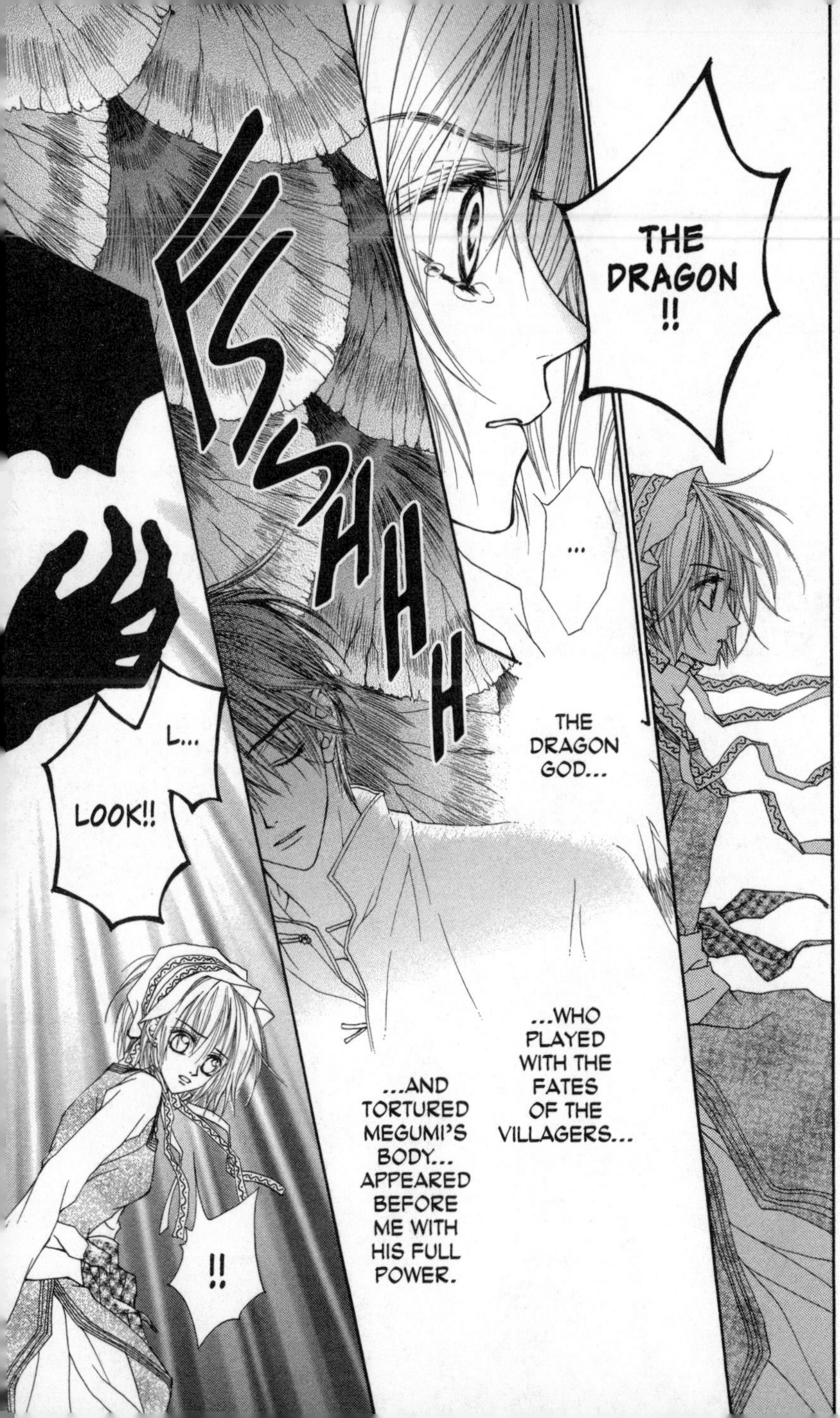
THE DRAGON!!
...
THE DRAGON GOD...
...WHO PLAYED WITH THE FATES OF THE VILLAGERS...
...AND TORTURED MEGUMI'S BODY... APPEARED BEFORE ME WITH HIS FULL POWER.
FSSHHHH
L... LOOK!!
!!

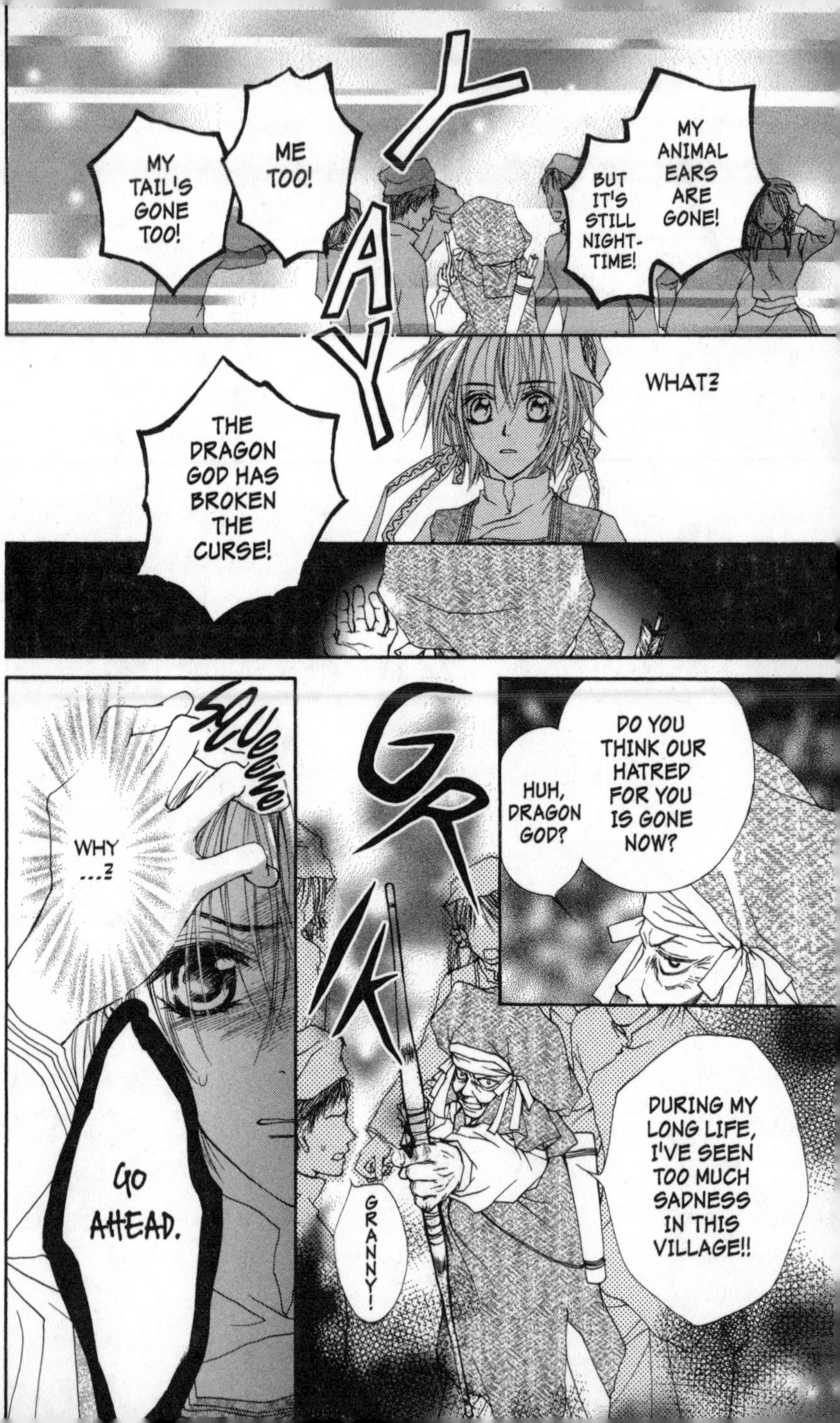
MY ANIMAL EARS ARE GONE!
BUT IT'S STILL NIGHT-TIME!
YAY
ME TOO!
MY TAIL'S GONE TOO!
WHAT?
THE DRAGON GOD HAS BROKEN THE CURSE!
DO YOU THINK OUR HATRED FOR YOU IS GONE NOW?
HUH, DRAGON GOD?
GRIK
DURING MY LONG LIFE, I'VE SEEN TOO MUCH SADNESS IN THIS VILLAGE!!
GRANNY!
SQUEEEZE
WHY ...?
GO AHEAD.

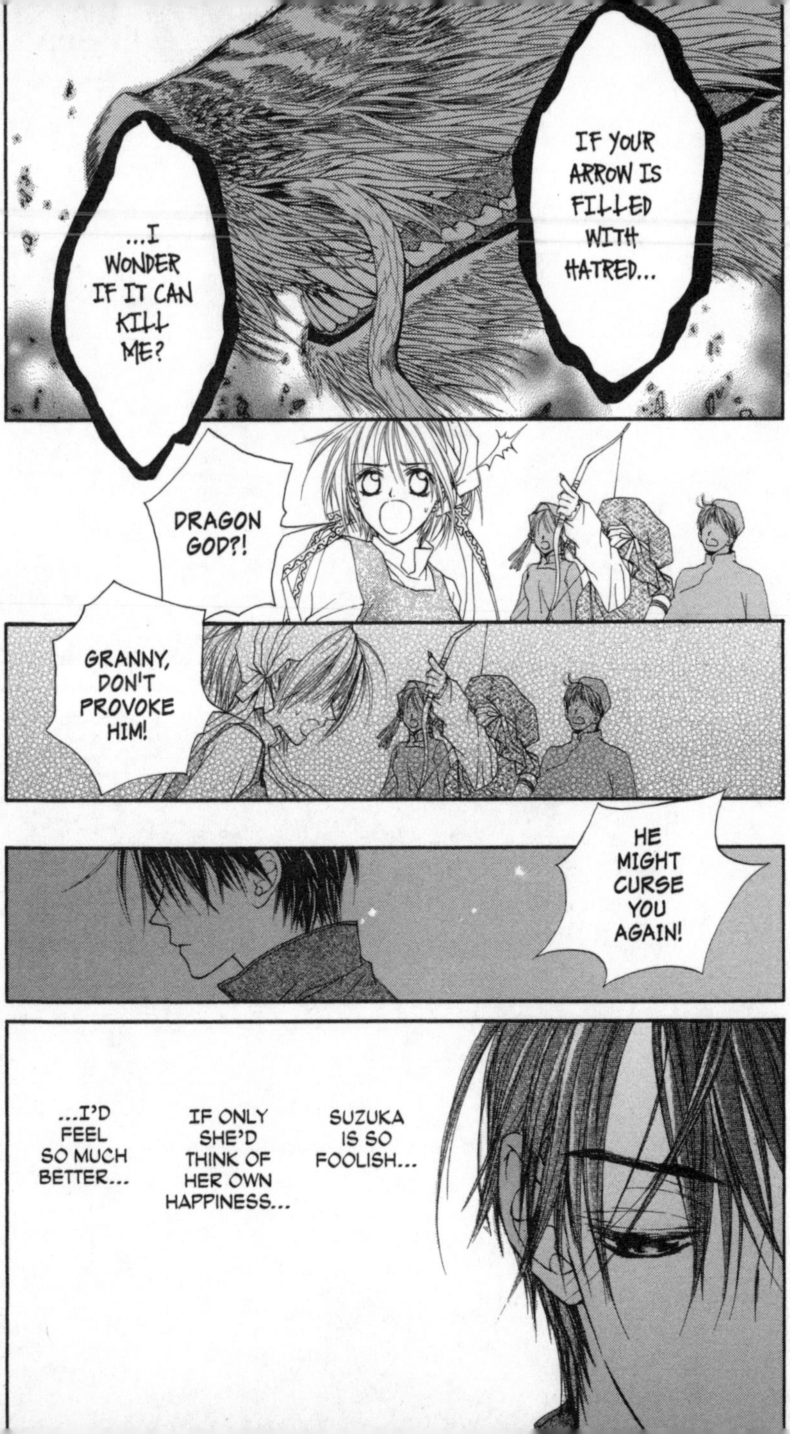
IF YOUR ARROW IS FILLED WITH HATRED...
...I WONDER IF IT CAN KILL ME?
DRAGON GOD?!
GRANNY, DON'T PROVOKE HIM!
HE MIGHT CURSE YOU AGAIN!
SUZUKA IS SO FOOLISH...
IF ONLY SHE'D THINK OF HER OWN HAPPINESS...
...I'D FEEL SO MUCH BETTER...

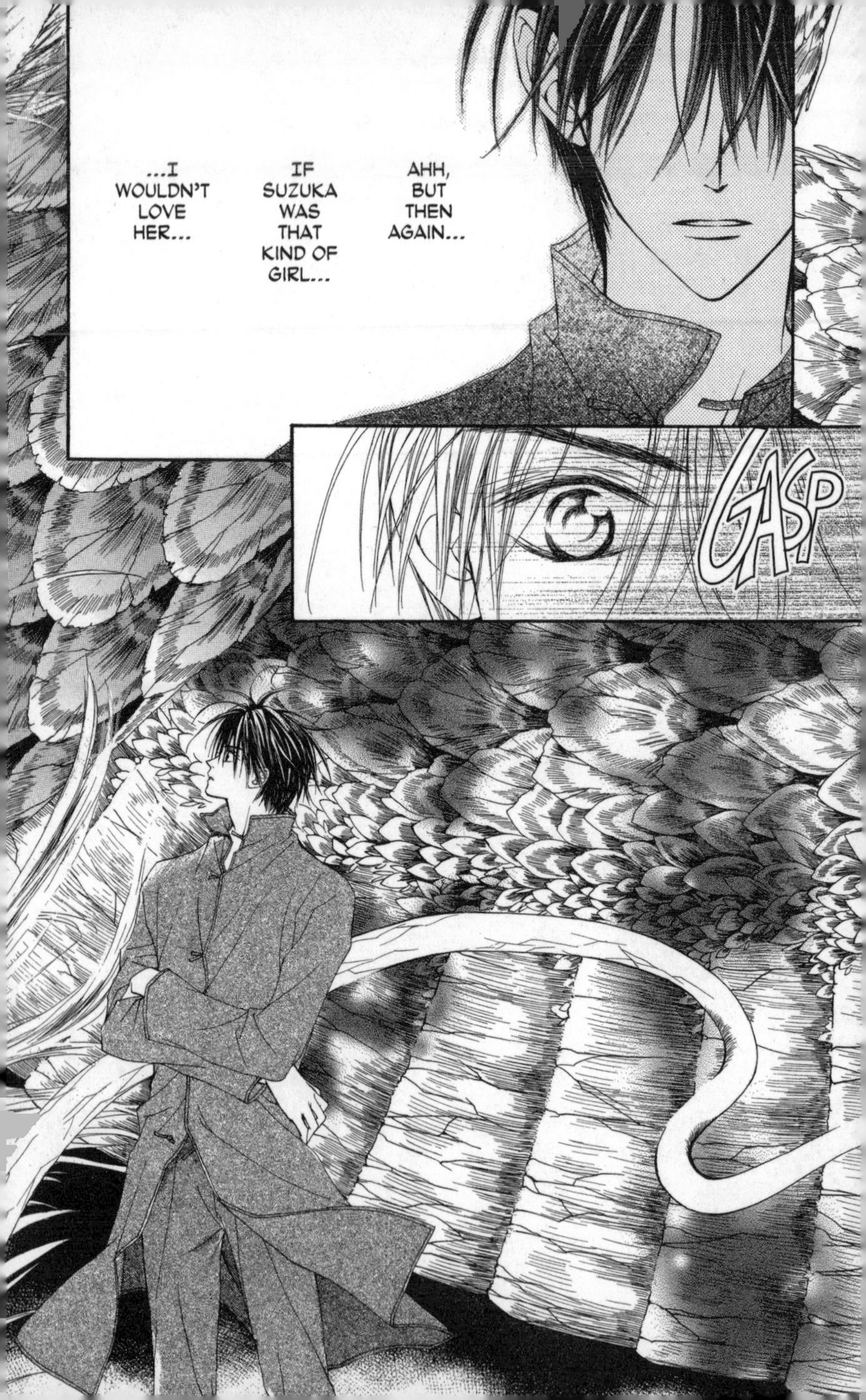
AHH, BUT THEN AGAIN...
IF SUZUKA WAS THAT KIND OF GIRL...
...I WOULDN'T LOVE HER...
GASP

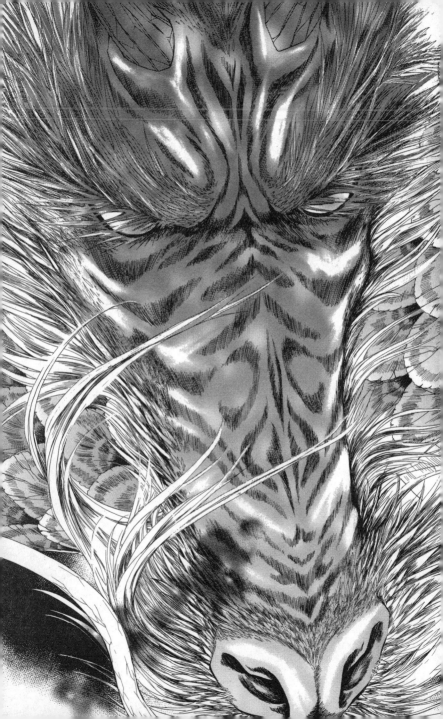

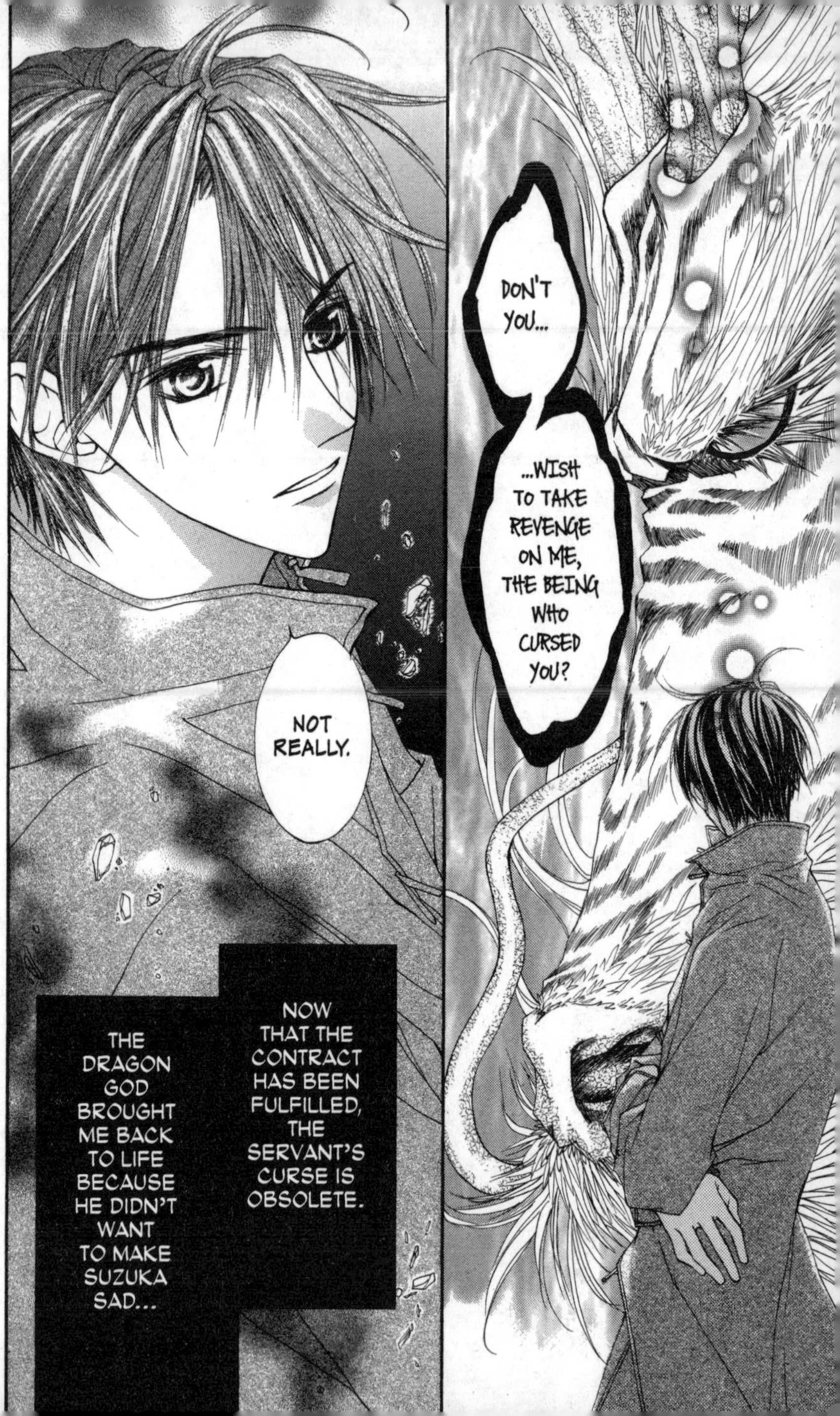
DON'T YOU...
...WISH TO TAKE REVENGE ON ME, THE BEING WHO CURSED YOU?
NOT REALLY.
NOW THAT THE CONTRACT HAS BEEN FULFILLED, THE SERVANT'S CURSE IS OBSOLETE.
THE DRAGON GOD BROUGHT ME BACK TO LIFE BECAUSE HE DIDN'T WANT TO MAKE SUZUKA SAD...

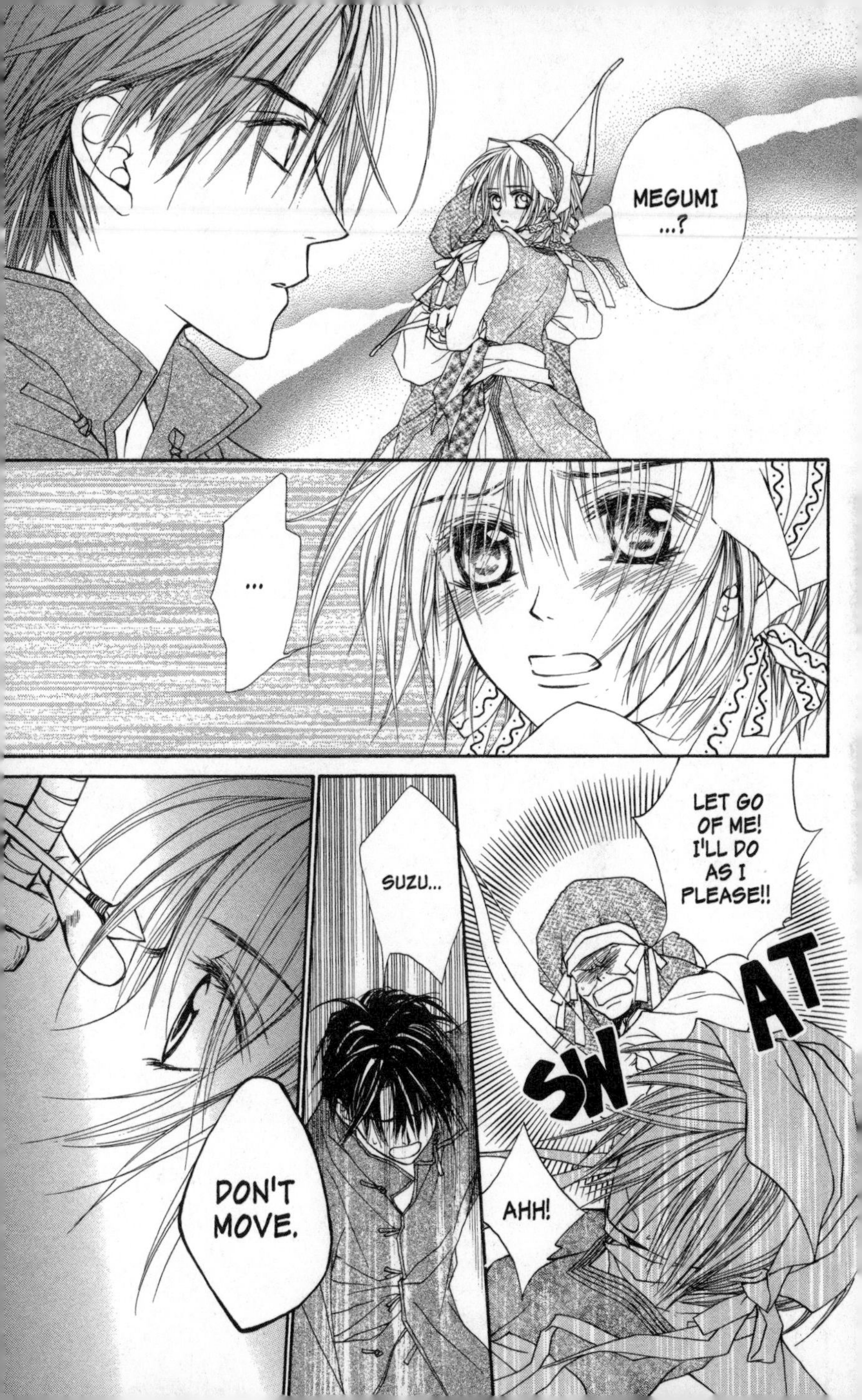
MEGUMI ...?
...
LET GO OF ME! I'LL DO AS I PLEASE!!
SWAT
AHH!
SUZU...
DON'T MOVE.

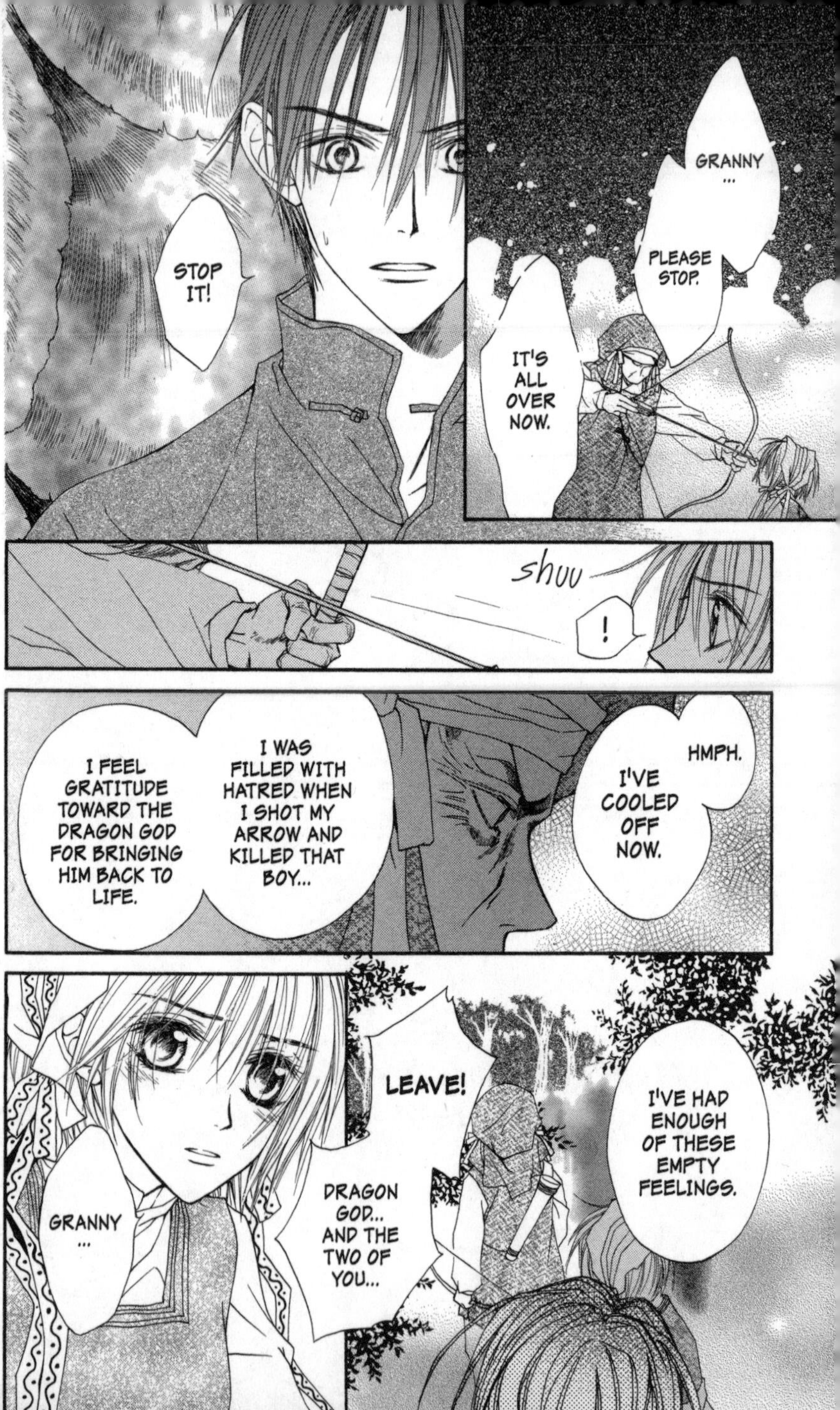
GRANNY ...
PLEASE STOP.
IT'S ALL OVER NOW.
STOP IT!
shuu
!
HMPH.
I'VE COOLED OFF NOW.
I WAS FILLED WITH HATRED WHEN I SHOT MY ARROW AND KILLED THAT BOY...
I FEEL GRATITUDE TOWARD THE DRAGON GOD FOR BRINGING HIM BACK TO LIFE.
I'VE HAD ENOUGH OF THESE EMPTY FEELINGS.
LEAVE!
DRAGON GOD... AND THE TWO OF YOU...
GRANNY ...

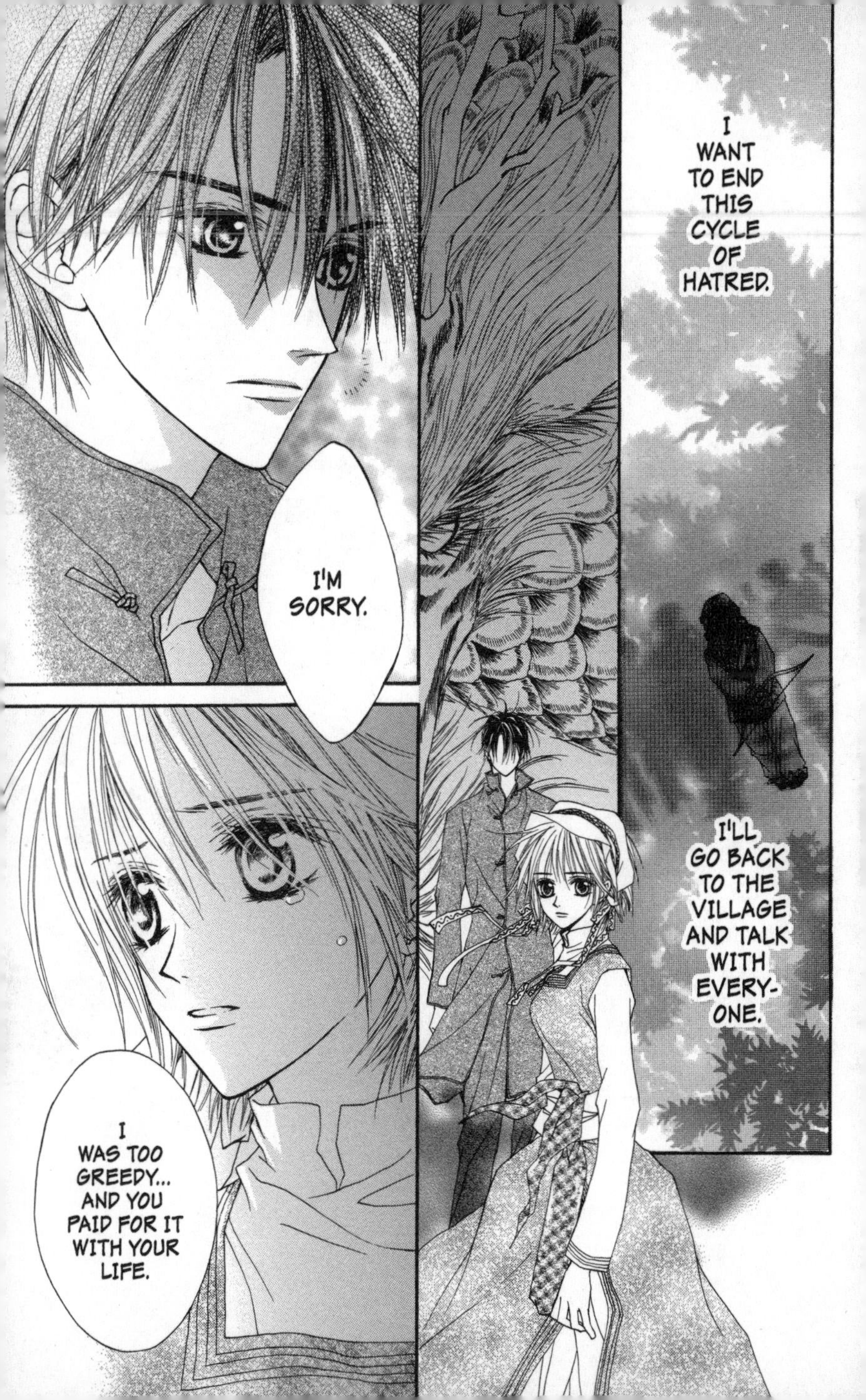
I WANT TO END THIS CYCLE OF HATRED.
I'LL GO BACK TO THE VILLAGE AND TALK WITH EVERY-ONE.
I'M SORRY.
I WAS TOO GREEDY... AND YOU PAID FOR IT WITH YOUR LIFE.

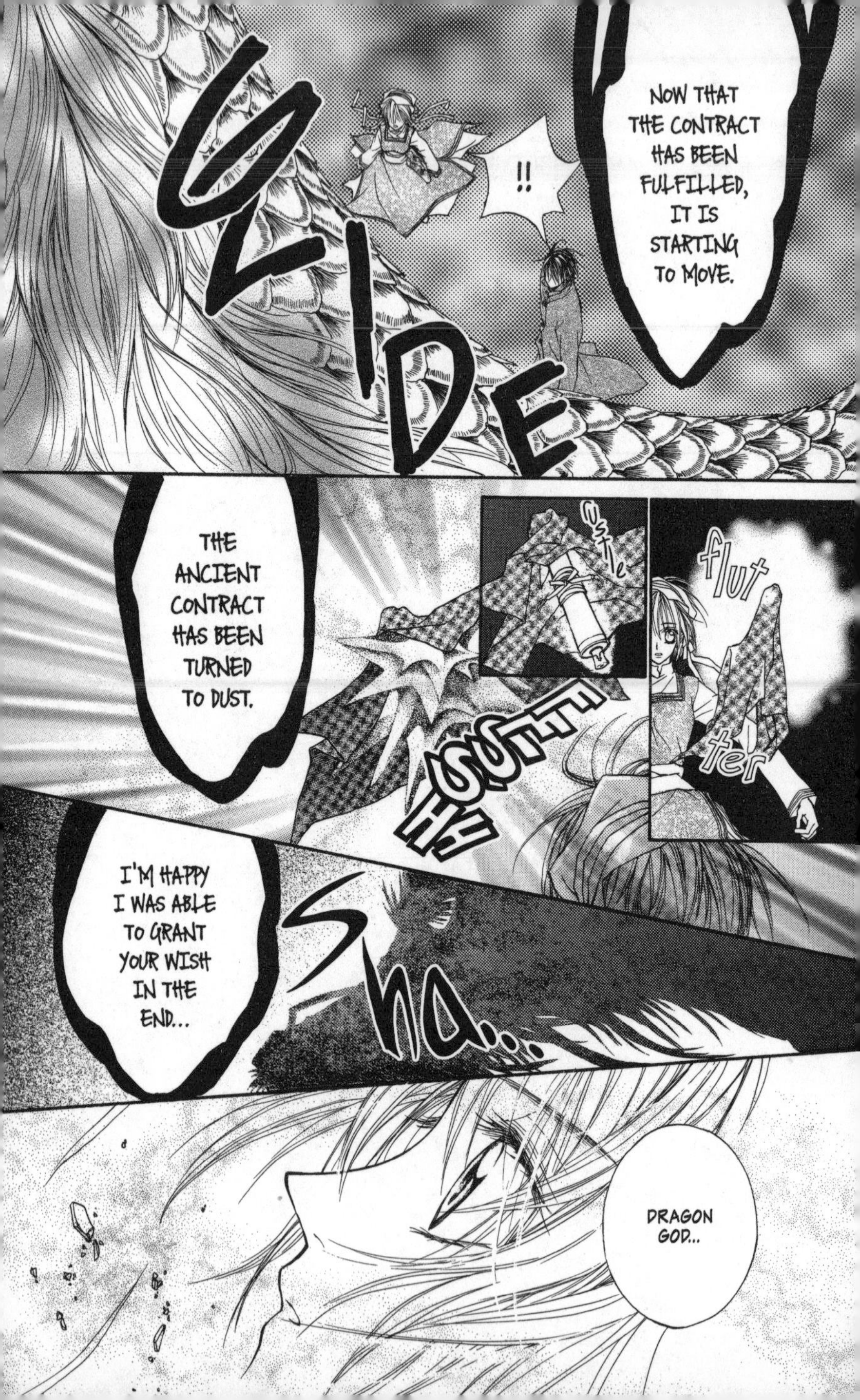
NOW THAT THE CONTRACT HAS BEEN FULFILLED, IT IS STARTING TO MOVE.
!!
SLIDE
flut ter
rustle
THE ANCIENT CONTRACT HAS BEEN TURNED TO DUST.
I'M HAPPY I WAS ABLE TO GRANT YOUR WISH IN THE END...
Sha...
DRAGON GOD...

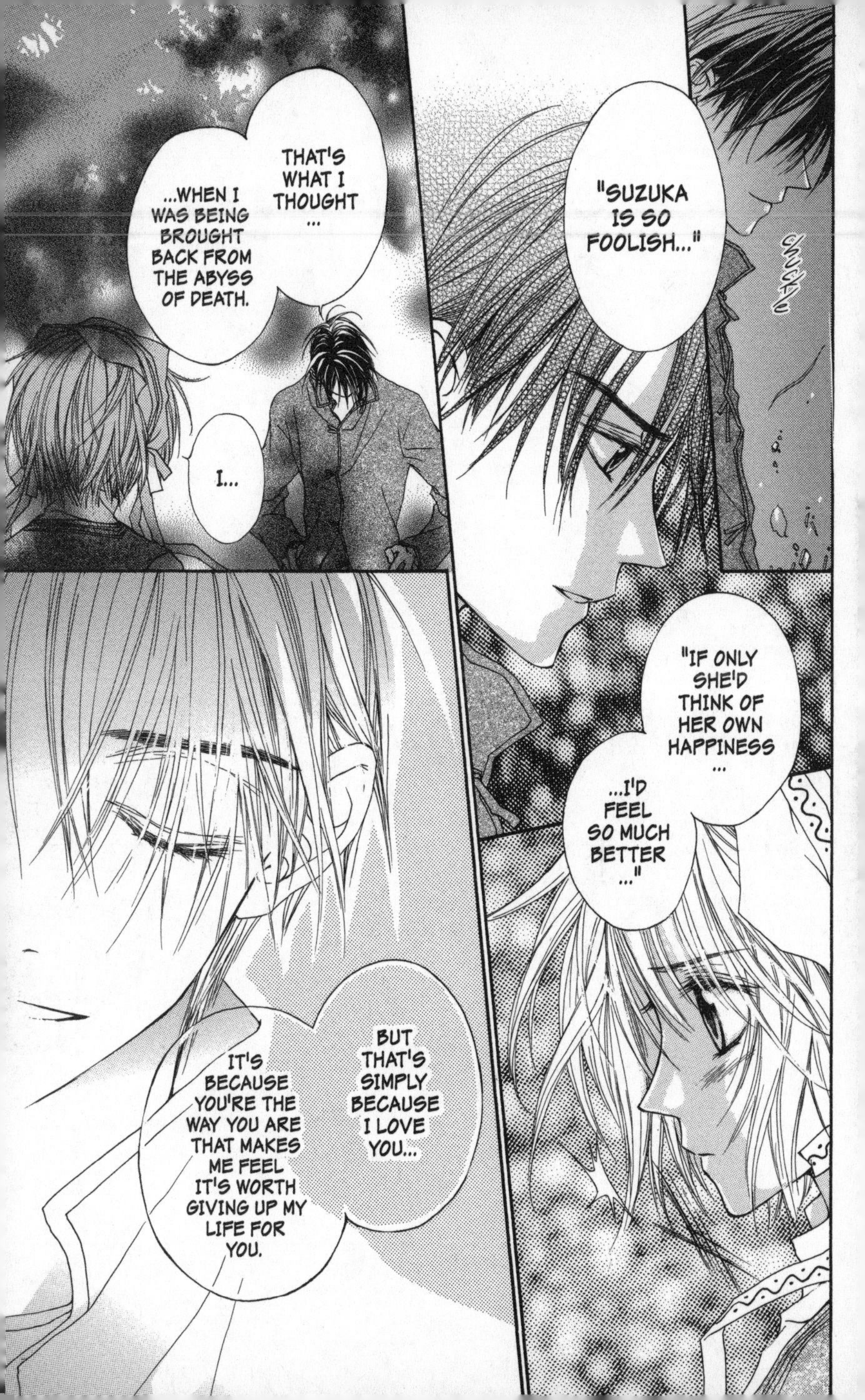
"SUZUKA IS SO FOOLISH..."
CHUCKLE
"IF ONLY SHE'D THINK OF HER OWN HAPPINESS...
...I'D FEEL SO MUCH BETTER..."
THAT'S WHAT I THOUGHT...
...WHEN I WAS BEING BROUGHT BACK FROM THE ABYSS OF DEATH.
I...
BUT THAT'S SIMPLY BECAUSE I LOVE YOU...
IT'S BECAUSE YOU'RE THE WAY YOU ARE THAT MAKES ME FEEL IT'S WORTH GIVING UP MY LIFE FOR YOU.

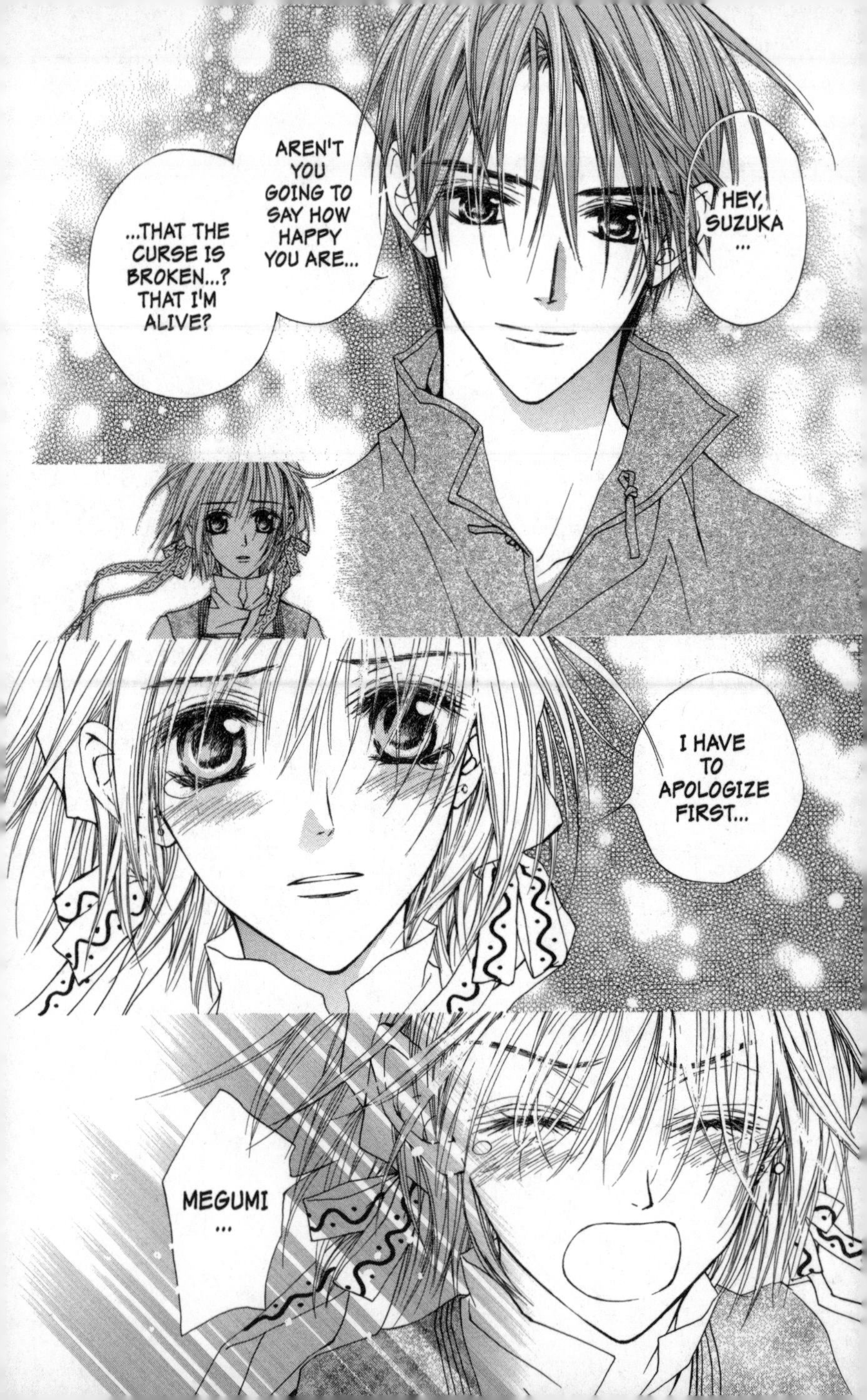
HEY, SUZUKA ...
AREN'T YOU GOING TO SAY HOW HAPPY YOU ARE...
...THAT THE CURSE IS BROKEN...? THAT I'M ALIVE?
I HAVE TO APOLOGIZE FIRST...
MEGUMI ...

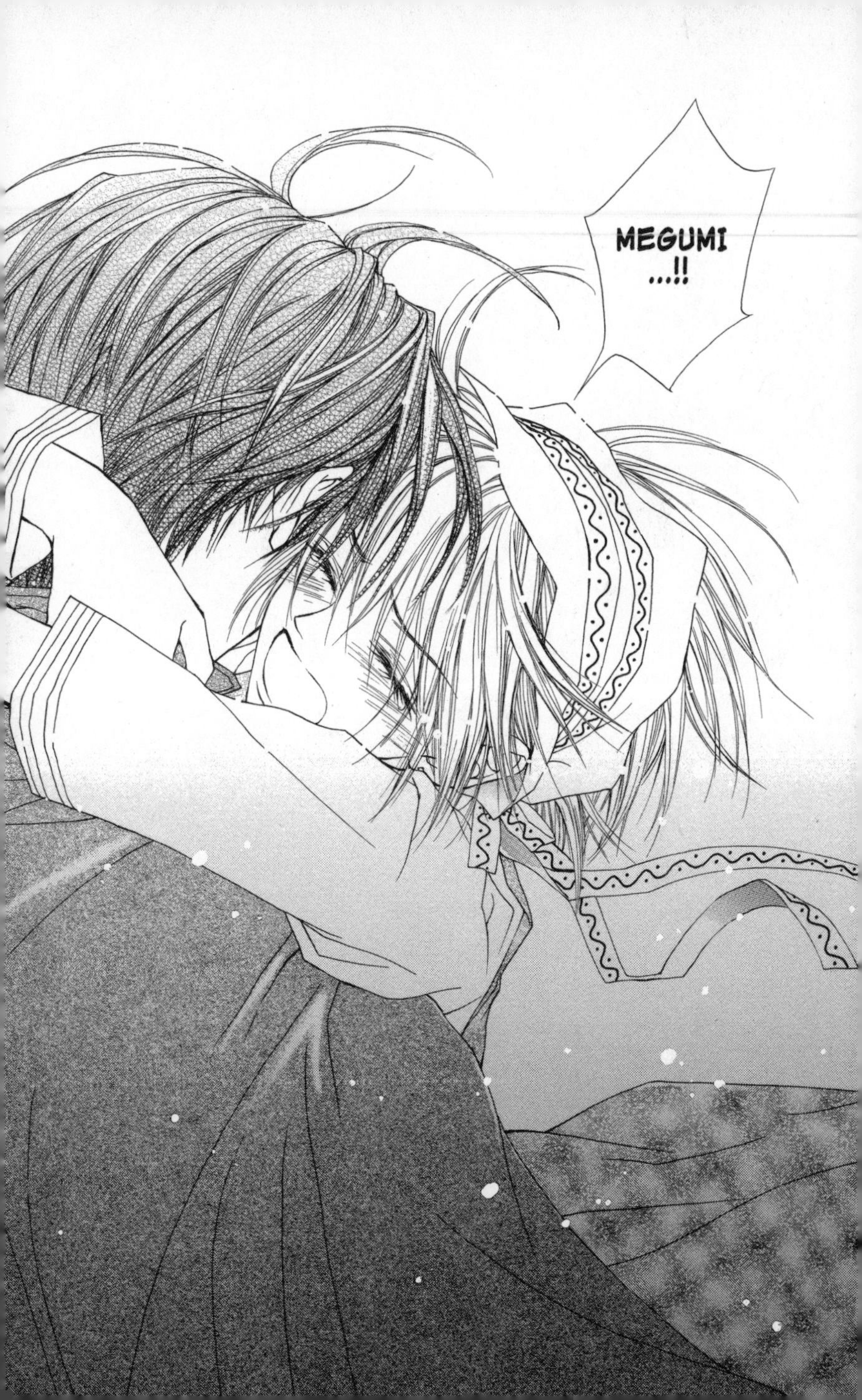
MEGUMI ...!!

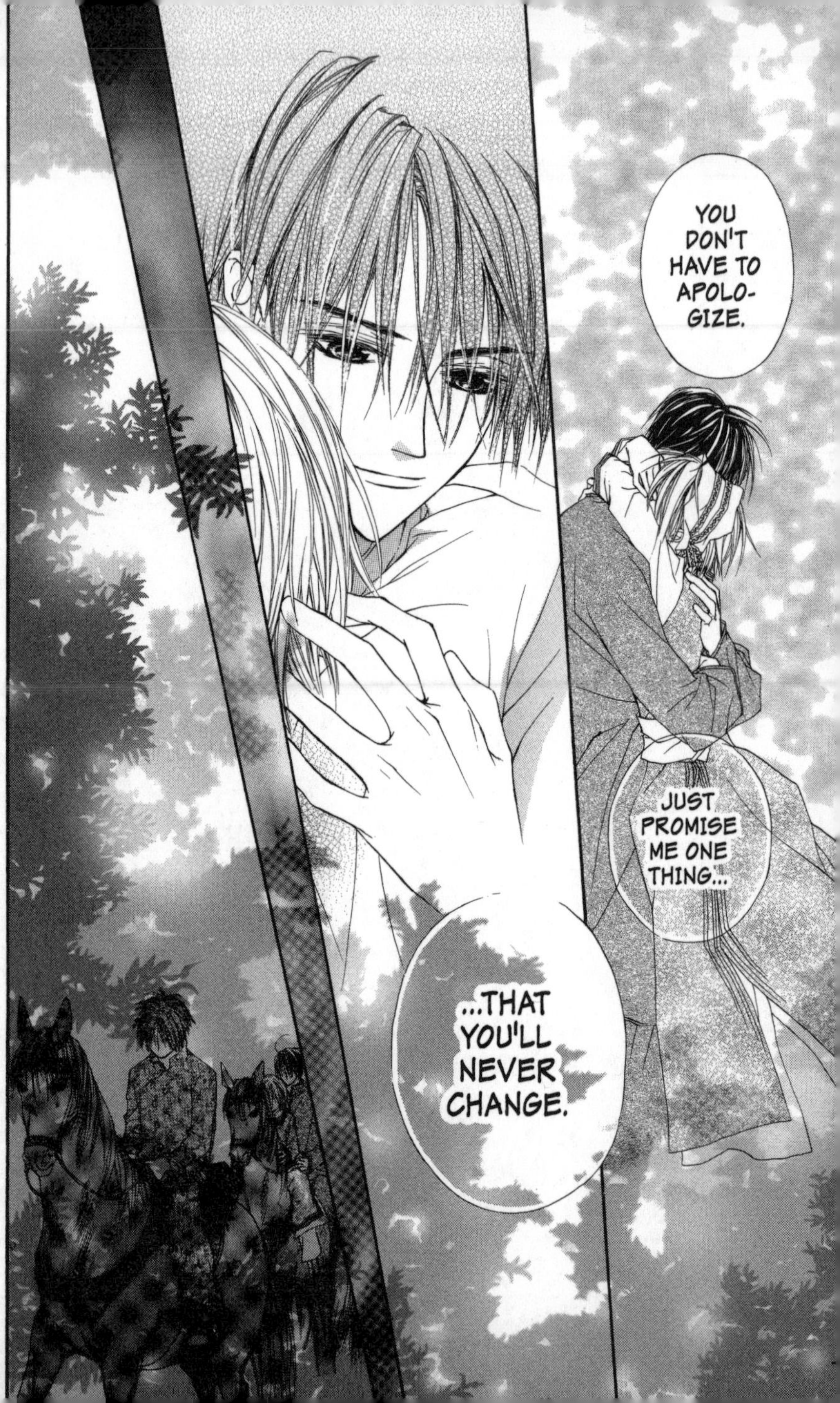
YOU DON'T HAVE TO APOLO-GIZE.
JUST PROMISE ME ONE THING...
...THAT YOU'LL NEVER CHANGE.

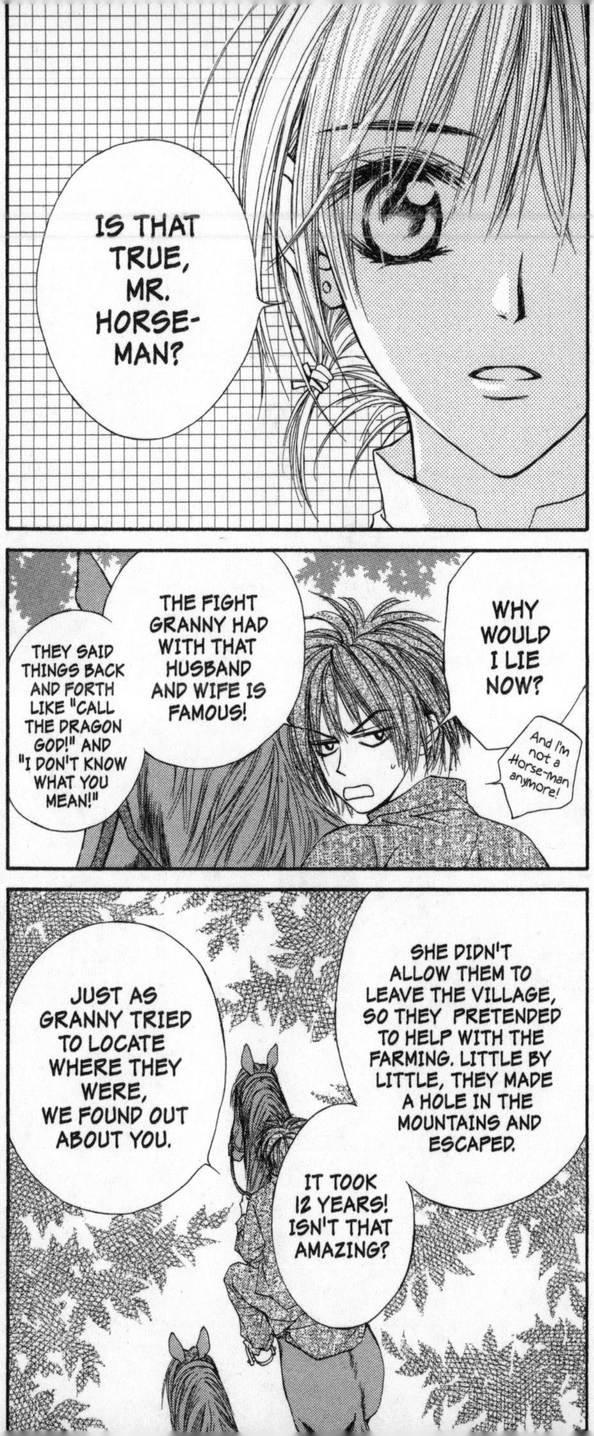
IS THAT TRUE, MR. HORSE-MAN?
WHY WOULD I LIE NOW?
And I'm not a Horse-man anymore!
THE FIGHT GRANNY HAD WITH THAT HUSBAND AND WIFE IS FAMOUS!
THEY SAID THINGS BACK AND FORTH LIKE "CALL THE DRAGON GOD!" AND "I DON'T KNOW WHAT YOU MEAN!"
SHE DIDN'T ALLOW THEM TO LEAVE THE VILLAGE, SO THEY PRETENDED TO HELP WITH THE FARMING. LITTLE BY LITTLE, THEY MADE A HOLE IN THE MOUNTAINS AND ESCAPED.
IT TOOK 12 YEARS! ISN'T THAT AMAZING?
JUST AS GRANNY TRIED TO LOCATE WHERE THEY WERE, WE FOUND OUT ABOUT YOU.

"Ooohh!" Drama CD Backstory, Part 3

I thought Megumi should have a normal voice that sounded like he had a good upbringing, but the rest was a mystery. I looked everywhere when someone suggested Ken Narita-san. He has a great voice and has done numerous roles playing handsome men in the past. But I wondered if he would be okay as Megumi's voice since it changes so much in tone due to the gags. ♡ We had Narita-san say some silly lines, and it worked! I was amazed he could sound like Megumi when he had those idiotic lines! The decision was made!!

Some Random Memories

- The scene with Megumi's looong monologue. It was like Narita-san was communicating with outer space! Maybe he actually made contact somehow.
- Narita-san was trying so hard in his scenes with all the dialog that he got oxygen-deprived. He almost passed out! I'm so sorry!! There were too many lines!
- The way Kawasumi-san said "Ohh!" as Suzuka was so cute. I almost fainted ♡♡ when she did her hair like Suzuka's on this page. ♡
- The lines where Kuroishi would come running. "Watch out, Miss Suzukaaaaa!" (etc.). The audio guy never knew when he was going to stop yelling! "Did I overdo it?" (Haha!)
- The way Narita-kun did Megumi's "changes" were hilarious! Tanaka-san said that as well, and I thought Tanaka-san's transitions were funny too!! (Laughs)
- I heard Takayama-san loves Kuroishi-san. So do I.
- Everyone except Narita-san is blood type B! Hahaha...

I was so happy with the voice actors' efforts. It turned out perfectly! ♡ Thanks so much!!

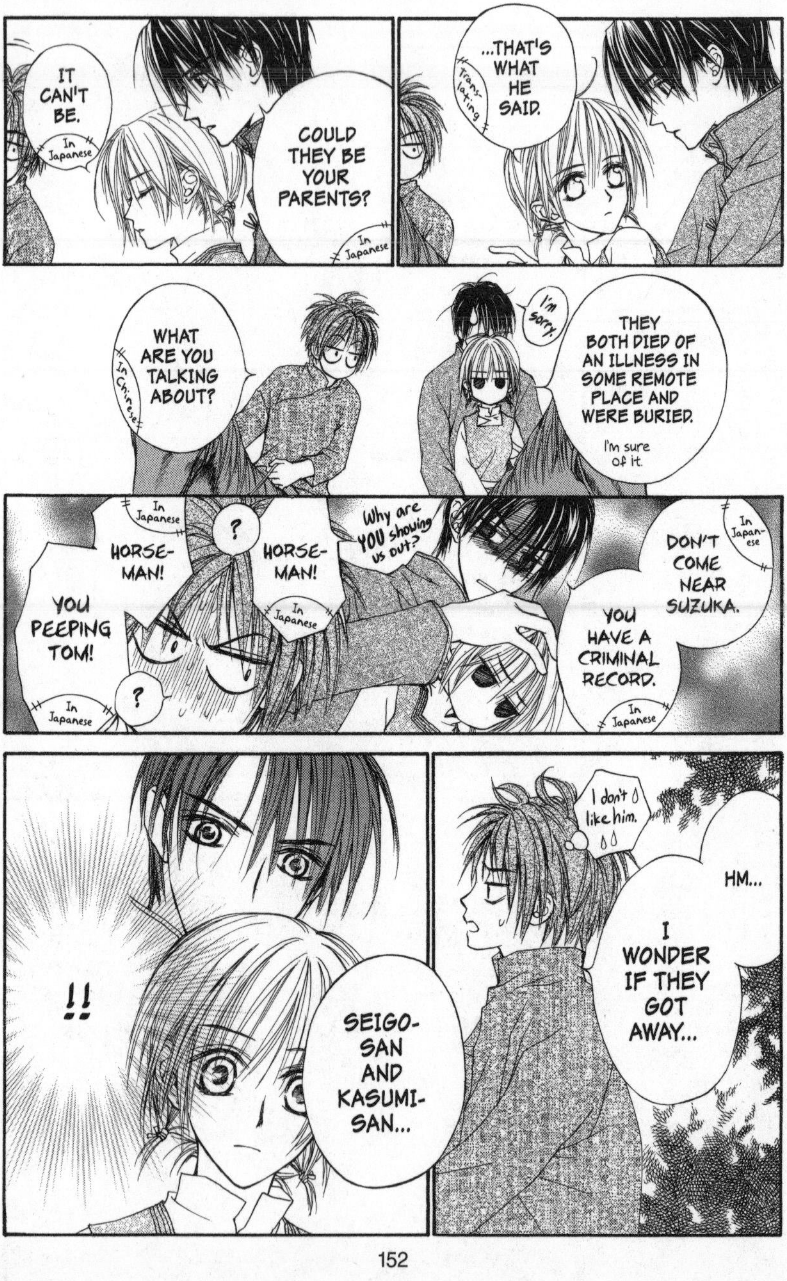
...THAT'S WHAT HE SAID.
Trans-lating
COULD THEY BE YOUR PARENTS?
In Japanese
IT CAN'T BE.
In Japanese
THEY BOTH DIED OF AN ILLNESS IN SOME REMOTE PLACE AND WERE BURIED.
I'm sure of it.
I'm sorry.
WHAT ARE YOU TALKING ABOUT?
In Chinese
In Japan-ese
DON'T COME NEAR SUZUKA.
YOU HAVE A CRIMINAL RECORD.
In Japanese
Why are YOU showing us out?
HORSE-MAN!
In Japanese
?
HORSE-MAN!
In Japanese
YOU PEEPING TOM!
?
In Japanese
I don't like him.
HM...
I WONDER IF THEY GOT AWAY...
SEIGO-SAN AND KASUMI-SAN...
!!

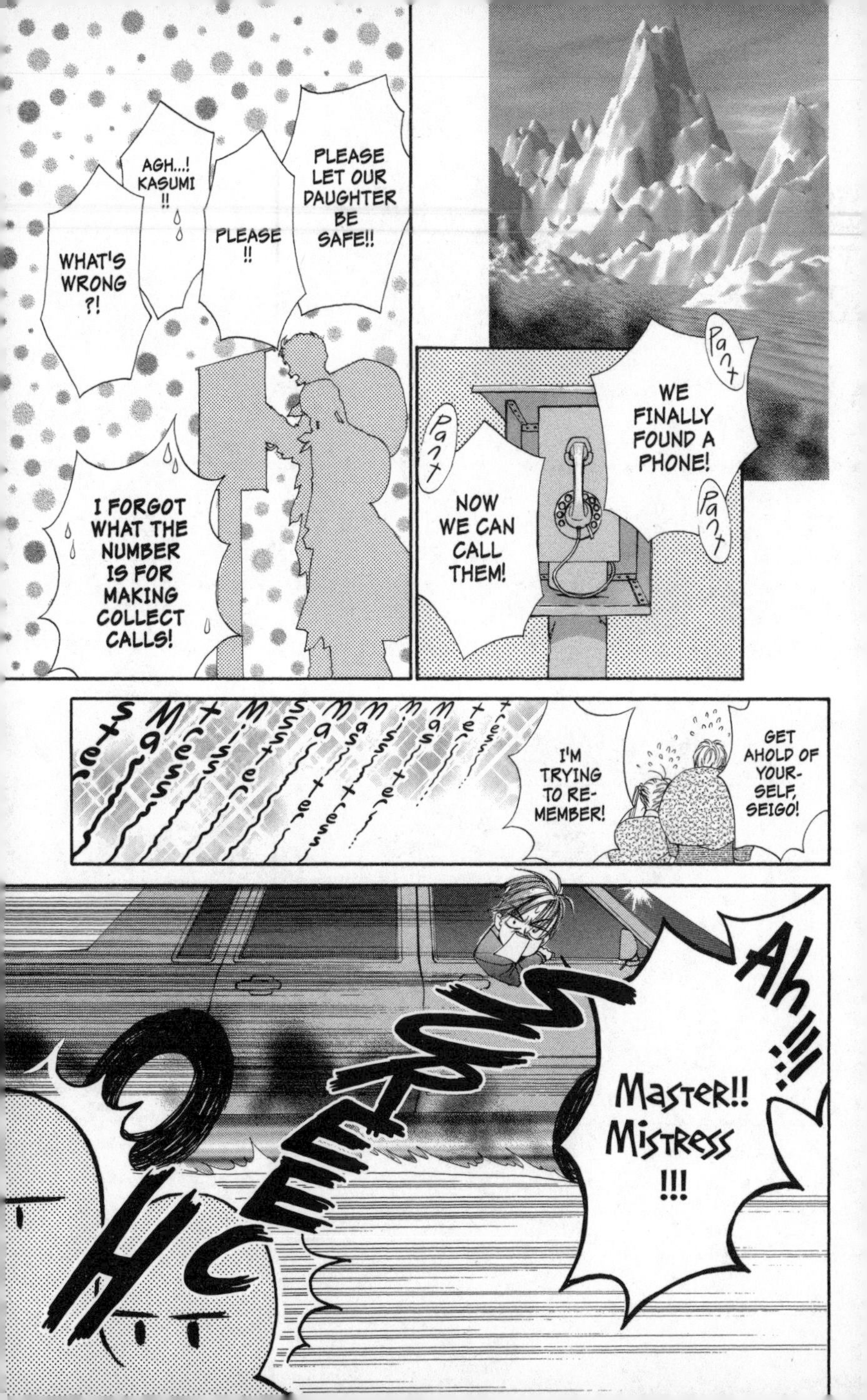
Pant
WE FINALLY FOUND A PHONE!
Pant
Pant
NOW WE CAN CALL THEM!
PLEASE LET OUR DAUGHTER BE SAFE!!
PLEASE !!
AGH...! KASUMI !!
WHAT'S WRONG ?!
I FORGOT WHAT THE NUMBER IS FOR MAKING COLLECT CALLS!
GET AHOLD OF YOUR-SELF, SEIGO!
I'M TRYING TO RE-MEMBER!
Ah!!!!
Master!! Mistress !!!

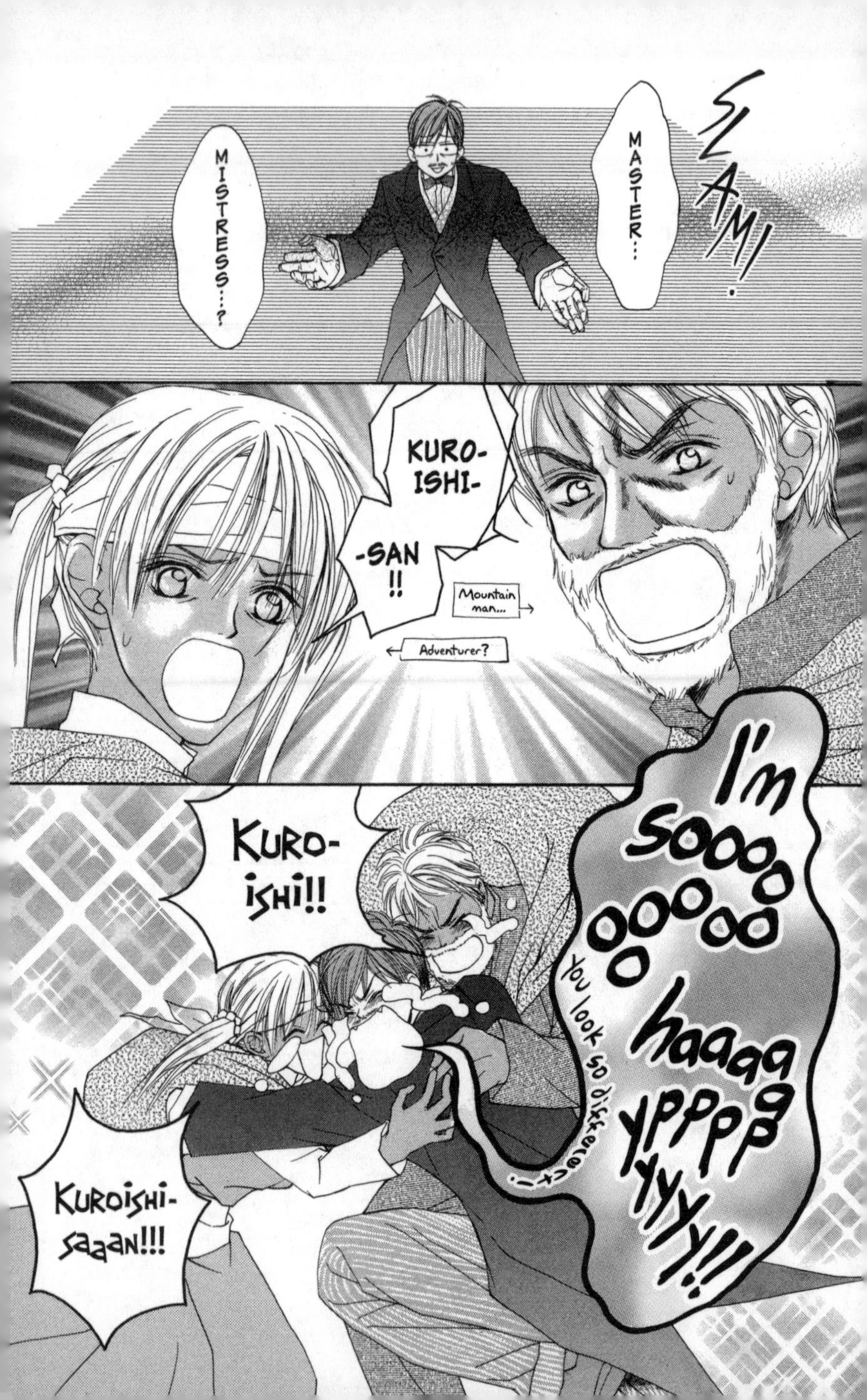
SLAM!
MASTER...
MISTRESS...?
KURO-ISHI-
-SAN!!
Mountain man...
Adventurer?
I'm soooooooooooo haaaaapppppyyyy!!
You look so differeeent--!
KURO-ishi!!
Kuroishi-saaan!!!

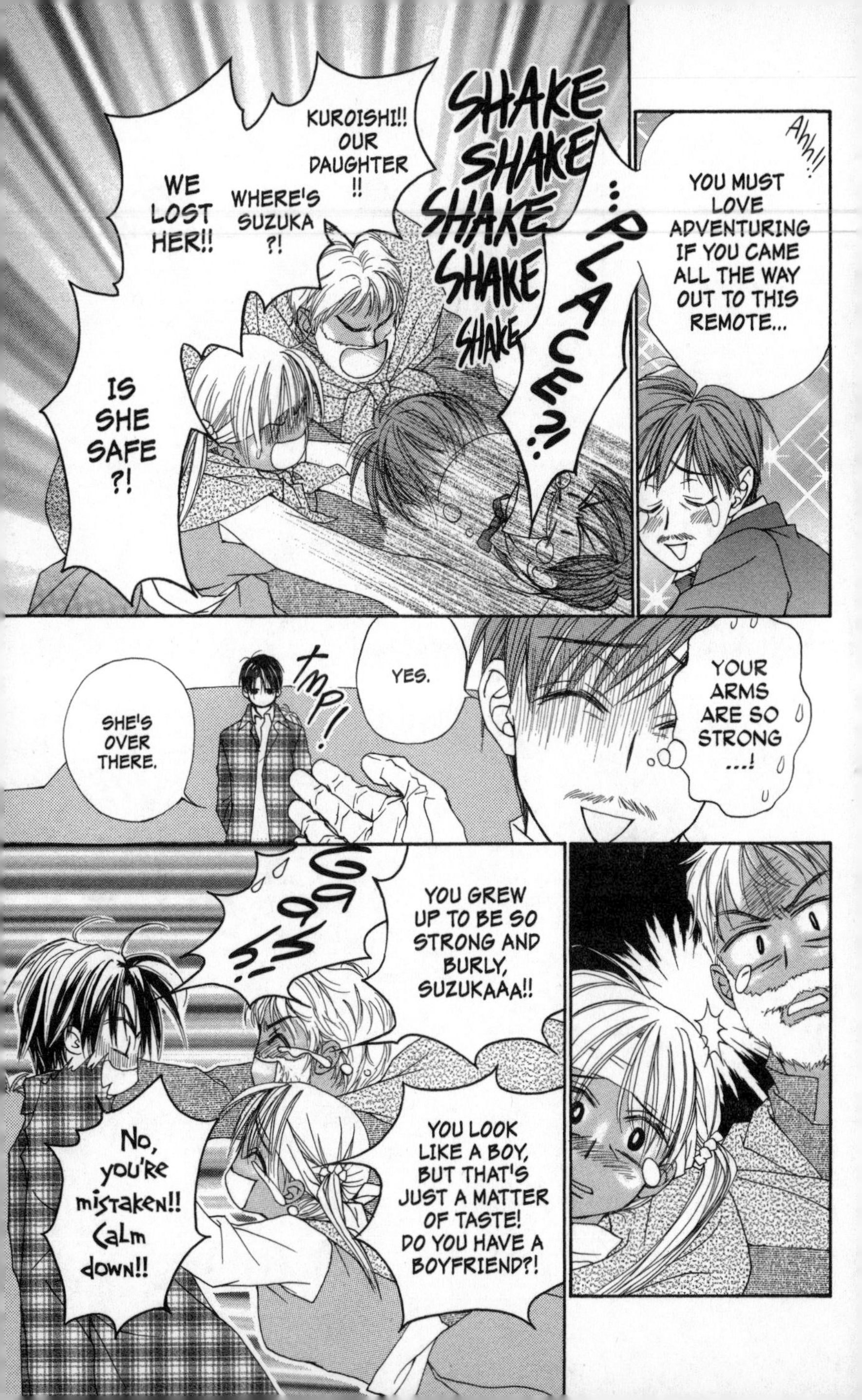

Ahh!!
YOU MUST LOVE ADVENTURING IF YOU CAME ALL THE WAY OUT TO THIS REMOTE...
...PLACE?!
SHAKE SHAKE SHAKE SHAKE SHAKE
KUROISHI!! OUR DAUGHTER!!
WHERE'S SUZUKA?!
WE LOST HER!!
IS SHE SAFE?!
YOUR ARMS ARE SO STRONG...!
YES.
tmp!
SHE'S OVER THERE.
YOU GREW UP TO BE SO STRONG AND BURLY, SUZUKAAA!!
YOU LOOK LIKE A BOY, BUT THAT'S JUST A MATTER OF TASTE! DO YOU HAVE A BOYFRIEND?!
No, you're mistaken!! Calm down!!

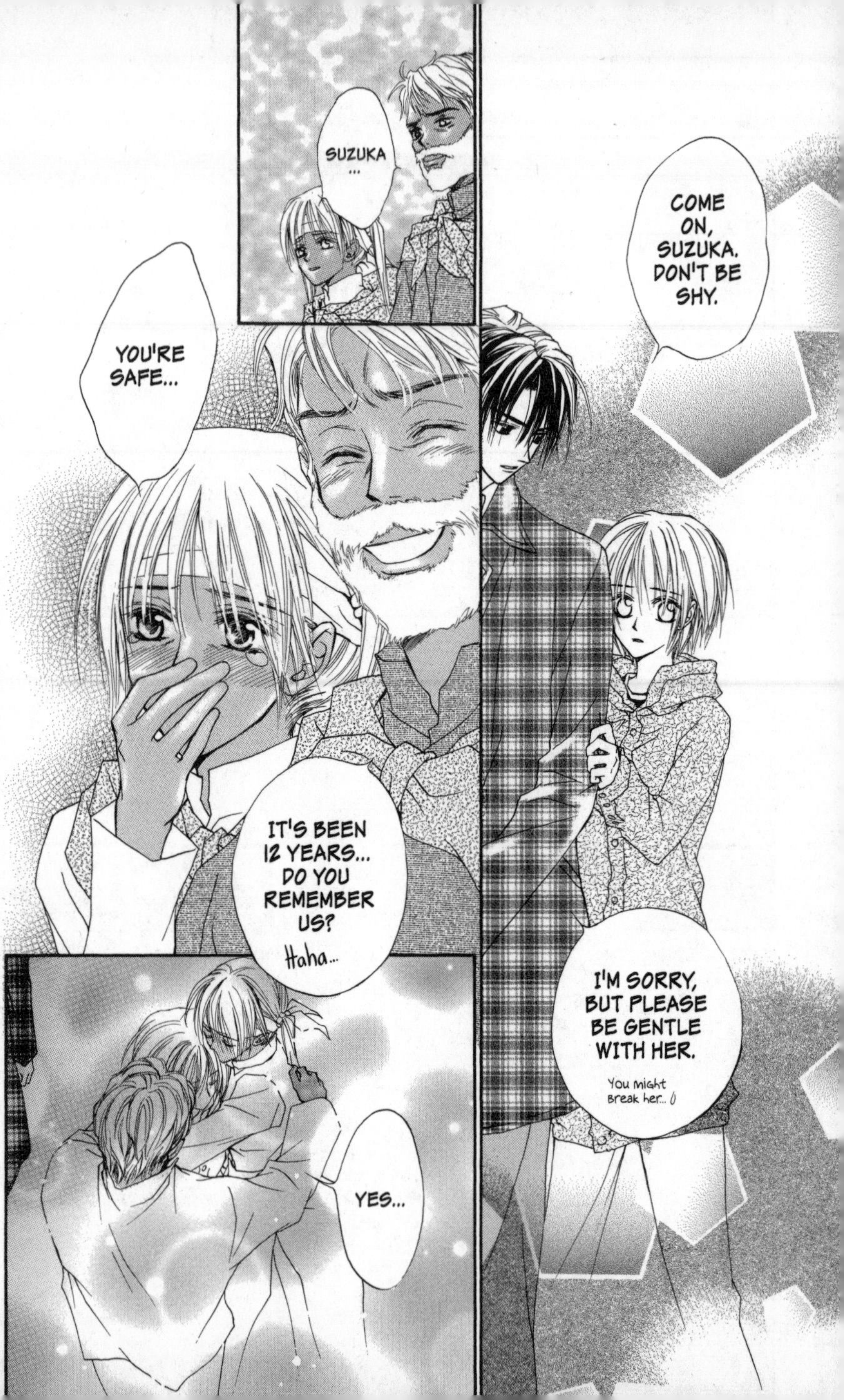
COME ON, SUZUKA. DON'T BE SHY.
I'M SORRY, BUT PLEASE BE GENTLE WITH HER.
You might break her...
SUZUKA ...
YOU'RE SAFE...
IT'S BEEN 12 YEARS... DO YOU REMEMBER US?
Haha...
YES...

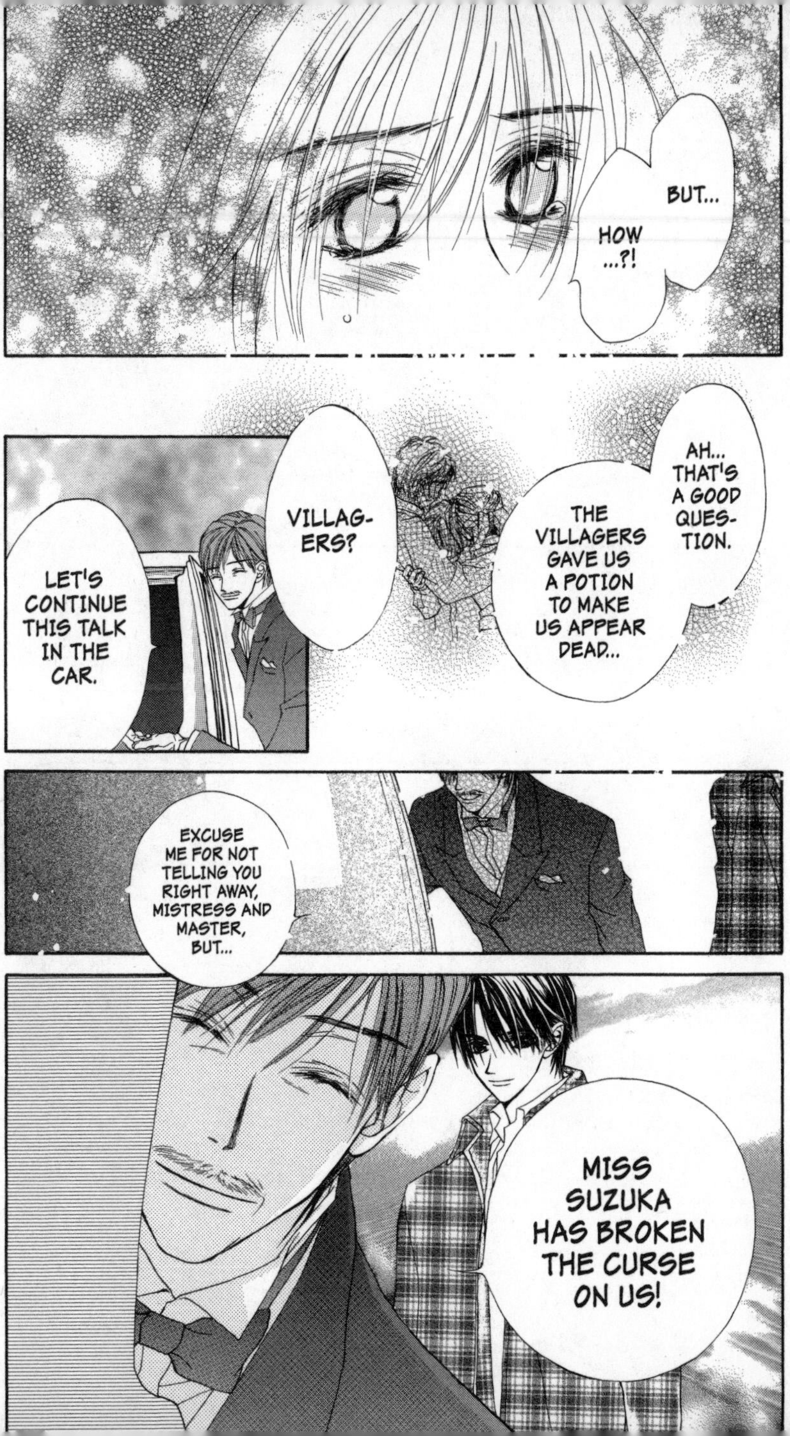
BUT...
HOW ...?!
AH... THAT'S A GOOD QUES-TION.
THE VILLAGERS GAVE US A POTION TO MAKE US APPEAR DEAD...
VILLAG-ERS?
LET'S CONTINUE THIS TALK IN THE CAR.
EXCUSE ME FOR NOT TELLING YOU RIGHT AWAY, MISTRESS AND MASTER, BUT...
MISS SUZUKA HAS BROKEN THE CURSE ON US!

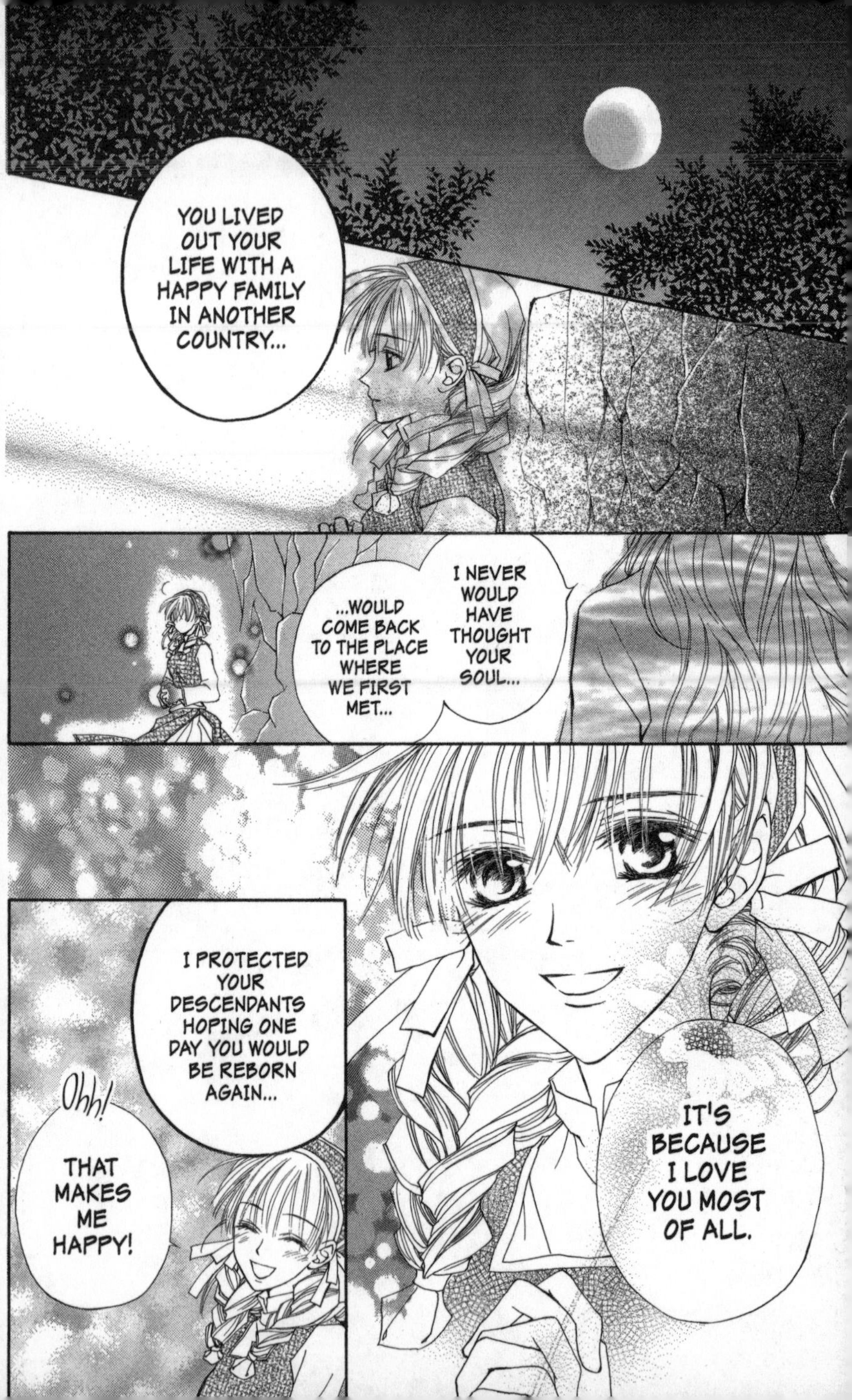
YOU LIVED OUT YOUR LIFE WITH A HAPPY FAMILY IN ANOTHER COUNTRY...
I NEVER WOULD HAVE THOUGHT YOUR SOUL...
...WOULD COME BACK TO THE PLACE WHERE WE FIRST MET...
I PROTECTED YOUR DESCENDANTS HOPING ONE DAY YOU WOULD BE REBORN AGAIN...
IT'S BECAUSE I LOVE YOU MOST OF ALL.
Ohh!
THAT MAKES ME HAPPY!

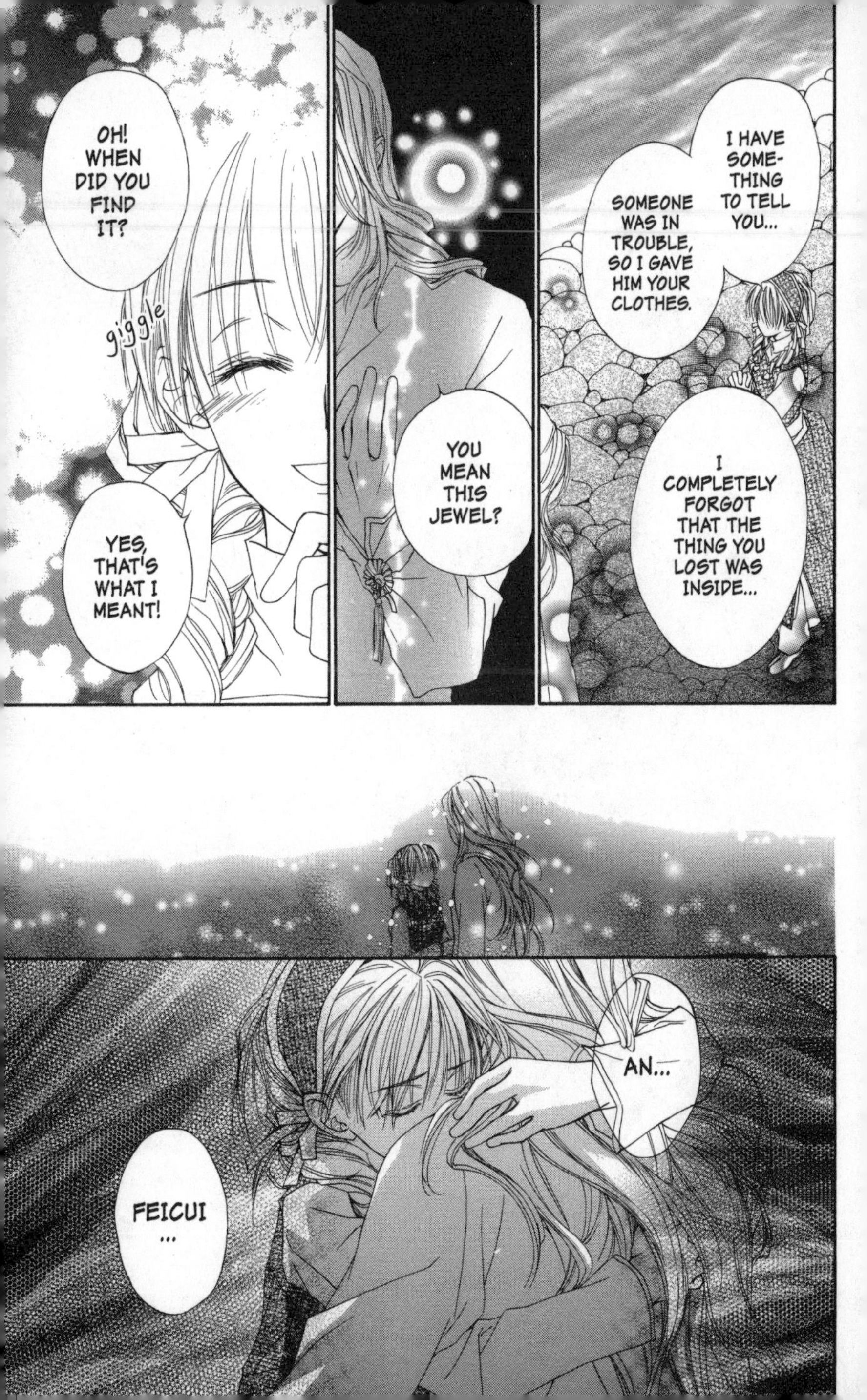
I HAVE SOMETHING TO TELL YOU...
SOMEONE WAS IN TROUBLE, SO I GAVE HIM YOUR CLOTHES.
I COMPLETELY FORGOT THAT THE THING YOU LOST WAS INSIDE...
YOU MEAN THIS JEWEL?
OH! WHEN DID YOU FIND IT?
giggle
YES, THAT'S WHAT I MEANT!
AN...
FEICUI...

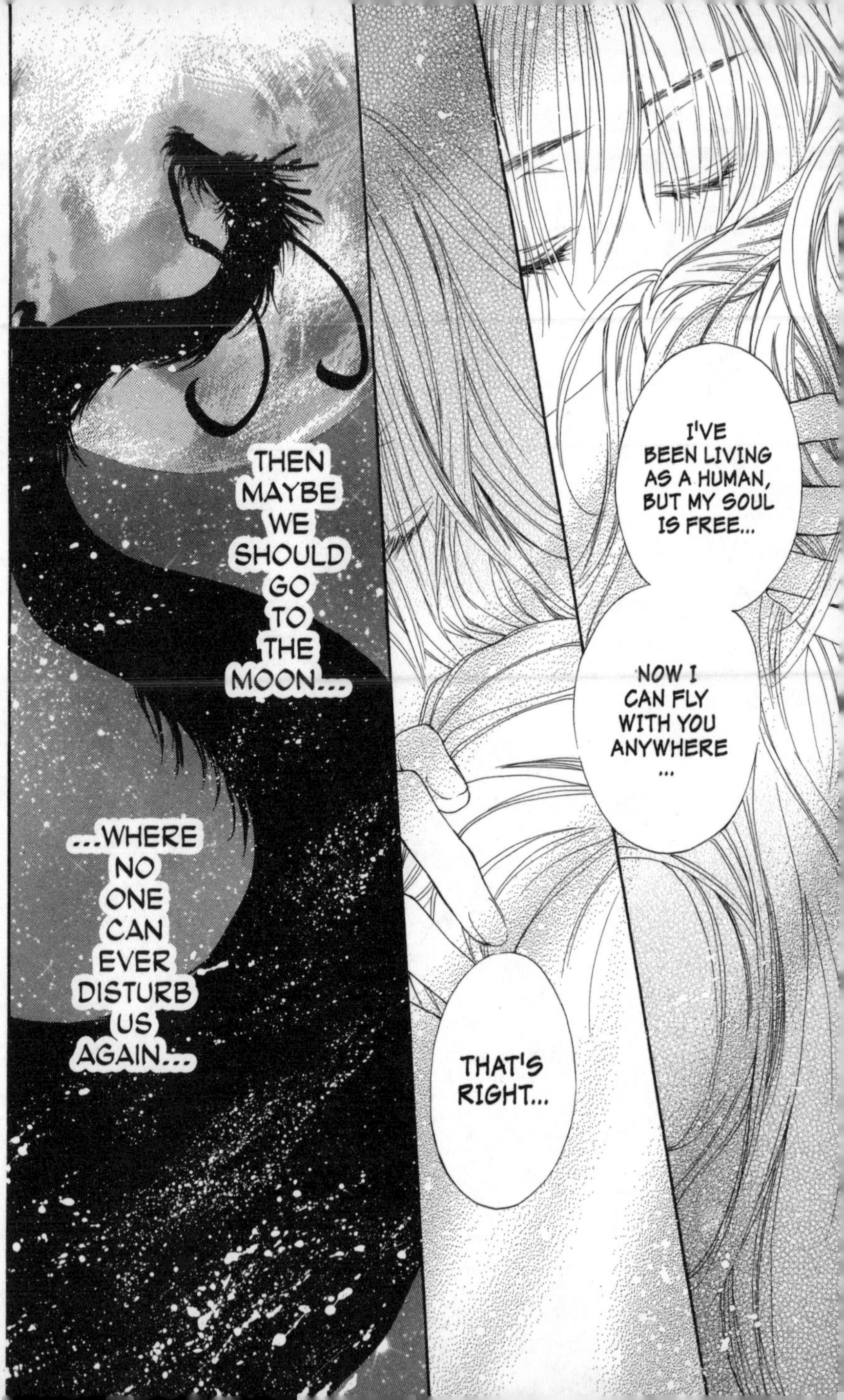
I'VE BEEN LIVING AS A HUMAN, BUT MY SOUL IS FREE...
NOW I CAN FLY WITH YOU ANYWHERE ...
THAT'S RIGHT...
THEN MAYBE WE SHOULD GO TO THE MOON...
...WHERE NO ONE CAN EVER DISTURB US AGAIN...

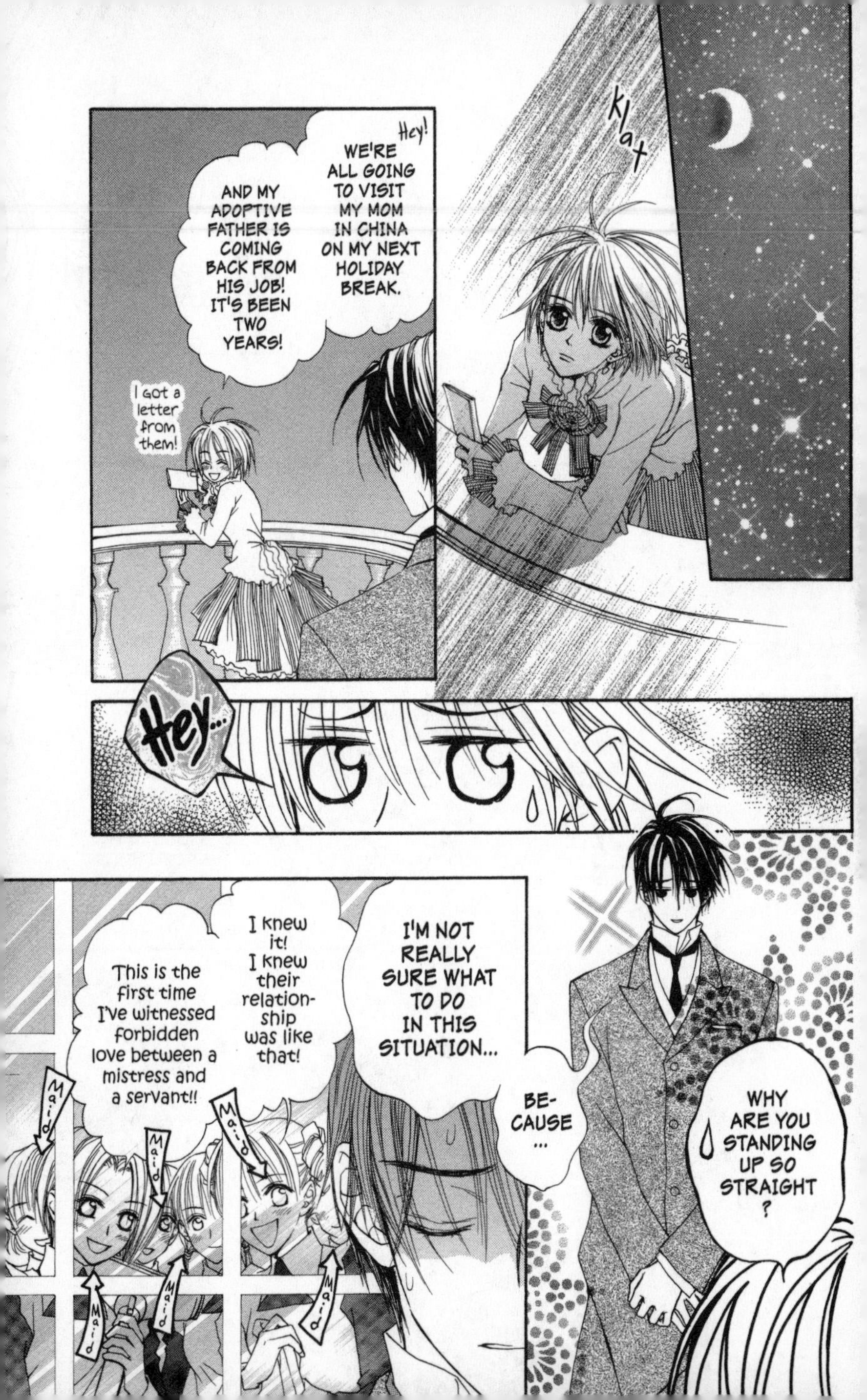
Klat
Hey!
WE'RE ALL GOING TO VISIT MY MOM IN CHINA ON MY NEXT HOLIDAY BREAK.
AND MY ADOPTIVE FATHER IS COMING BACK FROM HIS JOB! IT'S BEEN TWO YEARS!
I got a letter from them!
Hey...
WHY ARE YOU STANDING UP SO STRAIGHT?
BE-CAUSE...
I'M NOT REALLY SURE WHAT TO DO IN THIS SITUATION...
I knew it! I knew their relation-ship was like that!
This is the first time I've witnessed forbidden love between a mistress and a servant!!
Maid
Maid
Maid
Maid
Maid
Maid

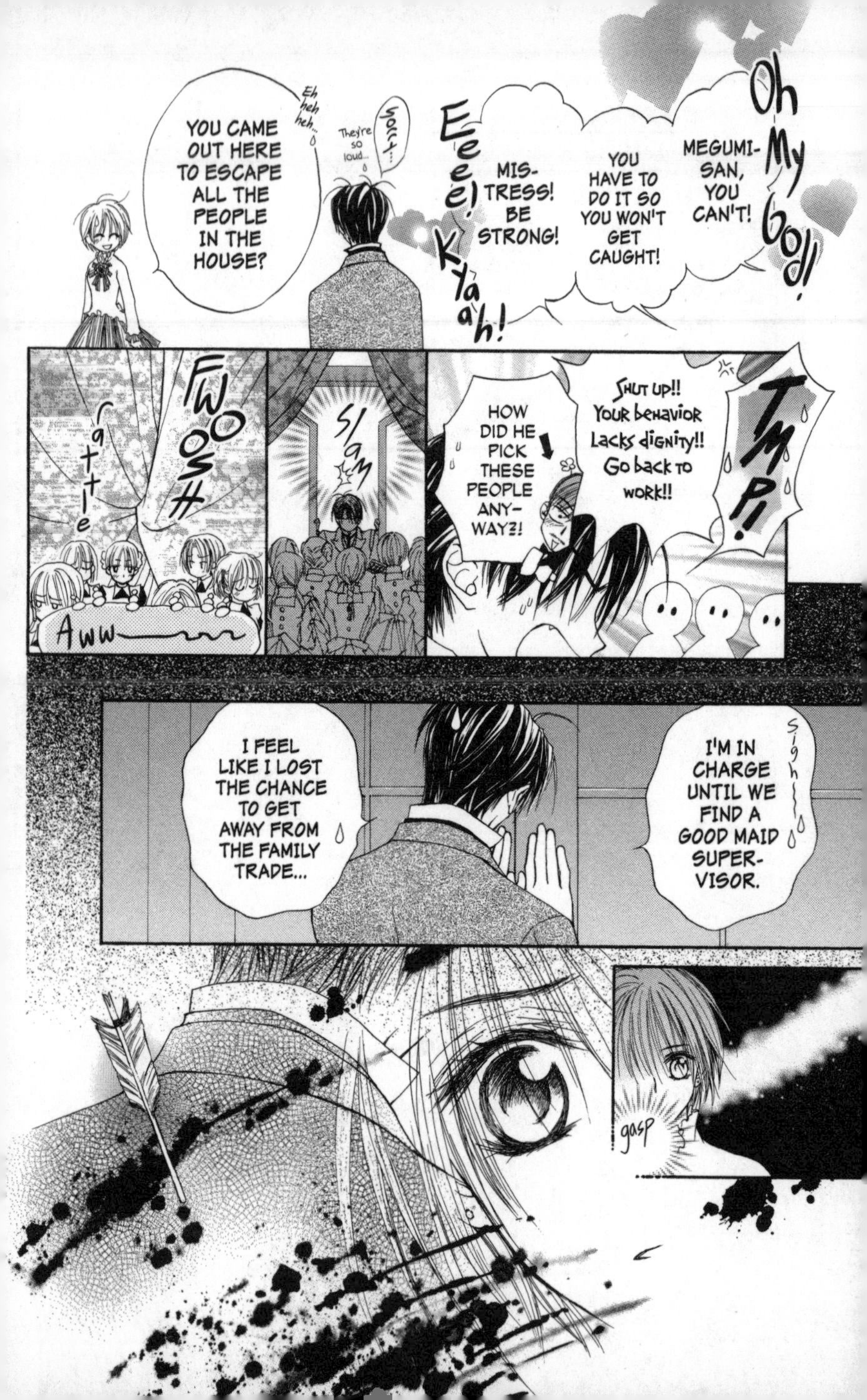
Oh My God!!
MEGUMI-SAN, YOU CAN'T!
YOU HAVE TO DO IT SO YOU WON'T GET CAUGHT!
MISTRESS! BE STRONG!
Eeee! Kyaaah!
They're so loud...
Eh heh heh...
YOU CAME OUT HERE TO ESCAPE ALL THE PEOPLE IN THE HOUSE?
TMP!
SHUT UP!! YOUR BEHAVIOR LACKS DIGNITY!! GO BACK TO WORK!!
HOW DID HE PICK THESE PEOPLE ANYWAY?!
SLAM
FWOOSH
rattle
Aww—
Sigh
I'M IN CHARGE UNTIL WE FIND A GOOD MAID SUPERVISOR.
I FEEL LIKE I LOST THE CHANCE TO GET AWAY FROM THE FAMILY TRADE...
gasp

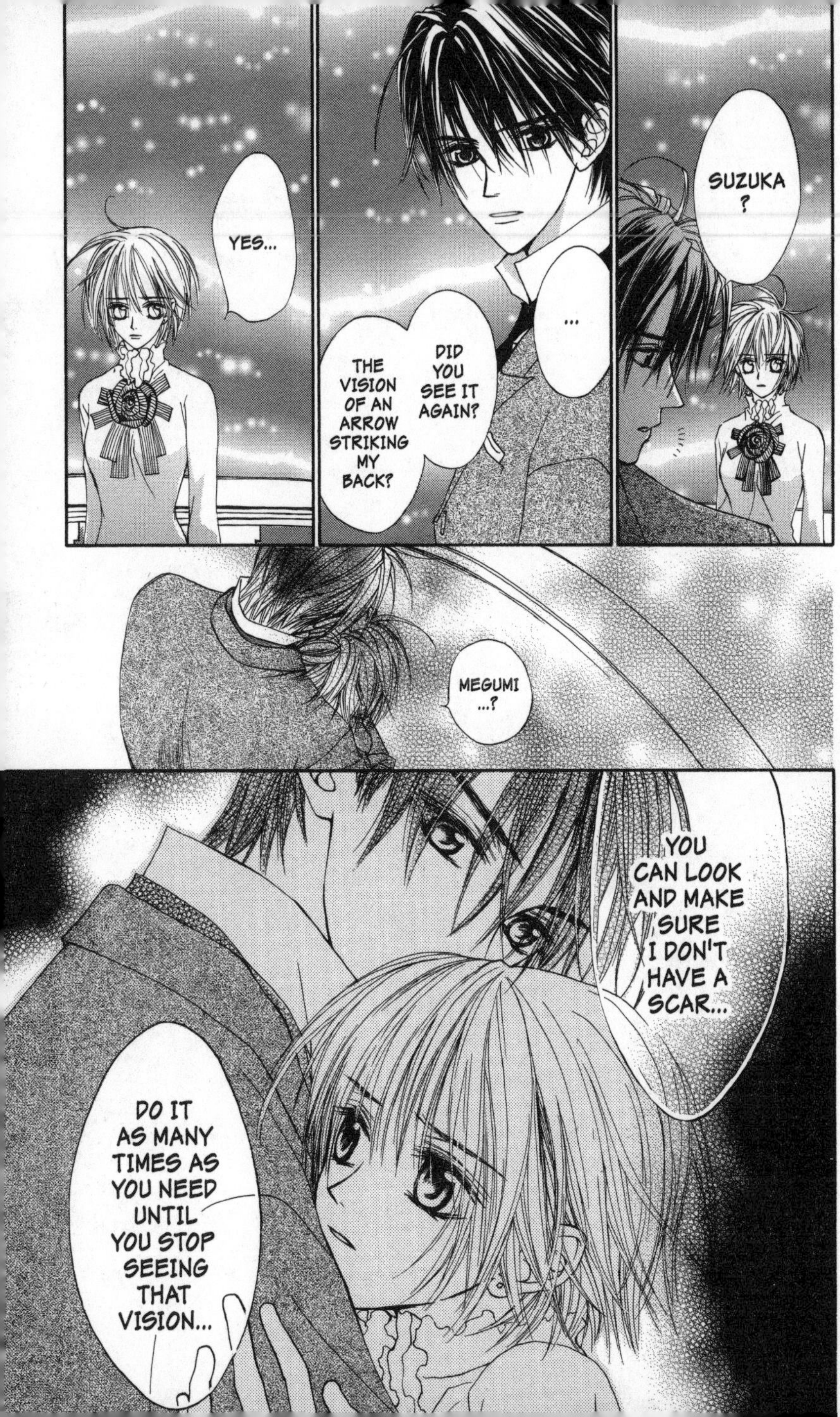
SUZUKA ?
...
DID YOU SEE IT AGAIN?
THE VISION OF AN ARROW STRIKING MY BACK?
YES...
MEGUMI ...?
YOU CAN LOOK AND MAKE SURE I DON'T HAVE A SCAR...
DO IT AS MANY TIMES AS YOU NEED UNTIL YOU STOP SEEING THAT VISION...

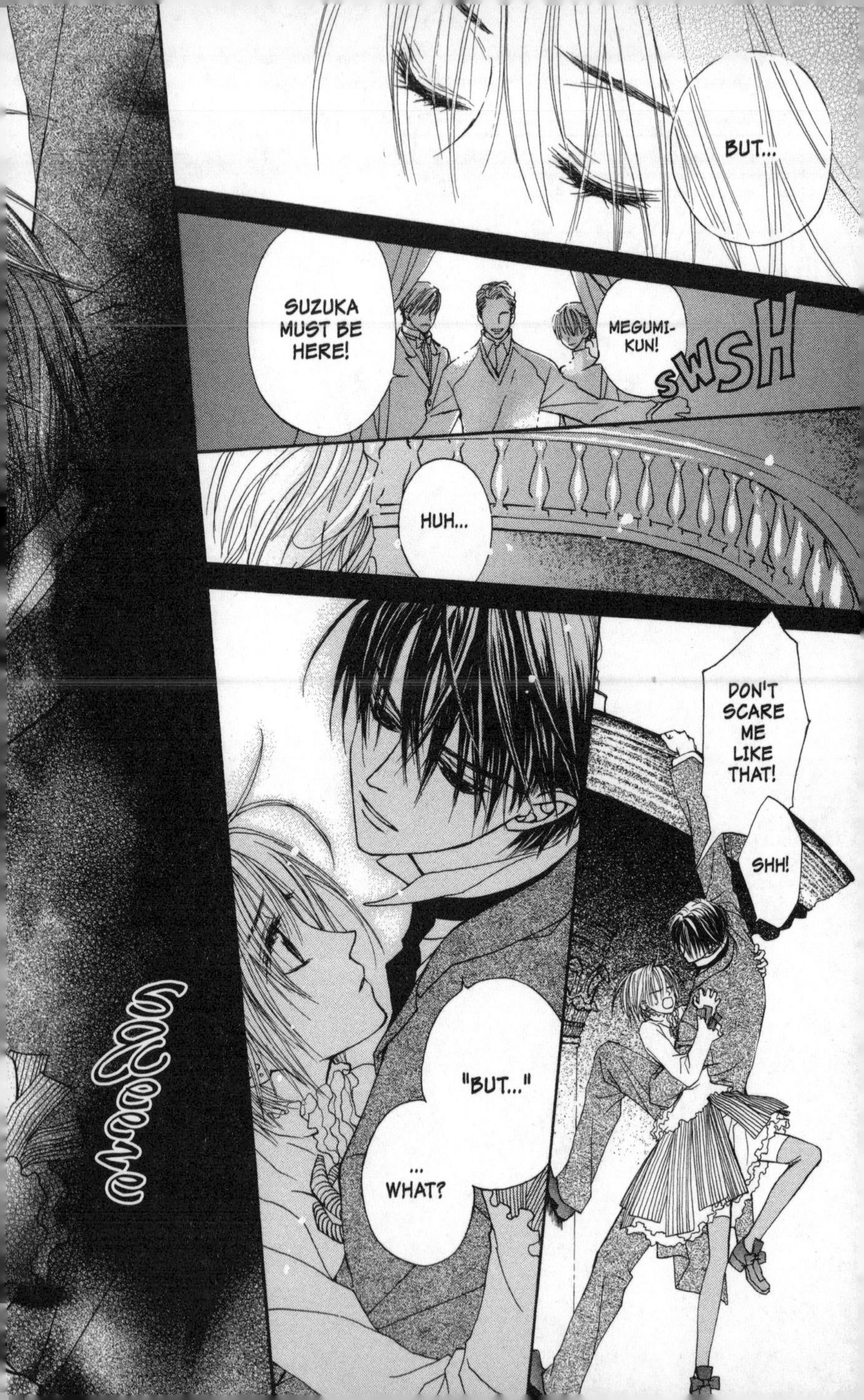
BUT...
SWSH
MEGUMI-KUN!
SUZUKA MUST BE HERE!
HUH...
DON'T SCARE ME LIKE THAT!
SHH!
"BUT..."
... WHAT?

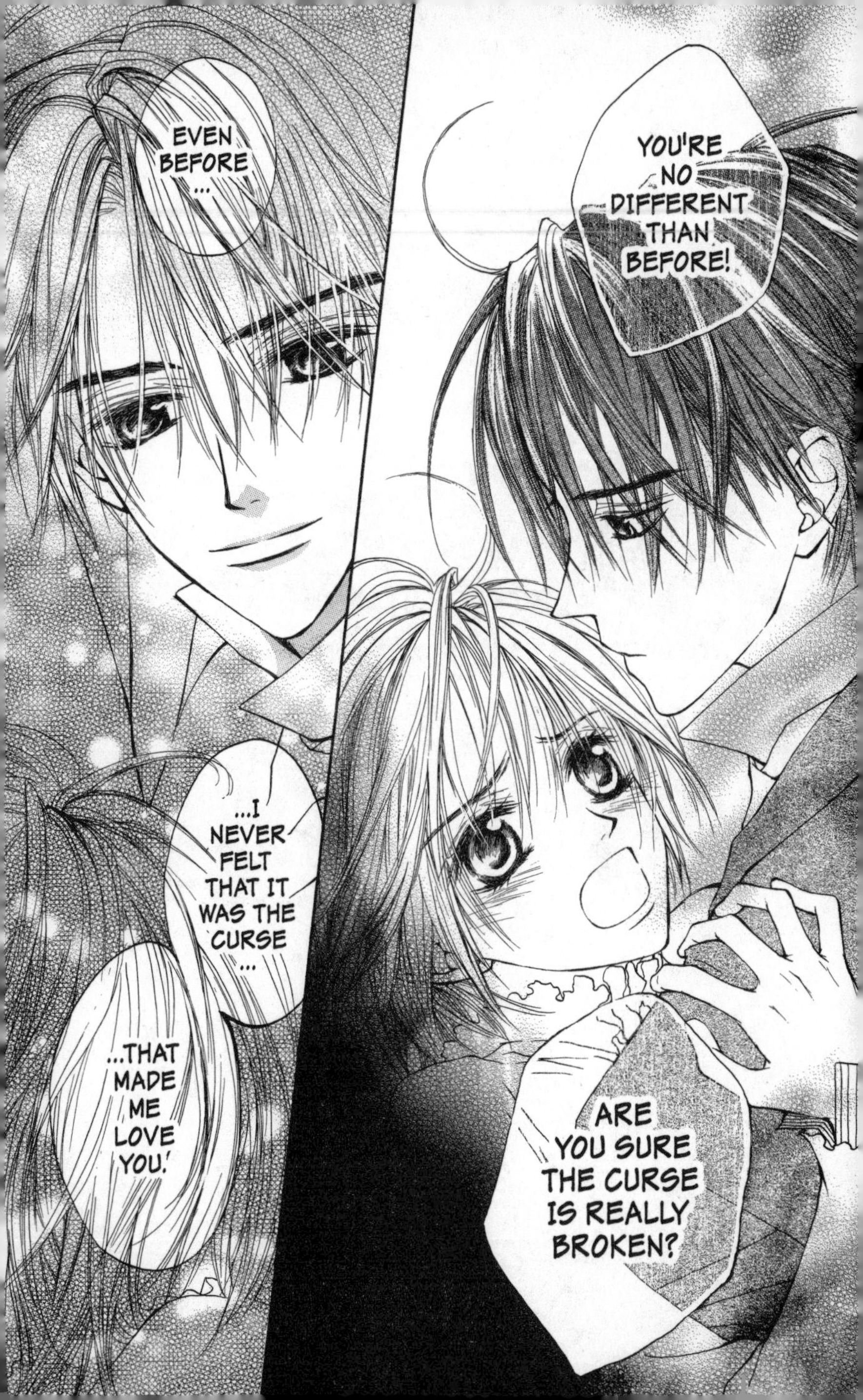
YOU'RE NO DIFFERENT THAN BEFORE!
ARE YOU SURE THE CURSE IS REALLY BROKEN?
EVEN BEFORE...
...I NEVER FELT THAT IT WAS THE CURSE...
...THAT MADE ME LOVE YOU.

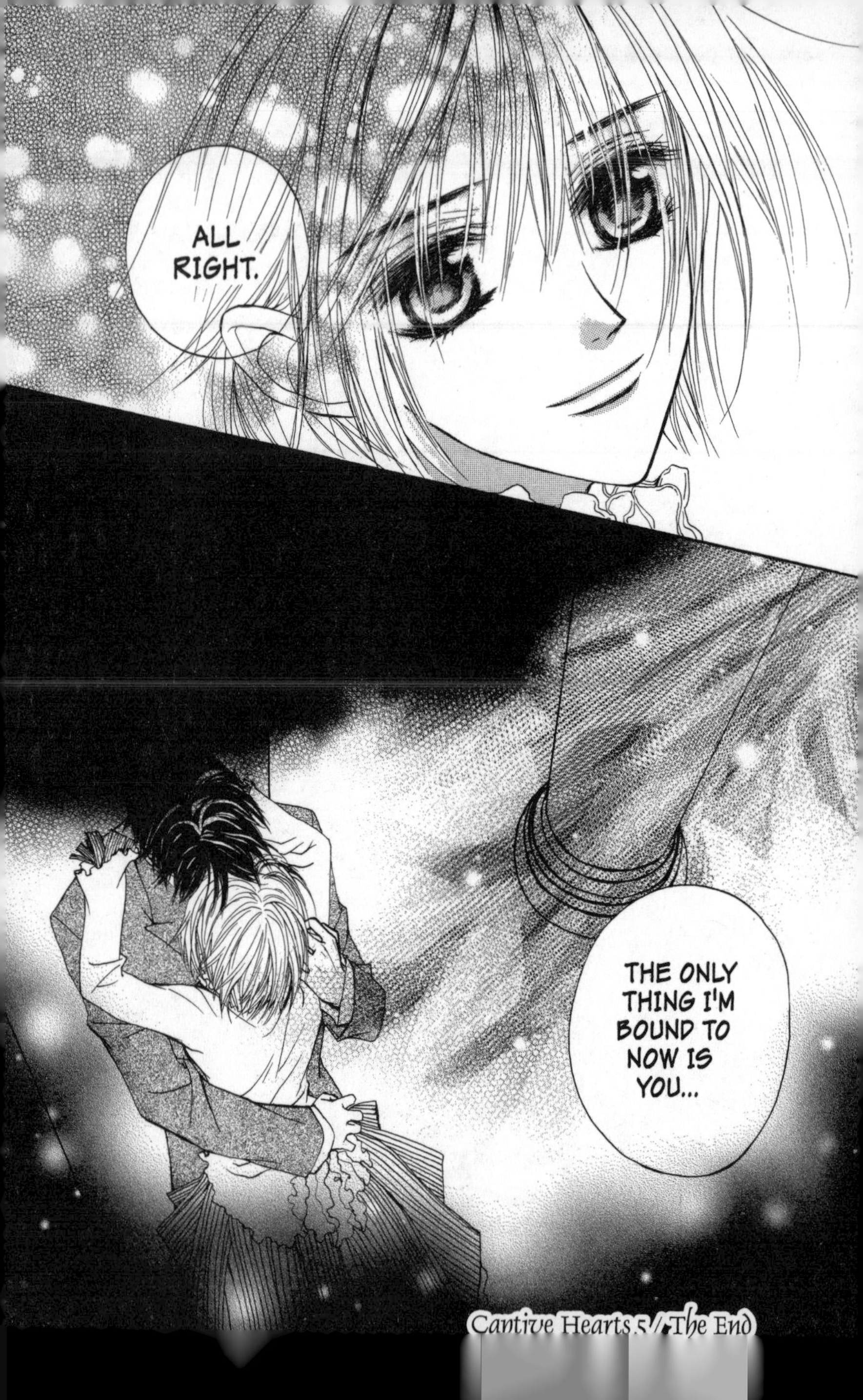
ALL RIGHT.
THE ONLY THING I'M BOUND TO NOW IS YOU...
Captive Hearts 5 / The End

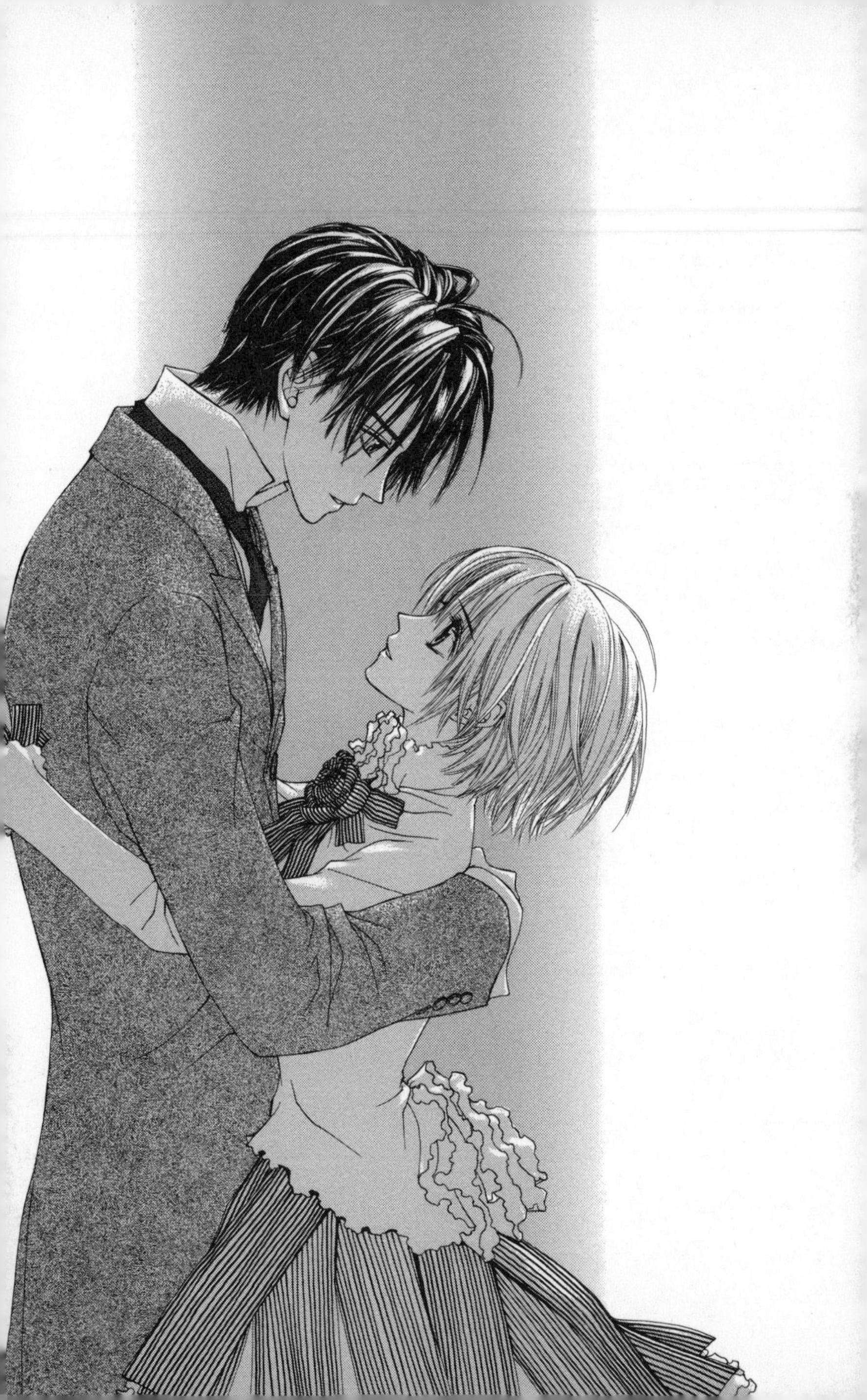

Tell Me the Real Meaning of That Kiss starts on the next page. The art is completely different from Captive Hearts. ▵▵ The illustrations from the beginning of Captive Hearts to the end changed a lot too though. ▵ I feel like it changed as I kept approaching my ideals of how I wanted the story to be.

I wrote this story seven years ago for LMS (the LaLa Mangaka Scouting course). In five days, I:
• Came up with the story → • Divided up the pages → • Decided on names → • Made a storyboard → • Inked → • and finished it right before the deadline. I remember I was in a huge hurry to finish it. I wanted to see the results so fast! (But I didn't end up debuting wth LMS. ♩ Even though I didn't get a job out of it, it was really good practice for me.)

So in other words, I have no memory of agonizing over this story at all. It just all appeared in my mind, and I wrote out the script for it.

So along with my supervisor (who was Ishihara-sama at the time), I aimed for debuting with LMG (LaLa Manga Grand Prix). I received a 2nd place prize from LMS for it (Diamond Rookie Prize). So these 16 pages appeared in LaLa and I got my first bit of fan mail for it. I have so many great memories from this story!

(I feel like Suzuka was Suzuka and Megumi was Megumi right to the very end.)

This is the end of the main story of Captive Hearts. I hope to write more about the characters in special editions and epilogues.

I'm going to do my best with my new one-shot stories and series, so if you see any of my work in LaLa or LaLa DX, please read it. ♡ Thank you!

So many people have supported me while I wrote Captive Hearts.

My supervisor, Taneoka-sama

My new supervisor, Ide-sama

Husky Sisters

Masami

Minako

Mom

And all my fans who read the books!

I'm grateful to you from the bottom of my heart.

(P.S.)
Megumi, Suzuka, Kuroishi-san, Sagara and all the other characters—please stay with me for a bit longer. ▵▵

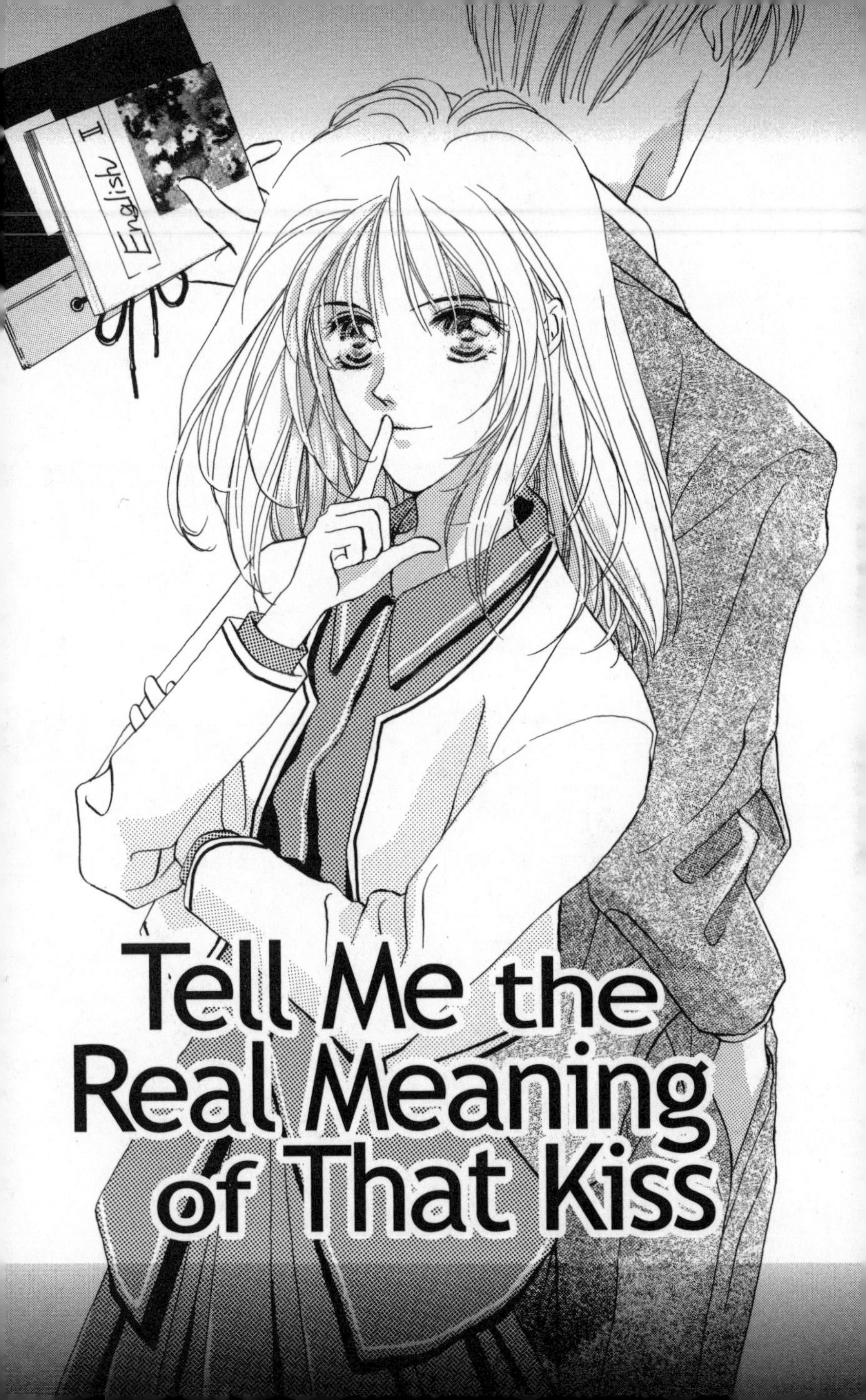
English II
Tell Me the Real Meaning of That Kiss

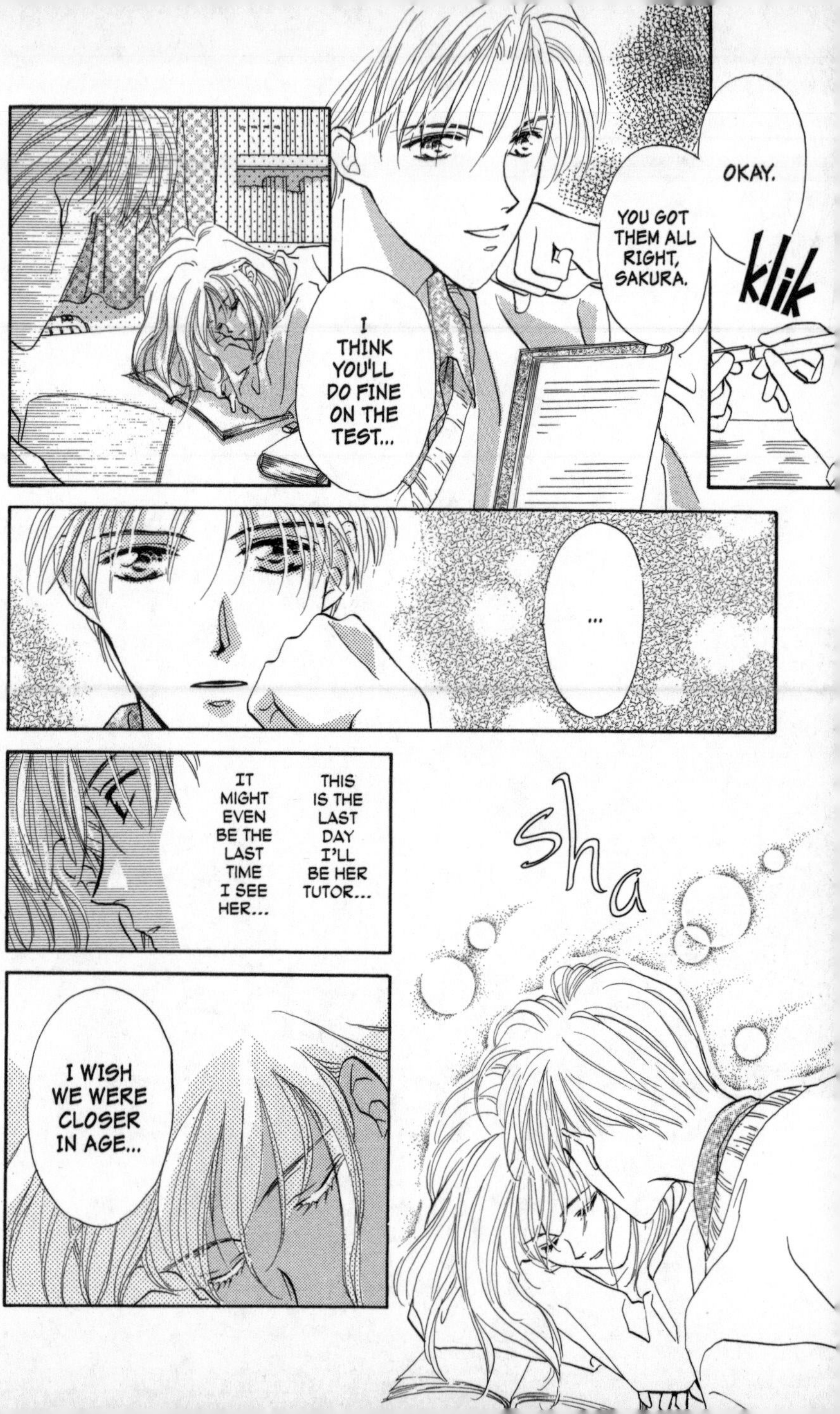
OKAY.
klik
YOU GOT THEM ALL RIGHT, SAKURA.
I THINK YOU'LL DO FINE ON THE TEST...
...
sha
THIS IS THE LAST DAY I'LL BE HER TUTOR...
IT MIGHT EVEN BE THE LAST TIME I SEE HER...
I WISH WE WERE CLOSER IN AGE...

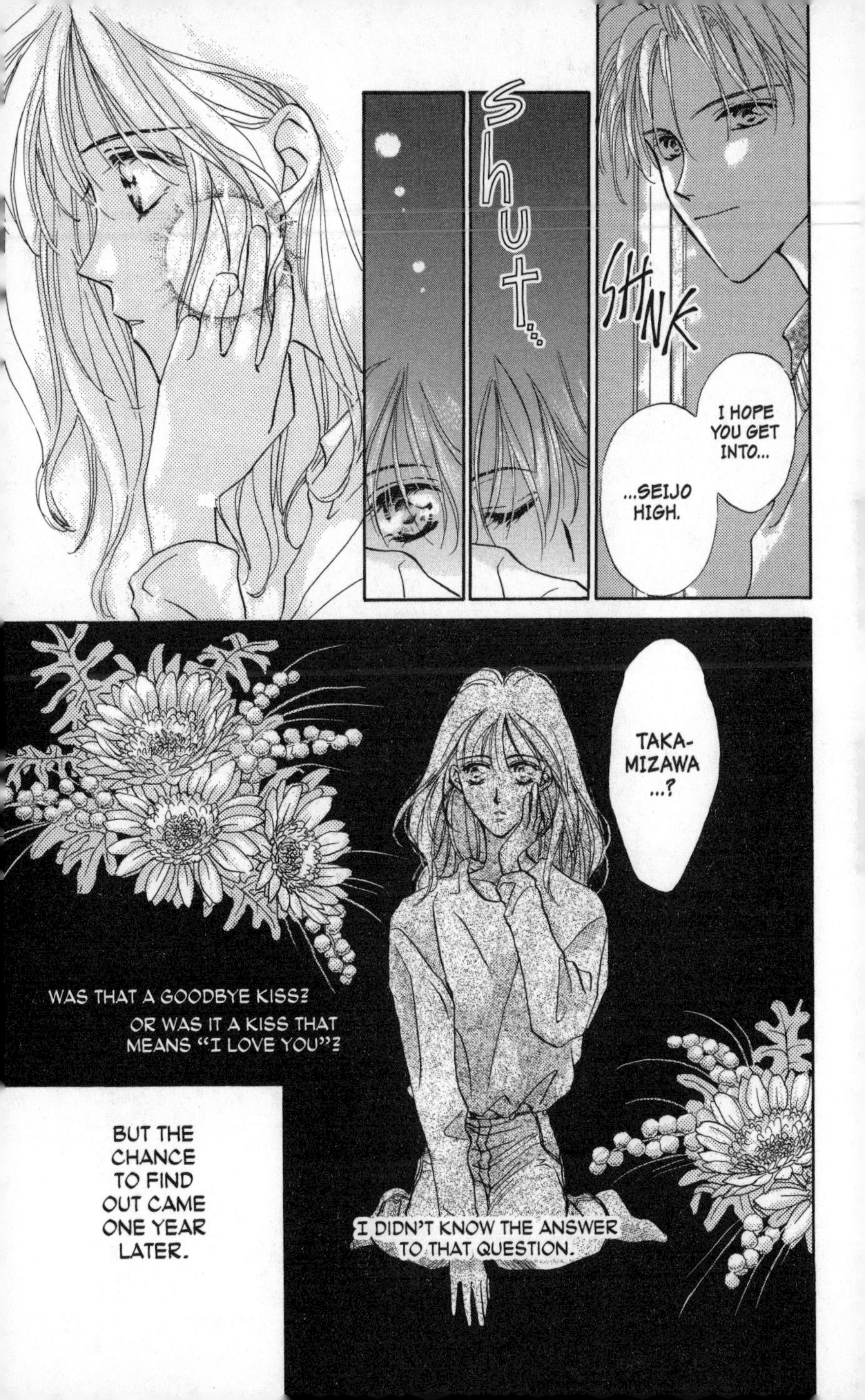
SHINK
I HOPE YOU GET INTO...
...SEIJO HIGH.
shut...
TAKA-MIZAWA ...?
WAS THAT A GOODBYE KISS?
OR WAS IT A KISS THAT MEANS "I LOVE YOU"?
I DIDN'T KNOW THE ANSWER TO THAT QUESTION.
BUT THE CHANCE TO FIND OUT CAME ONE YEAR LATER.

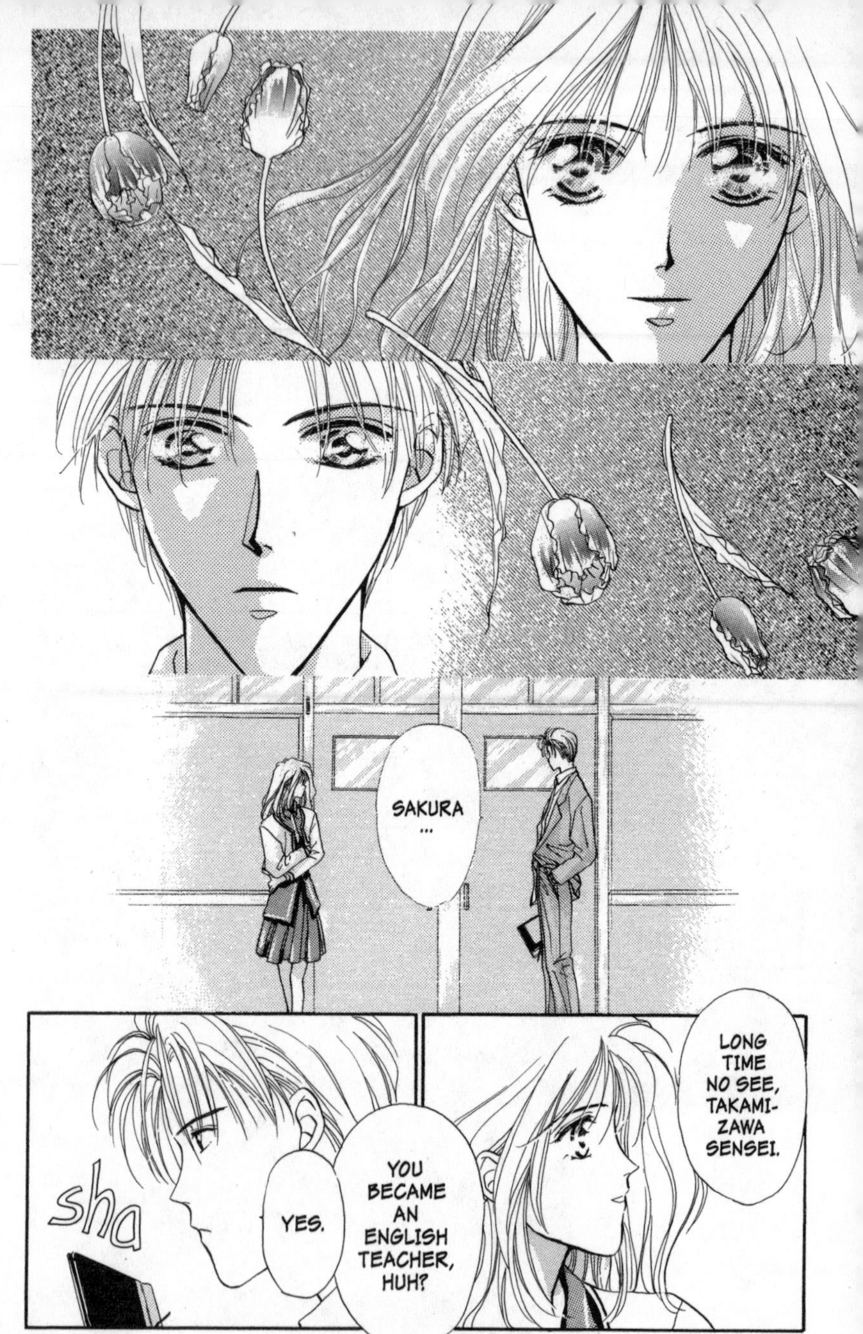
SAKURA ...
LONG TIME NO SEE, TAKAMI-ZAWA SENSEI.
YOU BECAME AN ENGLISH TEACHER, HUH?
YES.
sha

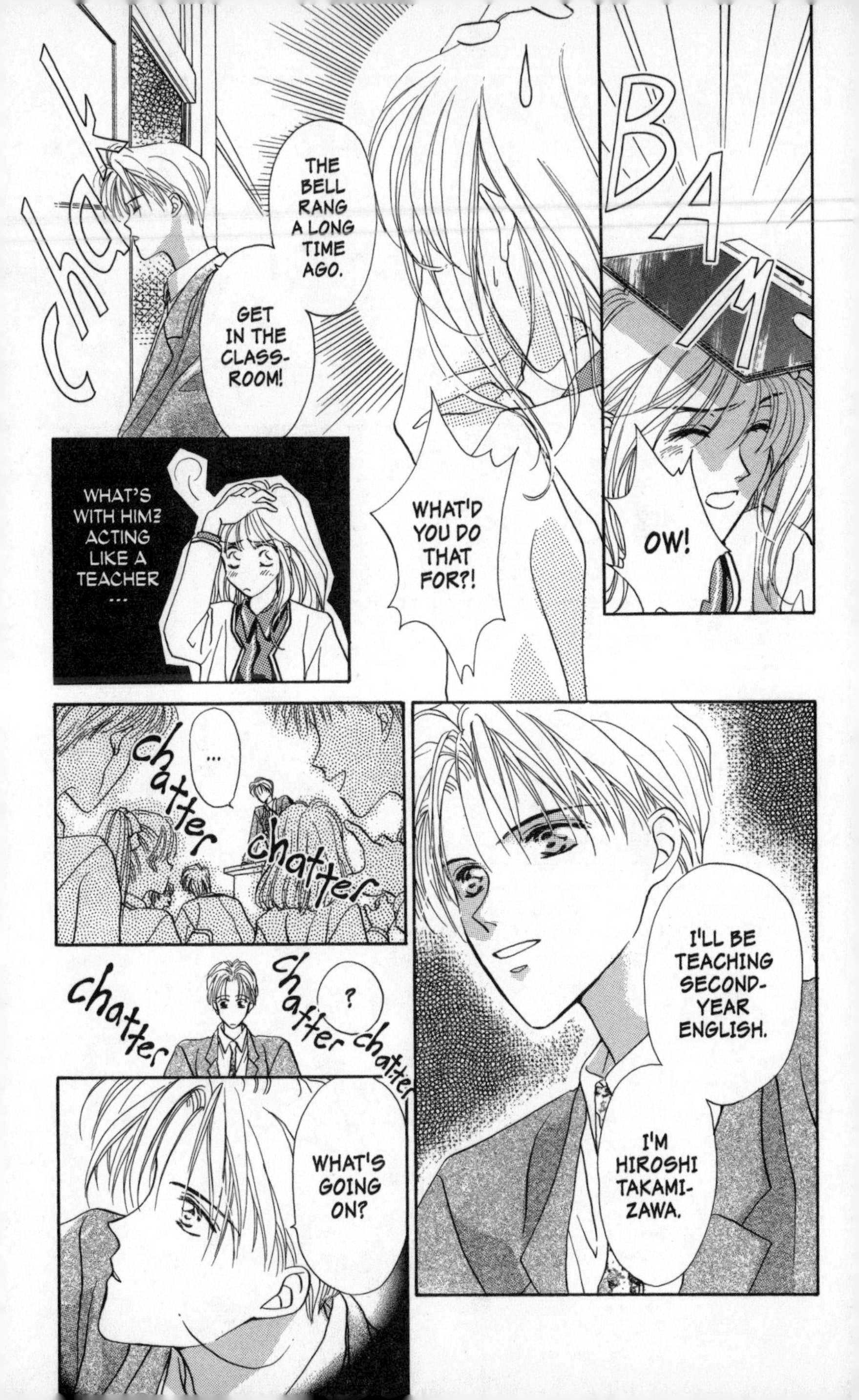
BAM
OW!
WHAT'D YOU DO THAT FOR?!
chak
THE BELL RANG A LONG TIME AGO.
GET IN THE CLASS-ROOM!
WHAT'S WITH HIM? ACTING LIKE A TEACHER...
I'LL BE TEACHING SECOND-YEAR ENGLISH.
I'M HIROSHI TAKAMI-ZAWA.
...
chatter
chatter
?
chatter
chatter
chatter
WHAT'S GOING ON?

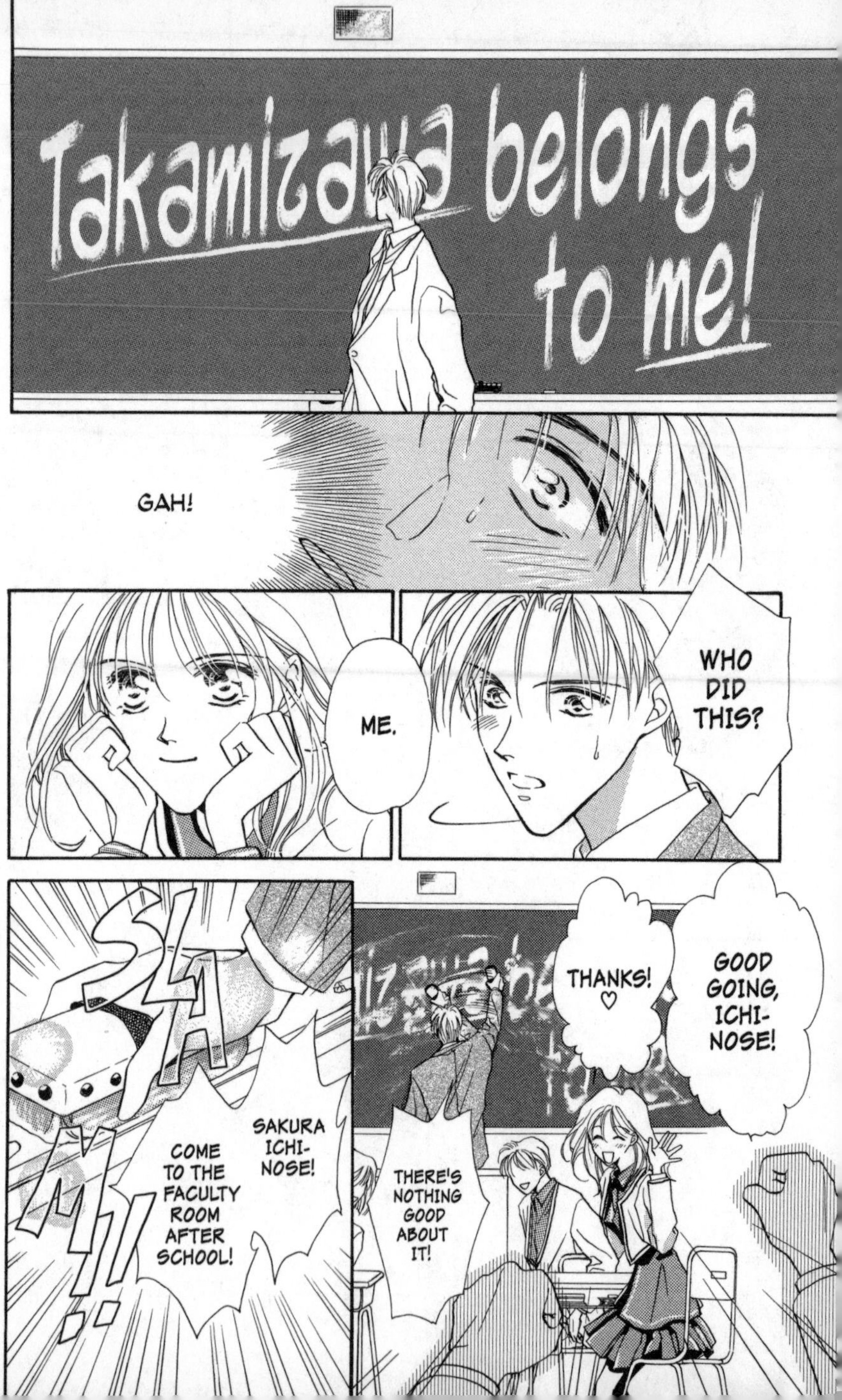
Takamizawa belongs to me!
GAH!
WHO DID THIS?
ME.
GOOD GOING, ICHI-NOSE!
THANKS! ♡
THERE'S NOTHING GOOD ABOUT IT!
SLAM!!
SAKURA ICHI-NOSE!
COME TO THE FACULTY ROOM AFTER SCHOOL!

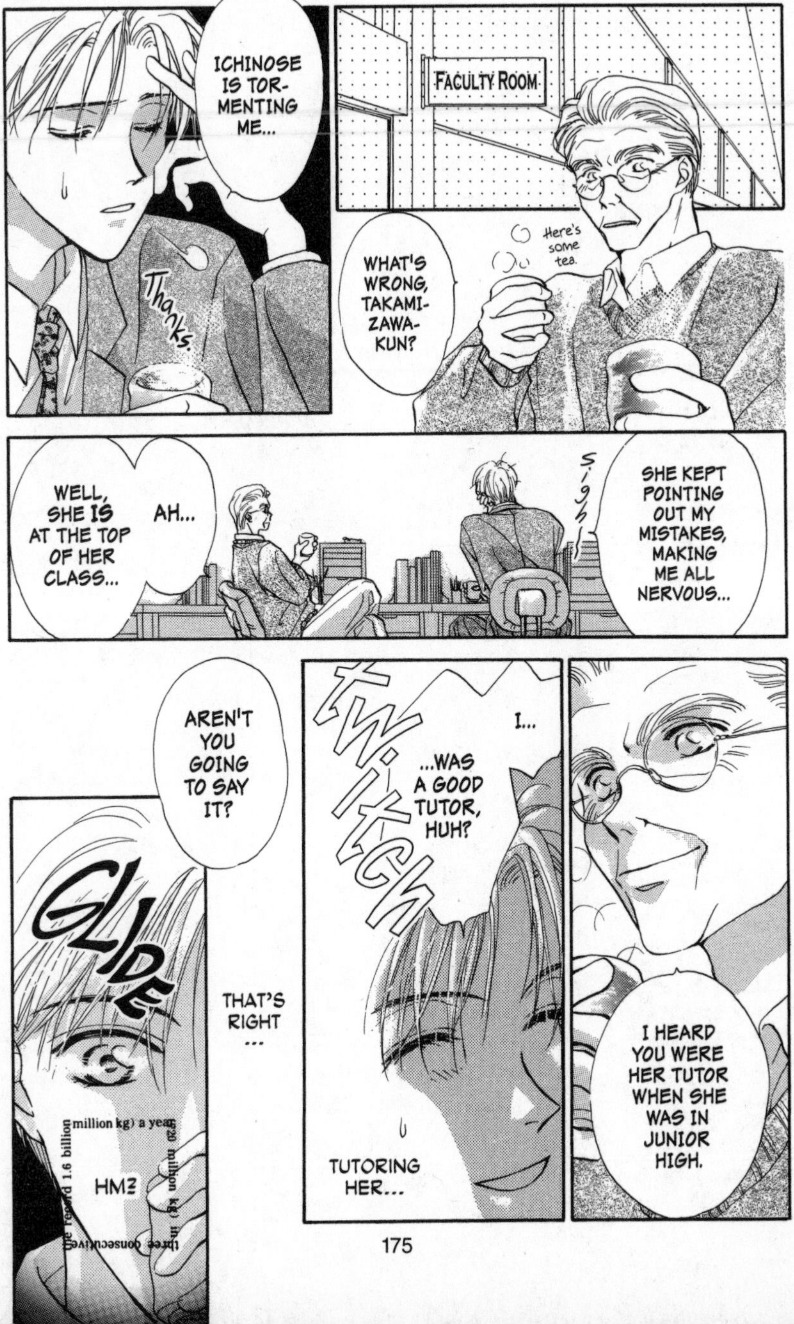
FACULTY ROOM
WHAT'S WRONG, TAKAMIZAWA-KUN?
Here's some tea.
ICHINOSE IS TORMENTING ME...
Thanks.
SHE KEPT POINTING OUT MY MISTAKES, MAKING ME ALL NERVOUS...
sigh
AH...
WELL, SHE IS AT THE TOP OF HER CLASS...
I HEARD YOU WERE HER TUTOR WHEN SHE WAS IN JUNIOR HIGH.
twitch
I...
...WAS A GOOD TUTOR, HUH?
TUTORING HER...
AREN'T YOU GOING TO SAY IT?
GLIDE
THAT'S RIGHT...
HM?

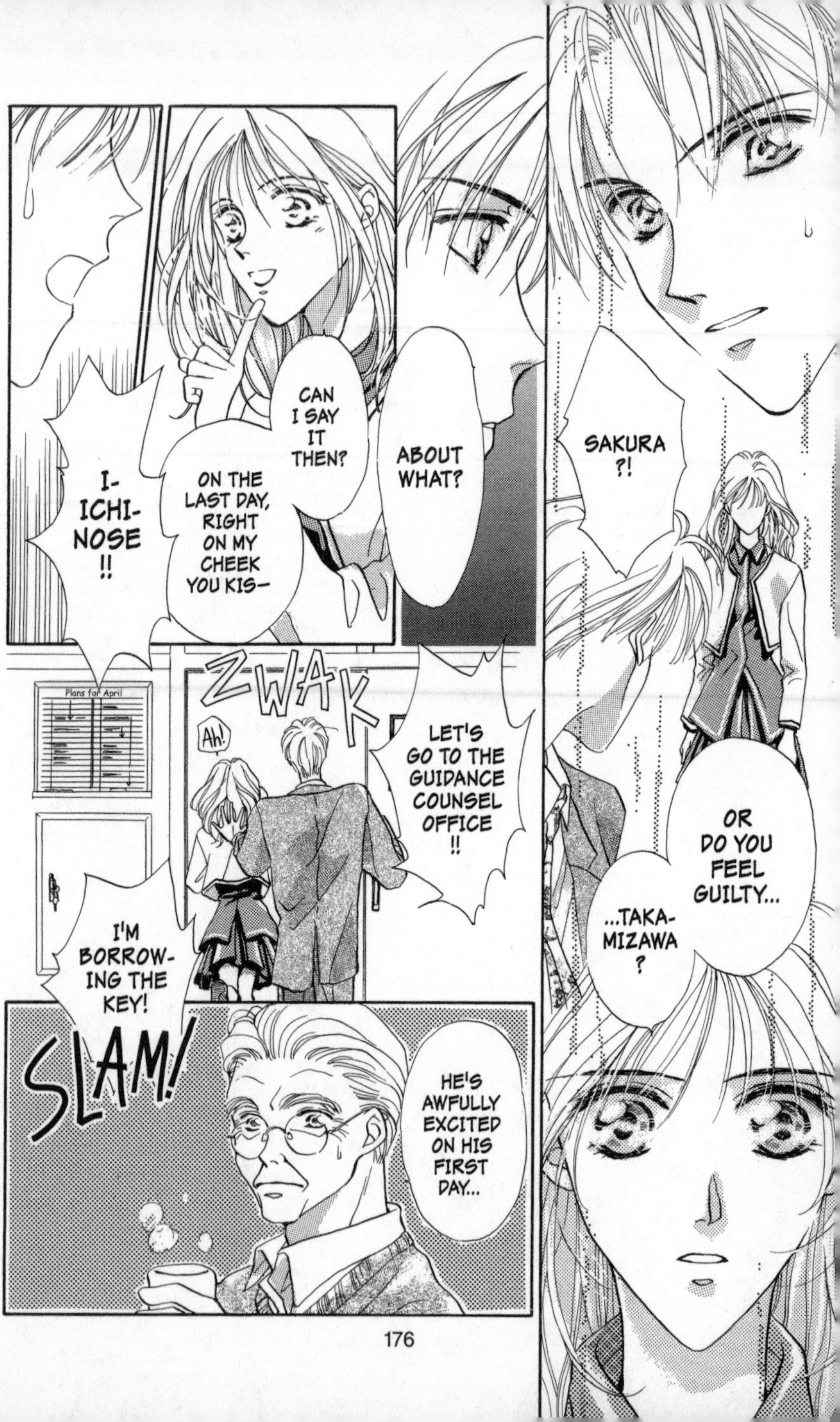

SAKURA ?!
OR DO YOU FEEL GUILTY...
...TAKAMIZAWA ?
ABOUT WHAT?
CAN I SAY IT THEN?
ON THE LAST DAY, RIGHT ON MY CHEEK YOU KIS—
I-ICHINOSE !!
ZWAK
LET'S GO TO THE GUIDANCE COUNSEL OFFICE !!
Ah!
Plans for April
I'M BORROWING THE KEY!
SLAM!
HE'S AWFULLY EXCITED ON HIS FIRST DAY...

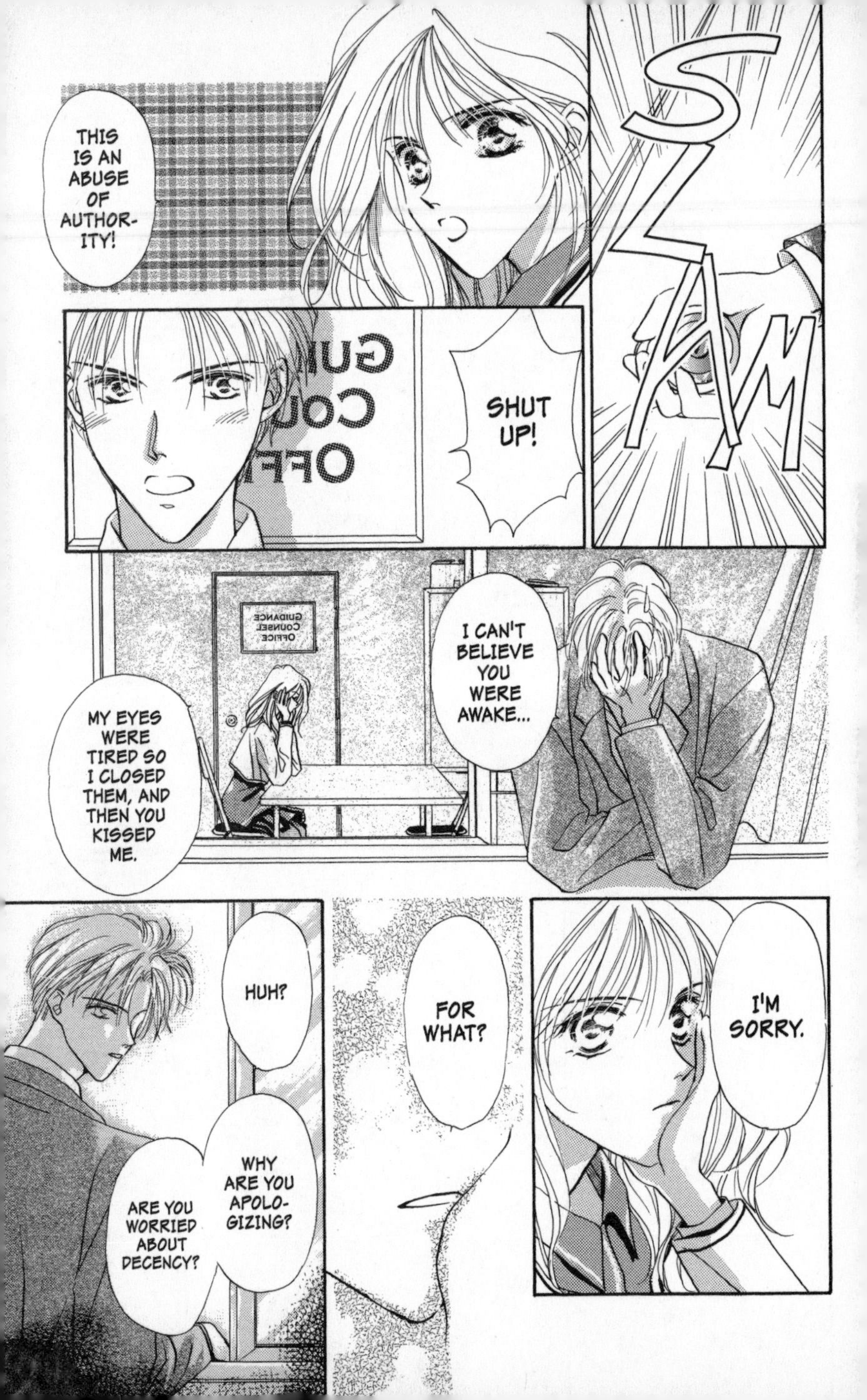
SLAM
THIS IS AN ABUSE OF AUTHORITY!
SHUT UP!
I CAN'T BELIEVE YOU WERE AWAKE...
MY EYES WERE TIRED SO I CLOSED THEM, AND THEN YOU KISSED ME.
I'M SORRY.
FOR WHAT?
HUH?
WHY ARE YOU APOLOGIZING?
ARE YOU WORRIED ABOUT DECENCY?

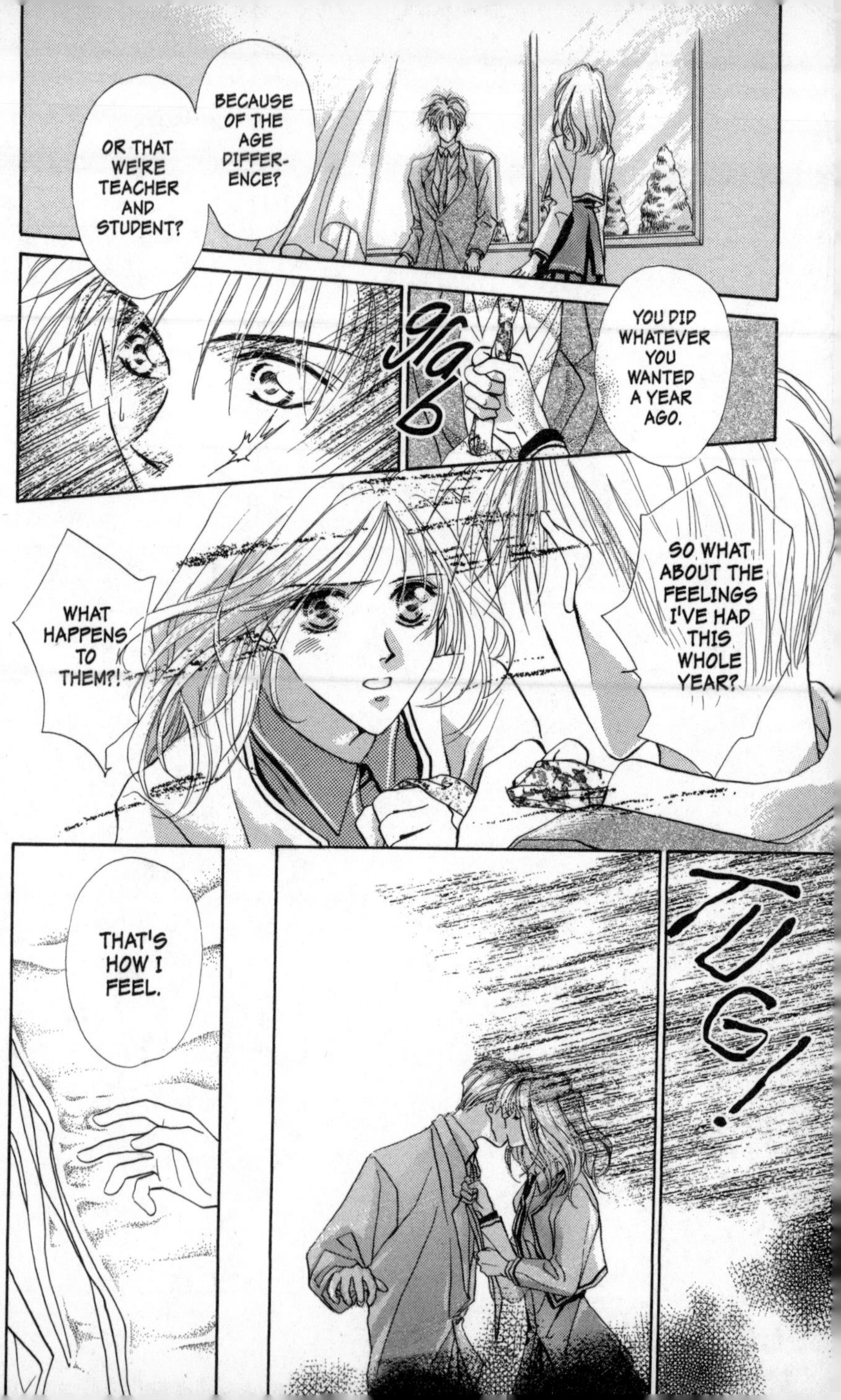
BECAUSE OF THE AGE DIFFERENCE?
OR THAT WE'RE TEACHER AND STUDENT?
YOU DID WHATEVER YOU WANTED A YEAR AGO.
grab
SO WHAT ABOUT THE FEELINGS I'VE HAD THIS WHOLE YEAR?
WHAT HAPPENS TO THEM?!
TUG!
THAT'S HOW I FEEL.

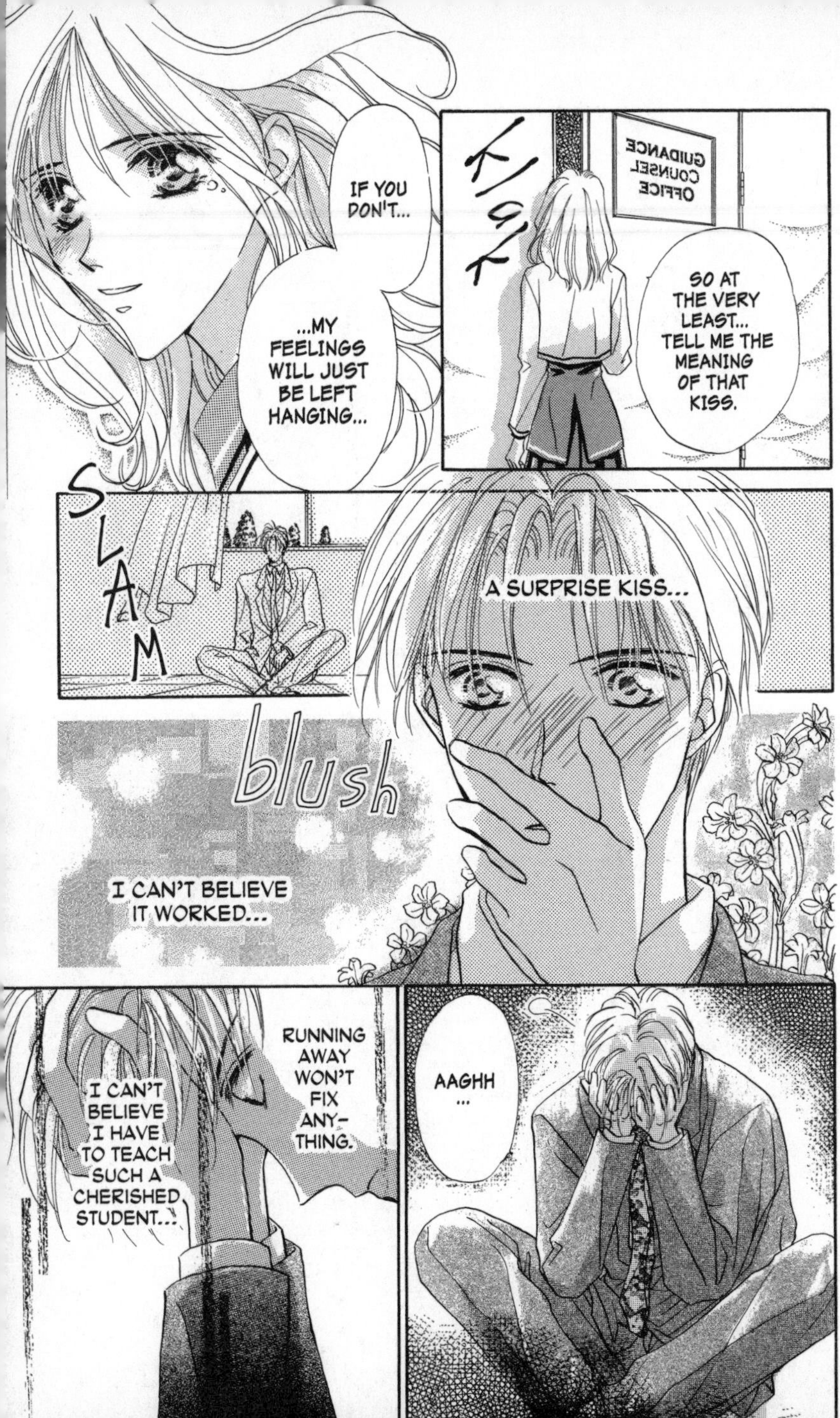
KICK
SO AT THE VERY LEAST... TELL ME THE MEANING OF THAT KISS.
IF YOU DON'T...
...MY FEELINGS WILL JUST BE LEFT HANGING...
A SURPRISE KISS...
blush
I CAN'T BELIEVE IT WORKED...
SLAM
GUIDANCE COUNSEL OFFICE
AAGHH ...
RUNNING AWAY WON'T FIX ANY-THING.
I CAN'T BELIEVE I HAVE TO TEACH SUCH A CHERISHED STUDENT...

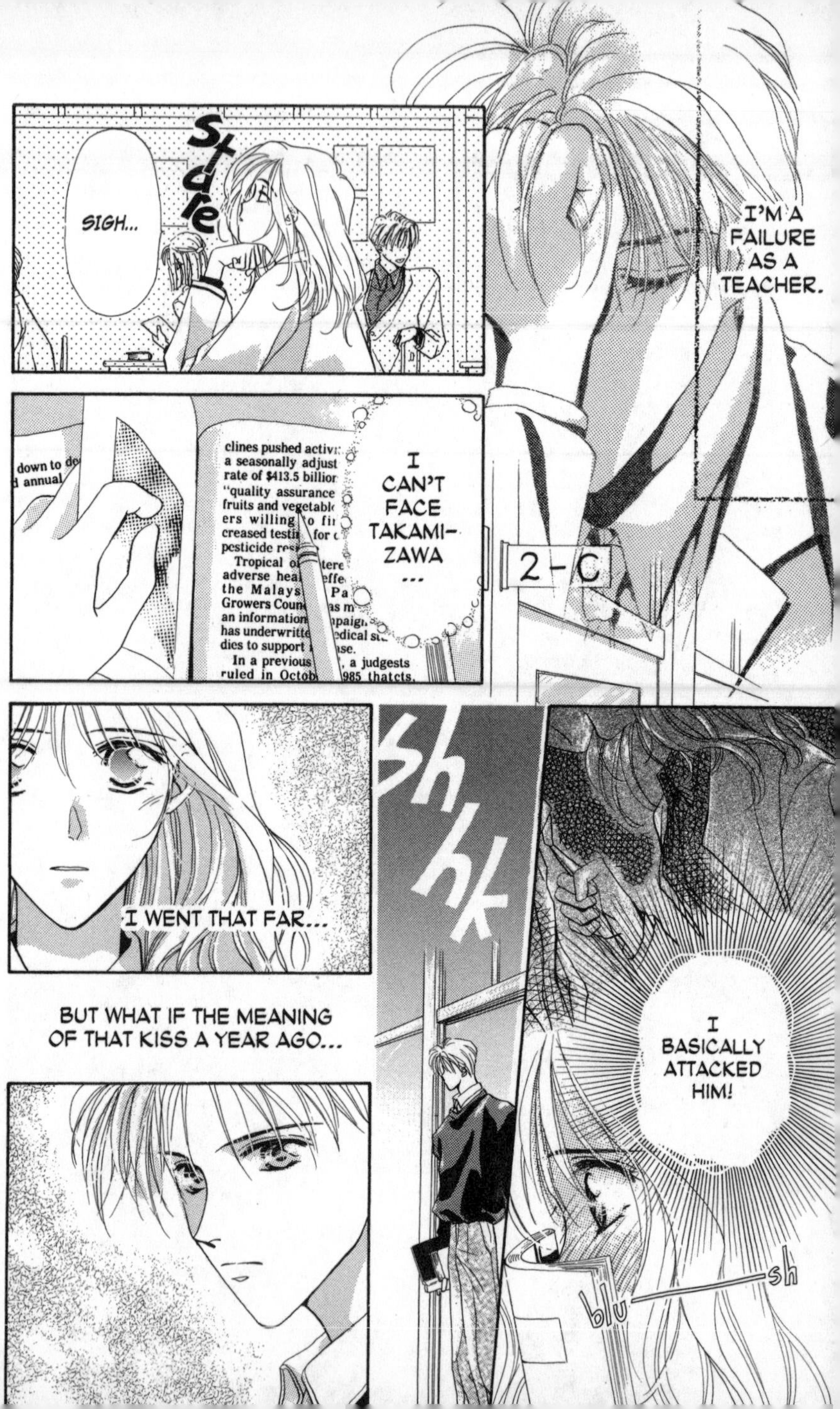
I'M A FAILURE AS A TEACHER.
2-C
Stare
SIGH...
I CAN'T FACE TAKAMIZAWA...
Shhk
I BASICALLY ATTACKED HIM!
blu———sh
I WENT THAT FAR...
BUT WHAT IF THE MEANING OF THAT KISS A YEAR AGO...

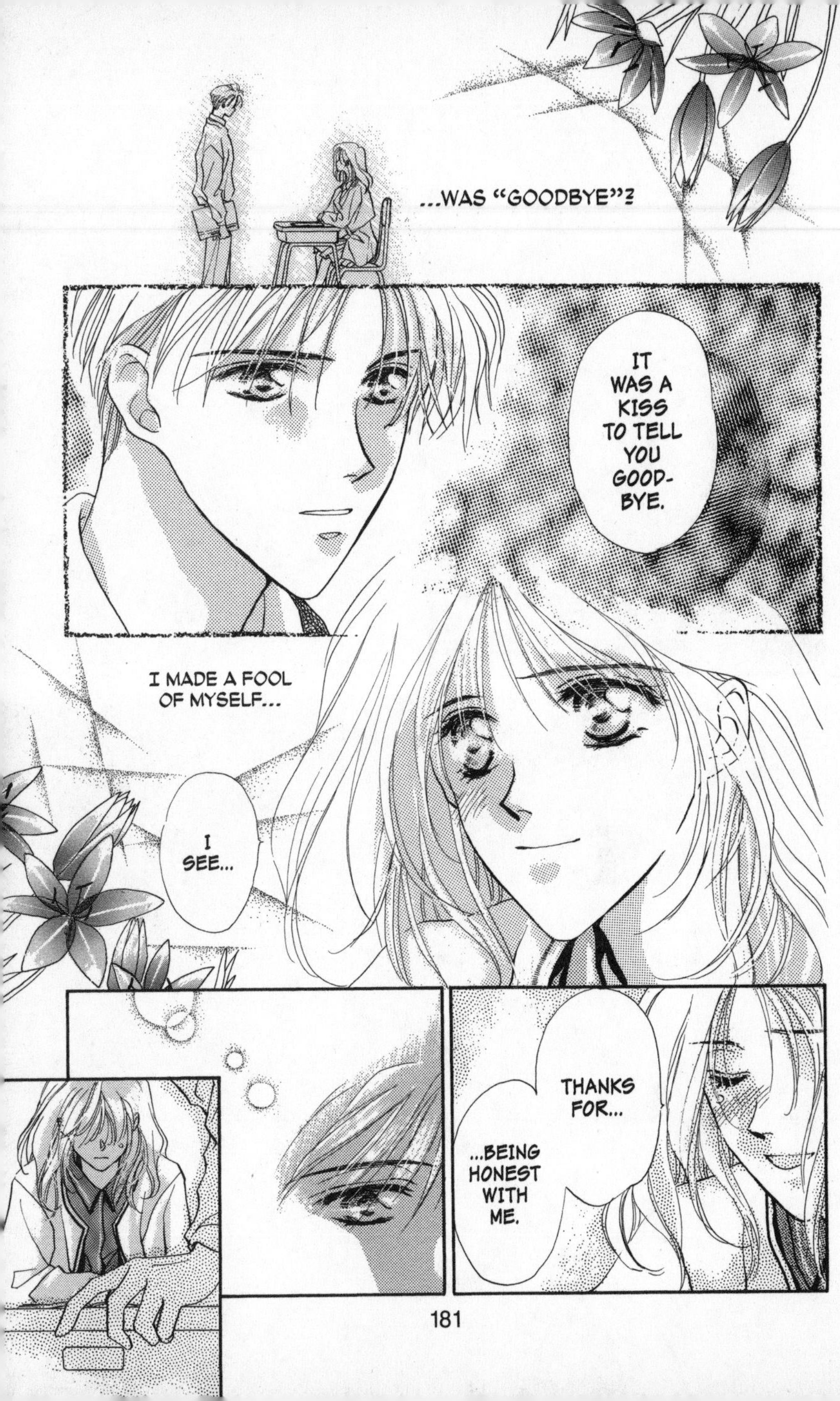
...WAS "GOODBYE"?
IT WAS A KISS TO TELL YOU GOOD-BYE.
I MADE A FOOL OF MYSELF...
I SEE...
THANKS FOR...
...BEING HONEST WITH ME.

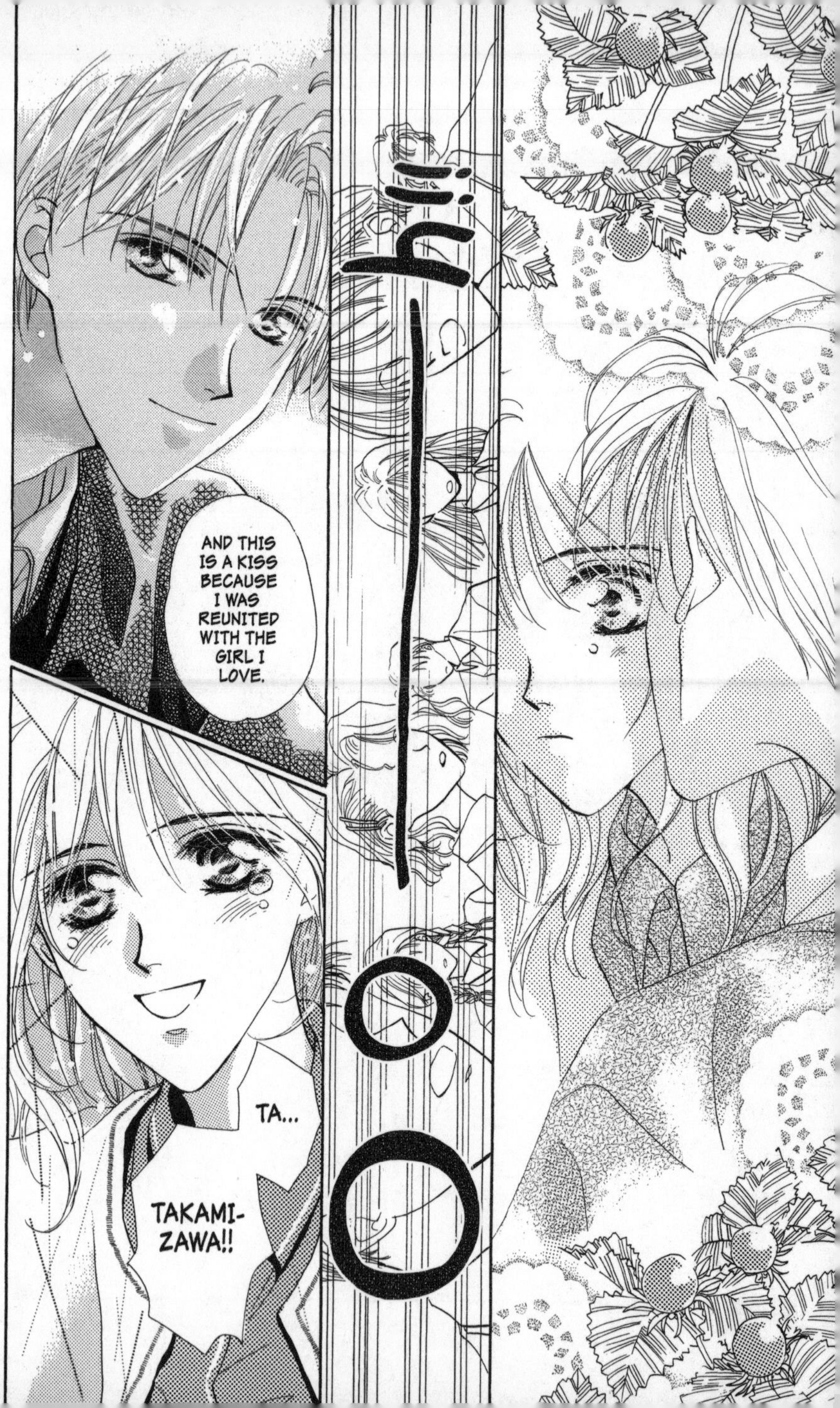
OO—h!!
AND THIS IS A KISS BECAUSE I WAS REUNITED WITH THE GIRL I LOVE.
TA...
TAKAMI-ZAWA!!

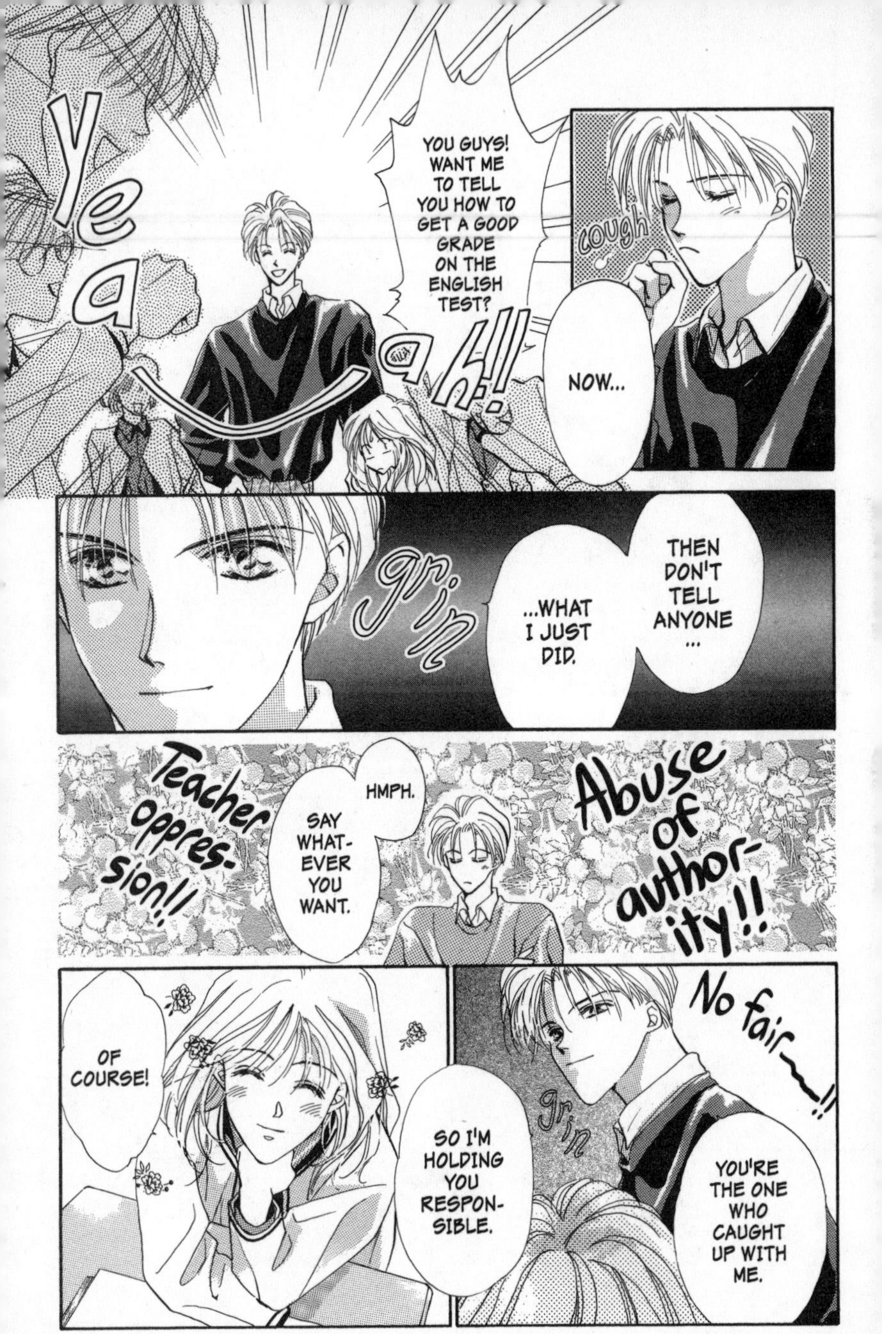
cough
NOW...
YOU GUYS! WANT ME TO TELL YOU HOW TO GET A GOOD GRADE ON THE ENGLISH TEST?
Yea—ah!!
THEN DON'T TELL ANYONE...
...WHAT I JUST DID.
grin
Abuse of authority!!
HMPH.
SAY WHATEVER YOU WANT.
Teacher oppression!!
No fair—!!
YOU'RE THE ONE WHO CAUGHT UP WITH ME.
grin
SO I'M HOLDING YOU RESPONSIBLE.
OF COURSE!

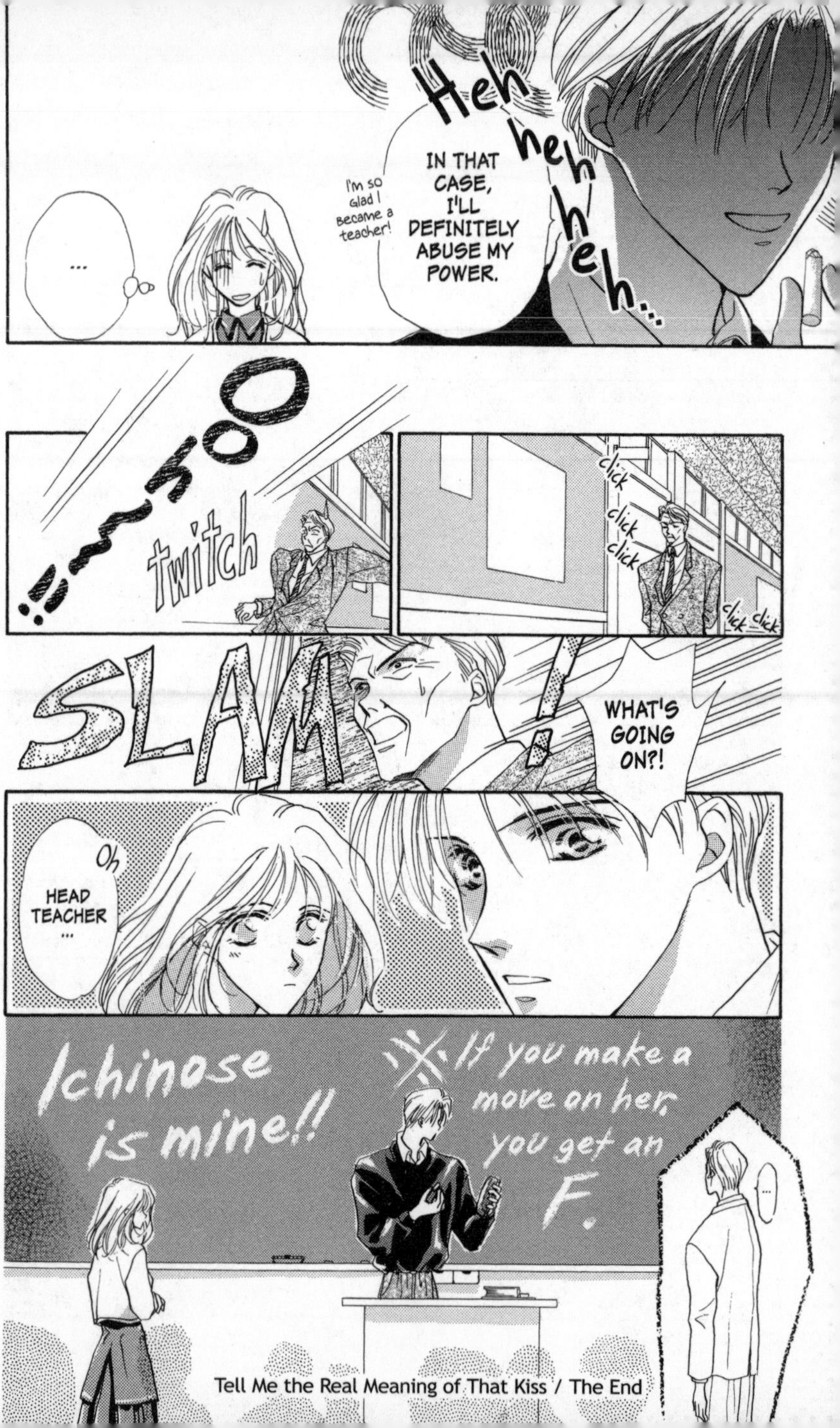
Heh heh heh heh...
IN THAT CASE, I'LL DEFINITELY ABUSE MY POWER.
I'm so Glad I Became a teacher!
...
click click click
click click
Ooh~!!
twitch
SLAM!
WHAT'S GOING ON?!
Oh
HEAD TEACHER...
※ If you make a move on her, you get an F.
Ichinose is mine!!
...

Tell Me the Real Meaning of That Kiss / The End

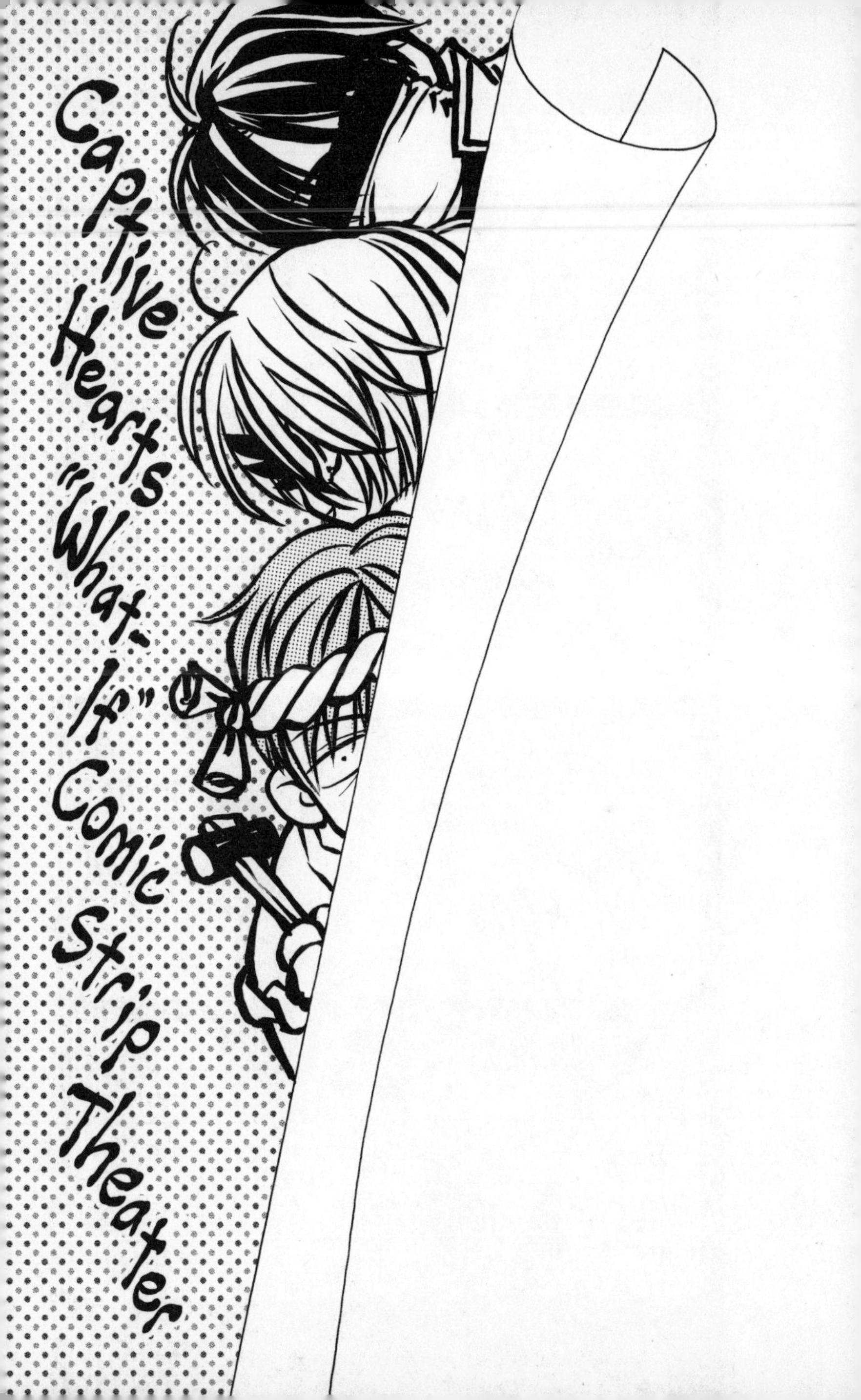
Captive Hearts "What-If" Comic Strip Theater

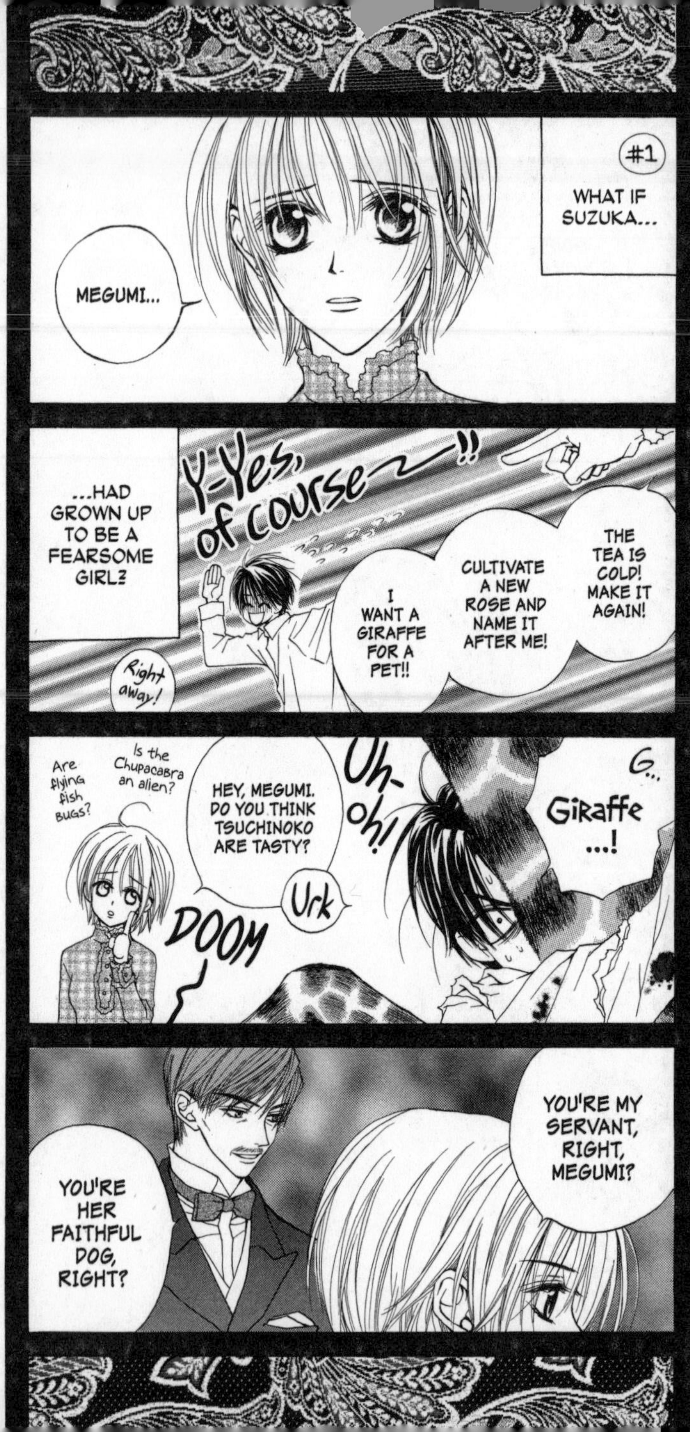
#1
WHAT IF SUZUKA...
MEGUMI...
THE TEA IS COLD! MAKE IT AGAIN!
CULTIVATE A NEW ROSE AND NAME IT AFTER ME!
I WANT A GIRAFFE FOR A PET!!
Y-Yes, of course~!!
...HAD GROWN UP TO BE A FEARSOME GIRL?
Right away!
G... Giraffe ...!
Uh-oh!
Urk
HEY, MEGUMI. DO YOU THINK TSUCHINOKO ARE TASTY?
Is the Chupacabra an alien?
Are flying fish bugs?
DOOM
YOU'RE MY SERVANT, RIGHT, MEGUMI?
YOU'RE HER FAITHFUL DOG, RIGHT?

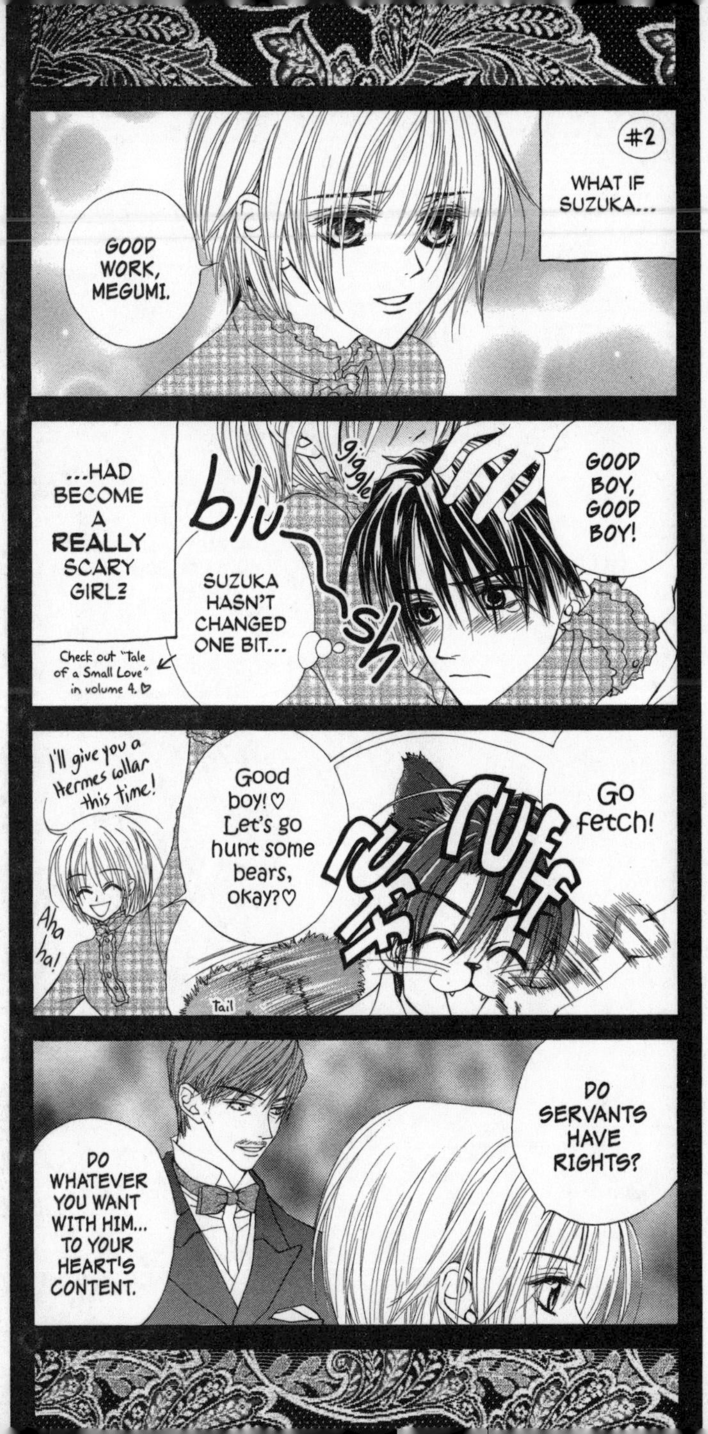
#2
WHAT IF SUZUKA...
...GOOD WORK, MEGUMI.
GOOD BOY, GOOD BOY!
giggle
blu-sh
SUZUKA HASN'T CHANGED ONE BIT...
...HAD BECOME A **REALLY** SCARY GIRL?
Check out "Tale of a Small Love" in volume 4. ♡
Go fetch!
ruff
ruff
Good boy! ♡ Let's go hunt some bears, okay? ♡
I'll give you a Hermes collar this time!
Aha ha!
Tail
DO SERVANTS HAVE RIGHTS?
DO WHATEVER YOU WANT WITH HIM... TO YOUR HEART'S CONTENT.

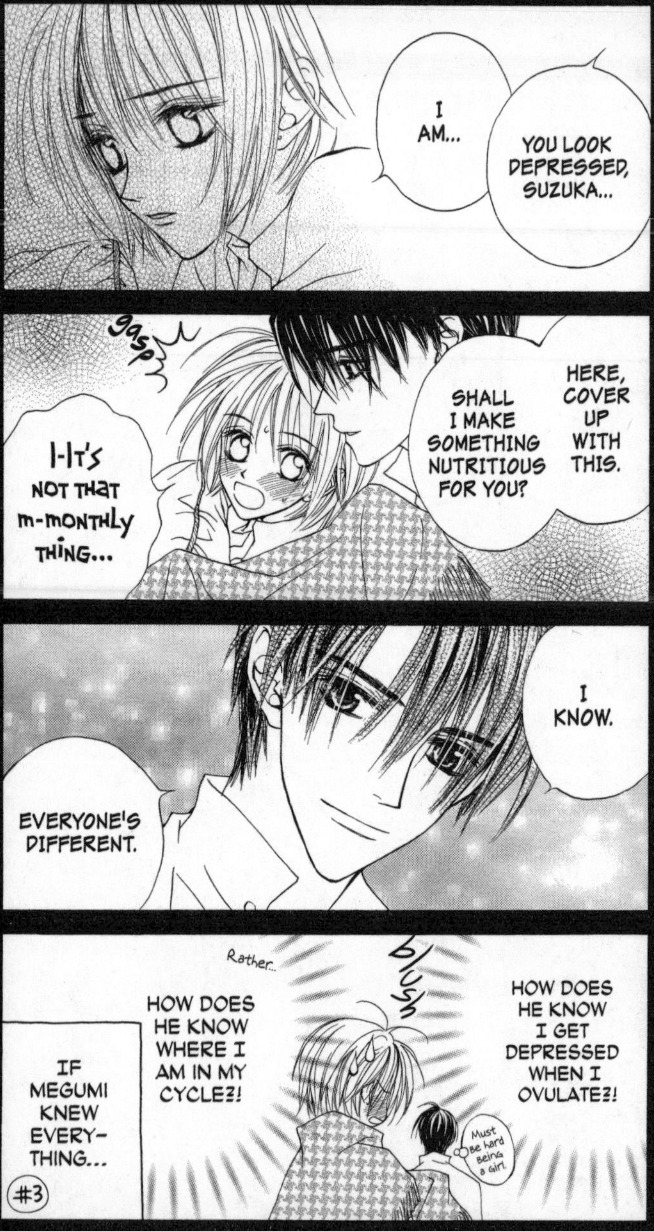
YOU LOOK DEPRESSED, SUZUKA...
I AM...
HERE, COVER UP WITH THIS.
SHALL I MAKE SOMETHING NUTRITIOUS FOR YOU?
gasp
I-It's NOT THAT m-MONTHLY THING...
I KNOW.
EVERYONE'S DIFFERENT.
HOW DOES HE KNOW I GET DEPRESSED WHEN I OVULATE?!
blush
Rather...
HOW DOES HE KNOW WHERE I AM IN MY CYCLE?!
Must be hard being a girl.
IF MEGUMI KNEW EVERY-THING...
#3

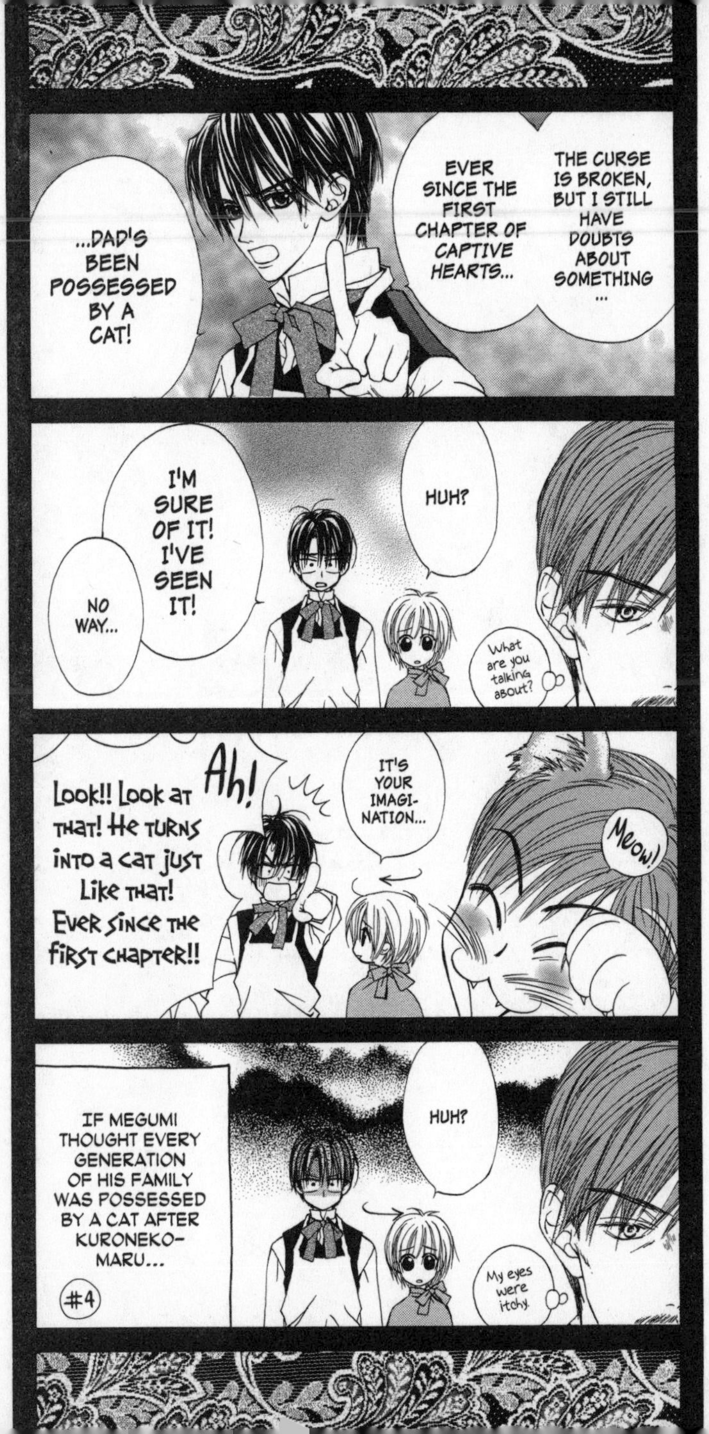
THE CURSE IS BROKEN, BUT I STILL HAVE DOUBTS ABOUT SOMETHING...
EVER SINCE THE FIRST CHAPTER OF CAPTIVE HEARTS...
...DAD'S BEEN POSSESSED BY A CAT!
What are you talking about?
HUH?
I'M SURE OF IT! I'VE SEEN IT!
NO WAY...
Meow!
IT'S YOUR IMAGINATION...
Ah!
Look!! Look at that! He turns into a cat just like that! Ever since the first chapter!!
My eyes were itchy.
HUH?
IF MEGUMI THOUGHT EVERY GENERATION OF HIS FAMILY WAS POSSESSED BY A CAT AFTER KURONEKO-MARU...
#4

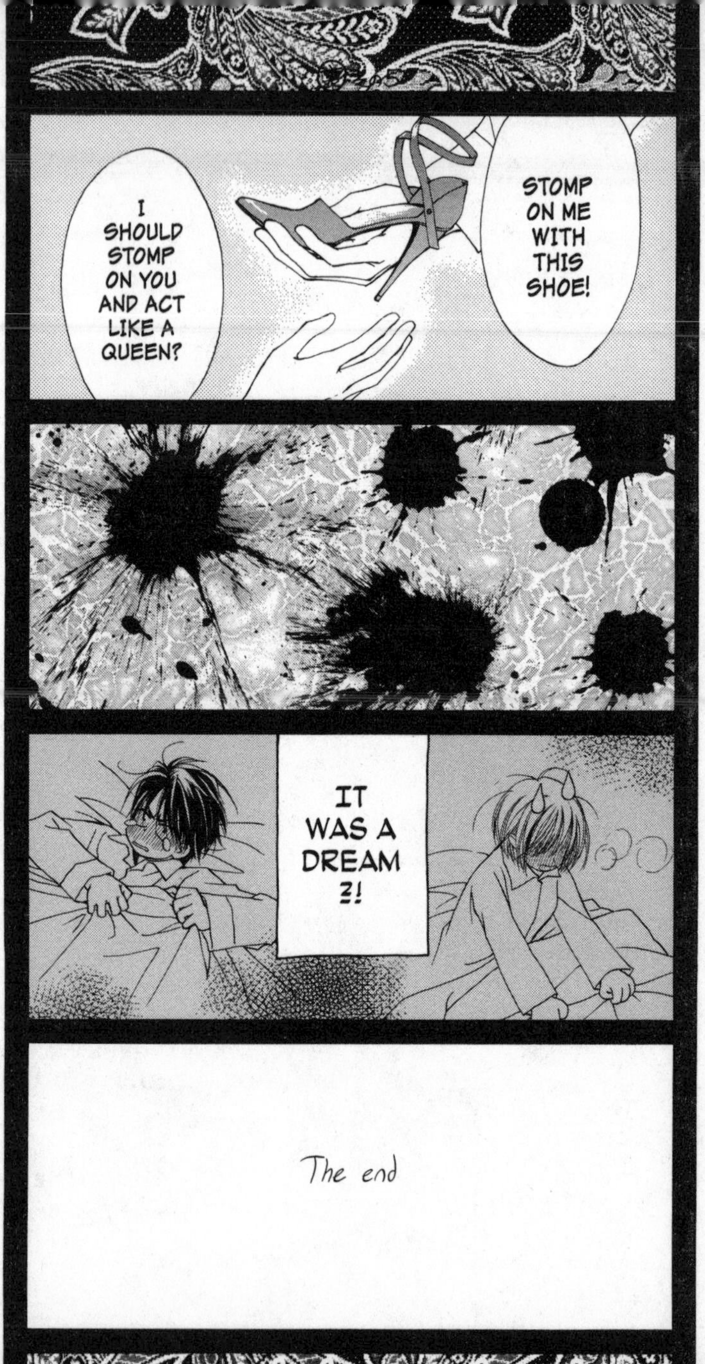
STOMP ON ME WITH THIS SHOE!
I SHOULD STOMP ON YOU AND ACT LIKE A QUEEN?
IT WAS A DREAM ?!
The end

Captive Hearts "What-If" Comic Strip Theater / The End

Captivated by the story but confused by some of the terms? Here are some cultural notes to help you out!

HONORIFICS

San – the most common honorific title; it is used to address people outside one's immediate family and close circle of friends.

Kun – an informal honorific used primarily for males; it can be used by people of more senior status addressing those junior to them or by anyone addressing boys or young men.

Sama – the formal version of *san*; this honorific title is used primarily in addressing persons much higher in rank than oneself.

Sensei – honorific title used to address teachers as well as professionals such as doctors, lawyers and artists.

NOTES

Page 113, panel 2 – **Kyoji**
Megumi uses the word *kyoji* (矜持) which means "pride" or "dignity," but Suzuka mistakes the kanji, thinking he is referring to the word *kyoji* (凶事) which means "calamity."

Page 168 – ***LaLa*** and ***LaLa DX***
Captive Hearts was originally serialized in *LaLa*, a Japanese shojo manga (girls' comics) magazine published monthly by Hakusensha. Some of Hino's stories have run in *LaLa DX*, *LaLa*'s sister magazine.

Page 186, panel 3 – **Tsuchinoko**
A mythical snake-like creature that is said to have a body that is much wider than its head or tail. While the existence of *tsuchinoko* has never actually been proven, legend says that these beings are able to speak but often lie.

MATSURI HINO burst onto the manga scene with her title
Kono Yume ga Sametara (When This Dream Is Over), which was published
in *LaLa DX* magazine. Hino was a manga artist a mere nine months after
she decided to become one.

With the success of her popular series *Captive Hearts* and *MeruPuri*, Hino
has established herself as a major player in the world of shojo manga.
Vampire Knight is currently serialized in *LaLa* and *Shojo Beat* magazines.

Hino enjoys creative activities and has commented that she would
have been either an architect or an apprentice to traditional
Japanese craft masters if she had not become a manga artist.

Captive Hearts
Vol. 5

The Shojo Beat Manga Edition

STORY & ART BY
MATSURI HINO

Translation & Adaptation/Andria Cheng
Touch-up Art & Lettering/Sabrina Heep
Design/Amy Martin
Editor/Amy Yu

VP, Production/Alvin Lu
VP, Publishing Licensing/Rika Inouye
VP, Sales & Product Marketing/Gonzalo Ferreyra
VP, Creative/Linda Espinosa
Publisher/Hyoe Narita

Toraware no Minoue by Matsuri Hino

First published in Japan in 2002 by HAKUSENSHA, Inc., Tokyo.
English language translation rights arranged with HAKUSENSHA, Inc., Tokyo.

Printed in Canada

Published by VIZ Media, LLC
P.O. Box 77010
San Francisco, CA 94107

Shojo Beat Manga Edition
10 9 8 7 6 5 4 3 2 1
First printing, July 2009

store.viz.com

RATED T FOR TEEN

PARENTAL ADVISORY
CAPTIVE HEARTS is rated T for Teen and is recommended for ages 13 and up. This volume contains suggestive themes.

ratings.viz.com

Oyayubi kara Romance

The Magic Touch

by Izumi Tsubaki

Romance from the Thumbs!

Chiaki Togu is the star of her high school's Massage Research Society club. But when she falls for the hottest guy on campus, she'll need to get over her insecurities—and the scheming of other girls—in order to win his attention. Will her heart prove to be as sturdy as her hands?

Find out in *The Magic Touch* manga—buy yours today!

On sale at www.shojobeat.com

Also available at your local bookstore and comic store.

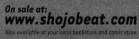

High Seas Hostage!

WANTED

BY MATSURI HINO, CREATOR OF *MeruPuri* **AND** *Vampire Knight*

In search of her kidnapped first love, Armeria disguises herself as a boy to join the crew of the pirate ship that abducted him. What will happen when the former songstress' cross-dressing cover is blown?

FIND OUT IN *WANTED*—MANGA ON SALE NOW!

On sale at **www.shojobeat.com**
Also available at your local bookstore and comic store